AF352651

The Papers of Howard Washington Thurman

VOLUME 3

The Bold Adventure, September 1943–May 1949

Senior Editor	Walter Earl Fluker
Associate Editor	Peter Eisenstadt
Managing Editor	Silvia P. Glick
Senior Advisory Editor	Luther E. Smith, Jr.
Consulting Editors	Quinton H. Dixie and Kai Jackson Issa

The University of South Carolina Press

© 2015 University of South Carolina

Published by the University of South Carolina Press
Columbia, South Carolina 29208

uscpress.com

Printed in the United States of America

Library of Congress Cataloging-in-Publication Data
can be found at http://catalog.loc.gov/.

ISBN 978-1-61117-541-7 (cloth)

Contents

Illustrations

Acknowledgments

"The movement of the Spirit of God," wrote Howard Thurman, often calls people "to act against the spirit of their times or causes them to anticipate a spirit which is yet in the making. In a moment of dedication, they are given wisdom and courage to dare a deed that challenges and to kindle a hope that inspires." With characteristic perspicuity, Howard Thurman introduced Alfred G. Fisk and identified his pivotal role in the development of the idea of the Church for the Fellowship of All Peoples in San Francisco, where he and Thurman served as copastors. Envisioning the future in complex social, political, and cultural contexts calls for more than sentimental aspirations—this was the underlying lesson Thurman sought to convey in the dedication to Fisk of his account of the Fellowship Church story. For Thurman, embarking on a vision of an interracial, intercultural, and interfaith experiment in the United States of America in 1944 required a certain blend of fortitude and faith.

Volume 3 of *The Papers of Howard Washington Thurman* is titled *The Bold Adventure, September 1943–May 1949.* From its beginning at Colgate-Rochester Divinity School (1992–98), continuing through its development at Morehouse College (1998–2010), until its move in 2010 to its current home at Boston University, the project has indeed been a "bold adventure," hazarding many unanticipated challenges and heralding many unforeseen rewards. Thankfully there were many foundations, organizations, and special individuals who made the risks worth our efforts and who now share in the project's visible accomplishments.

The Lilly Endowment, Inc., has been a steadfast contributor and has given the largest percentage of support to date for our work. Craig Dykstra, former senior vice president for religion, and Jean M. Smith, former religion program officer, found ways to keep the project alive when all the signs suggested otherwise. Christopher Coble, the new vice president of the Lilly Endowment, has continued this generous support begun by his predecessor. Michael Gilligan, president of the Henry Luce Foundation, and Lynn Swzaja, the foundation's program director for theology, faithfully supported the work of the project from 1998 to 2000 and most recently have funded both the editorial and public education components of our work for 2009–11 and 2012–13. I am also deeply indebted to James Lewis and the Louisville Institute for the Study of Protestantism and American Culture for grants in the fall of 1994 and the spring of 2005 that culminated in the publication of two edited volumes, *A Strange Freedom: The Best of Howard Thurman on Religious Experience and Public Life* (1998), coedited with Catherine Tumber; and *The Stones That the Builders Rejected: The Development of Ethical Leadership from the Black Church Tradition* (1998); these grants also contributed to the work on the present volumes. During the early development of the project, we received a three-year grant from the Pew Charitable Trusts, and the grant was subsequently renewed. The National Historical Publications and Records Commission (NHPRC) awarded the project consecutive annual grants for the years 1994 to the present and provided generous subvention support for the production of volumes 1 and 2 of the edition. Over the years our editors have benefited immeasurably from participation in the NHPRC-sponsored Institute for the Editing of Historical Documents, known as "Camp Edit." I am grateful to our longtime NHPRC program officer Timothy Connelly (now retired) for being a loyal supporter and adviser in every way. We also thank the Association for Documentary Editing, especially Beth Luey, the ADE's former education director, for running the institute.

I am thankful for the timely gift from the family of Virginia Scardigli, a close associate of Howard Thurman and secretary of the Fellowship Church.

I am honored that in 2009 and 2010 the project received National Endowment for the Humanities (NEH) funding under its *We the People* program, an initiative supporting projects that help advance knowledge of the principles that define America. Special thanks are due to Lydia Medici, our NEH program officer in the Division of Research, and Peter Scott, our NEH grants administrator, for their support, encouragement, and enthusiasm for our work.

The Thurman family has been supportive of the project from its beginning. I consulted with Anne Spencer Thurman and Sue Bailey Thurman from the project's conceptualization through its early implementation at Colgate-Rochester Divinity School and Morehouse College. For several years until her death in 2012, Olive Thurman Wong continued in this important role as a member of the Advisory Board. Her generous and wise counsel, along with the unwavering support of her son, Anton Wong, sustained our efforts as we moved closer to the edition's completion, and she is dearly missed. A special thanks is also extended to Suzanne Chiarenza, granddaughter of Howard Thurman and executor of the Howard Thurman Estate.

Early in my doctoral research on Howard Thurman, I met Professor Luther E. Smith. Luther encouraged me to pursue my research on Thurman and over the years has become a close colleague and loyal friend. As senior advisory editor to the Howard Thurman Papers Project, his encyclopedic grasp of the Thurman corpus and unfailing support have been of inestimable value. Luther's exceptional scholarship and gentle embodiment of Thurman's spiritual genius are constant reminders of what is at stake in our work.

Our home at Boston University School of Theology is a welcome and most fitting setting for the continuing work of the project. From 1953 to 1965 Thurman served as the university's dean of Marsh Chapel; he was the first African American to occupy such a position at a majority-white university. His early years at Boston University coincided with the matriculation of a young theologian and pastor who would shape the moral and legal landscape of twentieth-century America, Dr. Martin Luther King, Jr. Thurman's tenure at Boston University will be the focus of volume 4 of the edition.

For our home at the School of Theology we owe a great debt to the generous hospitality and graciousness of spirit embodied in Dean Mary Elizabeth Moore and the faculty, staff, and students who are part of a long and cherished tradition of producing prophetic leaders for the church and the world. The project has always greatly benefited from its close relationship with the Special Collections at Boston University, renamed in 2003 the Howard Gotlieb Archival Research Center to honor its founder. The late Howard Gotlieb and his entire staff provided assistance to the project and granted us access to Thurman's papers, along with the authority to catalog the bulk of the papers, which had not yet been organized. Vita Paladino, the present director of the Gotlieb Center, has been a fountain of inspiration and support. The late George Makechnie, founder of the Howard Thurman Center at Boston University and a close friend of the Thurman family, was an advocate for our work within the university and beyond, always demanding that we not forget the dream of community. Kenneth Elmore, dean of students, and Katherine Kennedy, the present director of the Thurman Center, deserve mention for the excellent work on diversity and student programming that marks the life of the center.

It continues to give me great honor to acknowledge my incredible colleagues, Peter Eisenstadt and Silvia P. Glick. Peter Eisenstadt, associate editor, has been with the project since its early days and continues to provide a sense of coherence and intellectual sophistication that astute readers will appreciate. Silvia P. Glick, managing editor and assistant director, has performed a herculean task in conquering some major logistical snares and placing the overall work of the project on a firm foundation. Former editors Quinton Dixie and Kai Jackson Issa deserve special mention for their early contributions to the present volume. Jamison Collier transitioned with the project from Morehouse College and provided support through his work with the Gotlieb Center. Research assistants Jennifer Quigley and Onaje Woodbine deserve special mention, and we are indebted to Marc Korpus for creating the map of San Francisco.

Many individuals, institutions, and organizations contributed to this volume through their generosity in granting permission to publish documents. We are grateful to the following rights holders for permission to publish corre-spondence and previously published writings: Frances Genung, wife of Dan B. Genung; Bernice Mays Perkins, niece of Benjamin Elijah Mays; the American Baptist Historical Society; the Bentley Historical Library, University of Michigan; *Christian Century;* the Church for the Fellowship of All Peoples in San Francisco; Colgate Rochester Crozer Divinity School; the Fellowship of Reconciliation U.S.A.; Grinnell College; HarperCollins Publishers; the Moorland-Spingarn Research Center, Howard University Archives; the National Council of the Churches of Christ in the U.S.A.; the Presbyterian Historical Society; the Presbyterian Mission Agency, Presbyterian Church (U.S.A.); the Rockefeller Archive Center; San Francisco State University; Sophia Smith Collection, Smith College; Time Inc.; the University of Chicago Press; and the YWCA of the U.S.A.

Numerous institutions have assisted us in our work. For invaluable contributions to the present volume, we thankfully acknowledge the following institutions for providing access to their collections: the Eleanor Roosevelt Papers, Franklin Delano Roosevelt Library, Hyde Park, New York; the Collections of the Department of History, Presbyterian Church (U.S.A.), Philadelphia, Pennsylvania; the Moorland-Spingarn Research Center, Howard University Archives, Washington, D.C.; and the Fellowship Church of All Peoples, San Francisco.

Mentors and friends such as Clayborne Carson, James Earl Massey, Randall K. Burkett, and Edward K. Kaplan have encouraged our work through the various stages of the project's development. Others who have worked with the project over time include Alton Pollard, Clarissa Myrick-Harris, Alma Jean-Billingsea, and Michael Joseph Brown.

Finally, I thank my wife, Sharon Watson Fluker, whose steadfast love and unwavering support make all things possible.

List of Abbreviations

Collections and Repositories

DH-PC   Collections of the Department of History, Presbyterian Church (U.S.A.), Philadelphia, Pennsylvania

ERP-FDR   Eleanor Roosevelt Papers, Franklin Delano Roosevelt Library, Hyde Park, New York

FC   The Church for the Fellowship of All Peoples, San Francisco, California

MSR-HU   Moorland-Spingarn Research Center, Howard University Archives, Washington, D.C.

Abbreviations Used in Source Notes

The following abbreviations describe the documents on which the transcriptions were based.

Script

A   Autograph (manuscript in author's hand)
P   Printed
T   Typed

Format

D   Document
L   Letter or memo
W   Wire or telegram

Version

c   Copy (carbon)
d   Draft

Signature

S   Signed

Biographical Essay

In July 1944 Howard Thurman took a leave of absence from his position as dean of Rankin Chapel at Howard University in Washington, D.C., to assume the copastorate of the newly formed Church for the Fellowship of All Peoples in San Francisco, an interracial, interfaith, and intercultural church. His decision surprised many of his friends and associates. They wondered why Thurman would leave—even temporarily—a prestigious ministerial position in the most academically accomplished of all the black colleges in order to assume the leadership of a tiny, fledgling church with uncertain prospects. The new position would pay only about half of what Thurman earned at Howard.[1] Yet Thurman never doubted that in undertaking what he called "the bold adventure,"[2] he had made the right decision. Thurman was generally a cautious man, certainly not one to gamble his carefully constructed career on a roll of the dice, but in many ways the decision to move to San Francisco was not difficult to make. It was a decision made through many years of preparation, the result of long periods of reflection on the theological and structural inadequacy of the existing church to address divisions of race, class, and creed.

Thurman first wrote at length about his intention to create an interracial church in 1947. He dated his dream of forming something like the Fellowship Church to 1936.[3] However, the initial stirrings date to the beginning of his ministry and to his first extensive interactions with whites in religious settings, usually at student Christian meetings. He was struck at how easy it was for whites to compartmentalize their dealings with blacks, to set limits on their religious fellowship, while practicing a religion that, as he wrote in 1925, "we surreptitiously label 'Christianity.'" He criticized those who "pussy-foot and wabble" on race and insisted that "to follow Christ means that *all* of life, not a segment here and there, must be increasingly permeated with the Spirit of Christ."[4] This included local churches, but in 1920s America there were few places for whites and blacks to worship together on a regular basis. Later in life Thurman would often tell the story of the Nigerian who visited a church when he was an assistant pastor in Roanoke, Virginia, in the summer of 1924 and said that Allah would laugh at the racial divisions within American Christianity.[5]

During his time in India in 1935 and 1936 as chair of the Pilgrimage of Friendship of the Negro Delegation to India, Ceylon, and Burma, Thurman carefully observed the differences between Christianity and Eastern religions, generally to the latter's advantage. In his conversation with Gandhi, the two men agreed that in terms of its racial practices, Islam was vastly superior to Christianity.[6] Toward the end of his time in India, in early February 1936 while visiting Peshawar (now in Pakistan) in the North-West Frontier Province, Thurman and his wife Sue Bailey Thurman (also a member of the delegation) took a brief excursion to the Khyber Pass, a famous path of trade and conquest through the towering mountains that mark the border between South Asia and Afghanistan. As Thurman remembered in 1947, when he and his wife reflected on the meaning of their journey, they spoke of the differences between the United States and India, especially the "fundamental contradiction that lay like a malignant growth at the heart of the Christian movement as it had expressed itself in our own country." This was the "will to separateness" within the church, making it "one of the strongest bulwarks in American life defending and exemplifying racial prejudice."[7]

Thurman determined that upon his return to the United States, he would challenge the separation between whites and blacks within institutionalized Christianity and create a church that would be expressly organized along interracial lines.[8] His work at Howard University gave him little chance to advance this goal. After discussions on starting an interracial church in a large eastern city with his friend Channing Tobias came to naught,[9] Thurman continued to speak about the need for a new kind of church. In a major address in Chicago in February 1941 before the International Council of Religious Education titled "Our Underlying Spiritual Unities," he spoke of the hypocrisy of segregated Christianity: "Can we expect more of the state, the body politic, of industry than we expect of the church? How can we teach love from behind great high walls of separateness?"[10]

Thurman was somewhat more explicit about the kinds of changes he demanded from the church in an important article, "The Will to Segregation," published in August 1943 in *Fellowship,* the journal of the Fellowship of Reconciliation.[11] He outlined a practical vision of how, in the near future, organized Christianity could combat the "will to segregation":

For the church this means a radical internal reorganization of policy and of structural change. I am realistic enough to know that this cannot be done overnight. My contention is that if the "will to segregate" is relaxed in the church then the resources of mind and spirit and power that are already in the church can begin working formally and informally on the radical changes that are necessary if the church is to become Christian. This of course, may not mean that there will be no congregations that are all Negro, or that are all white, but freedom of choice, which is basically a sense of alternatives, will be available to any persons without regard to the faithful perpetuation of the pattern of segregation upon which the Christian church in America is constructed.

Perhaps A. J. Muste, the editor of *Fellowship,* had this passage in mind when several months later, on 8 October 1943, he wrote to Thurman telling him about a church that was forming in San Francisco and that would be organized as an interracial church. The church would be led by the Presbyterian minister Alfred Fisk, who was looking for a black copastor.[12] Thurman's interest in the new venture was immediate, and after only a slight hesitation and some importuning from Fisk, Thurman agreed to become copastor.[13] The correspondence between the two men over the next nine months reveals the immensity of their challenge. Fisk originally was looking for (and had the budget only for) a student pastor, and more money had to be raised to bring Thurman's salary up to a minimally acceptable level.[14] In addition the temporary quarters for the church were clearly inadequate and would soon have to be replaced. Fisk wrote of splits and divisions within the congregation, the scramble for funding, and the myriad of challenges that typically beset new, experimental, and underfinanced ventures.

However, Fisk and Thurman also wrote of their shared hopes and dreams for the new congregation and considered whether, as Thurman wrote elsewhere, "there is enough vitality in the institutional expression of religion to deal creatively with the facts of racial conflict." Thurman hoped that the new church might become "an island of religious and racial community in a sea of religious and racial tension and animosity."[15] The largest question for both men was, in Thurman's words, "Is it possible for a Negro and a white man sharing full joint responsibility for the leadership of an institution of this kind to minister to the needs of the people on the basis of their respective gifts rather than their racial affiliations, and to do this over a time interval of sufficient duration to validate the idea?"[16] The answers to this and to other questions would be complex without straightforward answers, but the collaboration that developed between Thurman and Fisk was precious to both men. In 1975 Thurman reprinted most of the early correspondence that nurtured their partnership, in *The First Footprints.*[17]

If there was enthusiasm in San Francisco, there was considerable doubt and consternation among Thurman's friends and colleagues in Washington, D.C. Many questioned the wisdom of Thurman's plans. The first and most important skeptic was his wife, who in an interview late in her life said that she had initially "hated leaving her work in Washington, D.C. to come to San Francisco."[18]

Sue Bailey Thurman held various positions in Washington, D.C., including editor of the *Aframerican Woman's Journal*,[19] the official publication of the National Council of Negro Women.[20] Sue would soon change her mind, and the Thurmans and their two daughters had a "house meeting" in which the opportunities and the possible privations of the move were discussed. After two hours of intense discussion, the vote to move to the West Coast was unanimous.[21] Others required more convincing. Thurman had played a unique role at Howard University for a dozen years as teacher, preacher, and spiritual adviser. He had guided the careers of countless students and had helped direct some, such as James Farmer and Pauli Murray, toward a lifetime of civil rights activism. All this, his friends feared, would be lost in the move to an uncertain future with a tiny—predominantly white—congregation in San Francisco.[22] One of the skeptics was Howard University's president and Thurman's onetime mentor, Mordecai Wyatt Johnson. Johnson was reluctant to let Thurman go and questioned the soundness of Thurman's plans, noting the financial hardship it would entail for his family. In the end Johnson relented and allowed Thurman to take an unpaid sabbatical.[23] Ultimately almost all of Thurman's friends and colleagues came to support his decision, which he had never doubted was the right decision. As he wrote in March 1944 to an editor at Scribner about the Fellowship Church, "If Christianity cannot do this, then we shall have to find some other faith, and there is no other faith on the horizon."[24]

Thurman felt that in moving to San Francisco he was, as much as anything he had ever done in his life, responding to a divine call, and he worked to the limits of his energies and abilities to make the Fellowship Church a success. He became a diligent fund-raiser (something he had previously gone out of his way to avoid), patiently attended countless committee meetings, mediated disputes, and involved himself in every aspect of the life of the church. He greatly limited his outside appearances, although to help compensate for lost income, he continued to travel east every winter to undertake a grueling month-long speaking tour, often speaking in multiple locations a day and sleeping in Pullman coaches between stops.[25] (Any speaking fees in the Bay Area he donated to the church.) In December 1943, with the decision to move to San Francisco perhaps in mind, he wrote to a former student, "Yes, I do believe that there is a will of God. To me it is to be distinguished from mere desire, or whim in the life of the individual and is to be found primarily in the core of a man's yearning." He went on to distinguish between fate and destiny. According to Thurman, one had no control over one's fate. He stated, "A man's destiny is determined by what he does with his fate."[26] In the Fellowship Church, Thurman was convinced, he had found his destiny.

At a deeper level, Thurman's experimentation with religious experience as a resource within the church was concerned not only with interracialism but also with the transformation of culture. The underlying premise of the ecclesi-ological structure derived from this idea is that the church is, as he would write in 1954 in *The Creative Encounter,* "the organism fed by the springs of individ-ual and collective religious experience through which the Christian works in society."[27] For Thurman, the ministry of the church was twofold: it provided for an environment of worship in which experiences of spiritual unity were achieved; and it had both pedagogical (teaching) and hermeneutical (interpre-tive) functions for those engaged in acts of social transformation for a just and equitable society. Underlying the church's commitment to inclusiveness was the belief that the experiences of unity and fellowship are more compelling than the fears, dogma, and prejudices that separate people; Thurman believed that if these spiritual experiences of unity could be multiplied over a time interval of sufficient duration, they should be able to undermine any barriers, personal and social, that separate persons from one another.[28]

Thurman opened *Footprints of a Dream,* his personal history of the Fellowship Church, by asking, "What was the climate like in America in 1944 when Fellow-ship Church was launched?" There was only one possible answer: "Our country was involved in total war."[29] He had been enveloped in this reality for several years. Thurman was a pacifist, but regarding pacifism he was not, as he noted in a journal entry in July 1944, "an absolutist."[30] He counseled conscientious objec-tors and soldiers alike.[31] He felt that it was his duty, as mentor to so many How-ard men now in uniform, to support them and through his support to endeavor to fight racial segregation in the military. Thurman chose this course rather than—out of some higher ideological commitment to pacifism—completely wash his hands of the war effort.[32] He kept up a correspondence with dozens of his former Howard students serving in the military and wrote proudly of the combat record of blacks to those who would besmirch it.[33]

Thurman also expected, as did many Americans, that from the unspeakable carnage of the war some good might come, in the form of a new commitment to democracy and racial equality. As Thurman noted in a 1940 Chicago address, speaking about World War I, wars enlarge hopes and exacerbate fears. The total mobilization of the country under President Wilson forced those in positions of authority, however grudgingly and incompletely, to recognize the genuine citizenship of black Americans. But this was bitterly resented by a majority of whites, and amid postwar unrest and rioting, the faint promise of racial equal-ity was obliterated.[34] By 1942 Thurman was convinced that the social and po-litical forces that had been unleashed in the previous war were rising to the surface again: the push by blacks and their allies for equality, and the pushback by whites against such progress, with the ultimate victor unclear.[35] The war had generated much talk of a racially egalitarian democracy, much of it described in terms too abstract and flowery to be of any use. As Thurman wrote in "The Will to Segregation," war goals and postwar ambitions needed to be "concrete and specific. Mere slogans are completely meaningless."[36] But often the more people spoke of the ideals of American democracy, the more glaring their internal contradictions. "The measure of the frustration of Negroes is in direct proportion to the degree to which the meaning of democracy is made clear and definite."[37] But at least the war had made the possibility of genuine democracy more tangible and concrete.

This was Thurman's fight. He was fascinated by the sense of urgency the war created for average citizens, the need for involvement in an all-consuming cause. In February 1944 he wrote in a sermon titled "In Quest of a Life Worth Living," perhaps with thoughts of his impending move in mind, "We are all of us in quest of a way of life that is worth living. We want to feel that we are engaged in a total enterprise that is meaningful. . . . It is for this reason that war, despite its terror, wreckage and stark tragedy, makes so great an appeal to men, women and even children." People had not forgotten the horrors of war, Thurman argued, but "when war comes, something is at last at stake in the day's living. . . . A new kind of civic character appears sired by new and awful responsibilities. My country needs me—I fly to the rescue." This new civic urgency encompassed the usually excluded, among them African Americans. "The ordinary individual now counts in a strange new way. His country cares about what he does—all secondary and tertiary citizens become citizens, first class." He allowed that it was "one of the most tragic commentaries on modern life" that this happens only in wartime, but if it was a tragedy, it was also an opportunity.[38]

Thurman encouraged those who heard "In Quest of a Life Worth Living" to take advantage of these new circumstances, and in unusually exalted language he encouraged them to make a personal, spiritual commitment to create a better world: "How men treat each other, what they do to the environment in which little children must grow and develop, how they earn their living—all things in the making of which they play a significant part stand bare before the eyes of God. You must live and proclaim of faith that will make men affirm themselves and their fellowmen as children of God. You must lay your lives on the altar of social change so that wherever you are there the Kingdom of God is at hand!" There were many ways to accomplish this; for Thurman, it was his role in the creation of the Fellowship Church.[39]

Few areas of the country were changed as much by the war as San Francisco and the larger Bay Area were. Defense contracting, particularly the shipbuilding industry, fueled an economic boom and a reallocation of national resources that in a few decades would help make California the most populous state in the nation. San Francisco's black population, fewer than 5,000 in 1940 (out of a total population of about 630,000), increased by over 600 percent during the war. By 1945 there were approximately 32,000 African Americans living in the city.[40] When Sue Bailey Thurman first visited San Francisco in 1942, she observed that blacks were "scattered all over the city." When she moved to the city two years later, she noted large, discrete black neighborhoods.[41]

The rise of black San Francisco was overlaid on the tragic war-time plight of West Coast Japanese Americans, who had been forced by the War Department to abandon their homes and to enter internment camps. Thurman had visited two of the camps in 1942 and 1943.[42] When he arrived in San Francisco in 1944, the hatred of the Japanese was still palpable. The Japanese as real people had been replaced by the Japanese as billboard caricatures with leering, distorted faces, marking them, Thurman thought, as representatives of a subhuman race fit only for extermination.[43] He wondered as well if the virulent anti-Japanese racism had in effect transformed the war into a struggle between whites and non-whites, further contaminating American race relations.[44]

In San Francisco, as in many other West Coast cities, the recently depopulated Japanese neighborhood soon became a destination for recent black migrants from the South. Roughly five thousand Japanese Americans were expelled from the city, part of the approximately one hundred thousand Japanese Americans expelled from California.[45] Japantown had been one of the few areas of the city where nonwhites were welcome and could readily find places to live. As Fellowship Church minister Albert Cleage observed, "Twenty thousand Negroes were crowded into make-shift rooming houses and apartment houses which had accommodated about eight thousand Japanese."[46] Joseph James, a labor activist and the militant president of the local NAACP branch, wrote in 1945, "Caucasian San Francisco turned to the machinery already at hand [such as restrictive covenants] for the subjugation of the Oriental and applied it to the Negro."[47]

Largely because of the tiny black population, prewar San Francisco had enjoyed an undeserved reputation, as James wrote, "of being without a 'race problem' in so far as Negroes and whites were concerned."[48] This had always been an illusion. Not until 1942 would the first black be employed on San Francisco's public transportation system, and black representation in other municipal services was similarly marginal. Moreover, despite the existence of the Fair Employment Practices Commission, created in 1941 to prevent discrimination among defense contractors, unequal treatment was rampant in the area's burgeoning defense industry.[49]

In the fall of 1943, following the summer riots in Detroit as well as in Harlem and other eastern cities, many San Franciscans worried that something similar might happen in their city. When Albert Cleage arrived in San Francisco in February 1944, he found the city to be "suffering from a bad case of riot-jitters. Everywhere people seemed to be waiting for the signal which was to begin the fire-works. Both Negroes and whites were frightened and angry in the presence of something they couldn't understand."[50] This view was shared by Cleage's copastor at the Fellowship Church, Alfred Fisk. As Fisk wrote to Thurman in one of their first letters, "New Negroes pouring into this area in the tens of thousands; tension rising to the breaking point; the outbreak of violence in minor instances with more general rioting only averted by a hair's breadth."[51] A study of black war workers conducted in the fall of 1943 by the eminent Fisk University sociologist Charles S. Johnson was a damning indictment of the plight of local black workers and their families. Discrimination was rampant in housing, in schools, in access to employment, in the availability of public services and commercial amusements, and in access to political power.[52] At best, most white San Franciscans were indifferent to the newcomers; others were outright hostile. Thurman remembered a war-time acquaintance, "a sensitive, educated man of good will," confessing to him that "I feel squeamish and uneasy when I move around the city now because everywhere I look I see a Negro."[53] Established black San Franciscans were not necessarily less discriminatory toward other blacks, as the existing religious and community institutions were overwhelmed by the new arrivals.[54] Langston Hughes, in the spring of 1944, described old-time black San Franciscans who spoke contemptuously of "cotton-patch Negroes" as being "almost as prejudiced against the new dark arrivals from the South as are the reactionary white folks."[55]

Amid all this change and turbulence, in San Francisco and other large American cities, one thing remained the same: the racial attitudes of American Christianity. If every important institution in the country remained divided by race, the church was likely the most segregated of all. As Thurman would later note, of the country's eight million African American Protestants in the 1940s, the percentage of blacks that gathered together regularly with whites for worship services was "almost microscopic"—much less than one-tenth of 1 percent, perhaps one black in a thousand or even in ten thousand.[56] "What do we mean when we teach the brotherhood of man," he wrote in the summer of 1943, "when over and over again we give the sanction of our religion and the weight of our practice to those subtle anti-christian practices expressed in segregated churches and even in segregated graveyards!"[57] In private Thurman was even more scathing and despairing: "It is well within the range of possibility that the church through its own apostasy will be bypassed by God."[58]

One of the most creative efforts to deal with the problems of blacks' migration to war-time San Francisco and the racial rigidity of the church was undertaken by a small group of young women. They were Christian pacifists, most of them graduates of prestigious eastern colleges, who were living cooperatively in a house in the Fillmore area, in the heart of the former Japanese district.

Known as the Sakai Group, they were, as one correspondent wrote to Thurman in early November 1943, "a group of young people [who] are dedicating their energies to the interracial problem of San Francisco."[59] Members of the Sakai Group were involved in local civil rights struggles—such as Bayard Rustin's efforts to desegregate recreational facilities in the fall of 1943—and they opened their house to their neighbors, listening to their problems, playing with their children, inviting them for meals, and inviting them for prayer. Sometime in 1943 they had the idea of transforming their informal prayer meetings into something more fixed and established, and probably through mutual contacts at the Fellowship of Reconciliation, they got in touch with Alfred Fisk.

A native San Franciscan, Fisk had a reputation in the mid-1940s as one of San Francisco's leading liberal Protestant ministers. Born in 1905 and from solid Presbyterian stock—his father was the onetime moderator of the Los Angeles Presbytery—he was both a minister and a philosopher by training, and a member of the Fellowship of Reconciliation.[60] Fisk was a driven and determined man, rigorous and unrelaxed in pursuit of his goals. He does not seem to have been particularly easy to get along with. Two friends, writing after his too-early death in 1959, observed that "he was as near as being a personification of the Kantian man of duty as anyone we have known. He lived a life forthright to duty."[61] If this forthrightness sometimes led to tension with Thurman and others, without it and without Fisk's determination to create and lead an experiment in interracial Christianity, there would have been no Fellowship Church. Fisk arranged with the local presbytery and the National War Fund of the Presbyterian Church, U.S.A. to start providing some modest funds for the new venture. At the end of December 1943 Fisk offered the following description of the church's progress to an official at the Board of National Missions of the Presbyterian Church, U.S.A., which was providing funding: "After considerable preliminary work, those interested in the project were called together for an evening meeting on Dec. 1st. Forty-two were present and enthusiastically arranged for services to begin on Dec. 12th. The plan was to begin with morning church services and add a Sunday school the following week and other meetings as needed. This has been done. There were just 66 at our first morning service, about one third of whom were Negro. The following Sunday it was raining. There were 36 in attendance, but a larger proportion of Negroes."[62]

After seven weeks attendance was averaging about forty people, and many of those were merely curious; few newcomers had announced their intention to become regular participants in church events.[63] The church attracted persons from a variety of religious backgrounds, primarily middle-class professionals united by their commitment to racial equality. Joseph James, a distinguished concert baritone in addition to being a labor activist and president of the San Francisco chapter of the NAACP, was an early member. His wife, Alberta Mayo

James, was the church's first director of music.[64] Bayard Rustin's organizing efforts in San Francisco in the fall of 1943 attracted several persons who would shortly join the fledgling church, among them Thurman's good friend Virginia Scardigli, who was later secretary of the Fellowship Church, and Hope Foote, a member of the Sakai Group. Scardigli wrote to Thurman in October 1943 (before she knew about any plans for the new church) that she was "working like a beaver in a Race Relations Workshop led by Bayard Rustin" and that "tonight I am going to try a skating rink (4 of us) in an interracial group" to attempt to integrate it.[65]

From their earliest correspondence, Fisk and Thurman were in agreement on their vision for the church. It would be a place where whites and blacks would participate as full equals in every aspect of church life.[66] The church would not promote as part of its primary purpose any form of social outreach or assistance to blacks because, however well intentioned, such activities invariably reinforce attitudes of white superiority and black inferiority. Fisk and Thurman, especially Thurman, were adamant about the need for the church to avoid anything remotely smacking of Negro uplift or "mission work," but not everyone, both inside and outside the church, was as firm about this as Thurman.[67] Although the new church was inescapably attached to a controversial political agenda, Fisk and Thurman were insistent that the Fellowship Church was primarily and essentially a religious congregation, dedicated to deepening and enriching the personal and collective spiritual lives of its members.[68] At the same time, both men saw the Fellowship Church as something larger than its relatively small membership—as an experiment, a prototype for a new kind of Christianity. Its successes and failures would be carefully watched by a large number of interested observers, and Thurman, throughout his tenure, endeavored to create a national and even international reputation and standing for the church. These various aspirations were not always harmonious and at times clashed. Thurman often described the Fellowship Church as revolutionary. For example, in a 1946 letter to Elizabeth Eckert he referred to "this revolutionary experiment in which we are engaged," an unleashing of a hidden potential for social and spiritual transformation that had been buried deep within the inner recesses of institutional Christianity.[69] Revolutions rarely run smoothly.

Both men were determined that their church would be avowedly and purposively interracial, with blacks and whites participating equally. It would bear no resemblance to the common antebellum practice of slave masters and enslaved persons worshipping together, which dated back to the earliest days of New World Christianity.[70] Nor would it be a church, like Jehovah's Witnesses or certain Holiness sects, open to all, regardless of color, but unworldly, apocalyptic, and apolitical. Thurman wrote of such denominations that while, to their credit, "[t]he conditions for membership do not include ethnic, cultural, or national considerations; [their] [i]nclusiveness is incidental, never crucial."[71]

For Thurman and Fisk, the interracial nature of the church had to be part of its religious character. The Fellowship Church is often described as the first interracial church. It probably was not the first (it depends on one's definition of "interracial" and "church"), but the question of absolute priority is less important than the significance of the Fellowship Church as a herald of a new interracial church movement. Despite a few prewar precedents, notably Philadelphia's Fellowship House, churches self-labeled as interracial were war-time phenomena.[72] Examples included the short-lived Congregation of His People in Detroit, started in 1942, which was advertised as an "inter-racial congregation" dedicated to correcting "the evils of racism, anti-Semitism, [and] oppression" and to uniting "the peoples of the world."[73] In 1941 the onetime Indian missionary and Methodist minister E. Stanley Jones addressed a crowd of two thousand at the "Fellowship Church (Interracial)" in Pasadena, California, decrying the tragedy of race distinctions within Christianity.[74] Other examples soon followed.[75] By early 1947 the Unitarian minister Homer Jack could write with confidence about "the emergence of the interracial church" as a national movement.[76]

For Thurman, an interracial church that was not also interdenominational (and as he preferred, truly interreligious, embracing all faiths) was simply, in another way, reinforcing and recapitulating the divisions within humanity and Christianity. Fisk shared this belief, but it was never as central to his conception of the church as it was for Thurman. The emphasis by Thurman on interdenominationalism shaped worship at the Fellowship Church from the beginning. When, after India, he returned to Howard, where experimentation in interracial worship was a practical impossibility, Thurman introduced liturgical innovations that he saw as paving the way toward an interracial and interdenominational Christianity. Through the introduction of meditation periods, services without sermons, liturgical dance, and tableaux vivants (especially interracial Christmas representations of Mary and the infant Jesus), Thurman hoped to create worship experiences in which a sense of congregational unity transcended any confessional differences.[77] Thurman continued and extended all of these practices at the Fellowship Church, all intended to create a sense of interracial and interreligious harmony.

However effective as a worship strategy, these liturgical innovations did not efface all internal congregational differences, or what would later be called "the embroilment of membership in the church."[78] Indeed when Thurman arrived in San Francisco, he joined a congregation riven with factionalism and contention. The two original poles of the Fellowship Church, Fisk and the Sakai

Group, soon found themselves at odds over a whole host of church issues, with Fisk's rather conventional Presbyterianism clashing with what he called the "monastic group at Sakai House," whose Gandhian spirituality he deemed "not representative of Christendom as we understand it."[79]

Fisk also had problems with the two black assistant pastors with whom he worked before Thurman's arrival. Fisk found the first assistant pastor, Manley Johnson, to be incompetent.[80] A local divinity student, Johnson lasted only a few weeks after the founding of the church before Fisk's ire led to a parting of the ways. He was replaced by Albert Cleage, Jr., who was with the church from February until June. Cleage was at the beginning of a tempestuous career that would culminate in the 1960s with his gaining fame and notoriety as one of the leading advocates of a black nationalist Christianity. His politics were different in 1944, but they were just as fiery. Cleage came highly recommended, but Fisk's initial enthusiasm about him (before the two men had met) soon turned to deep disappointment. Fisk complained that Cleage took no interest in the religious school and neglected his pastoral duties.[81] Cleage's bluntness and political radicalism (especially his support of Communist-leaning CIO unions) brought the working relationship between the two men close to the breaking point and almost led to Cleage's dismissal. Cleage did leave San Francisco at the end of his contract at the end of June, a few days before Thurman's arrival. The two men, with their careers on very different ideological and theological trajectories, would never meet.[82]

After months of planning, and of dealing with the challenges of war-time travel, on Wednesday morning, 12 July 1944, the Thurman family—Howard, Sue Bailey Thurman, and their two daughters, Anne and Olive—arrived in San Francisco.[83] The five-day train trip from Washington, D.C., left them "tired and quite weary."[84] Thurman was met by Fisk, who had arranged for a full day of meetings with various officials. When the long day was finally over, Thurman noted in his diary, with a combination of exasperation and admiration, "This kind of experience after traveling across the continent. Everything that we did could have waited until the next day. This is the kind of zeal that Alfred Fisk has."[85]

Thurman's own zeal had taken him across the continent. He was perhaps thinking of the tasks ahead when in the first sermon at Fellowship Church, on 23 July, he quoted Lewis Mumford (speaking on Thurman's favorite novel, *Moby-Dick*) on the nature of the challenge or quest: "Where that sense is lacking, life shrivels into small prudences and weak pleasures and petty gains, and those great feats of thought and imagination which transform the very character of the universe and relieve human purpose from the scant sufficiency of toiling and eating and sleeping, in a meaningless, reiterative round, shrivel away, too."[86]

The most immediate challenge was finding a larger and more appropriate location for the church. Everyone associated with the church knew that its initial quarters, the former Japanese Presbyterian Church, with a sanctuary that held only one hundred people, were inadequate. Much energy was expended in the search for a new home for the church; most of the work was undertaken by Fisk. From late 1943 through mid-1944 Fisk investigated at least eight possible sites. These included potential rentals such as auditoriums of the Booker T. Washington Community Service Center (not "worshipful"), buildings owned by two white fraternal organizations (they would not rent to blacks), a Quaker meetinghouse, a Seventh-Day Adventist church, and two synagogues (unacceptable or unavailable for various reasons); and two prospective purchases that proved too expensive: a Baptist church and a Lutheran church, both congregations of which were intent on leaving the neighborhood because of its changing racial mix.[87]

For Thurman, the practical question of finding a new church building was perhaps less important than the need for the Fellowship Church to move from its current location. He did not want the church to remain in what was increasingly an African American neighborhood. At first Thurman found that few members of the church agreed with him about this. In his journal he described his first meeting with the church board: "I have found very little evidence that there was any clear cut notion as to what we are trying to do in this corner. It's interesting that again and again the reference is made to the fact that the church must be located in the heart of the Negro district. Is the idea that in some way this church is to bring into its walls the Negroes off the streets of the neighborhood? If that is the notion, then the church is merely repeating the pattern of Protestants and will be fought to the end by the Negro churches in the area."[88]

The issue was clear-cut for Thurman. He had come to San Francisco to preside over an interracial church. If it remained in a black neighborhood, he was convinced, the church would shortly become entirely black. People who thought otherwise were simply deceiving themselves about how race worked in American cities. For most other church members, the issues were more muddled.[89] Thurman's logic was directly opposed to the reasoning of many, if not most, members who wanted to get involved in a church located in the heart of black San Francisco. To "bring into its walls the Negroes off the streets of the neighborhood" was their main motivation. Thurman's insistence that the church focus on its interracial mission had profound consequences for its future, resulting in its relatively small size and its predominantly middle-class character. But as Thurman wrote in his diary, to do otherwise, to compete directly against the local black churches, would only generate ill will and divert the church from its mission. The best way, Thurman felt, to ensure that the

Fellowship Church would make an important statement about black equality, within the church and within American society in general, was to ensure that it remained interracial. A church whose chief goal was to work with the local black community would not achieve that result.

Thurman eventually persuaded the congregation to move to the other side of Van Ness Avenue, the informal line of racial separation. Although the new church, the former home of the Filipino Methodist Church, was only two blocks from this division, Thurman was gratified by the move and thought that it gave the church a chance to develop its interracial character. The church would move twice more, in 1946 to the Theater Arts Colony on Washington Street and in 1949 to its permanent home on Larkin Street[90] (see figure 1).

The meaning of interracialism in the Fellowship Church was oft-debated and continually evolving. On the most obvious level it was a matter of gross membership numbers. In 1949 the church had a local membership of about 285, with whites comprising about 60 percent of the members.[91] In 1951 the church had 345 members, a little over half of whom were white and about 40 percent black.[92] In December 1954, about a year after he left for Boston, Thurman was receiving reports, which proved to be an exaggeration, that the Fellowship Church was "becoming a Negro church."[93]

Beyond broad membership numbers, interracialism was a part of every facet of church operations. Careful attention was paid to racial balance and percentages. Thurman wrote to a church member in 1954 about a situation that had required his intervention: "I remember several years ago when the choir suddenly became 4/5ths Negro, I had a long conference with Corrine Williams [the choir director], calling her attention to what was happening and insisted that she work at restoring a more authentic inter-racial balance to the choir. This was deliberately done with positive and immediate effect."[94] At the same time there was recognition that attention to racial balances just heightens self-consciousness about race and is at cross purposes with the goal of relaxed and unforced racial interactions. Virginia Scardigli, an active member of the church, wrote in 1947, "In the early days we made a special effort to get a 'mixed bouquet' in all our groups and committees in order to demonstrate the interracial aspect. That is not done now."[95] This was probably too definitive a statement on Scardigli's part; conscious racial balancing was not finished in 1947, but maintaining the interracial ideal at the Fellowship Church required a number of strategies, among them knowing when to pay attention to racial percentages and when not to do so. In Thurman's words, maintaining "an authentic inter-racial institution in our kind of multi-racial society takes a special kind of ability, sensitiveness, and program."[96]

San Francisco was a city where interracialism was much broader than the white-black dyad typical of mid-century America. A pamphlet produced by

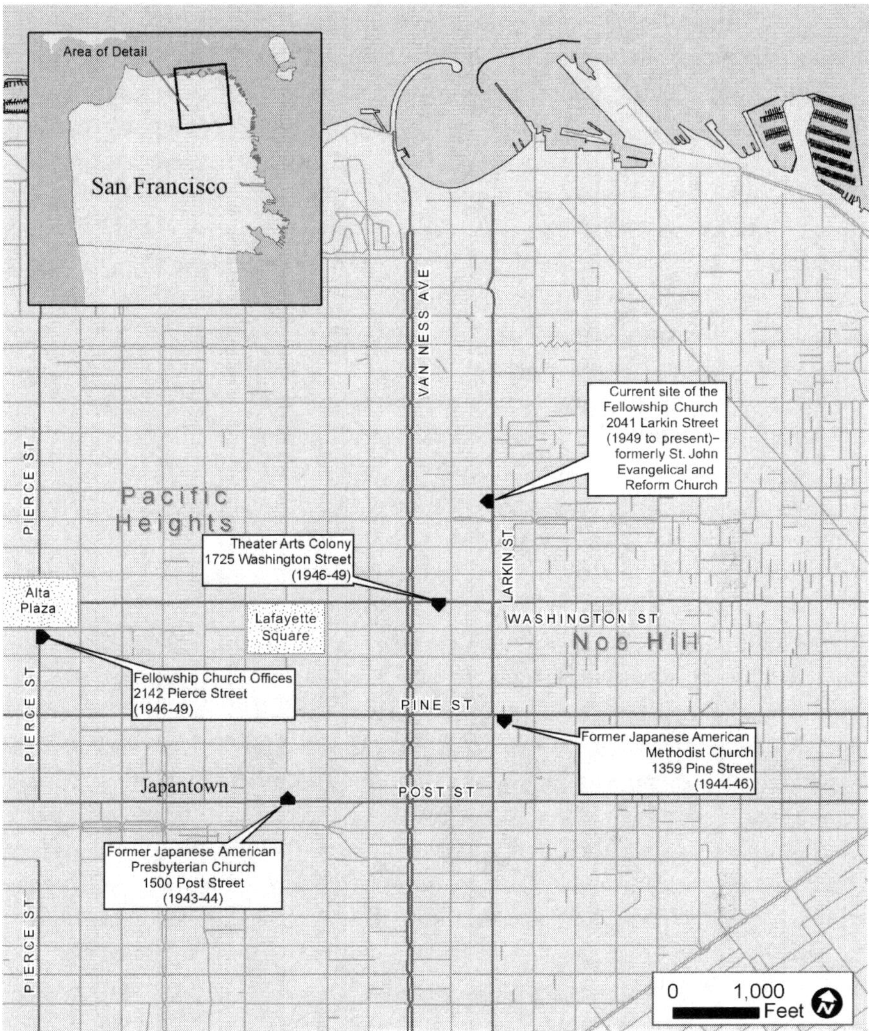

Fellowship Church locations in San Francisco. © 2013 Marc Korpus, used with permission.

the Fellowship Church stated, with some precision, that San Francisco had "sixty-three national and cultural background groups" and was a "gold mine" for interracial and intercultural activities.[97] Japanese Americans were active in the church from the outset; the president of the Japanese American Citizens' League, a recent returnee from the internment camps, was an early member of the church board of trustees.[98] The church had regular dinners, each devoted to a different ethnic group and cuisine, along with its Intercultural Concert

Series, the Intercultural Library of several hundred volumes, and the Intercultural Workshop for children.[99] In all of these activities, church members thought critically about the potential pitfalls of interculturalism, such as how to display the characteristics of an ethnic group without reducing them to a limiting stereotype, and how to view difference without superiority or condescension.[100] A description of the Young Adult Group on a retreat captures the church's intercultural ideal: "An open fire cracked and popped. Hearthside rays glanced from an East Indian reflected to the intense faces—the faces of young people in discussion—all young Americans—a Negro sailor from Chicago, a Nisei girl, a native San Franciscan, a Caucasian from a southern state, a Filipino youth leader. . . . [ellipsis in original] Questions, answers, opinions flew back and forth. Suddenly the mugs of cocoa appeared, the discussion drew to a close. . . . [ellipsis in original] The whole group joined in laughter, song, and fun."[101] The point of intercultural activities in the church was to free participants of any biases they had already absorbed, giving them, in Thurman's words, "a growing confidence in the naturalness of democratic living."[102]

Another arena in which "the naturalness of democratic living" was tested was politics. This was a special challenge for a church whose organizing rationale had an obvious political and ideological component that provided a prime reason for the involvement of many in the church. However, Thurman was adamant about keeping political commitments at arm's length from the actual work of the church. After his first meeting with the church board he noted in his diary, "The general impression was that this is a church of Pacifist[s]. Now, I am a Pacifist but I am also a human being. . . . The Pacifism of the church should express itself in the quality of life that emanates from the place rather than from pronouncements of one kind or another."[103] This was Thurman's approach to all political matters concerning the church. He wanted the political statement to be the "quality of life" of the church itself rather than external and extraneous policy statements or commitments. This was not always easy, especially with the vexed question of connections to the Communist Party, a divisive issue from the time of the founding of the church at least through the Henry Wallace campaign in 1948. Thurman was adamantly opposed to any sort of link or identification of the church with the Communist Party, although his own politics at the time were left of center and sympathetic to the Popular Front.[104] Official political positions of the church were largely limited to issues connected to its interracial mandate, such as ending discrimination in housing and employment.[105]

For the most part, Thurman thought that if the members of the church focused on its religious life, other concerns, such as race or politics, would tend to take care of themselves. He wrote in 1954, "In my judgment, the thing that kept the inter-racial character of the church important but secondary was my

Thurman at Fellowship Church with the Brewer family (from left: James Brewer, Howard Thurman, Barbara Brewer, and Jimmy Brewer). From the Howard Thurman Collection, Howard Gotlieb Archival Research Center, Boston University.

insistence that the heart of the church center around worship of God and not merely associations that were inter-racial in character. Wherever this is understood, there is immunity against the possibility of the church's becoming either black or white."[106] He said much the same for politics, regretting that some persons "experienced profound disappointment in the church because it was a *church* and not merely a social-protest group."[107] However, purely religious matters can also be contentious, and no issue was more important or more debated in the church in its first years than the nature of its religious character.

When Thurman first arrived in San Francisco, he was not terribly impressed with the church members' understanding of the purpose of the church.[108] From the beginning he pressed the board—and the church more broadly—to fashion and announce a programmatic statement about the nature of the church's religious ideals that would lay out with some specificity the church's religious purpose. In his journal Thurman wrote that at his first meeting with the board, he presented them with a statement that was written by him and Sue and approved by Fisk; this apparently was the first version of the Commitment, the statement of purpose. He wrote that it was approved by the board without changes.[109] This rather straightforward description of the origins of the Commitment seems at odds with Thurman's account in *Footprints of a Dream,* which recalls a more tortured process that involved wrestling day and night with the problem, "putting at the disposal of it my meditation, my prayers, and as much of a disciplined mind as I possessed," with many rewrites and reviews by Fisk.[110] Whatever the circumstances of its composition, in August 1944 Thurman preached a series of sermons on different aspects of the Commitment. At the end of that period, an invitation was extended for members of the congregation to sign the Commitment and formally affiliate with the Fellowship Church.[111]

Although Thurman generally had no interest in dogmatic propositions of faith, he insisted that a statement of purpose was necessary, for a number of reasons.[112] As a new and different kind of church, without any sort of tradition or precedent, it had to be defined as clearly and as unequivocally as possible. Thurman also felt that without a statement of religious purpose, the church would remain a purely local or a purely political endeavor. Above all he thought that signing the Commitment would help bind church members together and help them examine and scrutinize their reasons for involvement in the church. When the Commitment was adopted in the fall of 1944, it was with the understanding that it was "an immediate platform upon which to stand before the community and the world but not a ceiling either for our hopes or our achievement."[113]

There would be three versions of the Commitment.[114] The second version, approved in August 1945 at the time of the split from the Presbyterian Church, was prepared in what Thurman later described as a process of many meetings and a "vast fog of conversation."[115] The third and most enduring version was approved in 1948. The three versions of the Commitment show a steady evolution away from conventional Christianity. The Commitment first spoke of the church affirming "the highest manifestation of God—Jesus Christ." This was replaced in the second version with "God as revealed in Jesus of Nazareth." The Commitment was debated not only within the congregation but also by interested persons nationally. Some, such as George Haynes, the executive secretary of the Race Relations Department of the Federal Council of Churches and a strong supporter of the new church, thought that the move away from mainstream Christianity was not an improvement.[116] Others, notably John Haynes Holmes of the Community Church of New York, complained vociferously that the new version was still speaking in an exclusively Christian language.[117] The third and final version of the Commitment, which spoke of "God as revealed in Jesus of Nazareth and other great religious spirits," was probably more to Holmes's liking. The Commitment made no political statements, no call for the end of segregation, and no demand for racial equality; it simply expressed the "desire to share in the spiritual growth and ethical awareness of men and women in varied national, cultural, racial heritages united in a religious fellowship."

For Thurman and many other members of the church, one of the greatest pleasures of worship was the sense of transcending barriers, of "Jew and Gentile, black and white, rich and poor, clergy and lay, men and women, youth and age, sharing a spiritual unity in celebration of a concrete religious fellowship that in its daily functioning demonstrated that experiences of community are more compelling than all the things that divide."[118] The Fellowship Church encouraged dual memberships, enabling a person to remain involved in one's former congregation while actively participating in the Fellowship Church.[119] An anonymous member of the church in 1947 described the interdenominational and interreligious coming together that made the church unique: "Our membership includes people to whom the Sacraments of the Episcopal Church, the Catholic Mass, the Quaker silence, the communion as observed by the various Protestant denominations, or the age-old Jewish heritage of the consciousness of God's love and care are no less precious than the new fellowship."[120]

However interreligious in intent, the broad framework for worship at the Fellowship Church would always be Christian. The major Christian holidays were observed. The Lord's Prayer was recited. Communion was given on World-Wide Communion Sunday and at other times when a special need was felt. Because there was such a mix of denominational backgrounds in the church, baptisms were not provided.[121] Still, the goal of worship at the Fellowship Church was to move toward an ever more tangible common faith. Without "a common faith," which Thurman distinguished from a common religion, humanity would always remain split and divided. Perhaps he never expressed himself as clearly on this as in the spring of 1953, toward the end of his time at the Fellowship Church, in a sermon on the Brahman mystics of the Upanishads and the Bhagavad-Gita: "I may say almost in passing that at least from my point of view it is hardly a reasonable hope that there should ever come a time in human history when there shall be one world politically and socially until men find out how they can be sustained by one faith. And by one faith I do not mean one creed, one doctrine, one dogma, one church, but one faith, one pulse beat that is so fontal, so—that is so basic to all of the movements of life that it is capable of feeding all the little heartbeats and recognized as such. It takes more than a political dream and more than hunger of body to ground and sustain a neighborhood the size of a planet."[122]

The Fellowship Church's liturgy and religious education programs stressed intercultural and interreligious understanding, with particular emphasis on the development of a common faith that emerged from a collective religious experience. The theological basis for this, according to Thurman, was rooted in the notion that the church is the social institution that is entrusted with "the Jesus idea."[123] From this perspective Jesus is viewed as the central figure of the Christian church; however, Jesus is not a religious object of devotion and worship but rather is a religious subject and an exemplar of the quest for human community. According to Thurman, when Jesus is viewed as a religious object, the grounds are laid for a principle of exclusiveness that has implications not only for interreligious fellowship; because Jesus has been so deeply identified with Euro-Western culture and domination, worship of him becomes a tool of divisiveness and oppression.[124] Thurman asserted that whenever Jesus is rendered as a principle of exclusiveness, there are deleterious consequences for the poor, the disinherited, and the dispossessed. In *Jesus and the Disinherited,* he demonstrates how theological presuppositions were linked to ocular metaphors that served as cultural resources in the segregation of African Americans:

> Given segregation as a factor determining relations, the resources of the environment are made into instruments to enforce the artificial position. Most of the accepted social behavior-patterns assume segregation to be normal—if normal then, correct; if correct, then moral; if moral, then religious. Religion is thus made a defender and guarantor of the presumptions. God, for all practical purposes, is imaged as an elderly, benign white man, seated on a white throne, with bright, white light emanating from his countenance. Angels are blonds and brunets suspended in the air around his throne to be his messengers and execute his purposes. Satan is viewed as being red with the glow of fire. But the imps, the messengers of the devil, are black. The phrase "black as an imp" is a stereotype.
>
> The implications of such a view are simply fantastic in the intensity of their tragedy. Doomed on earth to a fixed and unremitting status of inferiority, of which segregation is symbolic, and at the same time cut off from the hope that the Creator intended it otherwise, those who are thus victimized are stripped of all social protection. It is vicious and thoroughly despicable to rationalize this position, the product of a fear that is as sordid as it is unscrupulous, into acceptance. Under such circumstances there is but a step from being despised to despising oneself.[125]

The "Jesus idea," therefore, is the essence of authentic fellowship and serves as the basis for the creation of common faith among Christians and others who are committed to equality under God. According to Thurman, Jesus placed before humankind three great truths with which the church is entrusted. First, Jesus gave to humankind the vision of a great creative ideal, community. The ideal of community affirms that the normal characterization of all human relations is in terms of inclusiveness. It maintains that the family of humankind is the family of God, and therefore all persons are inextricably bound to one another. Jesus proclaimed community to be the will of God, the intent of life at its most profound level. Second, Jesus taught that the method by which community is achieved is through suffering love. For Jesus, love transcends and gives meaning to all organic relationships and is the only means available to overcome divisions between human beings. The love of the enemy is the ultimate test of love. Third, Jesus gave the resource by which women and men can achieve community and by which they are empowered to love. Jesus called this resource God. The life of Jesus is an example of unrelenting loyalty to God and commitment to equality. He demonstrated in his living that the love of God is present as "an immediate available resource upon which man may draw in order to implement the ideal set before man."[126]

During his nine years at the Fellowship Church, Thurman found himself becoming more of a national figure than ever before. This was due in part to attention given to the Fellowship Church, which was the subject of articles in many leading publications, including *Time*.[127] But of equal importance was that during Thurman's time at Fellowship Church he started to publish regularly, and his message began to reach beyond the circle of his immediate admirers. His first book, *The Greatest of These,* a collection of prose poems, appeared in 1944, a few months after his move to San Francisco.[128] It was published by Eucalyptus Press, a private press imprint of Mills College, which a year later issued *Deep River,* Thurman's meditations on the spirituals. A similar work, *The Negro Spiritual Speaks of Life and Death,* Thurman's Ingersoll Lecture at Harvard, was published by Harper in 1947, his first book to be published by a major commercial house.[129] Also in 1947 Eucalyptus Press issued Thurman's first collection of meditations used in the Fellowship Church, *Meditations for Apostles of Sensitiveness;* a second edition, twice as long, was published the following year. In 1951 Harper reissued the book in yet another expanded form under the title *Deep Is the Hunger: Meditations for Apostles of Sensitiveness.*[130] A separate collection of Fellowship Church meditations, *Meditations of the Heart,* was published by Harper in 1953.[131] In 1949 Abingdon-Cokesbury Press published what has proven to be Thurman's most enduring work, *Jesus and the Disinherited.*[132]

Thurman had long thought of writing as a poor cousin to his preaching, claiming, "Until I came to San Francisco I had very little interest in writing."[133] This is something of an exaggeration. Before arriving in San Francisco, leaving collegiate writings aside, Thurman was the author of at least twenty-one published articles and sermons, eight book reviews, five book chapters, four published poems (some of them appearing in print multiple times), three published lecture and sermon series, and one sermon published as a separate booklet. If Thurman had not published a book with a major publisher before moving to San Francisco, it was not for dint of trying.[134] But most of Thurman's pre–San Francisco printed sermons or articles had appeared in relatively obscure publications with limited circulation or visibility. This would change during his years at Fellowship Church. The growth of Thurman's bibliography during these years is striking, a tribute to his growing stature and to his increasing confidence in putting his thoughts to paper, and a reflection of his personal and spiritual satisfaction with his role in the Fellowship Church.

Thurman's work during this period reflects both long-standing themes and his reaction to the situation in postwar America. Thurman was both hopeful and wary as the war ended. His wariness was evident in what was one of Thurman's most original essays, "The Fascist Masquerade," written in 1946.[135] One of Thurman's few forays into straight political commentary, the essay discusses "the basis of fascism as it has developed in America during the last decade and [attempts] to delineate the challenge which it presents to the Church." Thurman wrote broadly from a Popular Front perspective, deeply worried about the threat of domestic fascism emanating from organizations such as the Ku Klux Klan, which Thurman saw as dedicated to the principle of accentuating inequality between races, between economic groups, and between the empowered and the powerless.[136] For Thurman, these groups represented more than just lower-middle-class resentment and were funded by large and powerful antilabor business interests that usually kept their identities secret (hence the fascist "masquerade"). "American fascism" never became the national threat to democracy that Thurman feared. However, the Far Right groups labeled by Thurman as American fascists along with their ideological descendants such as the White Citizens' Councils were later in the forefront of the opposition to the civil rights movement.[137] One answer to the threat of the fascist masquerade would be provided by the "apostles of sensitiveness," a term Thurman often used during the war and immediate postwar years.[138] This represented an updating of a longtime Thurman theme: small groups of individuals who felt the contradictions of society more acutely than others and who would take the lead in addressing society's ills.[139]

Thurman summed up his religious and political thinking in what is arguably the most significant and personal of all his works, *Jesus and the Disinherited*, published in April 1949. The product of a lecture series he delivered in April 1948 at Samuel Huston College, a historically black college in Austin, Texas, the short book argues that the key to understanding the religion of Jesus (as opposed to the more complacent Christianity preached by the Roman citizen Paul) was his lack of Roman citizenship and then explores the lives of southern blacks, who, like the disinherited Jesus, lacked effective citizenship. After devoting one chapter apiece to the three great evils of social powerlessness—fear, deception, and hate—the final chapter, on love, provides a radical, nonviolent way out for those "who stand with their backs against the wall": learning to love their oppressors to establish their common humanity and to love their oppressors with enough forceful, concentrated, focused, and unsentimental love to destroy Jim Crow.[140]

The little book was a great inspiration to many in the civil rights movement, including Martin Luther King, Jr., who read it as a young seminarian within a few months of its publication and quoted it, without attribution, in several of his student papers. King quoted the story that Thurman's grandmother told him, about the exhortation of the slave preacher: "You—you are not niggers. You—you are not slaves. You are God's children." It was for King an example of how "being a child of God tends to stabilize the ego and bring new courage." King's quoting of Thurman was one of the few instances in his student papers that he discussed African American religion or cited, however obliquely, an African American religious thinker. *Jesus and the Disinherited* was one of King's first exposures to the ideas of radical pacifism.[141]

During Thurman's nine years at the Fellowship Church, the church continued to evolve. In the beginning, largely at the behest and arrangement of Fisk, the Fellowship Church was affiliated with the Presbyterian Church. But for a church as profoundly interdenominational and interreligious as the Fellowship Church, it always was going to be difficult to remain confined, however loosely, within the Presbyterian fold. From the outset there were those in the church who were determined that the church not have any denominational ties. Fisk, a lifelong Presbyterian, strongly opposed this.[142] On the one hand, a Presbyterian affiliation had never been Thurman's preferred approach. In a journal note from July 1944, he complained in scathing terms about the control the national Presbyterian Church wanted to exert over the church.[143] On the other hand, in the beginning he did not feel the Presbyterian ties to be too intrusive, and there were advantages, other than the obvious financial ones, in being supported by a mainstream Protestant denomination.[144] The connection quieted what Thurman said was a common reaction to the new church: "It's a fly-by-night group supported by the lunatic fringe of the community, and it can't possibly survive; and the man who came out from Washington is just out for a lark. Everybody's anxious to come to California for the weather anyway."[145]

However, by 1945 it was clear to Thurman that the national Presbyterian Church was viewing the Fellowship Church primarily as a mission church for blacks, with its interracial ideals put to the side.[146] Thinking back on this, he would write in 1947, "One of the simple devices by which the pattern of segregation spreads in American life is by the placing of institutions whose commitment is opposed to segregation into relatively segregated communities or neighborhoods and given in those neighborhoods a community assignment."[147] The debate on whether to end the Presbyterian ties was heated, and although many wondered how the church would survive without its Presbyterian subvention, the congregation voted on 1 August 1945 to sunder its denominational ties.[148] The church was now on its own. By the beginning of 1946, Thurman could write in a Christmas letter to his friends at Howard that the Fellowship Church was "no longer an 'experiment.'"[149]

Other changes soon followed the break from the Presbyterian Church. In May 1946 Thurman reluctantly decided not to return to Howard. His one-year leave of absence had been extended to a second year, but it would not be renewed again. By February 1946 Thurman was considering three options: full time in San Francisco, with several months a year for preaching in the East and teaching; full time at Howard, or if this proved impossible, some other campus in the East; or his preferred alternative, dividing his year between San Francisco and Washington, D.C., and using his time at Howard in part to nurture young pastors who could intern at the Fellowship Church.[150] He wrote to his friend Allan Hunter that month that "it is very difficult to decide between two things, both of which must be right, but one of which must be more completely in line with oughtness than the other."[151] Howard University's board of trustees largely made the decision for him when at the beginning of April they voted to end all war-time leaves of absence.[152] On 13 May 1946 Thurman submitted his resignation to Howard, doing so "with emotional lacerations and a deep sense of personal loss."[153]

Then that fall Alfred Fisk resigned his position and left the church. In his letter of resignation to Thurman, he wrote of the need for a Sunday school for his son, but Fisk had many other issues with the direction of the church.[154] Fisk had been upset by the decision to sever the relationship with the Presbyterian Church. He wrote in September 1945 that he was deeply regretful about the decision, and "this means that my own relation to this church will terminate in the near future."[155] He also felt that his personal relations with many members of the church were strained.[156] Thurman's response to Fisk's leaving is not known, but if his emotions were mixed, he probably thought this move inevitable. Thurman had previously worried that a church with two ministers with equal authority was unwieldy and artificial. He viewed the arrangement as more of a statement about racial equality than a practical method of church governance, and he had doubted whether the church could survive with copastors.[157] Thurman had become the effective leader of the church, and his decision to remain in San Francisco perhaps hastened Fisk's decision.

The parting between Fisk and Thurman was amicable, though they did not remain close friends, and Fisk had little or no involvement in the Fellowship Church after his departure. Fisk continued to teach at San Francisco State and developed a further career as a leader of global tours to places such as the Soviet Union and Eastern Europe, the Middle East, and South Asia in an effort to foster better international understanding. In 1959 Thurman dedicated *Footprints of a Dream* to the recently deceased Fisk and paid tribute to him as "a human being of acute sensitivity with a deep desire to extend the experience of brotherhood to all people."[158] No one, including Thurman, was more important to the birth of the Fellowship Church than Alfred Fisk. But with his departure in 1946, the Fellowship Church was essentially Thurman's, and it increasingly followed his spiritual emphases. In 1947 Thurman introduced a meditation service before the regular Sunday service and established an interreligious meditation room, with prayer books and religious figures from many different religious traditions. He also expanded his integration of dance into the service, along with other liturgical innovations.[159]

It was Thurman's fondest hope that the Fellowship Church would become a model, an exemplar. He wrote in 1945, "If in every community in the United States an experiment such as ours could be undertaken, the Church itself would once again set in motion those spiritual processes which gave to it its original impetus and power."[160] He sought a national audience for the church, creating a well-regarded, nationally circulated magazine, *The Growing Edge,* whose readers included Martin Luther King, Jr.[161] There was some thought, never realized, that the almost one thousand national members of the Fellowship Church might in some systematic way form the nuclei of interracial congregations in their own cities.[162] Certainly, Thurman did his best to publicize the church's achievements and promise. He wrote, "[W]herever I went to speak or to preach, the message of the church was carried."[163] Especially in Thurman's early years in San Francisco, he saw spreading the news about interracial religion as perhaps his chief mission. As he wrote to Mordecai Wyatt Johnson in 1946, "Ultimately, I hope to give all my time to developing the ideas of Fellowship Church in various parts of America."[164]

However, Thurman was adamant that though he wanted to spread the word about Fellowship Church, he did not want to replicate it, and above all he did not want to establish a chain of Fellowship Churches in other cities. This would only add to the existing divisions within Christianity. "To develop a church outside San Francisco," he was quoted as saying in 1950, "would mean starting a new church belonging to a denomination, [and] becom[ing] a fellow church with Fellowship Church, which would make this a new sect."[165] Instead he hoped that the church would be a model to interested groups elsewhere, and he was in contact with individuals seeking to create interracial churches in a number of cities.[166]

Up to a point Thurman's efforts were bearing fruit. In early 1947 the Unitarian minister Homer Jack hailed "the emergence of the interracial church." If this was still the tiniest of currents, no more than six or seven congregations—half in what was the interracial hotbed of northern California—Jack wrote of an effort "to create a pattern by which it will seem natural and practical for existing churches more nearly to adopt this interracial ideal."[167] This too was Thurman's goal, to make the interracial ideal seem so natural that it would be possible for a church to become interracial simply by doing it without calling any attention to itself. Thurman wrote in 1945, "It seems to me that if an established church is in a community that wishes to become an open church it should do so without dramatizing the fact. If this is done, the development will be normal and the assimilation of the various minorities would be a relaxed process."[168]

On the sensitive question of the potential impact of the interracial church movement on the black church, Thurman was equivocal. He had no illusions that the Fellowship Church and the handful of other interracial churches would in any way diminish the appeal of the black church, and he had no interest in doing so. The value of the Fellowship Church was as an alternative to, and not a replacement for, the black church. The Fellowship Church provided for the possibility of interracialism, and Thurman knew that this would not be of interest to everyone. As he wrote to Peggy Bremer in 1954, "The problem facing the Negro members is a peculiar one. At the moment, in San Francisco, Fellowship Church is the only place where these varied racial groups can have a common meeting ground without overtones of artificiality and limited association that characterizes most of the other inter-group associations in the community."[169] Over time, Thurman was convinced, more people of different racial backgrounds would feel the need for a Fellowship Church and would be glad to have the option. Thurman believed that whatever the future held, the distinctive traditions of the black church needed to be preserved.[170] However, he closed *Footprints of a Dream* by stating his hope that, in the fullness of time, there would be no black church and no white church: "The Negro has a rich and redemptive heritage which must not be lost in this effort to become an integrated religious fellowship. How to conserve the essential idiom that has kept alive in the spirit of Negroes a courage and a vitality that has sustained that spirit in all of its vicissitudes, and at the same time to bring into its fellowship more and more of those who are not Negroes, until at last from both sides there is a common meeting place in which there will be no Negro church and no white church, but the church of God—that is the task we all must work to finish."[171]

Thurman was immensely proud of the Fellowship Church and what he and its members had created there. His ministry at the church was in many ways the apex of his career. No other position was as satisfying. He wrote two books about his experience in the church. It was small enough to reflect directly his presence in almost every aspect of its operations, and it was large enough to have a national presence and significance. Unlike at Howard and Boston Universities, where he had to fit his religious ideas into the framework of an existing academic bureaucracy, Thurman was able to create the Fellowship Church largely in accord with his own lights and perspectives.

Notwithstanding his accomplishments at the Fellowship Church, when Thurman left for Boston University in 1953, much was left unfinished and incomplete. The interracial church movement never became a major factor in American Christianity. The membership of the Fellowship Church was never large and was always primarily middle class, with more white than black members. Success in reaching the black working class of San Francisco was always limited.[172] In addition, for all of his love of the Fellowship Church, it proved a fragile vessel, difficult to hold together, and without Thurman's charismatic presence, congregational divisions multiplied and the national stature of the church was lost.

Still, the founding of the Fellowship Church marked a decisive break with many long-standing Christian practices, in ways that have yet to be fully embraced by American Christianity. Although an interracial congregation is not quite the anomaly it was in 1944, it remains uncommon. In 2010 a survey found that 13.7 percent of American religious congregations were racially mixed. Among Protestant churches, the figure was far lower, a meager 5 percent.[173] Perhaps Thurman's other ambition for the Fellowship Church, that it become a model of a new style of worship—noncreedal, interreligious, and inclusive— has had more success, and the seeds Thurman planted in San Francisco have sprouted in progressive religious congregations across North America.

Speaking to *Time* in 1948, Thurman summarized his sense of how the Fellowship Church had grown and changed in the four years since his arrival. The church had originally been located in a section of San Francisco "crammed with Negro war workers." He persuaded the congregation to move, saying, "Until we became strong enough to have a character of our own, I thought we'd better get out of the atmosphere." He did not want the church to become "a dumping ground for do-gooders who would get an uplift once a week by coming into the Negro community and helping a struggling interracial activity. I wanted people to come because of the contribution it makes to their lives." The article closed with this quote from Thurman: "Our hardest job has been to keep our church from becoming a social whip. The radicals bear down, saying we are not in there fighting. Others want us to become an organization, a placement bureau, a mission that gets people jobs and gives away shoes. . . . We are a religious group. It is important that we give strength to people working on interracial problems, but the interracial character of our own group is becoming the least significant part of it. . . . We have remained a church."[174] For Thurman, this was the church's greatest accomplishment, making real, in some small part and in one small place, the "common desire for a better world."[175]

Notes

1. Thurman initially earned $2,400 (and received free housing) at the Fellowship Church. His salary at Howard had been $4,180. See To Alfred G. Fisk, 1 December 1943, printed in the current volume.

2. To Alfred G. Fisk, 3 January 1944, printed in the current volume. See also Howard Thurman (hereafter HT), *With Head and Heart: The Autobiography of Howard Thurman* (New York: Harcourt Brace Jovanovich, 1979) (hereafter *WHAH*), 137

3. HT, "The Historical Perspective," in *The Church for the Fellowship of All Peoples* (San Francisco: Church for the Fellowship of All Peoples, 1947), 3–6, printed in the current volume. Two years earlier he spoke of establishing an interracial church as "a dream which has haunted me for ten years," without mentioning its Khyber Pass origins (HT, "The Fellowship Church of All Peoples," Spring 1945, printed in the current volume).

4. HT, "Let Ministers Be Christians!," January 1925, printed in Walter Earl Fluker, ed., *The Papers of Howard Washington Thurman* (Columbia: University of South Carolina Press, 2009–), 3 vols. to date (hereafter *PHWT*), 1:43–46 (emphasis in original).

5. *WHAH*, 195; HT, "India Report," 10 February 1938, printed in *PHWT*, 2:138. Thurman's earliest use of the idea of Allah laughing at Christianity, in a different context, dates to the summer of 1924. See HT, "The Sphere of the Church's Responsibility in Social Reconstruction," July 1924, printed in *PHWT*, 1:41–43.

6. HT, "India Report," 137–38; Mahadev Desai, "With Our Negro Guests," 14 March 1936, printed in *PHWT*, 1:335.

7. HT, "Historical Perspective."

8. For Thurman's efforts to create an interracial church after 1936, see HT, *Footprints of a Dream: The Story of the Church for the Fellowship of All Peoples* (New York: Harper, 1959), 24–28.

9. By Thurman's own account, his thoughts at the Khyber Pass were stimulated by reading about Fellowship House, a religious experiment in interracialism in Philadelphia sponsored by the Quakers (HT, "Historical Perspective," printed in the current volume). When he returned to the United States, he preached there on multiple occasions and even considered becoming its spiritual leader if it became a full-time functioning church, rather than meeting once a month at different venues (From Marjorie Penney, 22 October 1942, printed in *PHWT*, 2:318–20). Thurman evidently first spoke at Fellowship House in 1938. See From Marjorie Penney, 25 April 1940.

The source of the majority of documents in the current volume is the Howard Thurman Papers, which are housed at the Howard Gotlieb Archival Research Center at Boston University. Where documents are from the Howard Thurman Papers, no source is indicated.

10. HT, "Our Underlying Spiritual Unities," printed in *PHWT*, 2:285–88.

11. HT, "The Will to Segregation," printed in *PHWT*, 2:337–44.

12. From A. J. Muste, 8 October 1943, printed in the current volume.

13. By his letter of 12 November, Thurman had largely committed himself to coming to San Francisco. See To Alfred G. Fisk, 12 November 1943, printed in the current volume.

14. From Alfred G. Fisk, 6 November 1943, printed in the current volume.

15. To Paul Robeson, 21 April 1944, printed in the current volume.

16. Ibid.

17. Alfred G. Fisk and Howard Thurman, *The First Footprints: The Dawn of the Idea of the Church for the Fellowship of All Peoples; Letters between Alfred Fisk and Howard Thurman, 1943–1944* (San Francisco: Lawton and Kennedy, 1975).

18. Albert S. Broussard, *Black San Francisco: The Struggle for Racial Equality in the West, 1900–1954* (Lawrence: University Press of Kansas, 1993), 185.

19. To Alfred G. Fisk, 1 December 1943, printed in the current volume; Broussard, *Black San Francisco*, 185.

20. The National Council of Negro Women was founded in 1935, with the intention of increasing the political visibility of black women. Mary McLeod Bethune, the chief advocate for its creation, was its president from its founding until 1949. Dorothy Height was its president from 1957 to 1997.

21. HT, *Footprints of a Dream* (hereafter *Footprints*), 32.

22. See To Alfred G. Fisk, 2 March 1944; To Alfred G. Fisk, 11 April 1944, both printed in the current volume.

23. HT, *Footprints*, 32; *WHAH*, 141.

24. To William L. Savage, 30 March 1944. Where documents are from the Howard Thurman Papers, no source is indicated.

25. HT, *Footprints*, 54.

26. To William Gardner, 30 December 1943, printed in the current volume.

27. HT, *The Creative Encounter: An Interpretation of Religion and the Social Witness* (New York: Harper, 1954), 135.

28. Ibid., 148–53; HT, *Footprints*, 24; *WHAH*, 148; Walter Earl Fluker, "America in Search of a Soul: Howard Thurman's Vision of the National Community," in *The Human Search: Howard Thurman and the Quest for Freedom; Proceedings of the Second Annual Thurman Convocation (Martin Luther King, Jr., Memorial)*, edited by Mozella G. Mitchell (New York: Peter Lang, 1992), 85–112.

29. HT, *Footprints*, 11.

30. HT, San Francisco journal, July–August 1944, printed in the current volume.

31. For Thurman's counsel to conscientious objectors, see From William Worthy, 24 October 1942, printed in *PHWT*, 2:320–21; From James Farmer, 15 December 1944, printed in the current volume. Thurman also tried to get black denominations to officially recognize conscientious objector status. See To Russell C. Barbour, 18 March 1940, printed in *PHWT*, 2:245–46.

In 1942 Thurman chose to register as a conscientious objector rather than opting for a ministerial deferment. See To William Stuart Nelson, 19 August 1942, printed in *PHWT*, 2:311–13.

For samples of Thurman's extensive correspondence with men in military service, see To William Gardner, 30 December 1943; From M. C. Merriweather, 5 January 1945; To James Russell Brown, 22 March 1945, all printed in the current volume.

32. To A. J. Muste, 20 September 1940, printed in *PHWT*, 2:265–66.

33. To Patricia Van Blarcom, 17 April 1942, printed in *PHWT*, 2:302.

34. HT, "A 'Native Son' Speaks," 17 May 1940, printed in *PHWT*, 2:246–52.

35. See To Kay H. Beach, 4 September 1942, printed in *PHWT*, 2:313–15. In the single year of 1943, forty-seven cities recorded 242 violent interracial incidents. See Danielle L. McGuire, *At the Dark End of the Street: Black Women, Rape, and Resistance—A New History of the Civil Rights Movement from Rosa Parks to the Rise of Black Power* (New York: Knopf, 2010), 22.

36. HT, "Will to Segregation," 338.

37. Ibid., 338–39.

38. HT, "In Quest of a Life Worth Living," 11 February 1944.

39. Ibid. For similar sentiments on the opportunities created by war, see also HT, "The Cultural and Spiritual Prospect for a Nation Emerging from Total War" (1945), printed in the current volume.

40. Joseph James, "Race Relations on the Pacific Coast: San Francisco," *Journal of Educational Sociology* 19, no. 3 (November 1945): 166–78.

41. Broussard, *Black San Francisco*, 133–42. Like his wife, Thurman had visited the Bay Area during the war before moving there in the summer of 1944. He was a featured speaker at the Institute of Interracial Relations at Mills College in Oakland the previous summer and had met Fisk in passing. See From Alfred G. Fisk, 15 October 1943, printed in the current volume.

42. In the summer of 1942 Thurman visited temporary confinement facilities for Japanese Americans at southern California racetracks (probably the tracks at Santa Anita or Tanforan). In June 1943 he visited the Granada Relocation Center in Amache, Colorado. See To Raymond Harvey, 29 July 1942; From Emiko Hinoki, 24 April 1943; To Emiko Hinoki, 31 May 1943.

43. HT, *The Luminous Darkness: A Personal Interpretation of the Anatomy of Segregation and the Ground of Hope* (New York: Harper and Row, 1965), 2.

44. HT, "Will to Segregation," 339.

45. For the best overview, see Greg Robinson, *A Tragedy of Democracy: Japanese Confinement in North America* (New York: Columbia University Press, 2009).

46. Albert B. Cleage, Jr., "Fellowship Church: Adventure in Interracial Understanding," *NOW*, (October 1944), printed in the current volume. The area did have some black population before the war. See James, "Race Relations on the Pacific Coast." The black population in war-time Los Angeles also grew in the space left by a depopulated Japanese neighborhood. See Scott Kurashige, *The Shifting Grounds of Race: Black and Japanese Americans in the Making of Multi-Ethnic Los Angeles* (Princeton, N.J.: Princeton University Press, 2008), 170–81.

47. James, "Race Relations on the Pacific Coast."

48. Ibid.

49. Broussard, *Black San Francisco*, 143–65.

50. Cleage, "Fellowship Church."

51. From Alfred G. Fisk, 30 October 1943, printed in the current volume.

52. Charles S. Johnson, *The Negro War Worker in San Francisco: A Local Self-Survey* (San Francisco: American Missionary Association, May 1944). For background on Johnson's survey, see Broussard, *Black San Francisco*, 136–42.

53. HT, *Footprints*, 13.

54. Johnson, *Negro War Worker*.

55. Langston Hughes, "Dixie in the Golden Gate," *Chicago Defender*, 6 May 1944.

56. HT, *Footprints*, 12–13, quoting Frank Samuel Loescher, *The Protestant Church and the Negro* (New York: Association Press, 1948), 76–78.

57. HT, "Will to Segregation," 342. He had used almost identical words two years earlier, in HT, "Our Underlying Spiritual Unities," 287–88.

58. To James E. Thompson, 10 November 1947.

59. From Joseph Conard, 2 November 1943; HT, *Footprints*, 29–30. They received their name from the name of the Japanese owner of their cooperatively shared house, who had been interned.

60. Alfred Grunsky Fisk (1905–59) received a bachelor's degree from Occidental College, attended Princeton Theological Seminary (1925–27), and earned a B.D. from Union Theological Seminary (1928) and a Ph.D. from the University of Edinburgh in Scotland (1930), for his dissertation, "The Fundamental Ideas of the Holiness Code in Relation to the Prophetic

Writings." Fisk then returned to his native San Francisco, where he served as pastor of Portalhurst Presbyterian Church (1930–35). Before his involvement with the Fellowship Church, he was supply (interim) pastor of the Howard Presbyterian Church (1941–43) to help offset a war-time shortage. He taught philosophy at San Francisco State College from 1932 until his death.

Fisk wrote relatively little. His one book, *The Search for Life's Meaning* (New York: Revell, 1949), was a work of popular philosophical theology. In the book he argues that we discover God through recognition of our intellectual, social, political, and interpersonal limitations: "O that we might catch a vision of the bigness of God, and some understanding glimpse of His purpose for our life and world! If [only] our self-reliant generation, proud of the greatness of its achievements, could see how far we have fallen short, how inadequate has been our concern for truth, and beauty, and the welfare of human personalities the world over" (quoted in "Service of Worship in Memory of Alfred G. Fisk," Temple Methodist Church, San Francisco, 19 April 1959, Howard Thurman Papers Subject Files, Howard Thurman Papers Project). Yet, as the authors of an obituary notice commented, *The Search for Life's Meaning* "is not an accurate reflection of the range of ideas he entertained" (Arthur Bierman and Jordan Churchill, "Alfred G. Fisk," *Proceedings and Addresses of the American Philosophical Society* 33 [1959–60]: 117–18). In the last decade of his life, Fisk traveled extensively, leading tours to the Middle East, Africa, the Soviet Union and Eastern Europe, and India. See his lecture brochure, "Alfred G. Fisk: Lecturer, World Traveler, Interpreter of World Events" (n.d.), Howard Thurman Papers Subject Files, Howard Thurman Papers Project. His publications on international affairs include "Is Peace Possible between Arabs and Jews?," *World Affairs* 118, no. 1 (Spring 1955): 5–8; and a posthumously published pamphlet, *Peace through Disarmament* (New York: Committee for World Development and Disarmament, 1961). Fisk's only published writing that discusses the Fellowship Church, "World Community Begins at Home," in *The Church for the Fellowship of All Peoples* (1947), printed in the current volume, also has an international focus.

61. Bierman and Churchill, "Alfred G. Fisk."

62. Alfred Fisk to A. L. Roberts, 24 December 1943, Department of History, Presbyterian Church, U.S.A., Archives.

63. From Alfred G. Fisk, 26 January 1944.

64. "The Fellowship Church of All Peoples," c. September 1944.

65. From Virginia Scardigli, 28 October 1943. According to Hope Foote, Rustin instructed the nascent CORE group in San Francisco on the proper tactics for challenging restrictive housing covenants and segregated restaurants and bowling alleys. See John D'Emilio, *Lost Prophet: The Life and Times of Bayard Rustin* (New York: Free Press, 2003), 55.

66. From Alfred G. Fisk, 15 October 1943, printed in the current volume.

67. To Alfred G. Fisk, 3 January 1944, printed in the current volume.

68. To Alfred G. Fisk, 12 November 1943, printed in the current volume.

69. To Mrs. Ralph Eckert, 5 December 1946, printed in the current volume. See also To Lois Wendell, 4 June 1946; To Alfred G. Fisk, 11 April 1944, both printed in the current volume.

70. John B. Boles has argued that "the normative worship experience of blacks in the antebellum South was in a biracial church." See John B. Boles, "Introduction," in *Masters and Slaves in the House of the Lord: Race and Religion in the American South, 1740–1870*, edited by John B. Boles (Lexington: University Press of Kentucky, 1988), 10. This had been

so for Thurman's grandmother Nancy Ambrose. See HT, *Jesus and the Disinherited* (New York: Abingdon-Cokesbury, 1949), 30, 50. Even the postemancipation sundering of black and white worship did not entirely end borrowings and shared worship between black and white Christians and churches, especially in larger prayer meetings and camp gatherings. See Paul Harvey, *Freedom's Coming: Religious Culture and the Shaping of the South from the Civil Rights Era* (Chapel Hill: University of North Carolina Press, 2005), 107–68.

71. HT, *Footprints*, 143–44.

72. For Fellowship House, see From Marjorie Penney, 25 April 1940; From Marjorie Penney, 22 October 1942; endnote 9, above. Perhaps the earliest church to describe itself as interracial was the Church of the Crossroads, a Congregationalist church in Honolulu, founded in 1923 and intended as a place of worship for whites, Asians, and native Hawaiians. See Betty Hemphill and Robert F. Hemphill, *The Crossroads Witness* (Honolulu: Church of the Crossroads, 1988).

73. Cedric Belfrage, *A Faith to Free the People* (New York: Dryden Press, 1944), 262; Angela Dillard, *Faith in the City: Preaching Radical Social Change in Detroit* (Ann Arbor: University of Michigan Press, 2007), 140. The church had close associations with the Communist Party.

74. E. Stanley Jones, *The Christ of the American Road* (New York: Abingdon, 1944), 97; "Here's Today's Events on Mission's Program," *Los Angeles Times*, 18 March 1941. The new church was a monthly Sunday afternoon meeting of many local churches. The Methodist minister Karl E. Downs (1912–48), who in 1948 would invite Thurman to give the lectures that became *Jesus and the Disinherited*, was one of the founders of the Interracial Fellowship Church in Pasadena.

75. For the All Peoples Christian Church in Los Angeles, see From Dan B. Genung, 29 February 1944, printed in the current volume.

76. Homer A. Jack, "The Emergence of the Interracial Church," *Social Action* 13, no. 1 (January 1947): 31–38.

77. HT, *Footprints*, 24–28.

78. From Ruth Coffin?, 11 December 1954.

79. From Alfred G. Fisk, 17 April 1944, printed in the current volume. When the Sakai Group broke up, shortly before Thurman arrived in San Francisco, Fisk was triumphant. See From Alfred G. Fisk, 8 June 1944, printed in the current volume.

80. From Alfred G. Fisk, 10 January 1944, printed in the current volume.

81. Alfred G. Fisk to the American Missionary Association, 18 October 1944, American Missionary Association Collection, Amistad Research Center, Tulane University.

82. Hiley H. Ward, *Prophet of the Black Nation* (Philadelphia: Pilgrim, 1969), 54–55.

83. HT, San Francisco journal; HT, *Footprints*, 40.

84. HT, San Francisco journal.

85. Ibid.

86. Ibid.; Lewis Mumford, *Herman Melville* (New York: Literary Guild, 1929), 361.

87. For the various efforts to obtain new quarters, see From Alfred G. Fisk, 28 December 1943; From Alfred G. Fisk, 17 April 1944; From Alfred G. Fisk, 16 May 1944; To Paul Robeson, 21 April 1944, all printed in the current volume; and HT, *Footprints*, 45–46.

88. HT, San Francisco journal.

89. See HT, *Footprints*, 43–46.

90. The church had its first services at its permanent home at 2041 Larkin Street (where, as of 2015, it remains) on 30 January 1949. See HT, *Footprints*, 43–46; Jane Sudekum, "S.F.—

The City of Churches: Fellowship Group Has 285 Members," *San Francisco News,* 24 March 1949; *Church for the Fellowship of All Peoples* (1947).

91. Sudekum, "S.F—The City of Churches."

92. "Trumpet Ready in the West," *Christian Century,* 12 September 1951, printed in the current volume.

93. From Ruth Coffin?, 11 December 1954.

94. To Peggy Bremer, 14 December 1954.

95. Virginia Scardigli to Elizabeth Jenks, 10 February 1947.

96. To Peggy Bremer, 14 December 1954.

97. "Intercultural Program and Workshop," *Church for the Fellowship of All Peoples* (1947), 9.

98. To Friends at Howard, January 1946, printed in the current volume.

99. "Intercultural Program and Workshop." The Intercultural Workshop, which was conducted from at least 1944 through at least 1946, was directed by Heather Whitton, a recent graduate of the Presbyterian Seminary at San Anselmo (north of San Francisco). In 1945 the program had twenty participants, ages ten to thirteen, with another, less elaborate program for younger children. For Sue Bailey Thurman, closely involved in its planning, the workshop was "teaching tolerance through songs, dance, and art." See Dorothy Margaret Bailey, "'One World in Embryo' Aptly Describes This Intercultural Workshop," *Christian Science Monitor,* 14 September 1946. A photograph in a San Francisco newspaper that summer shows the smiling faces and entwined arms of a black, a Japanese, a Chinese, and a white participant in the workshop. See Emilia Hodel, "World Workshop for Youth," *San Francisco News,* 24 August 1945.

100. See Alfred Fisk, "Stereotypes in Intercultural Education," *Common Ground* 7, no. 2 (December 1947): 28–33, which while not explicitly mentioning the church, clearly appears to draw on Fisk's experiences with intercultural education at the church and concerns the question of how to avoid stereotyping in teaching children about the distinctive cultural contributions of different races and ethnicities. After a discussion of a topic close to Thurman's heart, the mixed messages of pride and servility that the Negro spirituals can convey, Fisk asserts, "This does not mean, of course, that we are to discard the spirituals or the cultural contributions of any minority group. It does mean, however, accepting minority group cultural contributions without limiting members of those groups to the areas of cultural contribution with which they have been historically associated." He concluded, "The American culture of the future must not be the imposed culture of a dominant group upon all the others. We must recognize that to lose any of the cultural contributions of all the various groups would be to leave us all poorer. The America-that-is-to-be will gather up all the cultural strands of all peoples and weave them together into a garment of beauty. . . . So will we all, like Tennyson's Ulysses, become a part of all we have met."

101. "Young Adult Group," in *Church for the Fellowship of All Peoples* (1947), 8.

102. Hodel, "World Workshop for Youth."

103. HT, San Francisco journal.

104. *WHAH,* 145. The falling out between Alfred Fisk and Albert Cleage in May 1944 was largely over the issue of communism. There were concerns that FBI agents were regularly monitoring Fellowship Church services. See From Robert Meyners, 9 April 1948. For Thurman's anger that an article about the church in *Time* magazine mentioned a photograph of a church usher wearing a "Henry Wallace for President" button, see To Marion and Gilbert Banfield, 3 August 1948. On Thurman's suspicion of Communist-tied organizations, see

also To Gail Hudson, 26 June 1952, printed in *PHWT,* vol. 4, forthcoming. On the other hand, in no way was Thurman an anticommunist. He condemned red-baiting in "The Cultural and Spiritual Prospect for a Nation Emerging from Total War" (1945) and had occasion to work with many in or close to the party, including Max Yergan, Paul Robeson, and Louise Rosenberg Bransten. See To Paul Robeson, 21 April 1944, printed in the current volume. In his autobiography he proudly tells of providing a well-received prayer at the opening session of a constitutional convention of the National Union of Marine Cooks and Stewards, expelled from the CIO in 1950 for its Communist ties (*WHAH,* 145).

105. See "Your Voter's Supplement," Community Relations Committee, Church for the Fellowship of All Peoples, October 1947.

106. To Peggy Bremer, 14 December 1954.

107. HT, *Footprints,* 59 (emphasis in original).

108. HT, San Francisco journal.

109. Ibid.

110. HT, *Footprints,* 37.

111. A possible influence on the first draft of the Commitment was the Covenant adopted by another interracial church, the South Berkeley Community Congregational Church, founded a few months before the Fellowship Church. Thurman was familiar with the church and participated in a wedding service there within a fortnight of his arrival. See HT, San Francisco journal. For the text of the Covenant, see Edward E. France, "A Long Stride Forward" (South Berkeley Community Congregational Church, 1964), accessible at http://www .docstoc.com/docs/83440047/A-Long-Stride-Forward (accessed 16 December 2013).

112. HT, *Footprints,* 37–40.

113. Ibid., 38.

114. See "The Commitment," March 1949, printed in the current volume.

115. HT, *Footprints,* 51.

116. From George Haynes, 15 September 1945.

117. From John Haynes Holmes, 19 March 1946, printed in the current volume.

118. HT, *Footprints,* 108. See also To Ann Perry, 6 May 1948.

119. HT, *Footprints,* 55–57.

120. "A Lay Interpretation," in *Church for the Fellowship of All Peoples* (1947), 8.

121. HT, *Footprints,* 54–55.

122. HT, "Men Who Have Walked with God #3: Brahman Mystics," 26 April 1953.

123. HT, *Creative Encounter,* 135–53. See also Luther E. Smith Jr., *Howard Thurman: The Mystic as Prophet* (1981; repr., Richmond, Ind.: Friends United Press, 2007), 54–62, 70–72.

124. Fluker, "America in Search of a Soul," 90–91; Walter E. Fluker, *They Looked for a City: A Comparative Analysis of the Ideal of Community in the Thought of Howard Thurman and Martin Luther King, Jr.* (Lanham, Md.: University Press of America, 1989), 55–72.

125. HT, *Jesus and the Disinherited,* 43–44.

126. HT, *We Believe* (television series; WHDH Boston), 12 December 1958, Howard Thurman Collection, Boston University. For a discussion of Thurman's idea of love, see Fluker, *They Looked for a City,* 55–72.

127. "Religion: Fellowship Church," *Time,* 26 July 1948, printed in the current volume.

128. HT, *The Greatest of These* (Mills College, Oakland, Calif.: Eucalyptus Press, 1944).

129. HT, *Deep River: An Interpretation of Negro Spirituals* (Mills College, Oakland, Calif.: Eucalyptus Press, 1945); HT, *The Negro Spiritual Speaks of Life and Death* (New York: Harper, 1947). The former was reissued in an expanded form as *Deep River: Reflections on*

the Religious Insight of Certain Negro Spirituals (New York: Harper, 1955). Thurman's two works on spirituals were combined in *Deep River and The Negro Spiritual Speaks of Life and Death* (Richmond, Ind.: Friends United Press, 1975).

130. HT, *Meditations for Apostles of Sensitiveness* (Mills College, Oakland, Calif.: Eucalyptus Press, 1947). The book was reissued as *Deep Is the Hunger: Meditations for Apostles of Sensitiveness* (New York: Harper, 1951).

131. HT, *Meditations of the Heart* (New York: Harper, 1953).

132. HT, *Jesus and the Disinherited.*

133. HT, *Footprints,* 97.

134. See From William L. Savage, 21 February 1938, printed in *PHWT,* 2:142–43.

135. HT, "The Fascist Masquerade," 1946, printed in the current volume.

136. For a typical left-liberal discussion of domestic fascism, see Vice President Henry A. Wallace, "Wallace Defines 'American Fascism,'" *New York Times,* 9 April 1944.

137. Leo Ribuffo has labeled liberal and left-wing concerns about the rise of American fascism as the "Brown Scare," with ironic parallels to the subsequent "Red Scare." See Leo P. Ribuffo, *The Old Christian Right: The Protestant Far Right from the Great Depression to the Cold War* (Philadelphia: Temple University Press, 1983), 178–224.

138. Thurman delivered his address, "Apostles of Sensitiveness," printed in the current volume, at the Cathedral of St. John the Divine in New York City in February 1946. For previous uses of the phrase, see HT, San Francisco journal; and HT, "The Cultural and Spiritual Prospect for a Nation Emerging from Total War." Although Thurman's use of the phrase was at its height in the 1940s, it remained part of his vocabulary; he used it, for instance, in his eulogy for President Kennedy, printed in *PHWT,* vol. 5, forthcoming.

139. For earlier statements of similar themes, see HT, "The Sources of Power for Christian Action," 29 December 1937, printed in *PHWT,* 2:93–101.

140. See Quinton H. Dixie and Peter Eisenstadt, *Visions of a Better World: Howard Thurman's Pilgrimage to India and the Roots of African American Nonviolence* (Boston: Beacon Press, 2011), 183–94.

141. Clayborne Carson, ed., *The Papers of Martin Luther King, Jr.* (Berkeley: University of California Press, 1992–), 7 vols. to date, 1:281. For another borrowing from *Jesus and the Disinherited* in one of King's student papers, see ibid., 245.

142. From Alfred G. Fisk, 13 March 1944, printed in the current volume.

143. "[T]he Pres. church expects to exercise the same control [over the Fellowship Church] as it does over other Pres. Churches"; it views its connection with the church as more of an obligation than "a unique venture," and "the Pres. Church is fortunate to be able to participate in it" and should be "in some sense humbled by the magnitude of the opportunity" (HT, San Francisco journal).

144. HT, *Footprints,* 47.

145. "The Story of the Fellowship Church as Told by Dr. Thurman to Philips Academy Students," (n.d.).

146. From Jacob A. Long, 10 August 1945, printed in the current volume.

147. HT, "Historical Perspective." See also HT, *Footprints,* 47.

148. HT, *Footprints,* 46–50.

149. To "Friends at Howard," January 1946.

150. To Charles Gilkey, 19 February 1946; To William Stuart Nelson, 16 May 1946, both printed in the current volume.

151. To Allan Hunter, 9 February 1946.

152. From Mordecai Wyatt Johnson, 26 April 1946, printed in the current volume.

153. To Mordecai Wyatt Johnson, 13 May 1946, printed in the current volume.

154. From Alfred G. Fisk, 27 August 1946, printed in the current volume.

155. Alfred G. Fisk to Friends [War Service Unit], 15 September 1945, Presbyterian National War Board, Presbyterian Church (U.S.A.).

156. From Alfred G. Fisk, 27 August 1946, printed in the current volume.

157. To Adelbert Lindley, 14 March 1945.

158. HT, *Footprints*, 3, 29.

159. Ibid., 70–72.

160. "The Fellowship Church of All Peoples," Spring 1945, printed in the current volume.

161. See Carson, ed., *Papers of Martin Luther King, Jr.,* 6:661.

162. See HT, *Footprints*, 57.

163. Ibid.

164. To Mordecai Wyatt Johnson, 4 March 1946, printed in the current volume. See also To George Thomas, 4 May 1946, printed in the current volume; To Edmund Gordon, 5 June 1946.

165. "Special Meeting of Fellowship Church," 21 August 1950.

166. For examples of this advice, with the cities in question in parentheses, see To Calvin Keene, 29 May 1946 (Washington, D.C.); From Mrs. J. Otto Hill, 1 June 1945 (Newark); To George Thomas, 4 May 1946 (Portland, Ore., printed in the current volume); From Ellsworth M. Smith, 24 October 1946 (Detroit, printed in the current volume); To C. Durham Grandy, 17 March 1947 (Durham, N.C., printed in the current volume); From Interracial Church of All Peoples, 17 August 1948 (Cleveland); From J. J. Pruitt, 2 October 1948 (Seattle).

167. Jack, "Emergence of the Interracial Church," 31–38. For the prevalence of interracial churches in northern California after the war ended, see George Edmund Haynes, "Along the Interracial Front: An Interracial Experiment Station," Department of Race Relations, Federal Council of Churches, 5 October 1945.

168. To Adelbert Lindley, 14 March 1945.

169. To Peggy Bremer, 14 December 1954.

170. HT, *Footprints*, 155–57.

171. Ibid., 157. For Benjamin Mays's similar views on the future of the black church at midcentury, see Barbara Dianne Savage, *Your Spirits Walk Beside Us: The Politics of Black Religion* (Cambridge, Mass.: Harvard University Press, 2008), 217.

172. Broussard, *Black San Francisco,* 189.

173. Korie L. Edwards, Brad Christerson, and Michael O. Emerson, "Race, Religious Organization, and Integration," *Annual Review of Sociology* 39 (2013): 211–28. See also Kathleen Garces-Foley, "New Opportunities and New Values: The Emergence of the Multicultural Church," *Annals of the American Academy of Political and Social Science* 612 (July 2007): 209–23.

174. HT, "Religion: Fellowship Church."

175. HT, "Our Underlying Spiritual Unities," 286.

Editorial Statement

Document Selection

Spanning the years 1918 to 1981, *The Papers of Howard Washington Thurman* covers Thurman's formative period and tenure at Howard University, his founding of the Fellowship Church in San Francisco, and his tenure at Boston University, and it ends with his work as director of the Howard Thurman Educational Trust. The volumes are arranged chronologically, and each includes a biographical essay, a chronology, a selection of photographs, and an index. The array of Howard Thurman materials from which documents have been chosen for publication in this documentary edition is considerable: correspondence, public statements, sermons, lectures, speeches, articles, book reviews, interviews, recorded comments, unpublished manuscripts, essays, published articles, and more.

The documents selected for publication are those that the editors have determined best represent Thurman's thoughts and activities. Some published writings are included if they are not included in Thurman's later collections of sermons and essays. In the current volume, such writings include "The Inner Life and World-Mindedness," "The Quest for Stability," and "The Fascist Masquerade." Most of the writings in the current volume are published here for the first time, notably an excerpt from Thurman's personal journal, Thurman's final annual report as dean of the chapel at Howard University, and sermons preached by Thurman at the Fellowship Church. Three articles about the Fellowship Church that were not written by Thurman are included in the current volume: one by *Time* in 1948; another in the *Christian Century* in 1951; and an article by one of the church's first two pastors, Albert Cleage Jr. Correspondence to Thurman is included if it is from a prominent individual, relates to significant events in Thurman's life or the lives of his prominent associates, provides important historical context, or provides insight into Thurman's personality or interactions with other persons.

The transcriptions of Thurman's sermons, addresses, and lectures that are published in this volume were based on transcripts that, evidence indicates, were prepared in the 1970s by the Howard Thurman Educational Trust. The editors are confident that all of the transcriptions accurately convey the substance and style of each oration.

Documents have not been selected for publication if they are well known, still in print, and easily accessible.

The editors have excluded the several lengthy sermon series that Thurman preached to the Fellowship Church. These will be included in a volume of *The Papers of Howard Washington Thurman* exclusively dedicated to Thurman's sermons.

ANNOTATION

The editors of *The Papers of Howard Washington Thurman* have, in keeping with current documentary editing practice, followed a policy of parsimony in annotations, with the expectation that the documents speak well enough for themselves. Annotations for prominent persons are kept to a minimum, and well-known political events and institutions are not described. We have left without annotation those persons, places, and things that, despite extensive research, we were unable to identify. Annotations focus on Thurman's biography, and discussions of theology are limited to what is necessary to evoke Thurman's intellectual and religious world at the time of the document's composition.

However, ample annotations have been provided where they are necessary to adequately treat some aspects of Thurman's life and career. No comprehensive biography of Thurman has been written. Therefore it was necessary for the editors to perform a great deal of original research into many aspects of Thurman's life. Such research is reflected in the biographical essay that precedes the documents and in many of the annotations.

The best account of Thurman's life remains his autobiography, *With Head and Heart*. This will remain *the* essential source on Thurman's life, but like many autobiographies, it recounts many events that took place decades before its writing, lacks footnotes and other documentation, is selective in its choice of topics, and on some subjects—especially Thurman's relations with his close associates—is at times less than fully candid. *The Papers of Howard Washington Thurman* provides an alternative account of Thurman's life, at various points confirming, amplifying, modifying, and challenging the narrative in *With Head and Heart*.

EDITORIAL PRINCIPLES

In preparing transcriptions and annotations, general editorial principles established in other documentary editing projects have been followed. The editors were particularly influenced by the principles followed by the editors of *The Papers of Martin Luther King, Jr.*, and we acknowledge a special debt to the project's senior editor, Clayborne Carson. For questions of editorial style, we have been guided by *The Chicago Manual of Style*.

Most of the primary documents that have been consulted for the annotations are from the Howard Thurman Papers, which are housed at the Howard Gotlieb Archival Research Center at Boston University. Where documents are from the Howard Thurman Papers, no source is indicated. When cited documents are from other collections or repositories, these are indicated in the annotations.

In all documents, silent editorial corrections are made in cases of malformed letters and obvious errors in spelling, including words that are misspelled due to a one-letter mistake and words in which characters have been transposed.

Unless otherwise indicated, all ellipses have been reproduced from the original documents, and ellipses have not been added by the editors. In all documents, periods are silently added at the ends of sentences if missing.

Unless otherwise indicated, words in brackets ([ ]) have been added by the editors.

In typescripts of sermons and other writings, all misspellings have been silently corrected, minor grammatical errors have been corrected, and the editors have made corrections where it is apparent that errors were made by the transcriptionist, including instances of foreign words; names of people; and names of cities, countries, and other geographical entities. In these documents, the editors have also filled in lacunae where they were certain about the missing word or words, such as where names of individuals and places were missing, or where the word or phrase was apparent to the editors based on their knowledge of Thurman and of the surrounding context.

Hyphens and dashes in the documents have been modified by the editors in the following manner: end-of-line dashes are silently deleted unless the usage is ambiguous; hyphens between numbers are changed to en dashes (–); and long dashes are changed to em dashes (—).

Strikeovers and insertions in such minor cases as correcting misspellings or adding overlooked connective words are not reproduced. When significant, insertions (usually handwritten) are indicated by placement in curly braces ({}) and positioned to replicate their location in the original document as closely as possible.

Words of theological significance that are customarily capitalized, such as Christian and Lent, have been capitalized by the editors whether or not they are capitalized in the original text.

Line breaks, pagination, and vertical and horizontal spacing in the original document are not replicated.

In typescripts the underlining of book titles, court cases, and other words and phrases is reproduced by the editors.

Indiscernible words—or segments of words— in a document are indicated by the term "illegible," which is in italic type and placed within brackets, such as [*illegible*]. Conjectures of unclear text are indicated in the same manner, with question marks preceding the closing brackets. If the number of illegible words is known, it is noted, such as [several words are *illegible*].

Printed letterheads are not reproduced. Significant information in the letterhead is noted in the headnote or in an endnote.

Signed, original documents were selected in preference to copies. Signatures in both original documents and copies are reproduced in the following manner: [*signed*] name. For example:

Sincerely,
[*signed*] Mordecai Johnson
Mordecai W. Johnson

Most of the transcriptions of letters written by Howard Thurman are transcribed from carbon copies. Although the carbon copies are unsigned, the originals would have been signed. Unsigned documents, including unsigned carbon copies, are indicated in the following manner:

Sincerely,
Howard Thurman

If the closing includes neither a signature nor a typed name, and based on surrounding correspondence the editors have determined the letter's author, the name is placed in square brackets.

The date of the document is reproduced on the line below the title, and the place of origin is indicated on the line immediately below the date.

If the document does not contain a date and the editors have speculated on the date, it appears italicized in brackets. If the document does not contain a place of origin and the editors have speculated on the place of origin, it appears italicized in brackets.

If a document has been previously published, information about the previous publication (such as its name, date of publication, and publisher) is given immediately following the document.

Places in the United States are identified by state, and places in Canada are identified by province. For places located elsewhere, country identifiers are provided. Well-known cities, wherever located, are not further identified.

Places are identified by their historically appropriate names and orthography. Current names are indicated by, for example, [now Sri Lanka].

References to secondary works follow *The Chicago Manual of Style*.

SOURCE NOTES

The source of the majority of documents in the current volume is the Howard Thurman Papers, which are housed at the Howard Gotlieb Archival Research Center at Boston University. Where documents are from the Howard Thurman Papers, no source is indicated. When documents have been obtained from sources other than the Howard Thurman Papers, the sources are indicated in the source notes. A source note is in two parts (separated by a period and a space) at the end of each document. The first part is an abbreviated description of the document's script, format, version, and signature, as applicable (all categories do not pertain to all documents). The second part of the source note indicates the location of the original document. Thus the source note for a typed letter that is signed by Thurman, the original of which is held by the Moorland-Spingarn Research Center, Howard University Archives, will look like this:

TLS. MSR-HU

The *T* stands for typed, the *L* for letter or memo, and the *S* for signed.
Where no document format is given, the document is the original.

Howard Thurman Chronology

The following chronology has been compiled from Thurman's correspondence, scrapbooks, and writings and from secondary accounts of his engagements in newspapers. Although the chronology is comprehensive, it is not a complete register of Thurman's travels and speaking engagements. The chronology covers the period from 1 September 1943 to 31 May 1949. Unless otherwise noted, all of the locations set forth below are the sites of speaking engagements. The titles of addresses and sermons are provided when known. Asterisks mark extant writings or sermon transcriptions not published in Thurman's lifetime.

1943
11 September
Vassar College Liberal Association and Vassar Community Church, Poughkeepsie, New York

12 September
Vassar College Chapel

19 September
Wesleyan University, Middletown, Connecticut

26 September
"A High Priest of Truth," Hampton Institute, Hampton, Virginia

8 October
National Service Board for Religious Objectors, Friends Meeting House, Washington, D.C.

17 October
Rankin Chapel, Howard University, Washington, D.C.

21 October
19th Street Baptist Chapel, Washington, D.C.

24 October
Twilight Hours Service: Readings from the English Bible, Rankin Chapel

9–11 November
Offers three devotions at "The Minister and His Ministry Today," Howard University School of Religion Convocation

11–13 November
Retreat of the Fellowship of Religious Workers at Negro Colleges, Hanover College, Hanover, Indiana

21 November
Wellesley College Chapel, Wellesley, Massachusetts

21–22 November
World Affairs Club and Chapel, Dana Hall School, Wellesley, Massachusetts

5 December
Living Madonna Service, Rankin Chapel

12 December
Conference: "Youth's Role in Furthering Minority Understanding," Mt. Holyoke College, South Hadley, Massachusetts

26 December
"The Quest for Fulfillment," Council of Churches and Christian Education of Maryland-Delaware, Eutaw Place Temple (Jewish), Baltimore

1944
"The White Problem," in *The Society Kit: Discussion Topics and Program Suggestions for Young People* (Westminster Press)

January
"The Great Incarnate Words," *motive* (poem)

11 January
Federation of Churches Christian School, Washington, D.C.

14–16 January
Conference: "Brotherhood—Its Meaning Today," Buck Hills Falls Co-ed Conference, Buck Hills Falls, Pennsylvania

16 January
"What Must I Believe?," Howard University

18 January
"The Meaning of Man's Quest for Religion," Howard University

20 January
Day of Prayer, Howard University

21 January
YWCA, Southwest-Belmont Branch, Philadelphia

27 January
Founders Day Address, Howard University

6 February
Rockefeller Memorial Chapel, University of Chicago

13 February
Race Relations Sunday, Forest Street YMCA, Harrisburg, Pennsylvania

20 February
Bryn Mawr College, Bryn Mawr, Pennsylvania

27 February
Rankin Chapel

5 March
Baldwin School, Bryn Mawr, Pennsylvania

12 March
North Carolina State College for Negroes, Durham

20–24 March
Lenten Services, Second Baptist Church, Detroit

2 April
"Thy Kingdom Come on Earth," University of Wisconsin YMCA, Madison

3–7 April
Holy Week Services, Chicago Federation of Churches

4 April
"Not by Bread Alone," First AME Church, Gary, Indiana

5 April
Northwestern University, Evanston, Illinois

6 April
"Resources in Religion in Times of Stress," Social Work Division, Chicago Federation of Churches

14 April
Writes "A Hymn to Youth" (song) for YMCA in New York City

16 April
Rankin Chapel

23 April
Phillips Academy, Andover, Massachusetts

10 May
Bucknell University, Lewisburg, Pennsylvania

16–17 May
"Not by Bread Alone," "My God, My God, Why Hast Thou Forsaken Me?," and "Thou Shalt Not Tempt God," Rhode Island Baptist State Convention, Providence

21 May
Final Chapel Service as dean of chapel, Rankin Chapel

28 May
Baccalaureate sermon, Howard University

29 May
Commencement address, Bennett College, Greensboro, North Carolina

30 May
Testimonial dinner for Thurman, with First Lady Eleanor Roosevelt in attendance, Universalist National Memorial Church, Washington, D.C.

3–4 June
"Validity of Our Faith," Vassar College

5 June
"You Must Make a New City and a New Earth" (commencement address), Lincoln University, Jefferson City, Missouri

12–17 June
"The Cosmic Guarantee in the Judeo-Christian Message," Howard University School of Religion Institute

17 June
"Some Important Dilemmas of Jesus," Northfield League Girls Conference, Chestnut Hill, Massachusetts

23 June
Northfield League Conference, New York City

12 July
Arrives in San Francisco to serve as copastor at the Church for the Fellowship of All Peoples

22 July
United Service Organizations (USO), Oakland, California

23 July
"The Tragic Sense of Life" (first sermon at Fellowship Church)

2 August
"The Coming Faith in Racial Brotherhood," San Francisco State College

6 August
Sermon on the Commitment (Fellowship Church)

13 August
Sermon on the Commitment (Fellowship Church)

20 August
Sermon on the Commitment (Fellowship Church)

27 August
Sermon on the Commitment (Fellowship Church)

17 September
Booker T. Washington Community Center, San Francisco

8 October
Formal Service of Inauguration for the Church for the Fellowship of All Peoples
at the First Unitarian Church, San Francisco

24 October
"Prejudice as a Factor in Race Relations," San Francisco Junior League

24, 26 November
National Baptist Convention Congress, Second Baptist Church, Los Angeles

December
The Greatest of These (Eucalyptus Press)

4–5 December
Seattle and Spokane, Washington

6 December
World Order Conference, Portland, Oregon

24 December
"Christmas, 1944" (Fellowship Church)

1945
Deep River: An Interpretation of Negro Spirituals (Eucalyptus Press)
7 January
Connecticut College, New London
Battell Chapel, Yale University, New Haven, Connecticut

8 January
Fellowship Church Supper Meeting, Chestnut Hill, Massachusetts

9–11 January
Howard University

12 January
Emma Willard School, Troy, New York

13–14 January
Grinnell College, Grinnell, Iowa

15–16 January
Beloit College, Beloit, Wisconsin

17 January
Bonebrake Theological Seminary, Dayton, Ohio

18 January
Denison University, Granville, Ohio

20 January
Northfield League Faculty Conference, St. George's Episcopal Church, New York City

21 January
Vassar College Chapel

22 January
The Master's School, Dobbs Ferry, New York

24 January
Bucknell University

28 January
Mt. Holyoke College
Wesleyan University

February
"Interracial Church in San Francisco," *Social Action* (article)

1 February
McCollister Hall, Detroit

11 February
"Apostles of Sensitiveness" (Fellowship Church)

18 February
Negro History Week Address, San Francisco NAACP Chapter

February–April
"Mysticism and Ethics" (course), Berkeley Baptist Divinity School, Berkeley, California

Spring
"The Fellowship Church of All Peoples," *Common Ground* (article)
    "The Cultural and Spiritual Prospect for a Nation Emerging from Total War"* (Fellowship Church?)

1 April
"Sources of Strength for Christian Action: Jesus Christ" (Fellowship Church)

3 April
All Saints Episcopal Church, Carmel, California

15 April
In Memoriam [Franklin Delano Roosevelt] (Fellowship Church)

6 May
"The Quest for Peace" (Fellowship Church)

"The Inner Life and World-Mindedness," University of California, Berkeley

6–11 May
"The Inner Life and World-Mindedness," "What Shall I Do with My Life?," and "Apostles of Sensitiveness," Pacific School of Religion, Berkeley, California

7 May
First Methodist Church, Palo Alto, California

8 May
"What Shall I Do with My Life?," University of California, Berkeley

14–18 May
Portland, Oregon

20 May
"The Universality of the Prophets" (Fellowship Church)

22 May
"The Test of the Democratic Dogma," Stanford University, Stanford, California

3 June
Yosemite National Park Church, Yosemite Village, California

7 June
Quadrennial Meeting, Guild of the Evangelical and Reformed Church, Philadelphia, Pennsylvania

10 June
"The Vignettes of Life" (Fellowship Church)

12–15 June
Northfield Conference for Girls, Pendle Hill, Pennsylvania

15 June
Euclid Avenue Baptist Church, Cleveland

16–18 June
Washington, D.C. (primarily to visit dentist)

18–22 June
Visits mother, Alice Sams, in Daytona Beach, Florida

6 July
University of Iowa Chapel, Iowa City

15 July
Fellowship Church

29 July
"Vengeance Is Mine" (Fellowship Church)

12 August
"De Blin' Man Stood on de Road an' Cried" (Fellowship Church)

19 August
"Everybody Talking 'Bout Heaven Ain't Going There" (Fellowship Church)

22–23 August
Leads retreat, Belden Civilian Public Service Camp, Belden, California

26 August
"There Is a Balm in Gilead" (Fellowship Church)

27 August
Young Adults Conference, Christian Churches of Southern California, Idyllwild
Pines

2 September
"Deep River" (Fellowship Church)

9 September
Mount Hollywood Congregational Church, Los Angeles
Los Angeles Sunday Evening Club (radio broadcast)

24 September
"The Test of the Democratic Dogma," Sacramento, California

Autumn
"The Inner Life and World-Mindedness," in *Christian Leadership in a World
Society* (book published by Colgate-Rochester Divinity School)

30 September
"What Is Man?" (Fellowship Church)

7 October
"The Fellowship of His Suffering" (Fellowship Church)

18 October
"The Quest for Fulfillment," YMCA, San Jose, California

21 October
"Jesus and Reconciliation" (Fellowship Church)

22–24 October
Oregon State College, Corvallis

1 November
Council for Civic Unity, Vallejo, California

2 November
Planning Conference, World Student Service Fund, Oakland, California

4 November
"The Love Ethic and Social Change I" (Fellowship Church)

6 November
"Role of Religion in a New World Order," First Congregational Church, Los Angeles

8 November
"The Love Ethic and Social Change II" (Fellowship Church)

9–10 November
Pacific Coast Theological Group, San Francisco

24–26 November
Western Baptist State Convention Young People's Sunday School and Baptist Training Union Congress, Oakland, California

3 December
"Concerning Being Alive I" (Fellowship Church)

10 December
"Concerning Being Alive II" (Fellowship Church)

17 December
"Concerning Being Alive III" (Fellowship Church)

30 December
"Concerning Being Alive IV" (Fellowship Church)

1946
"God and the Race Question," in *Together* (Abingdon-Cokesbury)
   "The Fascist Masquerade," in *The Church and Organized Movements* (Harper)

5–7 January
Chapel Service, Vassar College (visits with daughter Olive, a student at the college)

12 January
Conference on Future of the Church, Chicago

13 January
Rockefeller Memorial Chapel
   "Deep River," Sunday Evening Club, Chicago (radio broadcast)

14 January
Beloit College

18–20 January
Howard University

21 January
"Deep River," Denison University
   "The Test of the Democratic Dogma," Monday Club, Newark, Ohio

23 January
Emma Willard School

24 January
Phillips Academy

25–26 January
Dana Hall School

27 January
Yale University Chapel
   Wesleyan University

1 February
Springside School, Chestnut Hill, Pennsylvania

3 February
Unitarian Church of Germantown, Pennsylvania

10 February
St. Paul's Church, Chestnut Hill, Pennsylvania
   "Apostles of Sensitiveness,"* Interracial Fellowship of Greater New York, Cathedral of St. John the Divine

14 March
American Women's Volunteer Services, San Francisco

29 March
Oregon State Teachers Association, Portland

4 April
First Methodist Church of Richmond, California

10 April
San Jose High School and San Jose Lions Club, San Jose, California

14–19 April
"The Five Great Dilemmas of Jesus" (Holy Week Services), Council of Churches, Portland, Oregon
   1) "The Dilemma of the Solitary Place"
   2) "The Dilemma of the Crossroads"
   3) "The Dilemma of Authority"
   4) "The Dilemma of the Garden"
   5) "Why Hast God Forsaken Me?"

26 April
Fresno Conference of Christians and Jews, and Fresno Church Council, Fresno State College, Fresno, California

1 May
Phi Beta Kappa Lecture, Mills College, Oakland, California

3–4 May
"The Fascist Masquerade," Pacific Coast Theological Group, San Francisco (presentation of paper)

7–8 May
Interracial Clinic, San Diego Council of Churches

18 May
Congregation Emanu-El (Jewish), San Francisco

23–24, 27–28 May
"The Quest for Fulfillment"
"The Apostles of Sensitiveness"
"The Dilemma of Jesus" (Vesper Series)
   1) "The Dilemma in the Wilderness"
   2) "The Dilemma of the Crossroads"
   3) "The Dilemma of Authority"
   4) "The Dilemma of the Cross"

11 June–11 August
"Mysticism and Ethics" (course), Visiting Professor of Religion, University of Iowa

23 June
Baccalaureate sermon, Doctor of Divinity (honorary degree), Wesleyan University

26 June
Women's Society of Christian Service of the Upper Iowa Conference of the Methodist Church, Cornell College, Mt. Vernon, Iowa

30 June
Church of All Peoples, Detroit

14 July
First Methodist Church, Iowa City, Iowa

17 July
"The Fascist Masquerade," University of Iowa Student Union

28 July
First Methodist Church, Iowa City, Iowa

18 October
Church of the Brethren District Conference, Fresno, California

Late October
Board Meeting of National Conference of Christians and Jews, New York City

12 November
Luther League of Northern California, San Francisco

15 November
Council of Presbyterian Women, Napa, California

28 November
United Thanksgiving Service, Hayward, California

1947
The Negro Spirituals Speak of Life and Death (Harper)
   "The Historical Perspective," in *The Church for the Fellowship of All Peoples* (pamphlet)
   Meditations for Apostles of Sensitiveness (Eucalyptus Press)

12 January
Mt. Hollywood Congregational Church, Los Angeles

14–17 January
YMCA Convention, Asilomar, California

18 January
Congregation Emanu-El, San Francisco

26 January
Fisk University Chapel, Nashville, Tennessee

30 January
Fellowship Church Membership Meeting, Washington, D.C.

1 February
All-Day Retreat, Northfield League, Boston

2 February
Northfield School for Girls, East Northfield, Massachusetts

4 February
Springside School

5 February
"The Religion of Jesus and the Disinherited,"* Religious Forum Lecture, Lawrenceville School, Lawrenceville, New Jersey

9 February
Germantown Interracial Forum, Pennsylvania
    Unitarian Church of Germantown
    The Master's School

10 February
Fellowship Church Supper, Church of the Reformation, Rochester, New York

12 February
Bucknell University

14 February
Germantown Friends School, Pennsylvania

16 February
Smith College, Northampton, Massachusetts
    Mt. Holyoke College

17 February
Choate School, Wallingford, Connecticut

18 February
Phillips Academy

19 February
Lenten Service, Nashua, New Hampshire
    First Presbyterian Church, Manchester, New Hampshire

23–26 February
Annual Religious Lectures, Wellesley College and Dana Hall School

2 March
Yale University Chapel
    Wesleyan University

5 March
"The Light That Is Darkness," Council of Churches Lenten Service, Jackson, Michigan

6 March
Lawrence College, Appleton, Wisconsin

9 March
Rockefeller Memorial Chapel
    "Concerning Love and Hatred," Sunday Evening Club, Chicago (radio broadcast)

11 March
Emma Willard School

12 March
Lutheran Church of the Atonement, Syracuse, New York
    West Genessee Methodist Church, Syracuse, New York

16 March
Fellowship Church

20 March
Girl Scouts Leaders Banquet, Berkeley, California

26 March
"The Message of Olive Schreiner," Book Day, Mills College, Oakland, California

13 April
St. Paul's Episcopal Church, Philadelphia

14 April
"The Negro Spiritual Speaks of Life and Death"* (Ingersoll Lecture on Immortality), Harvard University, Cambridge, Massachusetts

16 April
"Reflections Concerning the Democratic Dogma," YMCA, St. Louis

16 May
"The Negro Spiritual Speaks of Life and Death," Congregation Emanu-El, San Francisco

13 June
"The Genius of Democracy," Commonwealth Club, San Francisco

20 June
"The Religion of Jesus and the Disinherited," National Sunday School and Baptist Training Union Congress, Oakland, California

21 June
Officiating clergyman, commencement exercises, University of California, Berkeley

25 June
California Youth Workshop, Mills College

17–18 July
Northern California Japanese Young People's Christian Conference, Zephyr Point, Lake Tahoe, Nevada

20 July
First Methodist Church, Pasadena, California

1 August
"The Religion of Jesus and the Disinherited," School of Religion, University of Iowa

3 August
"The Religion of Jesus and the Disinherited," Central Methodist Church, Detroit

28 September
"Eulogy: Jessie Wickwire Overholt,"* Cleveland
   The Church of All Peoples, Cleveland

5 October
First Congregational Church, Berkeley, California

9 October
Council for Civic Unity, Wayfarer Church, Carmel, California

2–5 November
Religious Emphasis Week, Oregon State College, Corvallis

5–7 November
State College of Washington, Pullman

13–14 November
National Council of Negro Women, Washington, D.C.

16 November
"The Tabernacle of God," St. Paul's Methodist Church, Cedar Rapids, Iowa

1948
"Judgment and Hope in the Christian Message," in *The Christian Way in Race Relations* (Harper)

4 January
"Standing on Tip Toe"* (Fellowship Church)

5–6 January
"The Quest for Peace" and "The Tabernacle of God," American Friends Service Committee, Southern California Branch, Los Angeles

18 January
"The Good Man—The Dilemma of Human Suffering"* (Fellowship Church)
   Katharine Branson School, Ross, California

25 January
"Man and the Moral Struggle: Saint and Sinner" (Fellowship Church)

28 January
Council of Civic Unity Luncheon, San Francisco

30 January
"The Ultimate Basis of Self-Respect,"* Congregation Emanu-El, San Francisco

1 February
"Mahatma Gandhi: Eulogy"* (Fellowship Church)

February–May
"Men Who Walked with God," biweekly radio broadcasts, WSUI, Iowa City

6 February–5 June
"Religion in Human Culture" and "Men Who Walked with God" (courses),
School of Religion, University of Iowa

8 February
"The Ultimate Basis of Self-Respect,"* Unitarian Church of Germantown
   Fellowship House, Philadelphia
   "What Shall I Do with My Life," Bryn Mawr College

9 February
Denison University

15 February
Phillips Academy

19 February
St. Paul's Methodist Church, Cedar Rapids, Iowa

21 February
Bucknell University

22 February
Northfield School for Girls

29 February
Smith College
   Mount Holyoke College

7 March
Wesleyan University
   Choate School
   Dana Hall School

9 March
Men's Club, Cedar Rapids YMCA, Iowa

14 March
Emma Willard School
   Vassar College

28 March
"Easter Sermon"* (Fellowship Church)

11–16 April
"The Religion of Jesus and the Disinherited,"* Mary L. Smith Memorial Lectures, Samuel Huston College, Austin, Texas
   1) "Jesus' Technique of Survival"
   2) "The Fear of God—The Fear of Man, Which?"

3) "Let Your Words Be 'Yes' or 'No'"
4) "I Hate Them with Perfect Hatred"
5) "'Tis Love That Makes the World Go 'Round"

25–26 April
Cornell College, Mount Vernon, Iowa

25 April
Fellowship Church, Columbus, Ohio

2 May
Baldwin School
  Rankin Chapel

9 May
Church of the Good Shepherd, Chicago

23 May
Baccalaureate sermon, State College for Negroes, Pine Bluff, Arkansas

30 May
Baccalaureate sermon, Fisk University

18 June
Emanu-El Residence, San Francisco

11 August
National Baptist Convention Annual Meeting, North Oakland Baptist Church, California

21 August
"The Grace of God"* (Fellowship Church)

29 August
"Jacob's Ladder"* (Fellowship Church)

5 September
United Christian Youth Movement, Grand Rapids, Michigan

8–10 September
"The Religion of Jesus and the Disinherited," General Council, United Church of Canada, Vancouver

3 October
"Modern Challenges to Religion: Secular Radicalism"* (Fellowship Church)

17 October
"Materialism"* (Fellowship Church)

15–18 November
"Not by Bread Alone," "Life's Great Illusions," and "The Kingdom versus the Kingdom," United Council of Churchwomen, Milwaukee, Wisconsin

18 November
Lawrence College

21 November
Unitarian Church of Germantown
    Fellowship House, Philadelphia
    Bryn Mawr College

28 November
"The Tragic Sense of Life"* (Fellowship Church)

1949
"God, I Need Thee" (Galaxy Press) (sheet music)
    "The Religion of Jesus and the Disinherited," in *In Defense of Democracy*
(Putnam)

January
"Love Your Enemies," *The Growing Edge*

2 January
"He Looked for a City"* (Fellowship Church)

9 January
Katharine Branson School

23–24 January
Emma Willard School

February
"The Growing Edge," *The Growing Edge*

6 February
"The Quest for Stability I"* (Fellowship Church)

13 February
"The Quest for Stability II"* (Fellowship Church)

15–16 February
United Church of Canada, Toronto

20 February
"The Quest for Stability III"* (Fellowship Church)

27 February
"Skin of Our Teeth"* (Fellowship Church)

5 March
Congregation Emanu-El, San Francisco

7–12 March
"The Quest for Stability,"* National YWCA Convention, San Francisco

14 March
McCormick Theological Seminary, Chicago

16 March
Ohio Wesleyan University, Delaware, Ohio

17 March
Earlham College, Richmond, Indiana

18 March
Kalamazoo College, Kalamazoo, Michigan

20 March
The Master's School

22 March
Princeton University Chapel, Princeton, New Jersey
   Haverford College, Haverford, Pennsylvania

April
"The Quest for Stability," *The Woman's Press*
   Jesus and the Disinherited (Abingdon-Cokesbury Press)

4 April
"Your Life's Working Papers I"* (Fellowship Church)

10 April
"Jesus I: Your Life's Working Papers II"* (Fellowship Church)

17 April
"Jesus II: Your Life's Working Papers III"* (Fellowship Church)

24 April
"Your Life's Working Papers—Evil I"* (Fellowship Church)

29 April
"Better Co-operation through Inter-Faith Understanding," Western Young
Buddhist League Convention, San Francisco

May
Narrator, "Le Roi David" (composed by Arthur Honegger), San Francisco Symphony, War Memorial Opera House

6 May
Sunday Evening Club, Chicago (radio broadcast)

22 May
"Your Life's Working Papers VIII: The Inner Life"* (Fellowship Church)

27 May
San Jose State College, San Jose, California

29 May
"The Light That Is Darkness"* (Fellowship Church)

THE PAPERS OF
HOWARD WASHINGTON THURMAN

Volume 3

In the summer of 1943 Alfred G. Fisk,[1] a Presbyterian minister in San Francisco, was contacted by the Sakai Group, which was thinking about starting an interracial church in the city. The Sakai Group was a local, loosely organized female collective of Gandhian Christians, described by a contemporary as "a group of young people dedicating their energies to the interracial problems of San Francisco."[2] Fisk agreed to be one of the copastors, and he started a search for a prospective black counterpart. Given the limited resources available for the position—a mere one hundred dollars a month— Fisk sought out a young minister for the job. Thurman would later write, "Dr. Fisk took the initiative by writing to several people across the United States for suggestions that might help to secure a young Negro just out of seminary who would be willing to come out to California and devote all of his time to the fellowship."[3] One of those contacted by Fisk was A. J. Muste, who in turn wrote to Thurman about the new venture.[4] Thurman's response to Muste was enthusiastic, and he was immediately drawn to the possibility of his own involvement, writing a short note to Muste on 14 October: "Dear A. J.: Thanks for your note from Fisk. I have a man in mind.[5] If my position were different I would like to do it myself. I shall send a letter to him today. Thanks for calling my attention to it."

Professor Howard Thurman
Howard University
Washington, D.C.

Dear Howard:

Note the portion of this letter from Alfred Fisk, one of our very strong and capable people in the San Francisco Bay area, relative to a co-pastor for an interracial church. I have written Alfred that you would be the person most likely to have suggestions if the man they are hoping to get cannot make it.[6]

Will you think about this, and let Fisk have your suggestions? Fisk is tops for such a project as this.

Faithfully yours,
[*signed*] A. J.
A. J. Muste
ajm; herd
enc

                                                              TLS.

Notes

1. For Alfred G. Fisk, see the biographical essay in this volume.
2. From Joseph Conard, 2 November 1943.
3. HT, *Footprints*, 31.
4. Among the others Fisk contacted in the search for a black copastor was Charles S. Johnson, the Fisk University sociologist who had recently completed a survey of the black population in San Francisco, and Harold Chance of the American Friends Service Committee in Philadelphia, who would subsequently pass on Fisk's request to Thurman in early November (From Howard Chance, 8 November 1943).
5. Herbert King.
6. Probably Roy Nichols.

 ℘ From Alfred G. Fisk
15 October 1943
San Francisco, Calif.

After hearing from Muste, Fisk wastes no time in contacting Thurman directly, expounding enthusiastically on the possibilities of the new interracial church and on the support that the idea has already garnered.

Dr. Howard L. Thurman,
Dean of the Chapel,
Howard University,
Washington, D.C.

Dear Dr. Thurman,

You will probably remember speaking here during the Mills Institute,[1] and you may remember me as in charge of things. I am a good friend of your friend, Walter Homan.[2]

A. J. Muste may have written you about the new interracial church we are organizing in San Francisco. The Presbyterian Church is giving us the building of the former Japanese congregation, and a budget of $200 per month. I have resigned the church I am now serving and expect to become co-pastor of the new enterprise. But we don't want it to be in any sense run by whites "for" Negroes. It should be <u>of</u> and <u>by</u> and <u>for</u> both groups.

It was my hope that Roy Nichols,[3] whom you know, might be my colleague in establishing this work. But he is engaged in another project and we are looking for another man like him. He would not need to be a Presbyterian. We will call the church just "Fellowship Church" unless a better name is suggested.

We are committed to a real equality between the races in all aspects of church organization. The boards of the church, the choir, the Sunday School and its staff will all be of mixed character. The co-pastors will have absolutely equal status and will alternate Sundays in preaching and in taking other parts of the service.

Already, a very fine group of people are interested and have indicated that they will participate. Miss Venita Lewis[4] of the Children's Bureau,[5] whom I believe you know, has given a great deal of time and help to us. The director of the International Institute,[6] the principal of a High School and others of like character say they will attend.

We want, then, a young man of as high caliber as possible. But with our limited budget we can only pay part time salaries, at least to begin with. A student who would be finishing theological work (at the nearby Pacific School of Religion or Berkeley Baptist Divinity School) or a young man who would take a part time position at the Negro center here (where they need recreation leadership) would fit in very nicely. We could pay up to $100 per month, and there are living accommodations in the church.

It seems to me that within a year the work should grow and be able to support a full-time man. I would probably continue part-time.

Miss Lewis and many of us feel that this work is of much more than local significance. It should be a testimony to a principle, and a testimony that ~~will~~ should have wide significance. Because we are pioneering, it will be particularly important to have someone who has vision and ability to make community contacts. We have not been able to find anyone of that sort available here.

Could you suggest to us the man? We are very anxious not to delay too long, lest we lose the enthusiasm we have now. It would mean, I am afraid, that someone would have to drop other things and come out as soon as possible.

Any help you can give us will be very much appreciated.
Very sincerely yours,
[*signed*] Alfred G. Fisk
Rev. Alfred G. Fisk, Ph.D.
Chairman, Dept. of Psychology & Philosophy   TLS.

Notes

1. Thurman had been a featured speaker at the annual conference of the Institute of Interracial Relations at Mills College, in Oakland, the previous summer.

2. Walter J. Homan (1895–1963), a graduate of Boston University School of Theology, was chairman of the Department of Religious Education at Whittier College and subsequently taught at San Francisco State, where he was a colleague of Fisk. In the fall of 1943 he was chairman of the Northern California Branch of the American Friends Service Committee. He was the author of *Children and Quakerism: A Study of the Place of Children in the Theory and Practice of the Society of Friends, Commonly Called Quakers* (Berkeley, Calif.: Gillick Press, 1939), and with Lois H. Flint and Harry Edward Tyler, *Learning to Live: A Guidebook for Beginning College Students* (New York: Farrar and Rinehart, 1940).

3. Roy C. Nichols (1918–2002), a native of Maryland, was a graduate of Lincoln University in Pennsylvania and the Pacific School of Religion in Berkeley, California. He was a founding pastor in 1946 of the pioneering interracial South Berkeley Community Church. From 1949 to 1964 Nichols was pastor of the Downs Memorial Methodist Church in Oakland, and from 1964 to 1968 he was pastor of the Salem Methodist Church in Harlem. In 1968 he was named bishop for the northeast district of the United Methodist Church. Thurman knew Nichols fairly well. He wrote a letter of recommendation for him to the Oberlin School of Theology in 1941 in which he said that he had known Nichols for several years in connection with the Student Christian Movement and local student activities; described him as "a clean cut, engaging person" with a "keen sense of honor, and a well-balanced approach to life"; and expressed happiness on learning that Nichols had decided on a ministerial career (To Thomas K. Graham, 4 January 1941).

4. Venita V. Lewis was a graduate of Straight College (later absorbed into Dillard University in New Orleans), the University of Chicago, and the New York School of Social Work. In 1937 she became the first black professional social worker in the Children's Bureau of the U.S. Department of Labor. After the war she worked for the United Nations Relief and Rehabilitation Administration in China, the International Refugee Organization in Germany, and subsequently the Bureau of Indian Affairs. She was a national board member of the National Council of Negro Women.

5. The United States Children's Bureau was created in 1912 to research, investigate, and coordinate federal spending on child welfare agencies. Largely staffed by women, it was the first female-headed federal agency. Originally part of the Department of Labor, it is now within the Department of Health and Human Services.

6. Annie Clo Watson (1891–1960), born in Flint, Michigan, worked for the YWCA before becoming associated with the Association of International Institutes, and was director of the institute in San Francisco from 1932 to 1956. She was a leader of the fight against the war-time internment of Japanese Americans and discussed their plight in "Americans on the Fringes," *Journal of Educational Sociology* 17, no. 1 (September 1943): 14–19. She became an active member of the Fellowship Church. The first International Institute was founded in New York City in 1910, an offshoot of the YWCA's Department of Immigration and Foreign Communities. The International Institute of San Francisco, originally located in Oakland, was organized in 1919. It remains an organization committed to assisting immigrants and foreign residents in the United States.

Alfred G. Fisk, c. 1955. From the Howard Thurman Collection, Howard Gotlieb Archival Research Center, Boston University.

❧ To Alfred G. Fisk

25 October 1943

[Washington, D.C.]

Correspondence between Thurman and Fisk commenced on 15 October 1943. Thurman's first letter to Fisk, brief and matter-of-fact, says nothing of his potential interest in the copastor position but rather advances the candidacy of his friend Herbert King,[1] *whose position at the YMCA was coming to an end.*[2] *Fisk, who wrote to King shortly after receiving Thurman's initial letter, received a reply on 27 October in which King turned down the position for financial and other reasons.*[3]

In this letter Thurman remains largely noncommittal about his own possible involvement in the church project, but his statement "[I] wish very much that it were possible for me to take some time out and help you in the early days of the work" gave Fisk an opening that, in subsequent correspondence, he would strenuously try to exploit.

Dear Dr. Fisk:

I most certainly do remember you and it is a most pleasant memory.

You have doubtless received a letter from me already suggesting Herbert King.

Frankly, I am quite excited over the prospects of the venture and wish very much that it were possible for me to take some time out and help you in the early days of the work. It seems to me to be the most significant single step that institutional Christianity is taking in the direction of a really new order for America.

I shall see Herbert King in about two and a half weeks. At that time I shall certainly talk the matter through with him.

Thank you for your good letter and keep me in touch with developments.
Sincerely yours,
Howard Thurman
Dean of the Chapel

Dr. Alfred G. Fisk
San Francisco State College
San Francisco, Cal.

                                                                    TLc.

NOTES

1. King, undergoing a wrenching and traumatic separation from his position as a national secretary of the YMCA Student Division, was or shortly would be in need of a job. See *PHWT,* 2:332–33, 335–37. Thurman thought that the effort to relieve King of his position was "a very despicable piece of skullduggery" that revealed the latent racism of the YMCA (ibid., 332).

2. Thurman's letter in its entirety reads, "I am sending this note in response to a word from A. J. I have a very able man to suggest to you in the event that your present prospect does not prove to be acceptable. He is Herbert King, who at the present time is a National Secretary for the Student Division of the YMCA. He is a positive preacher and has had a

wide interracial experience among the colleges and universities of the country. If you are interested, I shall be glad to send you fullest particulars about him. If I can be of any further service, please let me know" (To Alfred G. Fisk, 15 October 1943). Even before the letter from Muste, Thurman was trying to help King land a new position. See To W. L. Wright, 12 August 1943. Wright was president of Lincoln University in Pennsylvania.

3. King thanked Fisk for the invitation, saying that he was "very much interested" and that it "would be a splendid opportunity for me and I should be glad to lose myself in it for a period." However, accepting the position would not be possible because of its low salary, and King wondered whether Fisk wanted someone who agreed with the Fellowship of Reconciliation's position on the war, telling him that "though I am a far cry from a militarist, I am not a Pacifist" (Herbert King to Alfred G. Fisk, 27 October 1943).

From Alfred G. Fisk
30 October 1943
San Francisco, Calif.

Fisk writes a vigorous letter to Thurman trying to persuade him to come out to San Francisco to work with the new interracial church and telling him that his participation in the church would be a "miracle" and that "the destiny of San Francisco hangs in your hands."

Dr. Howard Thurman,
Howard University,
Washington, D.C.

Dear Dr. Thurman:

Your letter has greatly excited me. If I could believe in miracles, I would dare to hope that the suggestion of you yourself coming to San Francisco might really be realized. Certainly nothing could be more wonderful!

Immediately upon the receipt of your letter I telephoned Miss Venita Lewis and read her your postscript. And she preached me a sermon (right over the 'phone) on faith in miracles! She said, "If Howard Thurman could be persuaded to come to San Francisco, it would be the most significant thing that could happen to us here in the West."[1]

The last two or three weeks of waiting as we have been searching for the Negro co-pastor have been difficult and discouraging. I wish that I could enable you to see the challenge of this situation as I see it. New Negroes pouring into this area in the tens of thousands; tension rising to the breaking point; the outbreak of violence in minor instances with more general rioting only averted by a hair's breadth.[2] Dr. Charles Johnson[3] of Fisk has been here for a month's survey. Bayard Rustin[4] has also been here for a month directing a group, in which I have participated, in the use of non-violent direct action in situations of race tension. And just yesterday Miss Venita Lewis gave the Friday luncheon address at the Commonwealth Club of California[5]—the highest honor of its kind that can come to an important person in California.

So you see, things have been on the move here in San Francisco. And now if Howard Thurman could come, it would be a climax in this movement toward the firm establishment of a socially integrated community. What a testimony it would be to "the new world a-coming."[6]

But I am conscious that all this is dreaming. To be realistic, I do not see how we can measure up to the coming of so "big" a man. We have no finances. The building at our disposal seats only about a hundred. We have no established organization. Were we to get a seminary student, I would have to say to him: You must be able to see the invisible, as a prerequisite for coming.

But somehow I feel that miracles would happen with you here. Finances would come, and a bigger building, and a work which would be significant not only here but to the whole nation. You might augment your income by lecturing at the Pacific School of Religion or elsewhere in the bay area. But of course I speak without any positive assurance.

Now please write me at once—and disillusion me if you must. But if there is a chance for the miracle, do let me know how and when and under what arrangements. We are naturally very eager to go forward as soon as possible. But we are even more anxious to start on the best possible basis when we do start.

After receiving your first letter, I had written Herbert King. He answered that he was very much interested in this sort of project, but that he was at a point in life where his financial obligations made it impossible for him to consider a position without more support. One or two other inquiries have likewise been negative, so we had absolutely no commitments—or positive hopes—at the time your letter arrived.

I think that I stated to you that the Presbyterian Board is giving us the use of the ~~former~~ building of the former Japanese Presbyterian Church and is making a grant of $200 per month for the project. We might ask them to increase the grant, with what success, I do not know. I will continue on here as Professor of Philosophy and Psychology, with part time through the week and all day Sunday at the disposal of the church. (I have resigned the church I have been serving the last three years,[7] in order to take up the work of this new project.)

There is so much that I would like to say, but I think that until I have heard from you further I have said enough.

Shall I say that the destiny of San Francisco hangs in your hands? No, that would be overly emotional. I must be realistic—but I hope for the best.

Sincerely yours,

[*signed*] Alfred G. Fisk

Alfred G. Fisk

                                                                         TLS.

Notes

1. Fisk evidently told many in his circle, on what were flimsy grounds, of Thurman's possible interest in the San Francisco position. It was an effective strategy. Thurman would receive a letter from Joseph Conard, executive director of the northern California branch of the American Friends Service Committee, on 2 November 1943 stating, "[Y]ou cannot guess how thrilled Alfred Fiske [*sic*] and I were to hear from you that there is even a <u>possibility</u> of your coming out to share in the work of a new interracial church in San Francisco." The letter had a postscript from Thurman's good friend Virginia Scardigli, who had just written to him on 28 October about her involvement with Bayard Rustin's interracial workshops: "[D]o I <u>have</u> to add any second to this very excellent idea. This is a fertile field and we need you" (From Joseph Conard, 2 November 1943).

2. If this sounds alarmist, it was a common sentiment at the time, among both black and white observers. Articles such as Horace Cayton, "Tension Areas: Sanity and Progressive Forces Have Prevented Outbreak in San Francisco," *Chicago Defender,* 18 September 1943; and "Increased Racial Tension Looms in San Francisco," *Baltimore Afro-American,* 15 April 1944, were common. Charles S. Johnson's study *The Negro War Worker in San Francisco,* conducted that fall, had as one of its main purposes developing strategies that might prevent the sort of rioting that had occurred that summer in Detroit.

3. Charles Spurgeon Johnson (1893–1956), a native of Bristol, Virginia, graduated from the University of Chicago in 1918, where he was a student of the sociologist Robert E. Park. He was a secretary for the National Urban League in Chicago and New York City and was the first editor of its journal, *Opportunity.* He taught at Fisk University after 1926 and in 1946 became its first black president. Johnson was one of the most prominent African American sociologists of his time, and his major works include *The Negro in American Civilization* (New York: H. Holt, 1930); *The Shadow of the Plantation* (Chicago: University of Chicago Press, 1934); and *Growing Up in the Black Belt: Negro Youth in the Rural South* (Washington, D.C.: American Council on Education, 1941).

4. Bayard Rustin (1912–87), a native of West Chester, Pennsylvania, was raised as a Quaker. After attending Wilberforce College and Cheney State, he moved to New York City in 1937. After a flirtation with the Communist Party, he became the Fellowship of Reconciliation's (FOR) secretary for student and general affairs in 1941. In January 1944 he was arrested and subsequently incarcerated for draft resistance. After his release he continued his work for the FOR and remained active in the organization until 1953. When the Montgomery Bus Boycott commenced in late 1955, he became one of the chief advisers to Martin Luther King, Jr. and with King helped organize the Southern Christian Leadership Conference in 1957. With King and his longtime associate A. Philip Randolph, he was a chief architect and strategist of the 1963 March on Washington. After 1964 he was a leading advocate for the reconciliation of the civil rights movement with the mainstream of the Democratic Party. In his later years he became a prominent advocate for gay issues.

5. Founded in 1903, the Commonwealth Club of California, located in San Francisco, was one of the oldest and most prestigious forums for public affairs on the West Coast. Thurman spoke at the Commonwealth Club in June 1947.

6. A reference to Roi Ottley's *New World A-Coming: Inside Black America* (Boston: Houghton Mifflin, 1943).

7. Howard Presbyterian Church.

 From Alfred G. Fisk
6 November 1943
San Francisco, Calif.

Continuing to give Thurman the hard sell, Fisk tells him that "San Francisco, so it seems to me now, is doomed if you do not come!" Fisk urges Thurman to start his ministry at the Fellowship Church by 1 December; he promises to seek additional funds for Thurman's compensation and if necessary to forego any salary for himself so that the money designated for him may "help toward our more necessary income."

Dr. Howard Thurman,
Dean of the Chapel,
Howard University,
Washington, D.C.

Dear Howard Thurman:

Since writing you a week ago today,[1] I have been wondering if my letter was not altogether too incredulous and perhaps did not seem to meet your suggestion realistically and sensibly.

Now that I have been thinking of the possibility of your coming, it seems as if nothing else can be realistically conceived! San Francisco, so it seems to me now, is doomed if you do not come! That is, we need you very much; there is no one in the nation who could do what you could do here; and after thinking about your coming, anyone else would seem woefully inadequate.

My main purpose in writing you again now is to say that I feel confident that we can rise to the challenge of the opportunity to have you by making the necessary arrangements. We will accept the responsibility of finding a furnished apartment for you and your family. We will campaign for extra funds, and if necessary I will forego all salary so that what was allotted to me may help toward your more necessary income.

Naturally, I have said nothing publically of the possibility of having you here in San Francisco. We would like word as soon as possible from you, so that we could make such an announcement and set to work on the necessary arrangements. If it would be possible for you to come by the first of December, that would enable us to get a fine start before Christmas.

I am eager to hear from you, and I hope that you will state frankly just what conditions we will have to meet. I will do all in my power to see that we meet them.

{Very sincerely yours,}
[*signed*] Alfred G. Fisk

                                                                    TLS.

Note

1. From Alfred G. Fisk, 30 October 1943, printed in the current volume.

❧ To Alfred G. Fisk
12 November 1943
[Washington, D.C.]

Thurman writes to Fisk explaining university requirements that prevent him from coming to San Francisco until the following summer and his need for an income adequate to meet his family's needs. He offers an expansive vision of the possibilities of the interracial church. Anticipating a large number of worshippers, he suggests that the church hold worship services in a theater rather than the small church auditorium.

Dear Alfred Fisk:

I have delayed writing because all of the thinking relative to the possibility of my coming involves many complications. The following is the result of my reflection.

1. I am very much interested in seeking a year's leave of absence from the university for the purpose of coming out to work with the experiment for that period. At the end of that time the decision can be made as to whether I return to Howard University or make a life job of this.
2. This release from the university cannot become effective until July 1, 1944. This is the regulation of the Board of Trustees governing leaves of absences. The action will be taken on the request for leave at the April meeting, 1944.
3. My financial responsibilities are so heavy that my income must of necessity be much higher than the figures indicated, as the situation now stands. I have a daughter[1] who enters college in the fall; a semi-invalidic mother, for whom I am responsible; a second daughter[2] who, though ten years old, is gifted with music and much money has to be spent in her training in piano. I think that if we could agree on a budget it would be possible to get it largely underwritten in my coming to work at the church for a year or more. One or two letters have come indicating that already.
4. The fact that I could not come until after July 1st may mean that it would do no good to come then because it would be too late. With reference to this, you and the committee there are in a much better position to judge. Personally, I think many things could be done during the winter moving in the specific direction of the plans which would be much more fully undertaken when I arrive.

5. Mrs. Thurman is thoroughly interested in the idea and would give to it her own wide experience and abilities.

6. I would not like for any announcement of any sort to be made relative to the possibility of my coming until the matter has been taken up officially with the President of the University and the Executive Committee of the Board of Trustees. This is of radical importance.

7. I conceive of the project as follows:

The church would provide a genuine source of religious experience and life for a group of interested and committed people. The structure would be simple and the actual membership may be small. It would minister through public worship to a much larger group than its specific membership. It may be that it would be better to have our morning public worship in a theatre, inasmuch as the auditorium of the church accommodates only one hundred people. We could have our Vesper Service in the Church Auditorium. The church itself would symbolize interracial brotherhood, which does not mean that its significance would be measured in terms merely of membership. It would be a clearing place for all kinds of activities in which racial groups may cooperate on the basis of a community of need and interest.

The going will be extremely difficult and there will be deep resistance to the idea both on the part of Negroes and white people for reasons that are not far to seek, but so significant is the idea as an expression of the true spirit of Christianity, that we should not be deterred. Herbert King is here this week-end, but I have not had a chance to talk with him about how far your negotiations with him have gone.

Thank you for your patience in waiting to hear from me.
Very sincerely yours,
Howard Thurman
Dean of the Chapel

Dr. Alfred G. Fisk
124 Buchanan Street
San Francisco, California

TLc.

Notes

1. Olive.
2. Anne.

✍ From Alfred G. Fisk

16 November 1943
San Francisco, Calif.

Fisk writes that he and others involved in the interracial church project share Thurman's appreciation for its potential, and he expresses his disappointment at Thurman's lack of availability until the summer.

Dr. Howard Thurman,
Howard University,
Washington, D.C.

Dear Howard Thurman:

I have discussed your letter [with] several of the group interested in the project of our inter-racial church. We feel in absolute accord with your expression of what you conceive the project may become, and we have already thought along similar lines—as, for instance, procuring a larger hall elsewhere for morning services. Our own building would become the center for recreation such as folk dancing, clubs, musical activities, exhibits, etc.

We are also agreed that the leadership of Howard and Sue Bailey Thurman would lift this work to high significance and give it an influence and effectiveness not possible under any other leadership we know.

As to finances, we are also agreed that we should provide adequately for your needs. Before receiving your letter I had made contact with the Rosenberg Foundation[1] and somewhat to my surprise they seem quite willing to consider a grant for such work and may supplement our budget to the necessary amount. I would appreciate from you a frank statement as to what figure you feel we should meet.

The only disappointing aspect of your letter is your statement that your release from Howard University could not be effective until July 1, 1944. We had hoped to begin this work on Oct. 15th and the Presbyterian Board notified the tenants of the building (a free lance gospel evangelist) to vacate on that date and the building has been idle since that date. It has been a bit difficult for me to explain to the board our delay so far. I have resigned my former church and they have already begun under their new pastorate.

Of course these are not the important considerations—the building and my personal situation—but the community readiness for the project, eagerness, I would say, and our feeling that following Bayard Rustin's and Dr. Charles Johnson's stays in the city this is a strategic time to go forward.

We are wondering whether, if we got a grant from the Rosenberg Foundation and financial concern did not enter into the situation, you could possibly make an arrangement to obtain a leave of absence from Howard University at this time. We would be very eager to see such an arrangement consummated.

As a second choice (though decidedly second in our minds) we wonder about the possibility of your coming out for a few weeks at the Christmas holidays or between your semesters, to start the project, lending the publicity value of your name and the great prestige you have in these parts to it, and let us carry on till the end of your school year with the help of say a Negro seminary student at the Berkeley Baptist Divinity School[2] who is available (a fine Christian boy, but hardly the community leader we want for the head of the project).[3] If you could come for such an opening and announce that you were coming back as co-pastor in July, I believe that we could hold the enthusiasm and do some very useful preparatory work in these intervening months. On the other hand, to wait {and do nothing} without even being able publicly to say that we were waiting for you would be an impossible situation, it would seem.

You will probably be seeing Miss Venita Lewis who has left {here} and is in Washington now. You will find her understanding of the local situation very complete, and I believe that it would be invaluable for you to talk with her about it.

With cordial good wishes, and praying that we may all be guided aright,
Very sincerely,
[*signed*] Alfred G. Fisk
Alfred G. Fisk

TLS.

NOTES

1. The Rosenberg Foundation was established in 1935 by the bequest of Max L. Rosenberg (1871–1931), a San Francisco businessman and philanthropist. In the 1940s the foundation's grants were primarily in the areas of intergroup and interracial relations, community planning, education, and public health. In 1944 the foundation gave $1,400.00 to the Fellowship Church for a "special project to develop an inter-racial summer vacation project and cultural project throughout the year" (Rosenberg Foundation, *Ten Years of Community Service, 1937–1946* [San Francisco: Rosenberg Foundation, 1947], 32).

2. Founded as California College in Vacaville in 1871, the school moved to Oakland in 1887 and to Berkeley in 1912, when it became the Berkeley Baptist Divinity School. In 1968, upon merging with the California Baptist Theological Seminary, the school became the American Baptist Seminary of the West.

3. Probably Manley Johnson.

⧽ To William L. Dawson
27 November 1943
[Washington, D.C.]

"God I Need Thee," Thurman's most popular poem, was set to music at least twice, both times by distinguished African American composers, John W. Work[1] and William L. Dawson.[2] On 10 November, Dawson wrote to Thurman telling him that he had set the poem, apparently unprompted by Thurman.[3] Dawson's setting of the poem was apparently not published.

Dear Professor Dawson:

Both Mrs. Thurman and I are quite pleased with the setting which you have made of my poem. As soon as I can get to it, I shall be very glad to make the changes which you suggest, so as to fit the music. Warner Lawson[4] was quite excited about what you had done and we are planning to use it in connection with our Sunday service in the new year. That you found the words stimulating and expressed your interest in so creative a manner, makes me very grateful, both to you and to God.

    With every good wish, I am
Very sincerely yours,
Howard Thurman
Dean of the Chapel

Professor William L. Dawson
Tuskegee Institute
Tuskegee Institute, Ala.

                                                                     TLc. MSR-HU

Notes

1. For the history of "God I Need Thee" and the setting of John W. Work, see *PHWT*, 2:240–42.

2. William Levi Dawson (1899–1990) was a celebrated composer, conductor, and educator. He graduated from Tuskegee Institute (1921) and received a B.M. degree from the Horner Institute of Fine Arts in Kansas City, Missouri (1925), and a master's in music composition from the American Conservatory of Music in Chicago (1927). He served as director of the School of Music at Tuskegee Institute (1930–55), where he also conducted the Tuskegee Institute Choir. Dawson's best-known composition is the *Negro Folk Symphony*, which premiered in 1934 by the Philadelphia Orchestra under the direction of Leopold Stokowski. During his tenure as director of the Tuskegee Choir, Dawson published a number of arrangements of African American spirituals such as "King Jesus Is a-Listening," "There Is a Balm in Gilead," and "Ezekiel Saw de Wheel." He also established his own music publishing business, printing his arrangements under the imprint Music Press.

3. Dawson wrote to Thurman in part, "[S]hould you desire to make it available for universal use may I suggest that lines 2 and 3 of all stanzers [*sic*] be revised so as to agree in meter with those of the first stanza" (From William L. Dawson, 10 November 1943).

4. Warner Lawson (1903–71) was born in Hartford, Connecticut, and was a graduate of Fisk University (1926) and Yale University (1929). He was a choral director and a pianist who studied with Artur Schnabel and was dean of music at Howard University from 1942 until shortly before his death.

✌ To Alfred G. Fisk
1 December 1943
[*Washington, D.C.*]

Thurman again tells Fisk that he will not be able to move to San Francisco until the following July but raises the possibility that he and Sue Bailey Thurman might spend their Christmas vacation in the city. He also discusses his salary needs, telling Fisk that while he "would not want the matter of money to make it impossible for us to come," he also did not want to have his "own energies divided by necessity in order to meet the demands of the family budget."

Dear Alfred Fisk:

I have delayed writing to you in reply to your good letter[1] because it was necessary for me to have a conference with the President of the University and he was out of the city for ten days. These are the facts.

1. He is of the opinion that I will have no great difficulty in getting a year's leave of absence from the university beginning next summer and going through the following summer.
2. The greatest difficulty in my getting away is in finding a man, or two men to take my responsibilities, both in the School of Religion and in the Chapel.
3. He is unwilling even to consider releasing me before the end of the school year, so that my only alternative is to wait until July.
4. Mrs. Thurman and I are willing to undertake the responsibility in connection with the church under the above conditions.

It would be a very wise thing, it seems to me, if it were possible for the two of us to come out to California for about a week or ten days during the Christmas holidays. I have a very important engagement at American University on January 6th, which engagement I shall try to shift. This would mean that I would be able to take a public religious service on January 2nd and if I can get my date shifted, remain to take a service on Sunday morning, January 9th, leaving for Washington Sunday night, January 9th. During the period that Mrs. Thurman and I are there, we could work in detail with the committee, talk with various people and lay our plans for beginning work in the summer. At such a time formal announcement could be made about our coming and the enthusiasm that has now been developed could be diverted to ground-work that could be done between January and July. This may not appeal to you and the committee at all because of the heavy cost that is involved. We are so concerned about it and regard it as being so necessary that by certain sacrifices on our own part, we may be able to have some share in the total cost of travel. I would not want to come alone because Mrs. Thurman should have the privilege of observing everything on the ground with me, inasmuch as so much will depend upon her cooperation in the execution of whatever plans to which I am committed.

With reference to finances, we should have a furnished apartment so as to make it unnecessary for shipping our furniture across the country. I hardly know what to say about salary because I do not know whether the cost of living in California is lower or higher than it is in Washington. My guess is that it is lower. My present salary is $4180. Out of that my contribution to my retirement is $206 a year, which amount is matched by the university. If I am on leave without pay, I shall have to pay the entire annuity instead of 50% of it as normally. This fact would be somewhat offset if I am not required to pay rent during the twelve months I am there. I mentioned to you in my previous letter about my personal responsibilities involving my two daughters and my mother, life insurances, and so forth.

Quite honestly, I do not feel that it is reasonable or ethical for the committee to pay me a larger salary as co-pastor than they pay you as co-pastor. Of course, if you will continue your teaching at the college that may make some difference, but it is important that both of us should run the same risks in doing what seems to be the great leading of the purposes of God. I would like a good statement from you on this point. Now that Mrs. Thurman and I are definitely committed to undertake the work I would not want the matter of money to make it impossible for us to come. On the other hand I do not think that it is fair to the difficult job ahead to have my own energies divided by necessity in order to meet the demands of the family budget.

When you reply, will you send me some information about the personnel of the committee which is sponsoring the church, and if possible, some word as to how they conceive of its function. I await your reply with eager interest.

With every good wish, I am
Sincerely yours,
Howard Thurman
Dean of the Chapel

Dr. Alfred G. Fisk
124 Buchanan Street
San Francisco, California
                                                                              TLc.

NOTE

    1. From Alfred G. Fisk, 16 November 1943, printed in the current volume.

❧ From Alfred G. Fisk
4 December 1943
San Francisco, Calif.

Although publicly Fisk (at Thurman's request) is still referring to Thurman as the "very outstanding Negro religious leader from the East" or the "illustrious Mr. X," he says that plans are proceeding for the new church (which as Fisk notes is not yet officially known as the Fellowship Church) and for Thurman's assumption of the role of copastor.

Dr. Howard Thurman,
Howard University,
Washington, D.C.

Dear Howard Thurman:

We are delighted with the possibility of your coming for a short visit in January. Before your letter[1] had arrived, I had called together those interested in the project for a discussion of plans. I did not feel that I or even a small committee should make decisions without consulting the constituency.

Something over 40 persons gathered together on Wednesday evening at the new church in response to invitations I had sent out to persons I knew to be interested, and in response, also, to public announcements at Negro meetings the week before. The group was fairly evenly divided between the two races, somewhat more white folk—due partly to the fact that some of our leading Negroes were away at meetings or conferences concerning a sudden (and very serious) discrimination in the ship yards—Negro workers who refuse to join the auxiliary unions of the A.F.L. being refused the privilege of work.[2]

A prominent Negro presided at our meeting. I was asked to give a statement concerning the situation and plans, which I did, mentioning that a very outstanding Negro religious leader from the East was planning to come out to the work the first of July (I did not feel free to mention your name). We discussed the question of whether we should wait till then or go ahead in a small way in the meantime. Many expressed their opinions, and it was practically unanimous that we should go ahead now and build up an organization that would be a worthy channel through which the "illustrious Mr. X" (!) could work when he arrived.

I felt greatly encouraged by the meeting, especially concerning the quality of the people who were present. The chairman of the Local NAACP accepted an appointment on a temporary committee; as did also the head of the Booker Washington Center, and the first Negro school teacher to be appointed by the city board of education (this fall). There seemed marked interest, I would even say enthusiasm.

The one point upon which we could come to no agreement was the matter of a name for the church; so that was left undecided. Perhaps you can give that some thought and bring us the answer. Personally, my choice was "Fellowship Church" with the subhead, "For All People." A great many liked the idea "The Neighborhood Church." That, however, does not seem to me to fit a project that is drawing members from all parts of the city, and at least one or two from across the bay. I also associate the term "Neighborhood" with settlements and "Neighborhood Centers." Other suggestions were, "The Friendly Church" and "The Church of All Peoples." The matter of name seems like a very insignificant matter, yet all publicity and announcements need it, and I wish that it could be decided at once.

So eager were people at this meeting to begin now, that it was decided to begin with a service of worship the morning of Dec. 12th. Mr. Manley Johnson,[3] a student in his final year at the Berkeley Baptist Divinity School, is to be associated with me in the leadership until "the leader from the East" is available. He is a fine recreation leader, and has built up interracial clubs under the Berkeley City Recreation Department.

By the time you come in January, we will have temporary "planning committees," "Finance Committee," etc. with which you can meet. If you have any further suggestion concerning things which we can do before you come in order to make the most of your stay here, please send them along. We have had the interior of the worship room painted, and a committee is now working on the heating problem.

You ask about the committee which is sponsoring the project. In answer, I will say that I proposed it to the Executive Secretary of the Church Extension Board of the San Francisco Presbytery, Dr. W. Clyde Smith.[4] He and I have conferred constantly concerning the project. Dr. Smith applied to the War Emergency Fund of the Presbyterian Church (which includes projects in defense areas) and received the appropriation of $200 per month of which I previously wrote. The matter was then laid before the Church Extension Board (a group of 20 or so, half clergymen and half laymen) and I was called in to outline my plans for the project, which I did. The Board approved the project without a dissenting voice and a committee of three clergymen were appointed to work with me on it.

Frankly, I haven't called together this committee, as I have felt the unofficial advice of people like Venita Lewis and Joe Conard[5] was much more valuable. The fact is, we have a complete free hand. The church will be technically Presbyterian, but need not be ostentatiously so. I have not inquired concerning the denomination of a prospective co-worker (I don't know what yours is) and my temporary associate will be Baptist.

As to financial arrangements, I would prefer to defer detailed comment until after I consult the Rosenberg Foundation, where I have an appointment for Tuesday. I agree with you that your effectiveness here should not be hampered by dividing your energies in order to support your family, and I am making a request to them on a salary basis of $4,200 per year.

As to my own salary, a hundred dollars a month from the church plus what I get from the college would bring it to slightly more than yours, but I am hoping that we may get the use of the building next [to] the church (owned by the Japanese who own the church building) for you to live in rent free. The church which I was supplying for the last three years paid me just $100 per month. I do not feel that I should take more than that while I am at the college; and I do not think that our new project can support two well-paid men at this time. My request to the Rosenberg Foundation is to make up the difference in your salary from the $100 the church would pay you, to the $350 you should receive. I am also requesting them for funds for a secretary and a part-time activities leader.

As to your coming in January, I don't know whether the Rosenberg Foundation would consider helping us there or not. If left to the church, it will be difficult for us to raise an adequate amount to bring both you and Mrs. Thurman here for so short a stay. We have spent more than we have so far on getting the building in shape. I share with you the desire to bring Mrs. Thurman as she will be very much involved in the whole project. I feel confident that we can raise $300 toward the January trip, and see that you have entertainment while here— at our home or with Mrs. Lucas.[6] That will not cover the entire expense, even if you use Tourist accommodations west of Chicago (which many of us always do). Would you be able to supplement that amount to enable you to come?

I shall write again after my conference with the Rosenberg Foundation committee.

The sooner I know definitely that you are coming in January, and the exact dates, the better use I can be made of your time. We would try to get you before groups meeting that week—such as NAACP, groups at the Booker Washington Center, etc.

I can't begin to tell you how thrilled we are at the prospect of having you here in San Francisco.

Very sincerely,

[*signed*] Alfred G. Fisk

TLS.

NOTES

1. To Alfred G. Fisk, 1 December 1943, printed in the current volume.

2. During World War II, AFL craft unions in San Francisco–area shipyards, most prominently the International Brotherhood of Boilermakers, segregated black workers into blatantly discriminatory auxiliary locals that skirted federal fair employment policies. Because most shipyards were closed shops, union membership was mandatory for employment.

3. After graduating from the Berkeley Baptist Divinity School, Manley Johnson worked with the YMCA in Berkeley and Los Angeles and subsequently taught at Citrus College in Glendora, a community college in suburban Los Angeles.

4. William Clyde Smith (1882?–1945) was a Presbyterian minister and administrator in Chicago until 1928 and thereafter in San Francisco, where he was executive secretary of the San Francisco Presbytery. He had a special interest in domestic mission work.

5. Joseph W. Conard (1911–65) was at the time of this letter a graduate student at the University of California, Berkeley, and executive secretary of the northern California branch of the American Friends Service Committee. He was also deeply involved in the problems of Japanese relocation and internment. He had written an enthusiastic letter to Thurman on 2 November 1943 upon hearing of Thurman's possible move to San Francisco. Conard had a second career as a respected academic economist and was the author of *Introduction to the Theory of Interest* (Berkeley: University of California Press, 1959) and other books.

6. Bertha June Richardson Lucas (1878–1944) was a lecturer and writer on current affairs and an influential civic leader in San Francisco. She served on the board of Fellowship Church. Lucas earned her B.A. from Smith College (1901) and studied biology and economics at Barnard College. In 1916 she worked for the Red Cross in France with her husband, and she recorded the experience in a book that she wrote under the name of June Richardson Lucas, *The Children of France and the Red Cross* (New York: Frederick A. Stokes, 1918). She was also the author of *The Woman Who Spends: A Study of Her Economic Function* (Boston: Whitcomb and Barrows, 1904). A collection of her papers is in the Hoover Institution Archives, Stanford University, Palo Alto, California.

❧ From Alfred G. Fisk
28 December 1943
San Francisco, Calif.

Fisk asks Thurman to clarify his views on his involvement with the fledgling San Francisco church and updates him on the challenges of getting funding and facilities. Fisk also tells Thurman that they have the opportunity to hire a young Oberlin Seminary graduate to help with the day-to-day work of Fellowship Church until the Thurmans arrive.

Dr. Howard Thurman,
Howard University,
Washington, D.C.

Dear Dr. Thurman,

We had a meeting last night of our temporary board and talked over our situation. While we would very much have liked to have you with us for a week in January, it does seem as though that were hardly possible. In view of the fact that we will not be able to confer in person with you, I want to take up by correspondence a number of matters with you.

First, our committee would like to know from you just how you view your participation in our project. Would you like to confine yourself almost exclusively to the local situation, doing considerable pastoral calling and giving intimate leadership to Sunday School, young people's work, etc.? Or do you feel that your place will be more that of guest preacher for a year and giving of your great experience in the over-all planning and direction (without the detail work or such intimate participation in detail program) while you also do considerable speaking on the outside—as for the Mills Institute, the Student Christian Association, and other groups which will urgently want you? Or will your view of your participation lie somewhere between these suggested alternatives, or be something quite different?

The divinity student who is associated with me now in the work is in many ways quite immature. Dr. Charles Johnson (who as you know was here for a month making a survey)[1] has recommended a young man, the Rev. Albert B. Cleage, Jr.,[2] a graduate of Wayne University, Detroit (major in Sociology and Social Work) and of Oberlin Seminary. Mr. Cleage is most highly recommended by all those with whom he has worked and by Walter Marshall Horton,[3] etc. His initiative and sociological understanding must be very marked. He is at present at the Chandler Memorial Church, Lexington, Kentucky, but is available to come here for the six months until your arrival. If your view of your work here is nearer the second alternative suggested above, and if we are able to finance your coming from some outside source, we might keep Mr. Cleage on after you come and work together as a staff of associates.

I am already finding the need for full-time work at the project; the divinity student has not been able to give us as much time as we had hoped and I would personally find great relief in the kind of leadership and help that a person like Mr. Cleage could give. Although the opportunities for Negro leadership are multiplying rapidly in the Bay area and Mr. Cleage could probably step into something else at the end of six months without any difficulty, he would nevertheless have to face the risk involved (which he seems willing to do). The Presbyterian Board is willing to raise our budget another hundred dollars a month to make possible Mr. Cleage's coming. (He is married and would live in an apartment in the church.) The arrangements with Mr. Cleage have not been finally consummated and if you feel strongly that it is an inadvisable move, I suggest that you wire me.[4] This has, of course, been talked over with Mrs. Lucas, who is a leading member of our board, and with Joe Conard who, though not participating in our church, is very much interested in its progress.

This brings me to the matter of finances. The Presbyterian Board is, as I have indicated above, willing to put as much as $300 per month into the project —$200 for a full-time Negro co-pastor, and $100 for myself half time. The house next door to the church belongs to the Presbytery and I have good reason to feel that we can secure it for your use. Now the difference between $2400 and house, and what we should pay you is our problem. We shall request the Rosenberg Foundation for a grant to cover your entire needs. Failing there we shall go to the Columbia or Rosenwald foundations. I am not sure whether they will aid so strictly a church program. If we get no foundation help, we will have to try individuals. We may then be thrown back upon fees in connection with such speaking as you could do for the Mills Institute, S.C.A., etc. But this would throw you into the role of the second alternative function suggested above. I state this frankly, so that you may help us by your suggestion and guidance.

You should also understand the inadequacy of our present building. We have fixed up the auditorium so that it is very worshipful, but it is small. We are glad for that just now as we begin, but with you here I am sure that we will need a larger room. The hall of the Negro Center (Booker Washington Center) would probably be available on rental basis. But it is frequently used as a dance hall on Saturday night. It has a stage and is not a worshipful room. Other halls may be available, and one can always add appointments to a stage that give worshipful symbolism. I want to tell you, however, that a large "white" Baptist church, the Hamilton Square Baptist Church, which is well located in the center of the new Negro Community, is for sale. This congregation wants to move out of the district! It is a fine building, of stone, with large auditorium, Sunday School facilities, etc., including pipe organ. They are asking $50,000. We are not considering getting the building, because we have no idea where to get the money, and I am simply telling you so that if you knew of any foundation or other source of money which would consider it, you would know of it. I am told that when the Sunday School auditorium is thrown in with the church auditorium, as at Easter, the seating capacity is 1000.

This covers the matters of immediate concern. I will be consulting you about other matters from time to time.

With very best wishes to yourself and Mrs. Thurman,

{Sincerely,}

[*signed*] Alfred G. Fisk

                                                                                      TLS.

NOTES

1. Published as Johnson, *The Negro War Worker in San Francisco.*

2. Albert Buford Cleage, Jr. (1911–2000) was the son of a prominent Detroit physician. He attended Wayne State University beginning in 1929 and spent the academic year 1931–32 at Fisk University. It was there that Cleage developed a friendship with the Fisk sociologist Charles S. Johnson, who recommended him more than a decade later for the position at the Fellowship Church. After spending some years in Detroit as a social worker, he graduated from Wayne State in 1942 and obtained his B.D. from Oberlin Graduate School of Theology the following year. Ordained in the Congregational Church in 1943, his first

congregation was in Lexington, Kentucky. After his time at the Fellowship Church, he briefly studied film at the University of Southern California before accepting the pastorate at St. John's Congregational Church in Springfield, Massachusetts, in 1946. In 1951 he returned to Detroit to lead the Central Congregational Church, which, after a quarrel with denominational authorities, became in 1953 the Central United Church of Christ. Dissatisfied with the direction of the civil rights movement, Cleage launched the Black Christian National Movement in 1967, renaming his church the Shrine of the Black Madonna and subsequently starting a new denomination called the Pan African Orthodox Christian Church. In the early 1970s he adopted the Swahili name Jaramogi Abebe Agyeman.

3. Walter Marshall Horton (1895–1966) was a theologian and leader in the Protestant ecumenical movement. He graduated summa cum laude from Harvard in 1917, was ordained a minister at the First Baptist Church in Arlington, Massachusetts, in 1919, and later earned graduate degrees from Union Theological Seminary and Columbia University. Horton joined the faculty of Oberlin College in 1925, teaching in both the Department of Religion and the Graduate School of Theology until he retired in 1962.

4. Fisk had already taken steps to secure Cleage's services, and by 18 December the War Services Unit of the Presbyterian Church (U.S.A.) had already dedicated two hundred dollars a month for Cleage's services for five months starting in January 1944 (A. L. Roberts to W. Clyde Smith, 18 December 1943, Presbyterian Church [U.S.A.] Archives).

To William Gardner
30 December 1943
[*Washington, D.C.*]

By April 1943 more than 675 Howard University students were serving in the United States military.[1] *Despite Thurman's pacifism and profound misgivings about the war, he kept up a voluminous correspondence with many Howard University students in the service, saying little about his own views on the war and instead providing encouragement and listening to complaints about racism in the military, religious musings and fears about the future, their homesickness, and their loneliness. William Gardner was one of Thurman's war-time correspondents and one of many who, with time on their hands, wrote to him lengthy, meandering letters. Writing to Thurman in September, he apologized for his letter's length, telling himself, "William, go back to sleep, Dean Thurman is a very busy man," but he kept on adding to the letter.*[2] *After having sent several letters to Thurman without receiving an answer, Gardner sent him a short, plaintive postcard on 29 December: "Dear Dean Thurman: I am waiting breathlessly for an epistle from you. I do hope that you find the time to answer all my many questions. I know that you are very busy."*[3] *The next day, presumably before receiving Gardner's postcard, Thurman wrote Gardner the following letter, which if it did not address all Gardner's questions, tried to answer at least one of them.*

Dear Bill:

I hope you had a good Christmas Season and that you are now all set for the adventures of the New Year.

Yes, I do believe that there is a will of God. To me it is to be distinguished from mere desire, or whim in the life of the individual and is to be found primarily in the core of a man's yearning. I think there is a distinction between a man's fate and his destiny, for fate has to do with the operation of individual law, or moral law upon him in ways under which he has no control and for which there is no logical personal responsibility. A man's destiny is determined by what he does with his fate. You will have to think this through. With reference to prayer, I do not think of it in terms merely of petition but rather prayer at its best is when the human spirit yields itself to the influence and the power of God without reservation, but with vivacious cooperation. I do not think God is interested in my diet, that is why I have a brain. I think He is definitely concerned about the kind of person I am and the direction I take in fulfilling his plan for human life. Life is raw material out of which the experiencer can make the most meaningful world of values possible.

Let me hear from you again sometime.

Sincerely,

Howard Thurman

Dean of the Chapel

Pvt. William Gardner

Station Hospital, Ward B-14

Camp Ellis, Ill.

                                                                                   TLc.

Notes

1. "Howard University Students," *Washington Post*, 30 March 1943.
2. From William L. Gardner, 29 September 1943.
3. From William L. Gardner, 29 December 1943.

 THE COMMITMENT

1944

The Fellowship Church went through at least three versions of their Commitment between 1944 and 1949. Each draft reflected a different phase in the history of the church and had different emphases. Although the interracial nature of the church was mentioned in each of the drafts, the main purpose of the Commitment was to vouchsafe the religious mission of the church. With each restatement, the Fellowship Church moved further from explicit ties and links to traditional Christianity and toward a freer spirituality—Christian in its origins but not its destination.[1]

First Version[2]

I desire to have a part in the unfolding of the ideal of Christian fellowship through the union of men and women of varying national, cultural, and racial heritage, in church communion.

In this commitment I am pledged to the growing understanding of all men as sons of God and seek after a vital interpretation of the highest manifestation of God—Jesus Christ—in all my relationships.

I desire the strength of corporate worship with the imperative of personal dedication which will be found through membership in the Fellowship Church of San Francisco.

Second Version[3]

I affirm my need for a growing understanding of all men as sons of God, and seek after a vital interpretation of God as revealed in Jesus of Nazareth whose fellowship with God was the foundation of his fellowship with men.

I desire to have a part in the unfolding of the ideal of Christian fellowship through the union of men and women of varying national, cultural, racial, or creedal heritage in church communion.

I desire the strength of corporate worship with the imperative of personal dedication to the working out of God's purposes here and in all places which will be found through membership in this Church for the Fellowship of All Peoples.

Third Version[4]

I affirm my need for a growing understanding of all men as sons of God, and I seek after a vital experience of God as revealed in Jesus of Nazareth and other great religious spirits whose fellowship with God was the foundation of their fellowship with men.

I desire to share in the spiritual growth and ethical awareness of men and women of varied national, cultural, racial, and creedal heritage united in a religious fellowship.

I desire the strength of corporate worship through membership in The Church For the Fellowship of All Peoples, with the imperative of personal dedication to the working out of God's purpose here and in all places.

NOTES

1. For a discussion of the evolution of the Commitment, see the biographical essay in the current volume.

2. HT, *Footprints*, 38.

3. Ibid., 52.

4. Ibid., 158. The date of the adoption of this version is uncertain, but it was no later than 1949.

The first home of the Church for the Fellowship of All Peoples, 1500 Post Street,
first half of 1944, prior to Thurman's arrival in San Francisco. The sign in front of
the church reads in part: "Fellowship Church / For All Peoples. . . . Albert B. Cleage,
Jr. / Alfred G. Fisk / Co-pastors." From the Howard Thurman Collection, Howard
Gotlieb Archival Research Center, Boston University.

 "The White Problem"
1944

*Thurman's short essay "The White Problem"[1] was commissioned and published by
the Board of Christian Education of the Presbyterian Church as part of* The Society
Kit: Discussion Topics and Program Suggestions for Young People, *an annual
publication that appeared between 1943 and 1947. Following the publication of
Gunnar Myrdal's influential study* An American Dilemma: The Negro Problem
and Modern Democracy, *there was a spate of essays, such as George S. Schuyler's
"The Caucasian Problem," which suggested that Negroes were not the race with the
"problem."[2] In 1944* The Society Kit *included four short essays under the heading "Is
There a White Problem?" In addition to Thurman's contribution, the publication included statements by the Chinese diplomat and educator Y. C. Yang, 1940 Republican
presidential candidate Wendell Willkie, and the Reverend Toru Matsumoto.[3]*

The myth of white supremacy finds no basis in science, religion or ethics. It is the child of fear and ignorance, kept alive by the willful processes of careful manipulation on the part of those who will seek to defeat life by building great walls of separation between the "white" minority and the world's population of "colored" peoples. It is a very sobering reflection that the so-called white race is a tiny minority as far as the population of the earth is concerned. Nevertheless, this minority at the present moment dominates all the other peoples of the earth. In the very nature of the case this is a temporary situation.

The present war is revealing the tragedy of a civilization built upon pride, arrogance and exploitation. There can be no peace tomorrow until all men are treated with a dignity becoming children of God. The will to brotherhood must be reenforced and the will to segregation relaxed and uprooted. This is the teaching of Jesus. He insisted that all of life is lived under the divine scrutiny from which there is no escape. Each person is precious in the sight of God, even to the numbering of the hairs on his head. It follows that the mood for each of us must be one of reverence—reverence toward one's self, towards one's fellowmen and towards life itself. This mood expresses itself in respect for personality—and what is that—it is meeting people where they are, and treating them there, as if they were where they ought to be. It means placing a crown over every man's head and using all of one's powers to enable him to grow tall enough to wear it. The test of Christianity is to be found in the degree to which it is able to order the life of man in the wake of such an ideal. If Christianity cannot resolve racial prejudice, notions of white supremacy and class conflict, it is doomed to become merely an esoteric sect stripped of all power and redemption.

The Society Kit: Discussion Topics and Program Suggestions for Young People (Philadelphia: Westminster Press, 1944), topic 45.

Td. MSR-HU

NOTES

1. Thurman's manuscript, as submitted to the Presbyterian Board of Christian Education, was entitled "The White Problem." It was published under the heading, "White Superiority is the Child of Fear and Ignorance, States Dr. Thurman." The text printed here is the published version, omitting a short coda probably not by Thurman.

2. Gunnar Myrdal, *An American Dilemma: The Negro Problem and Modern Democracy* (New York: Harper, 1944); George S. Schuyler, "The Caucasian Problem," in *What the Negro Wants*, edited by Rayford W. Logan (Chapel Hill: University of North Carolina Press, 1944), 281–98.

3. Thurman's essay is preceded by an introduction: "Dr. Howard Thurman is among the religious leaders in America. He is professor of philosophy and theology, an author, a minister, and dean of Howard University, Washington, D.C. He is, in fact one of the many distinguished Negro citizens of our country who, as a Christian leader, is making a significant contribution in the educational field. To have had the privilege of being guided

in worship by Dr. Thurman is an experience that few could ever forget. The Spirit of God has indeed taken possession of him."

꿩 To Alfred G. Fisk

3 January 1944
[*Washington, D.C.*]

Thurman agrees to curtail his hectic speaking schedule, and he accepts a steep reduction in his salary to assume the position at the Fellowship Church. Like Fisk, he is encouraged by the reports on Albert Cleage, the potential new assistant pastor. However, Thurman wonders if it would be fair to Cleage or good for the development of the church to hire him for only six months, creating a potentially damaging disruption in clerical personnel. Thurman asserts for the first time what will become a common theme in his letters: that for the Fellowship Church to succeed as an interracial church, it must avoid all funding from foundations that concentrate their benefactions on Negroes or Negro uplift, such as the Rosenwald Foundation,[1] lest the church be identified as primarily for blacks.

Dear Alfred Fisk:

With reference to your first query as to how I view my own participation in the church, I would like to confine myself very largely to developing the local situation giving as much leadership as possible. Naturally, I am interested in preaching and in addition I would like to experiment very definitely with some kind of worship vesper programs. I am not interested in signing myself up to do a lot of outside preaching and speaking for all kinds of organizations and groups outside of the city of San Francisco. During the course of the year ordinarily, I accept a large number of college and university, and city federations of churches invitations, but I am serving notice already that for the next year I shall be out of the picture. It is important, it seems to me, to know how well and intimately two men of different races sharing common leadership of a church can work themselves into the life of a community made up of different races. It is quite easy to become involved in a lot of activities so that there is very little of energy or time left for meditation and reflection. Naturally, I do not wish to make that mistake. On the other hand, I do not want to seem to be some kind of ecclesiastical prima donna. Somewhere between these two extremes I hope to find a place of effective leadership.

Secondly, I advise holding up proceedings with Mr. Cleage because I am afraid it will prove very embarrassing to him and the church, if at the end of six months it is necessary for his leadership with the church to be terminated. The understanding may be very clear and even contractual, but this will not make a great deal of difference if the emotions have become involved. If Mr. Cleage is able to do the things that are indicated, and is without any basic ties to prevent it, it may be best to think of him in terms of full-time use in the project, so that it will not be necessary for the church to have me come out at all. I say this quite objectively because it is not reasonable to me to come out for an interval of twelve, or even twenty-four months to participate in the work if the leadership that is required is already functioning in the church. If we could talk together, I would be able to make my position much clearer I am sure.

Now with reference to finances. Mrs. Thurman and I have talked the matter through very carefully and we are agreed that it would be very unfortunate if our coming out there was subsidized by the Rosenwald Foundation, or any of the uplift foundations with which we are acquainted. I have said nothing about the Rosenberg Foundation because I do not know anything about it. If any foundation can be persuaded to put money into the project, then it seems that the money should be invested in program activities, costs of operation, equipment, technical help of one kind or another. I think that it is spiritually unfortunate to have the ministers who are responsible for interpreting the meaning of religion to the people in any sense responsible personally to a foundation. In the light of this, we are willing to take our chances on the $2400.00 and a house that is rent free. As the work develops, we ought to be able to supplement this within the church fellowship itself, or from interested friends. If the job which we may undertake is right, and if there is any validity in our claim that God sustains His Kingdom in the world, we ought to be willing to venture in that kind of faith. As I have mentioned several times, I do not think that money should be the decisive factor in working out the success of the undertaking. I realize how practical the world is and that bills must be paid, and so forth, but to lift its consideration to the central point is not sound. This is not to suggest that you and the committee are not extremely wise in checking every detail as to the financial undertaking, but it is to say that there are risks involved in our bold venture and we must be prepared to take our share of them.

If the Hamilton Square Church is for sale in July, we might put our heads together on a plan to get it underwritten. I do think that it is critically important to have a good plant large enough to do our work and to move forward into the community without the psychology of our being some kind of a mission in the conventional sense. It is my faith that the money can be found, as our course is right!

The time has come for the university to make some formal announcement about my release. In your next letter please let me know if the mind of the group is clear at that point, so I can advise the university.

Personal greetings to you and Mrs. Fisk.[2]

Sincerely,

Howard Thurman

Dr. Alfred G. Fisk
316 San Benito Way
San Francisco, Calif.

TLc.

Notes

1. The Rosenwald Fund (also known as the Rosenwald Foundation) was created in 1917 by the retail magnate Julius Rosenwald (1862–1937), president and chairman of Sears, Roebuck. It is best remembered for its assistance to southern blacks and its support for educational opportunities for African Americans. Unlike most foundations, the Rosenwald Fund was not designed to last in perpetuity, and it ceased operations in 1948, having given away $70 million.

2. Eleanor Millard Fisk (1903–95) was born in China of missionary parents. Thurman described her as having "an amazing gift of grace, which gave warm assurance to the venture [the Fellowship Church] from the start" (*WHAH*, 143).

From Alfred G. Fisk
10 January 1944[1]
San Francisco, Calif.

Fisk responds to Thurman's acceptance of an offer to be the pastor of the Fellowship Church in San Francisco. He also outlines the role of Albert Cleage, who was to be brought on as an interim copastor until Thurman's leave would begin in July 1944.

Dr. Howard Thurman,
Howard University,
Washington, D.C.

Dear Howard Thurman:

Your letter[2] arrived here late Sunday night and I was immediately impressed by its fine spirit and the importance of the considerations you presented.

I called together a meeting of the more important members of our committee for this afternoon and we discussed our situation anew in the light of the considerations you have presented.

We are very happy over your statement as to how you view your own participation in the work of the church. It seems to us just right {from the point of view of the church}, though we are conscious of the fact that you are giving up a great deal—especially of the kind of work that brings the greatest recognition in our society. Only a very "big" man is willing to make such decisions.

We are agreed with you, also, that the spiritual ministry of the church should not be "beholden" to a secular foundation. The grants of the Rosenberg

Foundation, as I have known them have been without any "strings attached"; but I think that you are right in suggesting that grants for activity programs or building would be more appropriate than for ministerial support. Again we are humbled by your willingness to accept so small a salary, and we hope that it may be supplemented by private sources.

What you say about the coming of Mr. Cleage and the inevitable emotional involvements, seems to us also a matter of serious concern. If we could get along as we are until July 1st, we realize that it would be better than to complicate the picture with another individual. The committee wondered if some woman worker might be obtained who could do calling and promotional work among the Negroes in the community, especially in relation to Sunday School and young people's activities. Our crying need is to "get through" to the Negro "man on the street" in the community.

Before the committee meeting I called upon our Presbyterian Superintendent for National Missions, and discussed the Cleage negotiations with him. He urged me to have him come out to us with the understanding that he would not confine his work to our project, but help to develop work of a similar character at Hunter's Point (south of San Francisco where the world's largest dry dock is being built) and in a new Federal Housing Project in Oakland.[3] The idea would be that in the course of five or six months these projects would develop into full time work for Mr. Cleage, and he would make an easy transition to complete attention to them when you come out to our project.[4] And he would be invited to come out with that definitely in view.

After considerable discussion, our committee thought that such an arrangement would perhaps be the best thing we can do under the circumstances. We hope that you will agree with us, for we are anxious to work out arrangements that will be thoroughly satisfactory to you. I am not sure that Mr. Cleage will come on this new basis, but we did feel a little responsible to him in view of the preliminary negotiations we had opened up with him, and we do need someone to carry on the work right now. (Manley Johnson, our Divinity student, did not appear at all for our first young people's meeting last night, though we had planned together the previous week to have the meeting. He simply informed me in the morning that he might be late, as he was speaking at a meeting in Berkeley. This is typical of his behavior.)

I have written to Mr. Cleage enclosing a copy of your letter and telling of our committee discussion. I suggested to him that he might think of himself as coming to work for the Presbytery and loaned by them to our project until your arrival, with the understanding that he would be starting other work at Hunter's Point, Oakland, etc., to which he would give full-time after July 1st.

Please forgive me if my previous letter seemed impatient. Miss Venita Lewis will probably tell you that I find waiting very difficult![5] I think that I do need your ministry of spiritual quietness. (It is no accident that the hymn "Dear Lord and Father of Mankind" is the one I find most meaningful to me.)[6]

By the way, my wife, who was Eleanor Millard says that her sister, Ruth (Billy), knew your wife at Oberlin. It is a small world! Billy is thrilled at the prospects of you two coming to California. She is now Mrs. Bradford Bayliss, wife of a "Y" worker in Southern California.[7]

Greetings to you and Mrs. Thurman from us all,

Sincerely yours,

[*signed*] Alfred G. Fisk

Alfred G. Fisk

                                                                                              TLS.

NOTES

1. Fisk misdated the letter "10 January 1943."

2. To Alfred G. Fisk, 3 January 1944, printed in the current volume.

3. A commercial shipyard was built in Hunters Point, in the southeastern corner of San Francisco, in the 1870s. By 1920, when the shipyard was rented by the U.S. Navy, it had two one-thousand-foot dry docks and was among the largest in the world. In 1940 it was formally acquired by the U.S. Navy, becoming the San Francisco Naval Shipyard. It was closed in 1974. The federal government created more than thirty thousand public housing units in the East Bay during World War II, including thirty-five hundred in Oakland. This included several all-black housing developments, among them Bayview Hills, Cypress Village, Magnolia Manor, and Willow Manor Dorms. See Marilynn S. Johnson, *The Second Gold Rush: Oakland and the East Bay in World War II* (Berkeley: University of California Press, 1992), 97–111.

4. Both Fisk and the Presbyterian National Board of Missions were thinking of Cleage primarily in terms of "Negro work" rather than promoting interracialism.

5. Fisk's impatience would be noted by Thurman, in a less than flattering way, in the opening comments of a diary he kept on his arrival in San Francisco (HT, San Francisco journal, printed in the current volume).

6. This hymn to words of the poet John Greenleaf Whittier (1807–92) speaks of the need for divine calm: "drop thy still dews of quietness / Till all our striving cease." In response to a query from a newspaper editor, Thurman in 1947 provided a list of his favorite hymns, at the top of which was "Dear Lord and Father of Mankind," so perhaps it was Thurman's favorite hymn as well (To Carl Murphy, 24 July 1948, printed in the current volume).

7. Bradford Bayliss (1906–2001) was a director of education at several Presbyterian churches in Washington, D.C., and Pasadena. He married Ruth Millard in 1928.

❧ FROM ALFRED G. FISK

17 FEBRUARY 1944

SAN FRANCISCO, CALIF.

Fisk apprises Thurman of the latest church developments, including the agreement on the name "Fellowship Church," the decision not to host a summer program sponsored by the American Friends Service Committee, and the success of their Lincoln's Day Dinner.

Dr. Howard Thurman,
Howard University,
Washington, D.C.

Dear Howard:

We had a board meeting on Monday evening of this week and several important decisions have been made. We decided definitely against the name "Neighborhood Church" and are going to call it "Fellowship Church." It was generally felt that the term Neighborhood usually connotes a geographically restricted area, and we did not want that.

Secondly we decided against having an American Friends Service Committee Summer Project at our church.[1] I may say that the proposal had been not so much for a "work camp" such as the Friends put on in the East, as for an interracial project in cooperative living and in a recreational program for the children of our neighborhood.

I personally regret that our decision has the effect of "killing" one of the AFSC projects and that they do not feel it can be shifted to any other place in northern California. Mrs. Lucas feels strongly that the AFSC dominates everything it touches and gets all the credit for the enterprises in which non-friends do most of the work. She did not want our church eclipsed in that fashion. She also felt that AFSC projects are too loosely managed—if not actually mismanaged.

Our decision puts us in the position of having the moral responsibility of carrying on a summer project of our own—otherwise our action regarding the AFSC proposal is a "dog-in-the-manger" one. We will have to turn our thoughts to this at once. I am not sure just what we should attempt. A Vacation Church School for the children in the neighborhood might be very valuable to the church and to the community. We have not gone back to the Rosenberg Foundation, and we might ask for aid for such a project. With Mr. Cleage leaving July 1st, and you {just} arriving, and myself going off on vacation, we will need other leadership for such a project. And I know from an experience ten years ago that it will entail a very great amount of work.

Our Lincoln's Day Dinner was a great success. The room looked nice, the food was abundant and excellent, the musical program outstanding. Your friends the Brittons were present. (I got a note from the Bartlett Heards regretting that they could not come.) I read the page or two from "Meet the Negro"[2] describing you and your work, and made announcement of your coming July 1st. Of course there was great applause.

Mr. Walter Gordon[3] was called out of town and not able to be present. Mr. Cleage, who had arrived the day before, and Mrs. Lucas spoke—both very effectively. But the finest part of the evening was the feeling of oneness and good fellowship. This was very marked. There were something over 80 present about equally divided between Negroes and white folk. We had shared together in the planning, preparation, and serving of the dinner—as we did in the washing up.

You need not be concerned over the question of support from leading folk in the community. We have with us if not as constant participants, at least as supporters, all the leading Negroes—head of USO, paper editors, NAACP president and ex-president, Community Center[4] executives, etc. We borrowed silverware (it cannot be purchased) from the Community Center and are on most cordial relations with them. The Council of Churches is also heartily back of us. The President and Executive Secretary are among my best friends. They have set up an Interracial Commission and I am on it.

The results of the Johnson survey are not yet available. Dr. Johnson is returning early in March with the data. I will see that you get copies of whatever material is available.[5]

We are delighted with the prospect of a visit from Mrs. Thurman. Mrs. Fisk and I would be glad to have her as our houseguest while she is here. I think that it will be very valuable to have her see things first hand and meet with our board and other groups. If I could know well in advance when (and if) she is to arrive, I will try and plan things in relation to the visit. We might have another church dinner at that time.

I am sending you under separate cover copy of the "Reporter" and "People's Advocate"—San Francisco Negro papers,[6] and copies of our latest church bulletins.

With cordial good wishes to yourself and Mrs. Thurman,
Sincerely yours,
[*signed*] Alfred
Alfred G. Fisk

TLS.

NOTES

1. Quakers established the American Friends Service Committee (AFSC) in 1917 to give conscientious objectors during World War I an opportunity to aid civilian war victims, and their efforts expanded to work overseas. (Thurman's mentor Rufus Jones was one of the principal founders.)

2. Karl E. Downs, *Meet the Negro* (Los Angeles: Methodist Youth Fellowship, Southern California–Arizona Annual Conference, 1943), a collection of short biographical sketches of prominent African Americans.

3. Walter A. Gordon (1894–1976) received his undergraduate degree from the University of California, Berkeley in 1918 and subsequently became the first African American to earn

a J.D. from the UC-Berkeley School of Law. In addition to his law practice, Gordon's career included work as a police officer and a college football coach. He also headed the Berkeley NAACP in the 1920s and 1930s and remained a member in the 1940s. He served on the California parole board, the Adult Authority (1943–55), before being appointed governor of the U.S. Virgin Islands. He resigned that post in 1958 to accept an appointment as a federal judge in the Virgin Islands.

4. The Booker T. Washington Community Service Center, founded by the black community of San Francisco in 1919.

5. Johnson, *The Negro War Worker in San Francisco.*

6. The rapid increase in the black population of San Francisco led to a burgeoning of local black newspapers. The *Reporter* was founded in 1944 by Thomas C. Fleming but soon merged with the *Sun*, acquired in a poker game by Carleton Goodlett, Thurman's friend and a family physician, to become the *Sun-Reporter;* Goodlett remained the publisher until his death in 1997. The *People's Advocate* was a short-lived, left-wing, bi-monthly black newspaper in San Francisco founded in January 1944 by Angelo Herndon (1913–97). It did not survive the year. Herndon is best remembered as the central figure in a notable civil liberties case, when, as a 19-year-old Communist Party organizer in Atlanta in 1932, he was arrested and convicted for insurrection. He was released in 1937. See Charles H. Martin, *The Angelo Herndon Case and Southern Justice* (Baton Rouge: Louisiana State University Press, 1976).

From Dan B. Genung
29 February 1944
Los Angeles, Calif.

The Fellowship Church was part of an informal movement during the 1930s and 1940s to establish interracial churches in various urban centers of the United States. Dan Genung,[1] who moved to Los Angeles in 1942 to establish the interracial All Peoples Christian Church, introduces himself to Thurman.

Dr. Howard Thurman
Dean of the Chapel
Howard University
Washington, D.C.

Dear Dr. Thurman:

I was thrilled to read the other day that you will take a leave of absence from Howard and will aid in establishing an inter-racial church in San Francisco. May I welcome you to the coast, if not to Los Angeles.

Fresh from our graduate work, my wife and I came out here about 16 months ago to try and establish an inter-racial church in the former Japanese Christian Church property. We felt that work of this sort was the most critical and vital thing in the world. We still feel that way, and are encouraged to find that you, apparently, feel the same way.[2] It is sort of a pat on the back to us.

Of course, our work is quite different, for we are trying to "grow" a church through community work, almost altogether with the children so far. Also we found ourselves in a highly delinquent area and are trying to do something about that. But our primary motive is to build a church, where all men can worship together as brothers.

I can't help but admit a secret hope that your example may cause other leading ministers to take definite steps to either make their own churches inter-racial or to give up a "white" or "black" church and set out to build an inter-racial one. Perhaps I am not justified in so hoping.

Please accept my best wishes to you for taking the step you have, and may your work meet with the approval of God. I have heard you speak, and I know that He guided you in your decision.

Sincerely,

[*signed*] Dan B. Genung

TLS.

Notes

1. Dan B. Genung (1915–2008), a 1941 graduate of the University of Chicago Divinity School, arrived in South-Central Los Angeles in 1942 with his wife Frances to begin the All Peoples Christian Church, which was formally established in 1946 as a congregation associated with the Christian Church (Disciples of Christ). See Dan B. Genung, *A Street Called Love: The Story of All Peoples Christian Church and Center, Los Angeles, Calif.* (Pasadena, Calif.: Hope Publishing House, 2000). The church had close ties with the network of Christian pacifists, and visitors to the church during the war years included Glen Smiley of FOR, Bayard Rustin, and Thurman's protégé James Farmer (ibid., 49–50). W. E. B. Du Bois would attend the Easter service at the church in 1946 and would praise it as "an interesting and sincere ceremony" ("The Winds of Time," *Chicago Defender,* 8 June 1946).

2. Like the Fellowship Church, All Peoples Christian Church was located in a formerly Japanese church, in an area undergoing rapid transition from a Japanese to an African American population as a result of Japanese internment and in-migration of blacks. See Kurashige, *Shifting Grounds of Race,* 179–80.

⤳ To Alfred G. Fisk
2 March 1944
[Washington, D.C.]

Thurman shares reactions of students and faculty at Howard University to the announcement of his imminent leave of absence.

Dear Alfred:

I am very pleased to acknowledge your good letter.[1] Simultaneously with the meeting out there, the secretary of the University[2] released to the local press and the national Negro press an announcement of my leave beginning July 1st.[3]

It came as a distinct shock to the student body as a whole and to many of the faculty. Serious pressures are already being exerted in an effort to force a reconsideration but to no avail. I have received many thoughtful letters and telephone calls about the project. It is, indeed, reassuring that there is so wide spread an interest in the validity of the thing that is being undertaken.

A friend of mine in New York told me about meeting Mrs. Branston, I believe, who is one of the members of the board of the foundation of which you spoke earlier.[4] He told me that she spoke with definite enthusiasm for the project and its significance in terms of race relations. I am certain that your efforts to interest them will be fruitful. It will be a very good thing if a grant from them would make it possible for us to get the help we need for carrying on our program in the community.

I like the name Fellowship Church very much. I had thought of some such name as the Church of All Peoples, but Fellowship Church carries the same notion.

I received a full letter from the Britons. George Briton actually sent me a floor plan of the building and a detailed description even as to the color of paint; described the Sunday service, the Lincoln dinner, the number of people present, who spoke, what their points were. There was a special comment about the excellency of the singing of the quartette. They wished the church luck in trying to find a place for us in which to live.

I received the newspapers and the bulletins which you sent. You may be interested in seeing a copy of our University bulletin which I am enclosing.

I hope that Mrs. Thurman will be able to go that far when she makes her trip next week. She will not know exactly until she actually gets to Chicago. Everything turns on accommodations beyond Denver. If she cannot be there over Sunday, it would not be worth coming. Do not be surprised if suddenly you receive a wire saying that within the next four or five days she will be turning up. I cannot be more specific than that because it has been necessary to change her date in Denver due to the fact that the magazine which she is editing has been delayed in coming out. She has one more issue before her resignation takes effect. As soon as I get a chance, I will send several copies to you and Mrs. Fisk. It is the official Journal of the National Council of Negro Women.[5] This is enough for now. It is always good to have a visit with you. My personal greetings to Mrs. Fisk from both of us.
Sincerely,
Howard Thurman
Dean of the Chapel

Mr. Alfred C. Fisk
316 San Benito Way
San Francisco, California

                                                              TLc.

Notes

1. From Alfred C. Fisk, 17 February 1944, printed in the current volume.

2. James M. Nabrit Jr. (1900–1997) was a 1923 graduate of Morehouse College (in Thurman's class), a prominent civil rights lawyer, and president of Howard University (1960–65, 1968–69).

3. The first notices had already appeared, including "Dean Thurman on Leave to Establish Church," *Chicago Defender,* 19 February 1944.

4. Louise Rosenberg Bransten (1908–77), a niece of Max Rosenberg, inherited over a million dollars from his estate. She served on the board of directors of the Rosenberg Foundation for only a single year, 1936, but presumably remained active in its affairs for several years thereafter. See Rosenberg Foundation, *Ten Years of Community Service,* iii. Bransten was an active member of the Communist Party and prominent in both San Francisco society and left-wing circles during the war. In the late 1940s she testified before the House Committee on Un-American Activities on her Communist associations, especially questions on her war-time connection with the nuclear scientist J. Robert Oppenheimer. There has been some controversy over whether she was involved in espionage for the Soviet Union. One careful study is agnostic (John Earl Haynes and Harvey Klehr, *Venona: Decoding Soviet Espionage in America* [New Haven, Conn.: Yale University Press, 1999], 232–33).

5. *Aframerican Woman's Journal.*

From Alfred G. Fisk
13 March 1944
San Francisco, Calif.

Fisk asks for Thurman's views regarding an ongoing debate among members of the Fellowship Church on whether to continue their relationship with the Presbyterian Church.

Dr. Howard Thurman,
Howard University
Washington, D.C.

Dear Howard,

How I wish that you were here! There are many problems which I wish could be postponed until your arrival, but which some in our group are pressing upon us.

There is, for instance, the matter of our relationship to the Presbyterian Church. As I think you understand, and as I stated in the meeting at which we decided to go ahead with services (the minutes of which I recently sent you) ours is really a project of the Presbyterian Church. But some of our group, young people with interests at the Friends Center,[1] want us to be entirely independent.

Now I am not at all denominational in my thinking (I didn't know that you were a Baptist until last night—it never occurred to me to ask, and it does not matter) but our project was started by the Presbyterians, we use their building, and they underwrite our budget. I consider it entirely unrealistic to suggest, as one of the young people did last night, that we could go out and rent a store for services and raise our own budget.

The Presbyterians have given us completely a free hand and have backed us morally as well as financially.[2] We are not using "Presbyterian" on our sign board or publicity, and I cannot see that they are restricting us in any way. I see a certain value for us in a connection with a large national body, and I think that we can have an influence upon the church at large in that connection as we could not have otherwise.

I think that the Presbytery would feel it almost an insult for us to organize an independent community church now—as some are suggesting that we do. This matter came up last night at our planning meeting and was laid over for further discussion until our next meeting on March 27th.

In a real sense I do not think we have any right to discuss it. Certain commitments have already been made. We are a Presbyterian project. We have arranged for your coming on that basis—with funds from the Presbyterian Board and a further request for the house that belongs to Presbytery. I do not want {, however,} to squelch these enthusiastic young people by {seeming} dictatorial. I want to persuade them and keep their hearty support.

If you would care to write me a paragraph about your views concerning our relationship to the Presbyterian Church—whether you feel it would hamper our project and its significance, I think that it would be useful at the meeting in guiding the decision.

I am sorry that this has had to come up now.

The Brittons were at the meeting last night—and were very helpful. They certainly are very fine people. If Mrs. Thurman is able to come out, we plan a church dinner and Mr. Britton will be on the committee to arrange it.

On the whole, I think our project is going nicely. There is more and more community interest and support being manifested. Our services receive praise and approval from those who attend.

Our cordial good wishes to you,
Very sincerely
[*signed*] Alfred
Alfred G. Fisk
This letter has been written very much in haste, and is not very well expressed, I fear.

                                                                          TLS.

Notes

1. The Quaker Meeting House in San Francisco.

2. The Board of National Missions of the Presbyterian Church gave $3,600.00 a year for the Fellowship Church, $2,400.00 for Thurman's salary and $1,200.00 for Fisk's. In addition it placed at the church's disposal the property at 1500 Post Street—the former home of the Japanese-American Presbyterian Church—which included a small chapel and living quarters on the second floor, and which became the Thurmans' first home in San Francisco. See HT, *Footprints,* 33.

To Emerson O. Bradshaw

16 March 1944

[*Washington, D.C.*]

Thurman insists that the Church Federation of Greater Chicago find accommo-dations for him at a downtown hotel for his upcoming appearances in the city. The solution, communicated to Thurman on 29 March, would be that he stay at the Morrison Hotel,[1] *provided that Bradshaw accompany him at the registration desk upon Thurman's arrival, which the hotel was demanding.*[2] *This solution was acceptable, although not completely satisfactory, to Thurman.*

Dear Dr. Bradshaw:[3]

This is a hurried note to say that I shall mail you my list of subjects early next week from Detroit. You should have them not later than Wednesday or Thursday.

With reference to the hotel, it is my considered judgment that in the name of the Church Federation of Greater Chicago maximum pressure should be executed to get me accommodations. A far more important issue is at stake than my personal comfort. There are a dozen homes at least in which I could live with comfort and with some measure of privacy. I prefer a hotel for the reasons that you already know. It seems to me that this is an excellent oppor-tunity for the church to take a definitive position. I do not think that the hotels of Chicago will stand out against the organized will of the protestant church in the vicinity of Chicago. At this moment when so much is at stake for the future peace of the world, I do not see how we can afford to do less. I think that the hotels should be advised quite clearly that I am a Negro, that my complexion is dark, so that there would be no question as to their understanding as to what they are doing. Last year when I served the Council of Churches in Detroit this same question was up with reference to the Statler.[4] The group there insisted that I should be accommodated in the same way that the other guest speakers of the Council were accommodated. I understand that at first the hotel reneged but came through. I registered at the Statler and nothing happened except that

I had privacy and courteous treatment. This is the position that I have always taken in matters of this sort. Please let me know your decision in this matter. If you wish to get in touch with me before Friday morning, March 24th you can reach me at Hotel Statler in Detroit, or in care of the Detroit Council of Churches.

I hope that the luncheon meetings on Tuesday and Wednesday will not materialize because Monday, Thursday and Friday are heavy days. Thank you for your good letter.
Sincerely yours,
Howard Thurman
Dean of the Chapel

Dr. Emerson O. Bradshaw
Church Federation of Greater Chicago
77 W. Washington Street
Chicago 2, Ill.

                                                        TLc. MSR-HU

NOTES

1. The 45-story, 525-feet-high Morrison Hotel opened in 1925 in Chicago's Loop district. The hotel was demolished in 1965.

2. From Emerson O. Bradshaw, 29 March 1944.

3. Emerson O. Bradshaw (1881–1968) was for many years secretary of the Chicago Council of Religious Education and an official of the Church Federation of Greater Chicago. He authored *Unconquerable Kagawa* (St. Paul, Minn.: Macalester Park Publishing, 1952).

4. The one-thousand-room Detroit Statler Hotel opened in 1915. It was demolished in 2005.

🍃 "A HYMN TO YOUTH"
APRIL 1944

Evidently at the request of his old friend Channing Tobias, the senior secretary of the YMCA's Colored Work Department, Thurman agreed to write a hymn in honor of the organization's centennial.[1] The hymn, with music by Harry Robert Wilson,[2] was published by the International Committee of YMCAs.[3] Thurman's poem, which contains an early use of his favorite catchphrase "the growing edge," provides a glimpse of his revulsion at the carnage caused by World War II.[4]

1

Out of the welter of the years
Carried along with rhythmic
    beat—
The surging tide of moving feet
Of myriad youth have found their
    way.

2

We've come through many seas of
    blood;
Struggled in battles far and near—
Beset by terror, mad with fear
And yet our hope was
    never dimmed,

3

Our dream, the upward surge
    of youth,
The "growing edge" of life divine,
Has kept alive God's great Design
To make this world a holy place.

5[5]

O great, and understanding God
To thee we yield our total powers
Despite all hell, we shall not
    cower
Nor bring defeat of brotherhood.

6

In midst of carnage, hate and
    shame
The bitter fruits of sinning years,
We catch a glimmer through our tears
Of days of unborn, of promise bright.

Td. MSR-HU

NOTES

1. "The poem is quite acceptable and the prints are being made. I am very glad you did not let me say no to this" (To Channing Tobias, 28 April 1944).

2. Harry Robert Wilson (1901–68) was a choral composer, conductor, and educator; the author of numerous books on conducting; and chairman of the music education department at Teachers College, Columbia University, from 1958 to 1966.

3. *A Hymn to Youth: Written on the Occasion of the 100th Anniversary of the Young Men's Christian Association* (New York: International Committee of Y.M.C.A.'s, 1944).

4. To Paul Limbert, 15 April 1944. A careful craftsman, Thurman wrote that "the last line in the final stanza is weak, particularly the word bright," though it was unchanged in the printed version.

5. This stanza is misnumbered in the original.

To Alice Sams

[*2 April 1944*]¹
Madison, Wis.

In this letter to his mother, who was living in Daytona Beach, Florida, Thurman tells her about his growing fame with a combination of surprise, pride, and humility and talks about the looming move to San Francisco.

Dear Mamma

I am sending this note to you from up in Wisconsin. Tonight I am preaching at the Spring Religious Convocation for the University of Wisconsin. It is a meeting held in the large University Theater. All of these things continue to surprise me—I do not know how they happen or hardly what they mean. I do not suppose that it is mine to know the reasons. All I know is that God, for reasons best known to Himself, makes all kinds of openings for me to declare His Truth and here I am.

Tomorrow I go to Chicago where I shall be preaching until Friday at the Chicago Temple² in downtown Chicago, for the Federation of Churches of Greater Chicago. When I came through there yesterday I saw on the elevated platforms a big sign 4 feet high with my name written advertising the fact that I shall be preaching there all the week. There are 150 of those big announcements at as many platforms throughout the entire city. I pray that God will give me the strength and the wisdom to do His Purpose in all these things.

Sue's back from California. She went out there to meet the people at the church and to see about schools etc. for Olive and Anne and also about a place where we are to live. They wanted me to come but that was quite impossible and I asked her to go. She was there only 4 days.

Thanks for your good letter. I am glad that you are doing so well. Remember that you are not to worry but just keep on enjoying God and let Him carry your burdens. He is able and joyfully willing to do it all the way to the end and beyond.

Before I go West I am certainly coming home to see you. It will be great happiness for me to enjoy your blessed presence again in the flesh. I do not talk about it but I miss you oh so terribly.
Your Son
[*signed*] Howard

ALS.

NOTES

1. The letter is undated. Thurman went to Chicago on 3 April 1944 for a week of sermons and talks sponsored by the Chicago Church Federation.

2. The Chicago Temple is a combination church and twenty-three-floor office building and home of the First United Methodist Church of Chicago. At 568 feet high, it was the tallest building in Chicago from 1924, when it opened, until 1930.

꙳ TO ALFRED G. FISK
11 APRIL 1944
[*Washington, D.C.*]

On 29 March, Fisk sent a letter to Thurman about the possibility of purchasing the building of the First English Lutheran Church as a home for the Fellowship Church.[1] *The congregation was vacating its building in what was rapidly becoming an African American neighborhood. The church and its furnishings were available for about fifty thousand dollars, and his letter went into considerable detail about how, under the auspices of the national Presbyterian Church, this might be financed. Although the chairman of the San Francisco Presbytery, W. Clyde Smith, was somewhat skeptical about purchasing the building, Fisk was enthusiastic, writing that he had "fallen in love" with the church building, which "makes one feel the presence of God the minute one enters the sanctuary," and that "it would be the fitting place for Howard Thurman." In his response, Thurman returns Fisk's zeal, writing of the "profoundly creative, and in some ways revolutionary idea that we are trying to implement," and he promises to use his prestige and influence to help raise the funds necessary for the church to function at a high level. He also pledges to "stick by the venture until it is firmly established," including extending his leave of absence beyond the 1944–45 academic year. In the end the deal would not materialize.*

Dear Alfred:

I have just returned from conducting the Holy Week Services for the Church Federation of Greater Chicago. The services were held in the Chicago Temple down in the loop and it was a very interesting experience.

Last night Sue and I had some time to talk about her trip and about the plans for the future. I have read your letter under date of March 29th,[2] with very great care. My reaction is as follows. I shall follow the order in your letter.

(1) It is my opinion that if we are able to move into the Lutheran Church structure we will be able to draw into our constituency sufficient people to make it worth the venture. I feel very much happier about the whole prospect because I was not able to visualize holding worship services in an auditorium that only accommodated one hundred people. Some of my friends who are most critical of my leaving the East at this desperate time have called almost dramatic attention to the fact that I have no right to tie myself down to preach to a handful of people without regard to how great the idea is that sends me forth to do it. Some of the things which they have said relative to my ability and the necessity for using it in the widest possible manner are a little embarrassing to repeat. Suffice it to say that if we can negotiate for the church and move into it in the Fall it gives a tremendous lift to the entire venture.

(2) I do not know, as your question states it, if the Thurmans have the drawing power, but I believe that the Thurmans and the Fisks and the other people, and the Lord have the drawing power. If we are all consecrated to this great purpose it will draw. With reference to our staying only one year, I think that we ought to stick by the venture until it is firmly established. My leave is for one year, but I do not see how I can escape the necessity for having it renewed.

(3) I suppose that what Dr. Smith[3] says about the basic principle of church expansion is sound, namely develop the congregation first and get the building after. However, it must be remembered that this is the first venture of this kind in the history of the Protestant Church in the United States of America. There are no precedents to which appeal can be made. As I conceive of this Alfred, we have a profoundly creative, and in some ways revolutionary idea that we are trying to implement. We are trying to implement it because we feel that it is fundamental to the genius of Christianity. It is absolutely necessary that the launching of the idea should be under the most auspicious circumstances as to beauty and facility, therefore, this would call for the reversal, if necessary, of the normal policy for financing a church. Of course, I may be mistaken in this idea, but it is of the essence of sound judgment to protect ourselves from being the object of pity and compassion—this is an easy way to dismiss the challenge of our undertaking.

(4) It is a tribute to my faith in the undertaking that I shall do all I can to raise funds for the work even though I have never before given any thought, or energy to establishing the financial security of any undertaking. I have made many friends over the country, but never have my contacts been used for the purpose of money raising. There are people interested [in] any thing that I may be doing because of a confidence which they have developed in me. The simple

plan that I have is that I shall make a list of persons to whom I shall write personal letters seeking to interest them in investing in the idea. Some of these are persons of wealth who have been committed to some interracial ideal through the years. Everywhere I have been since I agreed to come West the adventure has been discussed. I think that without a single exception the interest has been spontaneous and genuine. Just last Sunday at the Lawrenceville Preparatory School[4] one of the Masters there said, "it must make you feel very humble to be pioneering in a venture of this sort. Please keep me in closest touch with everything that happens, so that the meaning that you discover may shed light on the job that I am doing." I am sure that such a man would contribute something if he felt that it were needed.

Are you much of a business man, or is there some young or older man of business experience who might help us work out the details for financing the church?

What is the attitude of the people in the church towards the possibility of our moving into the Lutheran structure? It is conceivable that new friends will be developed in San Francisco who would be challenged by our undertaking and who would be willing to put some money in it. If I may summarize my whole position. I think we ought to have the church. If the congregation is willing to join you and me in the venture, then I think we ought to do it. I am also willing to see friends in the East for the purpose of trying to get funds. It seems clear that such an undertaking will require a commitment on my part for longer than a year's duration. If the Presbyterian Board, locally and nationally were willing to make the loan up to 40% and give us a year for a campaign to raise the balance, the Lutheran Board may be willing to accept that kind of proposition. It may be that the promotion funds of some of the other denominations would be willing to invest some money in this idea. I shall write you again in a few days after I have had a little time to think a little further. This is really part one.

Olive and Anne were elated with the lovely gifts from Chinatown and all of us eagerly await the reunion of the Fisks and Thurmans.
Sincerely,
Howard Thurman
Dean of the Chapel

Dr. Alfred G. Fisk
316 San Benito Way
San Francisco 16, California

TLc.

NOTES

1. From Alfred Fisk, 29 March 1944, repr. in Fisk and Thurman, *First Footprints,* 29–31.
2. Ibid., 29–31.

3. The Reverend W. Clyde Smith was executive secretary of the San Francisco Presbytery.

4. During the 1930s and 1940s Thurman spoke regularly at the Lawrenceville School, an elite preparatory school in Lawrenceville, New Jersey. Founded in 1810, it was an all-male school until 1987. A collection of lectures delivered at the Lawrenceville Forum Series, published as Thomas H. Johnson, ed., *In Defense of Democracy* (New York: Putnam, 1949), includes an address by Thurman, "The Religion of Jesus and the Disinherited" (125–38). Delivered in 1947, it was a version of the first chapter of *Jesus and the Disinherited*, using Thurman's preferred title for the book.

To Alfred G. Fisk

13 April 1944
[*Washington, D.C.*]

In this follow-up to his letter of two days earlier, Thurman expresses a desire for more information and pictures of the Lutheran church building for sale. He was already beginning to work as copastor of the Fellowship Church. Here he tells Fisk that he has requested meetings with two prominent individuals who may be able to help the church's fund-raising efforts.

Dear Alfred:

I am wondering if it is possible for you to get some pictures made of the Lutheran structure—a good interior shot and one showing the building? I would like also, a picture of the present structure and the interior of the place of worship.

I am trying to locate a person to come out for the summer. I had in mind a very able young man who has been my assistant here, but he is coming back to do his senior B.D. year at Howard because he has been given a rather interesting offer. My first thought was that he could do his senior year at the Pacific School of Religion. Confidentially, Roy Nichols told Sue that he would consider coming over and working with us next winter because he is disappointed in the kind of cooperation he has been able to get, particularly from the Congregational Church.[1] I share this with you in greatest confidence. It is merely a possibility and there may be other reasons why it should not be considered.

I have written for interviews with several people, among whom are Paul Robeson and Earl Adams,[2] who is the director of the Promotion Fund of the Northern Baptist Convention. He and I were in seminary together and I do not see why they would not be willing to put some money in the program. It really is a conscience contribution, for how Christianity in America can maintain any measure of self-respect in the face of its iniquitous record of segregation and discrimination and even violence, is more than I can possibly understand. Paul Robeson is a very close friend to the important lady in the Rosenberg Foundation.[3] I want two things from him; first, a personal letter to her commending the whole venture. I do not think this is necessary because of the effective work you have done already, but if she knows that Paul is vitally concerned about it, it might heighten her own interest. The second thing that I want him to do, is to give me a benefit concert sometime next winter.

We would prefer a double bed in our bedroom. Our present plan is to bring only our linen and personal effects. We shall have to leave our house practically furnished. We may ship our radio. I am trying to keep down the item of expense for travel in this way. As the matter stands now, it will wreck the Thurman finances to pay one way transportation for four people from Washington to San Francisco with all of the other things that are necessary to close up affairs on this end. I hope it can be done without having to go in debt, but I do not know at this writing.

Sue wants me to say to you how happy she is as a result of the experience out there. She feels that there is a tremendous opportunity and that we are very fortunate that we have in you and Mrs. Fisk two persons of such extraordinary quality. I received a request from the Baptist Divinity School[4] to give a group of lectures in August, but I did not commit myself. This is all for now. More later.
Sincerely,
Howard Thurman

Dr. Alfred G. Fisk
316 San Benito Way
San Francisco, Calif.

TLc.

NOTES

1. The South Berkeley Congregational Church, an interracial church where Nichols was copastor.

2. Earl Frederick "Bud" Adams (1900–1956), a native of Palmyra, N.Y., graduated from Denison University and Rochester Theological Seminary and was ordained a Baptist minister in 1925. After serving congregations in Hillsdale, Michigan; Chicago; and Buffalo, he was general director of promotion for the Northern Baptist Convention (1939–45) and executive director of the Protestant Council of New York City (1945–48). He spent his last years as assistant general secretary of the National Council of Churches of Christ in the U.S., with special attention to international postwar relief efforts.

3. Louise Bransten.

4. In Berkeley.

☙ FROM ALFRED G. FISK
17 APRIL 1944
SAN FRANCISCO, CALIF.

Fisk describes the differences of opinion among the congregation of Fellowship Church about whether to move into a Lutheran church building and reports on other church developments, including his growing dissatisfaction with both the Sakai Group and Albert Cleage.

Dr. and Mrs. Howard Thurman,
Howard University,
Washington, D.C.

Dear Howard and Sue:

I have just come from a congregational meeting at the church, at which time
the project of making a move for the Lutheran building was thoroughly discussed. The first indication that anyone in the congregation had about the matter was at church yesterday (because the A.M.E. church is known to be considering purchasing it, I had felt it best to make no public statement regarding our
interest in it).

Many of the congregation, however, went over after church yesterday to look
the building over so that we would know what we were discussing. After the discussion tonight, I am reminded of the thing that is often said among ministers,
that differences of opinion in connection with the building of a church building are bound to be such that the minister who builds one must leave when it
is built and let some one else come in and carry forward the work in the new
building.

So the opinions tonight were various. Mrs. Lucas says that the stairs
would keep her and many others from ever climbing to the sanctuary. Several (to my amazement) do not like the general atmosphere—"old" and
"musty" and "Lutheran" it was described. The arrangement of the social
rooms down stairs was criticized, and the Amos's felt that {criticized it be-
cause} it had no place for young people to play basket ball and such games.
There was no point in arguing about such matters, and they were not the main
consideration.

The feeling that the project must grow out of San Francisco and meet the
needs of the San Francisco situation was felt by many to be a more important
consideration. If Howard Thurman could be here and by the response of the
community lead it to the point of purchasing such a building or of designing
and building one of our own—that, it was felt, would be the course we should
follow.

I am trying to interpret the sense of the meeting, which is not easy. No one
would make a motion, and it was suggested that I write you "the sense of the
meeting." The Brittons who were present and who had seen the building said, I
believe, nothing. Our choir director, who was not present, is very much in favor
of the building—she has an Episcopal background which gives her appreciation
of architecture that some others do not have. The Cleages said almost nothing,
though Mr. Cleage did speak highly of you and of confidence in your ability to
raise money.

My own feeling after the meeting tonight is that if we are meant to get that building (and personally I think the sanctuary is most beautiful and worshipful) it will be here and available when you come.

There were only about twenty people present tonight. After you are here a while, the tenor of the thinking of our congregation may be very different—being moulded by the thought of the sort of people that will be attracted by your message and what we stand for. Mrs. Lucas, as you may know, is not easy to work with. The monastic group at Sakai House[1] are not representative of Christendom as we understand it. But the general folk who have worshipped with us so far will not come out to business meetings, and that gives these other elements an undue voice in our discussions.

I do think that the work of the seven months we will {have} put into the project before you arrive will be to the advantage of the project after you get here. We are building slowly, but I think we are building. However, from many points of view we will have to "begin" after you come.

Later, April 18, 1944

My suggestion to you is to go ahead with the hope of purchasing the Lutheran building after you come out to the field, or of planning and building a building of our own as soon as that is possible. Any money that can be raised now would be very valuable both from the point of enlisting the interest of people throughout the country in our project, and in securing an adequate building.

Your suggestion of Paul Robeson giving a concert for our benefit is a thrilling one. If he comes West to San Francisco it would be of great significance locally if he would give such a benefit concert here.

I will have pictures of our present building and of the Lutheran building made for you and send them as early as possible. There is definitely no chance of renting the Lutheran building with option to buy.

I am not much of a business man. In drawing up a budget I would really like a committee to work out such a matter. Because I feel that you are anxious to get some rough statement right away I am enclosing the sketch of budget I have made out. This involves much guess work and I have probably not thought of some items. We could probably rent the auditorium of the Friends Center for $1.50 to $2 per Sunday, a mere nominal fee for janitor service. I have no idea what we would spend on postage and supplies, and I have put in no item for newspaper publicity. Also I have no way of knowing what audiences we would get and what their contributions would amount to.

It seems to me that we can easily expect to carry current expenses from current receipts with the exceptions of the three items I have checked in pencil: travel expense, salary supplement and salary for a secretary or part-time worker.

These items I would like to see included {in} (or come out of) any money you might be able to help us raise, though I do not think they need be itemized for the public. You could say that we will need between three and four thousand dollars to supplement our current expenses budget during the first year.

We may, of course, get a grant from the Rosenberg Fund to take care of the part-time worker. I will hear in a few days as to their summer grant, and the possibility of a continuing aid from them would be an open question to be decided during the summer. A letter from Paul Robeson to Mrs. Louise Bransten, 2626 Green St., San Francisco, who is on the Rosenberg Foundation, would be a help.

Your suggestion of Roy Nichols helping us next year would be a thrilling thing to happen. (I had hoped that Albert Cleage would turn out to be another Roy Nichols.) I know that Roy is committed to a summer project where he is, however; so that would not help us for then.

I think that our summer leader should be a Negro. I say this partly in view of the fact that some of the Sakai House girls think of themselves as quite able to lead such a project (though I definitely do not think so—an opinion which the Brittons share). Bringing in a Negro will not seem quite like overlooking them in the same way that paying a white young lady on our staff would. Also, and fundamentally more important, we are much more likely to get white volunteer help, and need a paid Negro to keep our staff balanced.

I feel that this letter, and our situation, will seem rather unsatisfactory to you. Please do feel free to tell me what to do. If you feel strongly that I should take a stand about the building in opposition to the feeling of the folk now part of the project, I will do so. I do know that the A.M.E. church has $30,000 in hand and may make a deal with the Lutherans at any time. The minister, who is a friend of mine, has been holding them off to hear from me. I do know, however, that the A.M.E. church is also considering another location. We could build a building of our own eventually that would be better than the Lutheran one, but building is impossible now. I feel no clear guidance as to what we should do.

Eleanor feels even worse than I do over the situation; she felt like weeping after the meeting last night, and neither of us slept very well after it!

We send you our very warmest personal greetings. We are eagerly awaiting the arrival of the Thurmans in San Francisco.

Sincerely,

[*signed*] Alfred

**Estimated Budget of Current Expenses for
Fellowship Church, San Francisco**

	Now	With Expanded Program	In Lutheran Church
Utilities, per month	$12	$15	$24
Postage, Supplies, etc.	8	15	15
Janitor service	0	20	40
Building maintenance & repair		10	20
Equipment	40	15	25
Building Insurance	2 ½	2½	10
Music	20–25	30	30
Total Per month:	$85	$107.50	$164.
Total Per Year:	$1020.	$1290. {+ $100}	$2000.

{for rent of Friend's
auditorium for Sun. a.m.}

In addition, the following items should be added:

x	Travel & moving expense for the Thurmans	$600.
x	Salary to supplement Board appropriation for H.T.	1600.
	Rental of house for the Thurmans	720.
x	Salary for part-time worker or secretary	<u>1200.</u>
		4120.

Our collections have been averaging about $15 per Sunday, in addition to
which gifts have come in (some solicited by Mrs. Lucas, some from people interested in the project but not participants; some from participants) amount-
ing to about $150 per month.

On this basis, I would expect about the following without any wide financial
drive:

Estimated collections @ $25 per Sunday	$1300.
Gifts by participants	<u>1000.</u>
	2300

TLS.

Note

1. The Sakai Group was a nucleus of young women affiliated with Fellowship Church
when Thurman arrived. They lived in a house owned by the Sakai family, who had been
incarcerated in a Japanese American Relocation Camp. Members followed the teachings

of the British pacifist Muriel Lester, and they wanted to share "a common life" among the African Americans who then lived in the neighborhood, which was in the vicinity of the first Fellowship Church. See HT, *Footprints,* 29.

❧ From Alfred G. Fisk
19 April 1944
[*San Francisco, Calif.*]

Fisk writes to the Thurmans about recent developments, including the Fellowship Church's search for a permanent home.

Dr. and Mrs. Howard Thurman
Howard University
Washington, D.C.

Dear Howard and Sue:

I feel constrained to write you again—though I haven't much new to say. I did get a phone call from Mrs. Lucas (who, I think, regretted the fact that she had been rather negative at the congregational meeting). Mrs. Lucas was afraid that maybe we had "let you down" by not rising to {the} challenge before us.

But Mrs. Lucas said—and I think this is very true— "We must not let a little group of unrepresentative individualists block what you and Howard Thurman feel should be done." The Sakai House group are unrepresentative, and they are individualists. What Fellowship Church stands for is much bigger than they. And when Fellowship Church becomes a sizeable movement, as it will in the not too distant future, they will not count for a very great deal in it.

So, as I said in my previous letter: let me know what you feel strongly we should do. And don't be greatly influenced by the lack of response upon the part of the group at our recent meeting. Mr. Cleage feels strongly that the Negroes of the community would be much more impressed by the importance of our enterprise if we had a fine building—and that would go for white people too.

The Lutheran building we have been considering is the "best available." It may need considerable repair before long. I am going to try to have that checked in the next few days. It is far from ideal in many ways, and I would rather see us build a modern building—but that is out of the question now. Buying this now would not preclude us from building our own building later on, would it?

I called on Mrs. Helen Coford Johnson today. She was deeply moved by your letter. She said to me, "If I hadn't tied up my main estate in another way, I would like to do something more for the project the two of you are giving your lives to."[1] This quite spontaneously on her part. If you should telegraph me to go ahead on the Lutheran building before the possibility of the A.M.E. church taking it, I will go to Mrs. Johnson, and I think that she may be able to rearrange her affairs so as to help us. I don't know how long Mrs. Johnson will be with us. She speaks lightly of her condition, but she was arranging with me details for a memorial service, disposition of her body, etc.

You may well imagine that I haven't been a very good teacher this year—what with the concerns that take up my time! Now I simply must do other things!

{Very cordially,}

[*signed*] Alfred

{P.S. The fact that buying the Lutheran building and house, would solve (though not perfectly) the problem of your living quarters, is a point in its favor.}

TLS.

NOTE

1. Fisk had written to Thurman about two weeks earlier that Helen Coford Johnson, a friend of Fisk who had terminal cancer, had decided to leave a significant portion of her estate to benefit either conscientious objectors or "the improvement of race relations." When Fisk told her of the Fellowship Church and Thurman's involvement in it, she told him that she and Thurman had a two-hour conversation at a conference at Mills College two years previously and that she considered Thurman "one of the outstanding mystics in the contemporary world, and it seems to have made her very, very happy to know that we will be working together." See From Alfred G. Fisk, 5 April 1944. Fisk suggested that Thurman write to Johnson, which he evidently did. The distribution of Johnson's estate is not known.

🐦 To PAUL ROBESON

21 APRIL 1944

[*Washington, D.C.*]

Thurman writes to the well-known African American actor, singer, and activist Paul Robeson requesting his help in securing the financial assistance of the San Francisco–based Rosenberg Foundation for the Fellowship Church.[1] Thurman concisely explains his hopes for developing a nonsectarian church that would approach worship through an understanding of ethnic, racial, and religious diversity.

Dear Dr. Robeson:[2]

In a telephone conversation with Max[3] a few minutes ago he said how involved you were during this particular period and suggested that I plan to see you sometime later on. Meanwhile, I want to give you some idea of the significance of the venture with the Fellowship Church of San Francisco as it seems to me.

(1) I am concerned as to whether there is enough vitality in the institutional expression of religion to deal creatively with the facts of racial conflict. I have no doubt as to its efficacy in the life of the individual but there is concern in my own mind about its vitality in lateral situations.

(2) Is it possible to create an island of religious and racial community in a sea
of religious and racial tension and animosity?

(3) Is it possible for a Negro and a white man sharing full joint responsibility
for the leadership of an institution of this kind to minister to the needs of
the people on the basis of their respective gifts rather than their racial affiliations, and to do this over a time interval of sufficient duration to validate
the idea?

(4) What may we learn definitively about the opposition to a venture of this
sort as that opposition may develop from the Negro church, or from the
white church, or from secular interests in the community who will see in
this interracial activity a challenge to the social pattern upon which the
security of their interests rests?

A word about the structure of the plan. Dr. Alfred G. Fisk, Chairman of the
Department of Psychology and Philosophy of the San Francisco College and I
will be co-ministers of the Fellowship Church of San Francisco. Services have
been held each Sunday since December 12th in a small building that was once
occupied by the Japanese. The building is owned by the Presbyterian Church
and has been released for the purpose of beginning this venture. The place of
worship accommodates only one hundred people. Obviously, it is necessary
for us to find more commodious quarters. It is important that the missionary
mentality shall not be permitted to short circuit the development, and the challenge of the idea be smoke screened by pity and compassion. If people can feel
sorry for this struggling effort then they may escape the necessity of facing the
challenge.

The church will function particularly in these areas: (1) creative worship experiences developed along a non-sectarian pattern; (2) special work with children, (representing as many races as possible), along lines of developing their
appreciation of religion as a part of life of other people and their culture as an
important increment of democracy. Some facilities in crafts and music, and
art that will deepen a sense of being at home in the midst of other peoples; (3)
special lectures of an inter-cultural, interracial, inter-religious nature, and (4)
a center of clearance and inspiration for persons who want guidance in matters
having to do with the enrichening of human relations.

You can see that this is a big order which may be impossible of attainment.
If we are necessarily free from economic anxiety and can have an adequate
place in which to function the test of the principle can be explored with some
measure of rational objectivity. A note from you to the Rosenberg Foundation
addressed to Mrs. Louise Bransten,[4] whom you know very well, expressing your
interest in the venture and your hope that they will give it financial backing will
help very much in this regard. I hope that I can have an opportunity to talk with

you before I leave for the coast during the last of June. Mrs. Thurman and I re-
member very warmly, even now, our meeting you in our home several years ago.
Sincerely yours,
Howard Thurman
Dean of the Chapel

Dr. Paul Robeson
Shubert Theatre
48 West 44th Street
New York, New York

TLc.

NOTES

1. This was a form letter of sorts that Thurman sent to prospective donors at this time,
with the identical queries and commentaries. For other examples, see To Henry M. Cra-
nem, 11 April 1944; To Elizabeth Matthews, 6 May 1944.

2. In 1944 Paul Robeson (1898–1976) was at the height of his career as a singer and actor,
appearing from October 1943 to July 1944 in the title role of an acclaimed production of
Othello on Broadway. After World War II, as the Cold War intensified, Robeson, a crusading activist for a number of African American and left-wing causes, was increasingly
circumscribed in his ability to earn a living in the entertainment field in the United States.

3. Max Yergan was Robeson's colleague on the Council on African Affairs. For Yergan's
early life, see *PHWT*, 1:69. After leaving the YMCA and South Africa in 1936, Yergan returned to the United States and settled in New York City. From 1937 to 1940 he taught at
City College of New York, as one of its first black faculty members, where he was one of the
first to teach African and African American history at a mainstream college. With Robeson
and others in 1937 he helped found the Council on African Affairs. Throughout these years
he was close to the Communist Party, until in 1948 he had a dramatic break with his former
politics and colleagues. Until his death in 1975 he was a prominent anti-Communist, supporting the U.S. State Department's African initiatives in the Congo and the white regimes
in South Africa and Rhodesia.

4. According to Robeson's biographer Martin Duberman, Bransten and Robeson were
occasional lovers. See Martin Duberman, *Paul Robeson* (New York: Ballantine Books,
1989), 244.

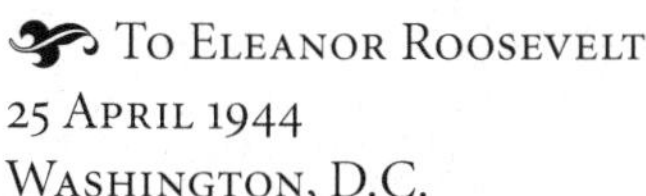 To Eleanor Roosevelt
25 April 1944
Washington, D.C.

Thurman makes a request for a meeting with Eleanor Roosevelt[1] *to get her support for Fellowship Church. She would grant Thurman's request for a meeting,
and he would later recall, "When I saw her she was most gracious and gave to me
the kind of encouragement that is so expressive of her amazing gift of intimacy."*[2]

In early June the First Lady was the featured speaker at a testimonial dinner held in Thurman's honor at the Universalist National Memorial Church in Washington, D.C., in which she encouraged Thurman to work with young people because "it is so much harder to combat discrimination and prejudice among older people because they have become set in their emotional habits."[3] Thurman always proudly claimed that Mrs. Roosevelt was the first person to become a national member of the Fellowship Church. In a memorial for her husband at the church in April 1945, Thurman called her "the president's conscience."[4]

My dear Mrs. Roosevelt:

I am writing to request the privilege of a thirty minutes conference with you at your convenience relative to the launching of an interracial, inter-denominational church in San Francisco to which I have been called as co-minister along with Dr. Alfred Fisk of the Department of Philosophy at the San Francisco College. In a conference with Mrs. Levy[5] in New York, she suggested that by all means I ought to talk with you about this important venture.

I can arrange to see you any afternoon between now and May 6th, except Sunday. Any consideration you give this request will be greatly appreciated. Sincerely yours,

[*signed*] Howard Thurman

Howard Thurman

Dean of the Chapel

Mrs. Eleanor Roosevelt

The White House

Washington, D.C.

TLS. ERP-FDR

NOTES

1. Anna Eleanor Roosevelt (1884–1962), First Lady of the United States from 1933 to 1945, was known for her support of civil rights and human rights efforts. In 1939 she personally integrated the seating at the Southern Conference for Human Welfare in Birmingham, Alabama, when she sat between white and black delegates. That year she also arranged for the African American concert vocalist Marian Anderson to sing at the Lincoln Memorial on Easter Sunday. In 1946 she was elected as head of the United Nations Human Rights Commission that drafted the Universal Declaration of Human Rights.

2. HT, *Footprints*, 32.

3. "Dr. Thurman Gets Farewell Dinner," *Baltimore Afro-American*, 10 June 1944.

4. Hjalmar Petersen, "A Brief Historical Sketch and Visit with President Roosevelt," April 1945. This typescript, in the Thurman Papers, recounts Petersen's visit to the church for the memorial service for Franklin Delano Roosevelt and his impressions of how Thurman spoke "eloquently" on Roosevelt's life. Petersen (1890–1968) was the Farmer-Labor Party governor of Minnesota (1936–37).

Testimonial dinner for Howard Thurman, Universalist National Memorial Church, Washington, D.C., 30 May 1944 (from left: Eleanor Roosevelt, Howard Thurman, Coleman Jennings). From the Howard Thurman Collection, Howard Gotlieb Archival Research Center, Boston University.

5. The philanthropist Adele Rosenwald Levy (1892–1960) of New York was a friend of Eleanor Roosevelt and the daughter of the magnate and philanthropist Julius Rosenwald. She corresponded with Thurman in 1944 concerning financial contributions to the Fellowship Church (To Mrs. David Levy, 2 May 1944).

❧ FROM ALFRED G. FISK
16 MAY 1944
SAN FRANCISCO, CALIF.

Fisk writes to Thurman about his difficulties in finding a suitable place of worship for the new church and his continuing problems with the Sakai Group. He also discusses his increasingly contentious relations with assistant minister Albert Cleage. Fisk's dissatisfaction with Cleage's performance of his pastoral and ministerial duties had been growing for months.[1] A forum Cleage organized in the church on 7 May on race relations and labor in Bay Area shipyards brought this tension to a head. The forum, on the blatantly discriminatory practices by Jim Crow AFL "auxiliary locals," was dominated by CIO unions close to the Communist Party.[2] Fisk later wrote that the forum had been "so overloaded" with communists that Cleage "gave our church the reputation of being a communist organization, and it was investigated by the FBI."[3] Fisk clearly found Cleage blunt and tactless, and as Fisk discusses in this letter, there was pressure exerted on him to fire Cleage. While this did not happen, rumors were circulating among San Francisco's black activists that Cleage had indeed been dismissed, rumors that Cleage himself helped suppress.[4] Cleage's stormy tenure at the Fellowship Church ended in late June, and he left San Francisco a few days before Thurman arrived.

Dr. and Mrs. Howard Thurman
Howard University,
Washington, D.C.

Dear Howard and Sue:

I have not been very successful in my endeavors since last writing you. The nearest and most beautiful synagogue will not be available to us. It contains one of the most beautiful worship rooms I have ever seen. I sent a friend over Sunday morning to verify the fact that it was not being used for Sunday School, but when I had a talk with the Rabbi about it the next day, he said that it would not be available because the Sunday School used it at that hour.

The other synagogue I had in mind, actually uses its temple room on Sunday morning for Sunday School. There are certain other buildings which have been suggested to me—the auditorium of the Jewish Community Center, a Seventh Day Adventist Church, etc. They do not appeal to me as ideal, and if we were to consider them, I think we can wait till you get here to decide.

Complaints about Mr. Cleage have greatly increased. He has irritated and alienated many individuals. He is said to stand for Negro "nationalism"—which I really doubt, but he certainly has a defeatist outlook, and his sermons are felt by many to be completely unreligious and very defeatist.[5] Complaints have even reached Presbytery offices. Dr. Smith[6] suggested that I ask him to resign—which I did not want to do. But after mounting complaints, particularly in relation to forums which he is putting on (where his dogmatism and discourtesy irritated many) I had a talk with Mr. Cleage in which I told him that since he is here for a temporary period anyway, and since I felt the best interests of the church would be served if he left at the time Miss Myles[7] comes, I would be glad to have him terminate his work at that time.

Mr. Cleage agreed as though it were a matter of no particular consequence. But then he stirred the Sakai group up. I realized that it would be interpreted that one co-pastor had attempted to get rid of the other, so after the Sakai group came to me about the matter, we agreed to leave arrangements as they are through June.

The Sakai group are increasingly difficult to work with. They have criticized me severely for arranging with you for the employment of Miss Myles and they want to run the vacation program. They do not want to make it a church program at all. I have had in mind the usual Vacation Church School program—an assembly period with a worship service, stories—Bible and secular, Bible memory work, and then an hour and a half of crafts. With excursions in the afternoon—to the beach, to parks, to museums, etc. The enclosed folder soliciting volunteers will give you an idea of my notions.

I wish that you would advise me as to procedure. With Mr. Cleage here during the time when program plans will be made (and for the first week of the school), and with the Sakai group (with no Negro representation) outvoting me at every step in the planning (if I submit the planning to vote at each point) I am in a difficult position. I have conducted Vacation Church Schools in the past and feel I know something about it; I have consulted with the Council of Churches Vacation Church School promotion office (an excellent group). But to consult with Council of Churches officials, or with Presbytery officials simply infuriates the Sakai group. They want us to be independent and do whatever we (i.e. they) decide. I would appreciate your suggestion as to procedure I should follow; also your idea as to what our summer program should be.

My own feeling is that the program of the church should build up the church. The Sakais however, got an appropriation from the church treasury for $25 for craft materials and some afternoon craft work is now being conducted—some at the church, some at Sakai House—where no mention of its connection with our church is made. If I raise any question concerning this I am asked: Are you interested in helping people, or in building an institution?

My own feeling of the importance of worship and religious education makes me want to include that in our program (contrary to the Sakais notion). What do you think?

It is a shame to worry you with these problems when you must be very busy winding up your affairs in Washington.

I am working on the house problem and hope to have something to report to you soon. I do want an estimate of your moving costs.

This is all for now—too much perhaps! Most cordial greetings to you.
Sincerely yours,
[*signed*] Alfred
Alfred G. Fisk

                                                                TLS.

Notes

1. See Fisk's litany of complaints about Cleage in Alfred G. Fisk to American Missionary Association, 18 October 1944, a letter written apparently to undermine Cleage's chances of obtaining another ministerial position.

2. For the struggle to end segregation in the San Francisco shipyards, see Albert S. Broussard, *Black San Francisco: The Struggle for Racial Equality in the West, 1900–1954* (Lawrence:

University of Kansas Press, 1993), 159–165; Joseph James, "Race Relations on the Pacific Coast: San Francisco," *Journal of Educational Sociology* 19, no. 3 (November 1945): 166–178.

3. Fisk to American Missionary Association, 18 October 1944.

4. See From Angelo Herndon, 12 May 1944, a letter containing a never-issued press release from his newspaper, the *People's Advocate,* "San Francisco Presbytery Dismisses Negro Minister in Surprise Move: Albert B. Cleage Dropped as Co-Pastor of New Inter-Racial Church After Militant Stand Against Auxiliary Unions for Negroes." Herndon writes Thurman that he had held up circulation of the press release because "Rev. Cleage advised against publication of the story because he felt that it might impede your work here in the church." In his response to Herndon, Thurman notes that his wife had told him of Herndon's interest in the Fellowship Church and his occasional attendance at Sunday services. He is grateful to Herndon for not circulating the story because "the general opinion is that venture[s] of this sort simply cannot work. Any publicity revealing friction simply jeopardizes the possibility of the fulfillment of the idea." Thurman praises Cleage for his role in persuading Herndon not to run the story, To Angelo Herndon, 18 May 1944.

5. Fisk's statement about Cleage as a supporter of "Negro 'nationalism'" raises the question of how nationalist Cleage's politics were in 1944. There is no doubt that he was already an outspoken and radical defender of black rights, suspicious of liberal attempts at racial amelioration, sympathetic to violent black responses to racism (as in the Detroit riots of 1943) and well-disposed to the racial politics of the Communist Party; for this see Albert B. Cleage to Fred Brownlee, 18 January 1944, American Missionary Association Collection, Amistad Center, Tulane University, New Orleans. However, there is no doubt that in his public and private statements at the time, he was supportive of the ideas of interracialism, as he understood them. As he told Angelo Herndon at the time of the 7 May forum at the church, "as long as I am connected with Fellowship Church it will be a live and vital force in the community concerning itself with all problems effecting the rights of the Negro people," From Angelo Herndon, 12 May 1944 [Enclosure]. See also Albert B. Cleage, "Fellowship Church: Adventures in Interracial Understanding," October 1944, printed in the current volume. Many years later, when Cleage had moved far beyond the interracialism of the Fellowship Church, he would tell his biographer that Fisk and the church had been "well-meaning" but an "interracial church is a monstrosity and an impossibility," Ward, *Prophet of the Black Nation,* 54–55.

6. W. Clyde Smith.

7. Jacqueline Myles (later Jacqueline Myles Smith, b. 1920) was the young woman Thurman hired as codirector of the first summer camp program at Fellowship Church in July–August 1944. She was a longtime friend of the Thurman family. She had graduated from Bennett College in North Carolina and had completed a year of graduate study in social work at Howard University. See To Alfred Fisk, 12 May 1944; HT, *Footprints,* 34. She later worked for the San Francisco Public Welfare Commission and the Bay Area Urban League.

☙ To Alfred G. Fisk

19 MAY 1944

[*Washington, D.C.*]

Thurman encourages Fisk in the search for a larger sanctuary for the church, relates the progress of his fund-raising efforts, and discusses new developments

*that may complicate their attempt to launch the church as an interdenomina-
tional effort. Thurman also tries to defuse the growing tensions between Fisk and
Cleage without taking sides, and he stresses the need to keep Cleage at the church
to avoid the perception that the interracial organization of the Fellowship Church
was a facade. He makes some suggestions about the summer program, and he
urges that the church experiment boldly with forms and practices, reflecting the
unique nature of their venture.*

Dear Alfred:

I was very glad to get your letter. I am sorry that to date it has not been possible to find an adequate place for worship. We must not be discouraged in our
quest but continue to seek.

I had a long conference with John Thomas of the Baptist Board. He was
quite surprised to learn that the venture is not completely a Presbyterian one.
He had been told by some Presbyterian representative who is a friend of his
that the Fellowship Church was their venture. He looked on with envy, he said,
but wished the Presbytery every success in so important an undertaking. He informed me that he would be happy to present the whole matter to his Board for
the purpose of getting support if he can be assured that it is the official decision
of the church to be inter-denominational. This means that the matter must be
held in abeyance until I arrive in San Francisco and we have a chance to discuss
the entire thing informally together. Meanwhile, he is asking a group of men in
New York representing more than one denomination, I believe, to meet me for
luncheon Tuesday, June 13th when I am again in New York. At this luncheon
the philosophy of the whole plan and what I see as its possibility will be discussed. In my discussions thus far, I have been frank, open and above board in
my approach. I feel profoundly that a large share of the responsibility for racial
conflict must be made at the door of the church because it has systematically
upheld a pattern of segregation, even as it has preached a gospel of brotherhood. Again and again the question of the possibility of inter-marriage is raised
by individuals with whom I have talked. I have said to all and sundry that if
young people of different races associated together as friends and perhaps fall
in love; if they do, I shall take the same attitude towards them as I would take
towards any other couple who fall in love. We shall talk more about this when I
see you. I shall advise you about the results of the June 13th luncheon meeting.

On Monday, May 30th, an interracial committee in the city here is having
a testimonial dinner meeting in honor of me and Sue and this venture. They
expect about 200 people. Mrs. Roosevelt is giving one of the main addresses and
I shall give a talk on the implications of the thing which we are undertaking.[1] I
am trying to give the widest possible spread to the knowledge concerning the

venture because it will help a climate in which this sort of thing can take place effectively in other parts of the country. It may be that the idea which you have projected is [of] far more significance for the future of democracy than many of the people who are associated with you can perhaps realize. One of our jobs will be to school them in the height and depth and breadth of so creative a task.

I am uneasy in my spirit because of the crisis that has arisen relative to the Cleages and the church, and so forth. I am happy to know that he is remaining until the end of June. To have released him would have been a terribly costly thing because of the presuppositions are against the possibility of any two ministers working together on a church without tension and if one is a Negro and the other is white the final assumption is that the thing simply cannot work. Whatever may have been the justification, and I trust your judgment here, it would have been a bad mistake in strategy. It is good to know that this was the way you felt also.

Now, with reference to the program. I would suggest that you select a committee responsible to the church for carrying out the summer program. I would put on that committee some of my most level-headed people, being sure to have the Sakais represented. It would not be a bad idea to have one of the Brittons on it also. You can reason with a small committee with power to act. Mr. Cleage would not be a member of the committee, but certainly should be in on the discussion if he wishes. My own idea is that we should have a children's program that includes all of the character building aspects of the daily Vacation Bible School but that the emphasis should be more along the lines of giving the children an interpretation of the spiritual significance of life, other people's and their gifts including crafts and music. As I see it, we are trying to do two things. First, develop the religious experiences of these children and broaden their horizon at the same time, so that the carry over to their community relationships will be effective and definitive. We shall need to experiment profoundly in these particulars. I have talked with Miss Myles[2] about it and shall do so several times before she leaves. I am very sorry that the Sakais may offer psychological resistance to her presence, but I am not disturbed particularly.

I agree with you that the program of the church should build up the church, but we must keep in mind constantly that the kind of church that we are building has never been built in the United States before. We must not hamper the creative form that the spirit of God may inspire, by clinging to the patterns with which we are ordinarily familiar. Of course, we shall make many errors, but we shall not be mistaken in the soundness of the thing we are undertaking.

With reference to moving expenses, Sue and I are trying to arrange for our two daughters to join us after we have become settled out there. We are trying to persuade my sister to take a vacation in San Francisco and bring them with her. Our railroad fare, that is for the four of us, will amount to approximately $365.00. We expect to ship our radio and perhaps 150 pounds of household things, the barest minimum and maybe the same amount of books. I have no idea what this would cost, but will see after it the first time I get a moment to breathe. I am working day and night for the past two weeks, and I have averaged about five hours sleep. I hope that I will not pay too heavy a price for this before commencement. I am enclosing a copy of a poem I wrote on Jesus,[3] I thought you would like to have it.

Sincerely,

[Howard Thurman]

Dr. Alfred G. Fisk
316 San Benito Way
San Francisco, California

TLc.

NOTES

1. The testimonial dinner was held at the Universalist National Memorial Church, which was, as Thurman later wrote, one of the few places in Washington, D.C., "in which a 'mixed group' could meet in those years" (HT, *Footprints,* 32). Eleanor Roosevelt, Thurman, and Mordecai Wyatt Johnson spoke at the dinner. A photograph in the *Baltimore Afro-American* shows Mrs. Roosevelt shaking Thurman's hand, the pair flanked by Thurman's friend Coleman Jennings, the sponsor of the dinner, and Mordecai Wyatt Johnson ("First Lady at Farewell for Dr. Thurman," *Baltimore Afro-American,* 10 June 1944).

2. Jacqueline Myles.

3. Probably "The Great Incarnate Words," *motive* 4, no. 4 (January 1944): 24–26. The poem was reprinted later that year in Thurman's first book-length publication, *The Greatest of These.*

FROM ALFRED G. FISK

27 MAY 1944
SAN FRANCISCO, CALIF.

In this correspondence Fisk is more measured in his comments on developments in the church than in his previous letter. He discusses both the Sunday school program and plans for the summer program, and he queries Thurman about how he wants to handle publicity surrounding his arrival in San Francisco.

Dr. Howard Thurman
Howard University
Washington, D.C.

Dear Howard:

I am sorry to know that you are working so hard. Maybe you should stop off for a few days rest before coming out to San Francisco. Things are going very well here, and I hope that you are not unduly worried about them.

We had a very harmonious meeting last night of all those interested in our Vacation Project. Mr. Cleage was present and the Sakais and several others. In some ways I got to understand the Sakais better than previously. They are opposed to Sunday Schools and Religious Education because they have experienced so much bad religious education, but they have not come through to an understanding of the best in modern religious education, and they confessed that they would not know what to tell children or what to teach them in regard to religion.

This, I believe, is a very challenging situation for you and me to meet. Unfortunately Mr. Cleage has been in the same position as the Sakai group (openly making derogatory remarks about the Sunday School) and our Sunday School has dwindled to five pupils. But as we talked last night, I think that they realized that that kind of negative attitude was unconstructive. At any rate they will not oppose the rest of us in including a worship service in our Vacation School—though they frankly admit they wouldn't include it if they were running the school.

As a matter of fact, only one of the Sakai House group will give us regular help in the summer school, the rest being tied up with regular jobs. Also Hope Foote,[1] who was formerly at Sakai House, will help. These two will give us regular time with the craft work.

A young lady who has had a year at the San Anselmo Theological Seminary (training in religious education) will be one of our all-summer volunteers.[2] I have word from a similar young lady in Chicago who is considering the same. A couple of my college students are coming for shorter periods.

It was suggested that we build our program around the cultural contributions of groups in San Francisco. We might build up to a {public} program and exhibit each two weeks. The first two weeks might be spent on the Chinese; then the Japanese (who in the not too distant future will return to our very section of the city where they hold property); then others. No definite decision, however, as to program has been made, as we feel that Miss Myles[3] should be consulted.

I am very happy to say that I am making arrangements with the American Women's Voluntary Services[4] to serve a hot lunch to the children. This will be a great drawing card, and will relieve us of a great deal of trouble. Also will bring our project in touch with other community forces.

It was suggested by the group last night that we begin our school at 10:00 a.m. instead of 9 as children do not get up so early during vacation. Also it was suggested that we do not begin immediately after public schools close but allow a week or two of vacation to elapse before we start our school. I think that the first suggestion is a good one, and it will give the staff time to prepare materials for the day. I am not so sure about the suggestion of a two week vacation intermission. We may lose the children in such an interim. The local public school will allow us to pass out handbills announcing our summer project to the children in school classes, and if we begin the Monday after school closes there is no great "forgetting."

On the other hand, if Miss Myles does not get here till the 16th, it would give her more time to prepare for the program. Perhaps an eight weeks school, July 10 to Sept. 1, will be enough to "kill us off" anyhow. My own school, however, is out June 16, and if we began on June 26th I would give full time to the Summer School the first two weeks. It is important that we decide dates immediately, so I would appreciate hearing from you and /or Miss Myles regarding this. The argument for postponing the opening was that children like to have a few days of free vacation, and until they get tired of being "free" don't want to come to a Vacation school. (Most of the church schools that are run for two weeks, however, come the first two weeks of vacation.)

Another suggestion of the Sakai group, about which they felt rather strongly, is that we should not call our project a "Vacation Church School"—both <u>church</u> and <u>school</u> being unattractive words. They suggest the term "Summer Camp-at-home."

Now I would like to ask you about a personal question. If we let the matter of a more adequate place for worship go until you come out, should I plan quite a publicity splurge at the time of your arrival? Or do you wish to begin quietly with the group we have and then make a wider publicity appeal later. There is certainly psychological value in publicity at the time of your arrival—even though the middle of July is not the best time of year. I think that I can have the use of the mailing list accumulated by the Johnson survey (those attending the meetings and helping or sponsoring it) and of course there is newspaper publicity—for a price.

Another question: What arrangement did you make with Miss Myles regarding salary? We will expect to take care of her board and room during the project. Whatever arrangement you make will be unquestioned by us. But as we will need some money for craft material and board expenses for volunteers, I was asked if there would be anything left from the $500 grant. I think that we will have no great difficulty in raising whatever we need.

{I won't burden you with a further page this time!}
{Very cordial good wishes to you all from us all,}
[*signed*] Alfred G. Fisk

                                                                TLS.

Notes

1. Hope Foote was a member of the San Francisco branch of CORE established by Bayard Rustin during World War II. She worked on investigating and protesting restrictive housing covenants and segregated bowling alleys and restaurants. See D'Emilio, *Lost Prophet,* 55.

2. Heather Whitton was a white graduate student in religious education at the San Francisco Theological Seminary in San Anselmo, California. She codirected the summer

program with Jacqueline Myles in 1944 and then ran the program herself in 1945 and 1946. See HT, *Footprints,* 34. In 1946 Whitton described the main workshop as open for children ages nine to fourteen. (There was a separate program for younger children.) They would come to the church on Saturday mornings and could return to finish their weekly projects on Monday and Wednesday afternoons. On Sundays the participants would take excursions to different parts of the city. Whitton described their excursions as attracting considerable attention: "people always gape at us—all our little total of different hues—on the streetcars" (Bailey, "One World in Embryo").

    3. Jacqueline Myles.

    4. The American Women's Voluntary Services was founded by Alice Throckmorton McLean (1886–1968) in 1940 to support war preparedness and, after Pearl Harbor, the war effort. The organization was noteworthy for its efforts to open its membership and services on an egalitarian and interracial basis.

🎏 To Albert Cleage, Jr.

2 June 1944
[*Washington, D.C.*]

Thurman writes a friendly and supportive letter in which he says he looks forward to getting the young minister's perspective on recent church events in a face-to-face meeting, but Cleage left San Francisco before Thurman's arrival.

Dear Mr. Cleage:

    I was very happy to get the two mimeographed sheets announcing the various growing activities about which we are all vitally concerned.

    Your friend, Horace White,[1] has told me many fine things about you and Mrs. Cleage.[2] I am anxious to know both of you. Mrs. Thurman enjoyed her visit with you also, even though it was very short as to time.

    When we arrive in San Francisco, I hope you and Mrs. Cleage will give us the privilege of having a long thorough discussion with you about your experiences and about the opportunity there as you see it. In a venture of this kind, we need all of the wisdom and help that are available because there are so few precedents if any, by which our feet may be guided. This is a tremendous advantage and a terrific responsibility. This is beginning to be a letter, so I will close hoping to see you next month.

Sincerely,

Howard Thurman

Dr. Albert B. Cleage, Jr.
1500 Post Street
San Francisco 9, California

                                                TLc.

Notes

1. Horace A. White (1909–58), a native of Rome, Georgia, was a graduate of Drew Seminary, Western Reserve University, and the University of Michigan. He was minister of Plymouth Congregational Church in Detroit after 1936 and also had a significant political career, serving on the Wayne County Board of Supervisors and, after the 1943 riots, on the Detroit Housing Commission.

2. Doris Juanita Graham Cleage (1923–82).

From Alfred G. Fisk

8 June 1944
San Francisco, Calif.

Fisk continues to offer his opinions on the current state of affairs at the Fellowship Church. Given the sharp divisions within the church and the controversies that have swirled around him, Fisk is unsure of what role to take after Thurman arrives.

Dear Howard and Sue:

Your letters are a great help—and make me look forward to the closer association with you in the work ahead. I have not received the programs of your dinner yet (they will come by slower mail doubtless) but there are several things for me to write you about. I did note Eleanor Roosevelt's comment about attending your dinner, and had a telephone call from Time's correspondent here. (I am holding my breath about the Time write-up till I see it, for the correspondent had talked with Mr. Cleage. Frankly I spend most of my week trying to mend the damage Mr. Cleage does us. He has alienated the Ministerial Alliance of Negro ministers;[1] the Negro A.W.V.S.—who might otherwise have helped us in our Vacation school—and countless people of importance in the community.)

This leads me to ask you your frank opinion regarding my vacation dates. I would like to have you here in San Francisco at the earliest possible moment, of course; but my feeling is that perhaps you ought to take a few days after the rush of getting away from Washington and rest at some quiet place in Michigan or Yellowstone Park (I name these at random—you would know better where). Then if you feel that it would be quite important to you to have me here the first month after you arrive, I would postpone my vacation.

I want to be of maximum benefit to you and the project. Everything personal is secondary. I have no fear of community response after your arrival. You will so easily make the proper contacts with the Ministerial Alliance and other groups and individuals. But Mrs. Lucas (who has been very disturbed by the Sakai group and Mr. Cleage's behavior) thinks I should be here "to set you right" regarding many things. But I wouldn't want it said that I did this—or as some might interpret it, that I passed on my "prejudices" to you! Sometimes I feel that after a brief period of consultation together you might like really to be alone for a while to draw your own conclusions and to feel out the community for yourself. At other times I feel that Mrs. Lucas is right and that I should be here after you come for as long a period as possible.

The biggest problem I have had this last month (and I have tried not to worry you with it) is the matter of [a] house for you, and I think it is being solved most satisfactorily. After combing the district and following many a "wild goose chase," it seems that the house next door that belongs to the Presbytery will be available. We are getting another place for Mrs. Turner and her roomers (none other than the Sakai House—which is splitting up!) We will plan to have the whole place redecorated (it surely needs it) and to store some of the antique furniture in the basement. But as I should think that you would like to determine on the decorating, we will probably leave that till you come.

As I write the telephone has rung and the Time correspondent tells me that the story of Fellowship Church and your coming to it will be postponed until your arrival here.[2] I had hoped that the banquet to you in Washington would be the occasion for the story. I am sorry that it is not going in now, as it would help materially in getting us financial aid—toward redecorating the house, and perhaps the purchase of the Lutheran Church.

Your letter[3] and the fact that the city Health Department will not give us clearance for serving meals to children during our summer project (because the building is rat-infested) have spurred me regarding the matter of building. I would very much prefer to have you here to help determine what should be done regarding building. Since you want me to go ahead, I feel that the Lutheran building is the best available place. I took our Presbytery representative of the Presbyterian War Emergency Fund to see the Lutheran building today. Again I am under the spell of its very beautiful place of worship. This man is very enthusiastic about our getting it and thinks the War Emergency Fund will make the first payment. He is much more of a businessman than I, and I am putting the matter in his hands.

Meanwhile we have had a Congregational Meeting and elected a "Church Board Pro Tem" which is to serve until you and I feel we should make other arrangements. It is an excellent, representative board—five Negroes and five white. Mr. Britton is a member, and only one of the Sakais.

With the receipt of your letter, we have decided definitely to wait until July 10 to begin our Summer Program. Your arrangement with Miss Myles regarding salary is very satisfactory.

I must hurry off to a meeting, so will let this suffice for now. I can imagine with what pull of the heart strings you {both} are quitting Washington. Our hearts go out to you. O Pioneers!
Sincerely,
[*signed*] Alfred
Alfred G. Fisk

                                                                          TLS.

Notes

   1. The Ministerial Alliance was a local organization of black ministers.
   2. The article did not appear until 1948: "Fellowship Church," *Time* 52 (26 July 1948): 40–42, printed in the current volume.
   3. To Alfred G. Fisk, 19 May 1944, printed in the current volume.

❧ Annual Report, The Dean of the Chapel
30 June 1944

Thurman's final report as dean of the chapel at Howard University provides an overview of his approach to shaping a religious community and is a model of the approach he would employ in building the Fellowship Church. His commitment to rooting religious experience in an ecumenical, interreligious, and interracial setting is a thread running through all of his varied activities as dean of chapel.

ANNUAL REPORT
1943–1944

Dean of the Chapel
Howard University
Washington, D.C.
June 30, 1944

I. Religious Services
The following is the calendar of the formal all-university religious services held in the Andrew Rankin Memorial Chapel for the academic year 1943–44.

Fall Quarter
Chapel Speakers (Exhibit A)

   October 3   FRESHMAN CHAPEL
        10   Mordecai W. Johnson, D.D.
              President, Howard University

17   Howard Thurman, D.D.
      Dean of Chapel, Howard University

24   C. Victor Brown, D.D.[1]
      Vassar College
      Poughkeepsie, New York

31   William Stuart Nelson, LL.D.
      Dean, School of Religion
      Howard University

November 7   M. C. Otto, Ph.D.[2]
              University of Wisconsin
              Madison, Wisconsin

14   Herbert King, S.T.M.
      National YMCA
      New York, New York

21   SERVICE OF SONG
      The University Choir

28   THANKSGIVING RECESS

December 5   LIVING MADONNAS

12   Mordecai W. Johnson, D.D.
      President, Howard University

19   CANDLELIGHT SERVICE

26   CHRISTMAS RECESS

January 2   CHRISTMAS RECESS

Winter Quarter

January 9   Mordecai W. Johnson, D.D.
             President, Howard University

16   Howard Thurman, D.D.
      Dean of the Chapel
      Howard University

20   DAY OF PRAYER

23   SERVICE OF SONG
      The University Choir

30   Robert M. Williams, D.D.[3]
      Pastor, Asbury Methodist Church
      Washington, D.C.

February 6   William E. Carrington, S.T.M.
              School of Religion
              Howard University

        13   Ralph Harlow, Ph.D.
              Smith College
              Northampton, Massachusetts

        20   Rabbi David Wice[4]
              Temple B'nai Jeshurun
              Newark, New Jersey

        27   Howard Thurman, D.D.
              Dean of the Chapel
              Howard University

March 5   Melvin H. Watson, S.T.M.
              Dillard University
              New Orleans, Louisiana

        12   Mordecai W. Johnson, D.D.
              President, Howard University

        19   RECESS—End of Winter Quarter

Spring Quarter

April 2   PALM SUNDAY
              Service of Song

April 9   EASTER RECESS

        16   Howard Thurman, D.D.
              Dean of the Chapel
              Howard University

        23   Mordecai W. Johnson, D.D.
              President, Howard University

        30   Harold B. Ingalls, M.A.
              Northfield Seminary
              East Northfield, Mass.

May 7   Douglas Steere, Ph.D.
              Haverford College
              Haverford, Pennsylvania

        14   Mrs. Harper Sibley[5]
              Rochester, New York

21   Howard Thurman
      Dean of the Chapel
      Howard University

28   BACCALAUREATE

The total number of services held during the year was twenty-nine. The list of visiting preachers breaks down as follows:
Men—fourteen
Women—one
Rabbis—one
Institutions of Learning—seven
Denominations—five
Negroes—seven
White—eight
Pastors—three
Music services—three
University faculty—four
Services preached by the Dean of the Chapel—six
Services preached by the President—five
Visiting preachers—thirteen

The institutions of learning represented were Howard University; University of Wisconsin, Dillard University, Vassar College, Smith College, Haverford College, Union Theological Seminary and Northfield Seminary.

The all-university services during the past academic year reached a new high in all-over attendance. The undergraduate student attendance was very much better than in previous years. Uniformly, the standard of preaching has been of a high order. An interesting cross section of the community continues to worship with us each Sunday.

Services began at ten fifty-five with an organ prelude and were usually over by twelve fifteen. Too much credit cannot be given to Dean Lawson,[6] Mr. Kerr and the choir for the services which they have rendered during the academic year.

The choral response in the first half of the service was written by the Dean of the Chapel and set to music by William Dawson of Tuskegee.[7] (Exhibit B.)

Dean Lawson and I have been experimenting with various worship patterns until at last we have been able to evolve a thoroughly integrated and creative non-sectarian pattern of worship. There is a bit of the liturgical and the non-liturgical element present. Very enthusiastic indeed have been the comments of all kinds of people as to the qualitative significance of the service.

A. Memorial Service

By vote of the Trustees of Howard University, the Howard University Women's Club was given permission to install a memorial window in the Chapel in honor of Dean Lucy Diggs Slowe[8] on Sunday afternoon, November 7, 1943. A special service of dedication was held in the Chapel (see Exhibit C). The service was very impressive and was attended largely by Dean Slowe's friends in the city of Washington. It was most unfortunate that there was practically no representation of the young women of the university. We have yet to become sensitive to the necessity for keeping alive the memory of the persons who have given their lives in leadership and service. I do hope that at some future date it will be possible to dedicate a window to Dean Adams[9] of the School of Medicine.

B. Twilight Hours

As in previous years the Chapel has conducted a series dealing with worship through art. The twilight hours have now become a tradition. This year there were six such services.

1. <u>October 24th.</u> This was a service built around the English Bible giving the story of Creation, the Ten Commandments, certain selections from the Prophets, several devotional Psalms, sections from The Sermon on the Mount and the Crucifixion. Mr. Kerr[10] provided a background of organ music and the Dean of the Chapel read the selections continuously for fifty-five minutes. This twilight hour was publicized as one having to do specifically with the reading of the Bible. It was expected that a maximum of 150 people would come out to such a service. To our joy, more than 300 came. The greatest tribute to the service was found in the fact that for a full two minutes after the benediction the audience remained seated in meditation and reverie.

2. <u>November 14th.</u> The Chapel presented the Lincoln Players directed by Joseph Hill in a one act play dealing with the life of Brother John[11] one of the Disciples of St. Francis of Assisi. This service served two purposes: (1) It deepened our sense of appreciation for the life of one of the great exponents of Christianity who sprang from the loins of the Roman Catholic Church and it provided a new level of cooperation between Lincoln University and Howard University.

3. <u>December 5th.</u> Living Madonnas were not produced this year. It was impossible to secure the services of Mrs. Sewell because of the unusual demands that were placed upon her incident to the resignation of the Head of the Department of Home Economics. I did not feel that pressure should be placed upon her to do this service which involved more than one hundred hours of extra work without being able to give some compensation.

Since this was impossible, that type of service had to be cancelled. Instead, we were able to rent from the Metropolitan Museum of New York, a group of colored slides of paintings of various Madonnas. Professor Herring[12] of the Art Department made a special trip to New York to secure these for me. In addition, I gave an interpretation of the Madonna concept showing that its moods were deeper than the liturgy and the ceremony of the Catholic church. This discussion was of very great importance for the entire university community because of the concept of Madonnas is associated primarily with Catholic worship; to see the wider implications of the facts at the disposal of all Christians, the richness of the concept. There was great disappointment because we did not have the Living Madonnas, but those who came to the substitute service were lifted up and strengthened.

4. January 16th. As a part of the Annual Religious Emphasis series, which will be discussed in another part of the report, we presented Mr. And Mrs. Modak, originally of India and now associated with the East and West Association of New York City in an evening of Hindu Worship and ceremonials. They were dressed in Indian clothing and reproduced on the platform scenes from Hindu domestic life and temple worship. It was an exciting and informing evening.[13]

5. February 27th. Dr. Clarence Ward,[14] Director of the Memorial Art Gallery of Oberlin College gave an illustrated lecture on French Cathedrals. For this twilight hour we were able to get the cooperation of the Department of Architecture and the Department of Art. More than one hundred graduates of Oberlin College came out to the lecture which fact gave the university an additional tie into the life of the community. Dr. Ward remained over for a part of Monday to visit the Department of Architecture and our Gallery. He is sending to the university a group of reprints and slides which will be of very great value in carrying on the work of the Art Department.

6. May 7th. Mrs. Meta Warrick Fuller,[15] the celebrated sculptor of Framingham, Massachusetts gave an illustrated lecture covering still another phase of the arts. She discussed various objects that she had created and interpreted them in the light of man's struggle for a sense of meaning and security in life. She remained our guest for four days during which time she appeared before several of the public schools and other groups. Once again the Chapel was able to go beyond the campus in providing inspiration and instruction to groups in the community.

It was impossible to present a special event this year because Dr. Archibald MacLeish[16] who was scheduled for a lecture-recital on his poetry, but had to cancel it in order to fulfill an assignment given to him by the President of the United States.

C. Religious Emphasis Week

The Annual Religious Emphasis Week was conducted January 16–20. It was decided that the series this year should deal with "Man's Quest for Religious Values" (see Exhibit D). The series opened Sunday morning at eight o'clock with an Inspirational Service in Crandall Hall under the joint sponsorship of the Women's Dormitory Council of the three dormitories. About one hundred women were present after which there was a breakfast. At eleven o'clock, the Dean of the Chapel preached on "What Must I Believe." In the evening the Twilight Hour was "Religious Values found in Hinduism." Monday evening, the Drama Workshop of the School of Religion with its supporting cast presented a Catholic play, "Shadow and Substance."[17] This play portrayed the quest of religious values from the point of view of Roman Catholicism. Tuesday morning in the regular Freshman Assembly, Reverend Modak gave a talk on Christianity as it is being developed in India in the midst of old world religions like Hinduism and Mohamedanism. At eight o'clock the same evening Dr. Felix Valyi,[18] the Hungarian Orientalist gave a lecture on the "Buddhist's Quest for Religious Values." This was a dinner meeting to which one hundred people, students and faculty were invited. It was an occasion long to be remembered to those who attended. On Thursday, the Day of Prayer, Dr. Walter Judd, Junior Congressman from the State of Minnesota gave an address on "Christianity's Answer to World Chaos."[19] The attendance for this service was the largest that we have had for the Day of Prayer since I have been here. In addition to these activities, discussion groups were held in Cook Hall, led by Dean Thurman, in Truth Hall by me, Crandall Hall, by Dean Nelson,[20] Frazier Hall by Director Snowden[21] and in Miner Hall by Reverend Charles King. The unusual feature about these discussions was the fact that the students had prepared questions on religion, answers to which they sought in the discussions. The average attendance was seventy-five for each discussion. It is safe to say that there was more campus-wide participation in this religious emphasis series than has been true during the past ten years. Our experience therefore, shows that it is possible to have a religious emphasis series that captures the mind and energy of the university community.

II. Personal Counselling and Group Activities

The ministry of the Dean of the Chapel becomes each year more useful in helping individual students and faculty and their friends in trying to find the answer to their personal problems and questions. To the most casual observer it is clear that the collapse of so many stable things in our world has heightened a deeper sense of social and personal stability in the lives of countless people. It is at this point that the Chapel has rendered a service unique in the university and of profoundest significance.

A voluminous correspondence with men in the armed forces is a part of another aspect of this ministry. It is a pleasant privilege to send some word of counsel and inspiration to young men who are scattered all over the earth and who are living in constant jeopardy of their lives and ideals that to them are either unreal or hypocritical.

The demands for counselling grow out of the Sunday services [and] move in a continuous stream. All of this means that the Dean of the Chapel finds it impossible to get any one single day of complete rest. He has no Sabbath, no day of rest!

A. *Group Activities*

It has not been possible (as I indicated last year that it would not be) for the Dean of the Chapel to maintain intimate contact with the Fellowship Council. The reason for this has been largely physical. The trustees have not been able to recondition the downstairs of the Chapel as a place for activities for student groups. Lacking this provision, the only other place has been either the home of the Dean of the Chapel or the Fellowship Room of the School of Religion when it was not otherwise engaged. Fortunately, however, we were able to secure the support of Mr. Edmund Gordon,[22] a middler in the School of Religion. He has worked intimately with the Fellowship Council in all of their meetings and activities. As compensation, we have given him an average of thirty dollars a quarter taken from the funds realized from the sale of calendars. The activities sponsored by the Council this year were: Get-Acquainted Week; small social activities of groups of students; religious conferences; the annual faculty-student dinner; college exchanges; World Student Service Fund Campaign.

1. <u>Get-Acquainted Week</u>. Get-Acquainted Week came during the first full week of school. The purpose of this activity is to acquaint our students with the geography of the university. Campus tours to the various colleges were conducted. Three faculty members, including the Dean of the Chapel at "at homes" one evening during the week to which more than two hundred students came. The first weekly meeting of the Fellowship Council was held during this period at which time the ideals and aims of the organization were set forth (see Exhibit E).

2. <u>Conferences</u>. The Fellowship Council sponsored the 7th Annual Howard-Lincoln Conference. It convened this year on the campus of Lincoln University. The theme had to do with post-war educational and specific opportunities for Negro young men and women. Because of travel limitations, we were able to send only twenty students to the conference.

   Mr. Gordon attended a special conference at Johns Hopkins university on Work with Trainees on the campus.

Two student representatives attended the conference at Pendle Hill, Pennsylvania having to do with vocational opportunities involved in Postwar Reconstruction. We are sending one delegate to the Middle Atlantic Student Movement Conference to be held at Kanestake, Pennsylvania.

3. <u>Faculty-Student Dinner</u>. The Fifth Annual Faculty-Student Dinner was held January 29th. The attendance was 200 with a smaller Liberal Arts Faculty representation, but a larger representation from the administrative staff of the university. The program consisted of community singing, a skit, and a talk by the Secretary of the University. A sense of community spirit was more evident at this dinner than at any previous dinners. When the students were in line to get their coats from the cloakroom, there was quite a bit of spontaneous group singing. This is a manifestation of definite health (Exhibit F).

4. <u>Student Exchanges</u>. Travel limitations have made curtailment in this program mandatory. Nevertheless, we were able to send eight girls to Smith College for a long week-end and thereby establishing a new relationship with another college. Our schedule calls for student exchanges during the next academic year with Smith and Mount Holyoke Colleges. Five girls and one faculty representative visited Keuka College in upstate New York for a long week-end. This marks the greatest distance that we have ventured in our plan of student exchange. The social significance of this activity cannot be over-estimated.

5. <u>World Student Service Fund</u>.[23] The campaign of the World Student Service Fund is under the general chairmanship of the Dean of the Chapel. The Omega Psi Phi Fraternity gave the bulk of its proceeds from its annual dance to this venture, this was in addition to the regular Tag Day. Our total was $166.25. This was a decided increase over last year. The educational value of this activity is only exceeded by its social significance (Exhibits G & H).

III. Other Group Activities

The regular monthly meetings of the Ushers were held at the residence of the Dean of the Chapel. These meetings provided an opportunity for checking on the services and much informal discussion about many things of a personal nature. The Annual Banquet was held at the residence of the Dean of the Chapel.

Beginning in late October and each Tuesday evening throughout the academic year, a discussion group on religion was held for the men of Cook Hall. It is to be noted that this group was developed as a result of a special request from the men. The average attendance was thirty throughout the year. The final meeting was held in the residence of the Dean of the Chapel as a supper. The discussions had to do with the Life of Jesus and the Great Doctrines of the

Church and the relationship between men and women. The nucleus of men who will return next year hope to carry on this activity with the Acting Dean of the Chapel.

We followed the custom again of inviting small groups of faculty and students in for dinner or supper with university guest preachers. As always, these occasions provided very much of inspiration and information.

IV. The Wider Ministry

The services of the Dean of the Chapel have been in demand for the performance of many marriage ceremonies. These ceremonies have been conducted for the most part in the Little Chapel of the School of Religion. Many of the persons were not even connected with the university. During Holy Week, this year, the Dean of the Chapel was the guest preacher of the Church Federation of Greater Chicago. The services were held in the Chicago Temple downtown in the loop. The Christian Century had a special word of commendation about this.[24]

The Dean of the Chapel's office made special Christmas cards for all of the trainees on the campus. In addition more than 500 booklets having to do with private devotion were given to them and to some of the other students (Exhibit I).

The Fellowship Council conducted a census of the trainees and made their religious affiliations available to all of the local ministers involved. This was done through the Office of Dr. Robert W. Williams,[25] President of the Minister's Alliance.

The Student Council collected more than 300 pounds of clothing and so forth and contributed twenty-two dollars in cash for the sharecroppers in Chicho County,[26] Arkansas.

The Dean of the Chapel has been given a leave of absence from the university to undertake a very important venture in San Francisco. The expressions of goodwill and affection from all sections, particularly in the student community have been a most stimulating tribute to the ministry of the Chapel. It is to be devoutly wished that the same fine cooperation that the administration has given to the Dean of the Chapel and its ministry will be given to Professor Melvin H. Watson who will be acting in that capacity in the interim.

Conclusion

On the whole the year has been a very good one. The most urgent physical need is for space to carry on the student activities. Recommendations have already been made relative to the preparation of the ground floor of the Chapel for that purpose. So urgent is this that it is impossible to carry on any organized activities another year unless there is some place provided. Students must be able to build their contacts around a place with reference to which they are able to develop a sense of ownership and responsibility. We have arrived now to the point that it is impossible to expect any further development of a committee like the Fellowship Council, or even its maintenance, unless there are rooms set aside for such activities. If the downstairs of the Chapel is completed all of the activities of the Dean, including office space, etc., will be housed under one roof. This will make for efficiency and effectiveness. It continues to be difficult to administer to the needs of the university under the psychological handicap of being completely identified with the School of Religion. This does not mean at all that there has not been the completest cooperation on the part of the Dean of the School of Religion.

It is to be desired that the recommendation concerning repairing the interior of the Chapel will be carried over into the new fiscal year. The Department of Buildings and Grounds was unable to do it during this year because of circumstances over which they had no control.

PUBLICATIONS

"A Hymn to Youth," a hymn written for the 100th Anniversary of the National Young Men's Christian Associations, June, 1944.[27]

"O God I Need Thee," a poem written in 1938, and set to music in March, 1944 by William Dawson of Tuskegee, Alabama.[28]

"The Great Incarnate Words," motive, Vol. IV., No. 4, (January, 1944), Nashville, Tennessee.[29]

"The Cosmic Guarantee in the Judeo Christian Tradition," Institute of Religion, Howard University, June, 1944.[30]

A review of William Douglass Chamberlain's The Manner of Prayer, Journal of Religious Thought, Howard University, Spring, 1944.[31]

A review of Douglas Steere's On Beginning from Within, Journal of Religion, University of Chicago, Spring, 1944.[32]

TD.

Published courtesy of the Moorland-Spingarn Research Center, Howard University Archives.

NOTES

1. The Reverend C. Victor Brown, a graduate of Chicago Theological Seminary, was a chaplain in the U.S. Navy and at Vassar and Union Colleges. After serving as minister for several years in the mid-1950s at First Congregational Church in New Milford, Connecticut, in 1957 he became dean at Elmira College. He was named pastor at the Presbyterian Church in Barrington, Illinois, in 1964 and served until his retirement in 1981.

2. Max Carl Otto (1876–1968), born in Germany, came to the United States at age five. He lived in Wisconsin for most of his life, and he taught philosophy at the University of Wisconsin at Madison for many years. Otto was a prominent antitheistic Unitarian. His works include *Things and Ideals: Essays in Functional Philosophy* (New York: H. Holt, 1924) and *The Human Enterprise: An Attempt to Relate Philosophy to Daily Life* (New York: Crofts, 1940).

3. Robert Moten Williams (1896–1956) was a native of Galveston, Texas, and a graduate of Wiley College and Gammon Theological Seminary. He became minister of Asbury Methodist Church in Washington in 1931 and stayed in the position for the remainder of his life.

4. David H. Wice (1908–2002) was rabbi of Temple B'nai Jeshurun in Newark from 1941 to 1947 and of Congregation Rodeph Shalom in Philadelphia from 1947 to 1981. From 1973 to 1980 he was president of the World Union for Progressive Judaism.

5. Georgianna Farr Sibley (1887–1980), generally known as Mrs. Harper Sibley, married Harper Sibley of Rochester, New York, in 1909. She was extremely active in Episcopal affairs and became a leader in the international ecumenist movement, traveling extensively in Asia in the 1930s. She also held leadership positions in a number of national organizations, including the presidency of the USO during World War II, and was named American Mother of the Year in 1945. In addition she was a national leader in liberal attitudes toward race relations. In 1939, as president of the National Council of Church Women, she called for a full acceptance of interracial marriages, and she played a significant role in fostering interracial relations after the Rochester riots of 1964. When she first met Thurman is unclear, though their paths likely crossed during his years at Rochester Theological Seminary. He invited her to speak at Howard several times.

6. Warner Lawson.

7. This is presumably Dawson's setting of "O God I Need Thee."

8. Lucy Diggs Slowe (1885–1937) was a native of Virginia. She graduated from Baltimore public schools and then attended Howard University (1908) and Columbia University (1915). While at Howard, she became one of the nine founders of the Alpha Kappa Alpha sorority. In 1917 she won the women's singles title in the inaugural national tournament of the all-black American Tennis Association. After teaching in Baltimore and Washington, D.C., public schools, she became the first dean of women at Howard, remaining in the position until shortly before her death.

9. Numa Pompilius Garfield Adams (1885–1940) became the first African American dean of the Howard University Medical School in 1929 and remained in that position until his death.

10. Thomas M. Kerr Jr. was a 1935 graduate of the Eastman School of Music.

11. Holy Brother John Della Penna of Ancona.

12. James V. Herring.

13. Ramkrishna Shahu Modak (1891–1968) was a minister and later an archbishop in the Indian Orthodox Catholic Church. He spent many years in the United States as an author and lecturer. His American wife Manorama Ramkrishna Modak (b. 1895, née Margaret Groves) was a prolific writer on Indian topics.

14. Clarence Ward (1884–1973) was an expert on medieval cathedrals, an architect, a pastor and a longtime professor of art history at Oberlin College (1917–47), and founder of the college's art museum.

15. Meta Vaux Warrick Fuller (1877–1968) was born and raised in Philadelphia and became one of the most prominent African American sculptors of the first half of the twentieth century.

16. Archibald MacLeish (1892–1982), one of the most prominent American poets of his time, was assistant director of the Office of War Information during World War II.

17. Probably *Shadow and Substance* (1937) by Paul Vincent Carroll (1900–1968), a play dealing with the Catholic Church in contemporary Ireland.

18. Felix Valyi was the author of many books on the Middle East and South Asia, among them *Spiritual and Political Revolution in Islam* (London: Kegan Paul, Trench, and Trübner, 1925).

19. Walter Henry Judd (1898–1994) had been a missionary in China and a surgeon before he was first elected to the House of Representatives from Minnesota in 1942, where he served for ten terms. He was an influential voice on foreign affairs.

20. William Stuart Nelson.

21. Frank M. Snowden Jr. (1911–2007) taught at Howard for half a century and was the premier African American classicist of his generation. He was the author of, among other works, *Blacks in Antiquity: Ethiopians in the Greco-Roman Experience* (Cambridge, Mass.: Harvard University Press, 1970) and *Before Color Prejudice: The Ancient View of Blacks* (Cambridge, Mass.: Harvard University Press, 1983).

22. Edmund W. Gordon (b. 1921), a graduate of Howard School of Religion, had a distinguished career as an educator at Yale and Columbia Universities.

23. The World Student Service Fund was an organization created in 1937 to aid students in nations that were in distressed circumstances.

24. "Thurman Fosters Unity in Chicago," *Christian Century* 61, no. 16 (19 April 1944): 508. The article claimed that "there may be many other men—and it is to be hoped there are—who can match the distinguished dean of Howard University in combining a devout spirit with a disciplined mind, but most of those who followed him through a week of services will doubt if there are any who would exceed him." The article also estimated that about one-third of those in attendance were African Americans, evidently a high percentage for services in downtown Chicago.

25. Robert M. Williams.

26. Probably Chicot County.

27. Printed in the current volume.

28. The song was first published as "God, I Need Thee" (New York: Galaxy, 1949). For Thurman's original poem, versions of which date back to 1935, see *PHWT*, 2:240–42.

29. This was printed in *motive* 4, no. 4 (January 1944): 24–26. Thurman's poem was part of a special issue of *motive*—which was published by the Board of Education of the Methodist Church—on the theme of "Race: The Color of Christian Democracy." The editor's note for Thurman included the following statement: "Perhaps more than any other speaker he has been in demand as a speaker at conferences."

30. For the history of this article, see "Judgment and Hope in the Christian Message," printed in the current volume.

31. HT, "Review of William Douglass Chamberlain, *The Manner of Prayer*," *Journal of Religious Thought* 2 (Spring–Summer 1944): 179. In this short review Thurman says, in part, that "the volume is not a plea for piety or devotion in isolation from the squalid scaffolding of human life but it indeed is intimately a part of the development of holiness, of brotherhood, of Christian living," and he approvingly quotes Chamberlain to the effect that the realization of the Kingdom of God "may require a rearrangement of our whole manner of life."

32. The review appeared in the October 1944 issue of the *Journal of Religion*; it is printed in the current volume.

❧ San Francisco journal
July–August 1944
San Francisco, Calif.

*On his arrival in San Francisco, Thurman briefly kept a diary, recording
his first impressions of the Fellowship Church; these initial impressions
were written with more candor than any of his subsequent accounts. From
the beginning, while he appreciated Alfred Fisk's contribution to the church, he
found him "highly nervous and tense" and with a "stifled" imagination. Thurman also appreciated the commitment of the church's members, but he felt that
no one had "any clear cut notion as to what we are trying to do," especially in the
practical requirements for creating an interracial church. In addition, from the
outset he found Presbyterian officials patronizing and limited in their understanding of the new venture. Thurman writes candid appreciations of the members of the church and provides an important statement of his understanding
of the role of pacifism in the church. In some ways he was dismayed by what he
found in San Francisco, but he ended his initial fortnight in the city with a sense
of purpose and with clear ideas about the role that he must play in the
new church.*

San Francisco
Sunday—July 15 1944[1]

This is our first Sunday here. I wonder what it would be like finally. The week
has been very full.

We arrived Wednesday morning, tired and quite weary. We were met at the
ferry by Alfred Fisk, co pastor and George Britton, young friend of ours. George
was glad to be with us and stole away from his business in order to give us a
personal welcome. He invited me there to go to the "Merry Widow"[2] on Friday
night.

Alfred Fisk is a highly nervous and tense individual with a deep sense of
mission and a profound sincerity. His goal tends to stifle his imagination. As
an example—we were met about 11 15 o'clock. We were carried immediately
to see the proposed Baptist Church and then the present structure and then to
a conference with Dr Clyde Smith. ~~and~~ This conference lasted for nearly two
hours—after which we went to lunch for another long conference with Rev.
Simpson. In time, when we reached our room at the Fisks' home, it was about 6
o clock. This kind of experience after traveling across the continent. Everything
that we did could have waited until the next day. This is the kind of zeal that
Alfred Fisk has.

I am impressed with several things in this situation.

1. I have found very little evidence that there was any clear cut notion as to what we are trying to do in this corner. It's interesting that again and again the reference is made to the fact that the church must be located in the heart of the Negro district. Is the idea that in some way this church is to bring into its walls the Negroes off the streets of the neighborhood? If that is the notion, then the church is merely repeating the pattern of Protestants and will be fought to the end by the Negro churches in the area.

In San Francisco as all over the world where there are racial barriers, mixing of the races takes place in the secular world particularly in matters of vice and certain form of recreation.[3]

4. The general impression was that this is a church of Pacifist[s]. Now, I am a Pacifist but I am also a human being. I am not an absolutist because I do not have the wisdom to be that. The Pacifism of the church should express itself in the quality of life that emanates from the place rather than from pronouncements of one kind or another.[4]

The Presbyterian Church.

The P.C. is on the ground floor of the venture. From the beginning they have been supporting it outright with their funds. The church is so completely dominated by secularism that it expects to behave just as business does with reference to investments. I suppose this is to be expected. At any rate, the Pres church expects to exercise the same control as it does over other Pres. Churches that are not self supporting. The fact that this is a unique venture and that the Pres. Church is fortunate to be able to participate in it and should therefore regard itself as in some sense humbled by the magnitude of the opportunity and responsibility must yet be released in their minds as a great and powerful lesson. But this is a part of our own job in the church.

First Board Meeting.

At the first Bd Meeting I presided. A very interesting passage from Dr. Otto's book_______was read. It had to do with the oak tree.[5] There was silent prayer. (I may throw in here that there are some who feel that there is too much lip prayer in season and out.) We discussed the minutes and old business etc. Then the agenda I had prepared was worked out. I asked each [and] every member of the Board to say to me why he was interested in a church such as this one.

Summary

Mr. Russell—interested because he wanted to worship in a place that was not bound by racial or class barriers. He came the first time and liked what he found so much that he has been coming ever since. If we keep to our original purpose it ought to be a very tremendous gesture for a new world.

Mrs. _____ Had shopped around quite a bit in all kinds of churches but was unable to find anything that spoke directly to her condition. When she became a part of the Fellowship Church it was a very satisfying experience and continues to be. She hopes that such a church can actually develop.

Miss Anderson[6]—(Norwegian) Came to this country as an immigrant. Suffered so much as a foreigner and stranger as a little child that she prepared early to work for the eradication of such attitudes from the life of her new home. Early developed an interest in Negroes. As a teacher in the public schools she initiated the observance of Negro History Week. She heard about Carter Woodson's organization[7] and became a member etc. Now Negro History Week is rather widely observed in the city through her influence. She regards the F. Church as an important step in advance of Xt and is glad to have a share in so important a venture. In the church she finds a modicum of religion and spiritual fulfillment unique in her own experience.

Mrs. Lucas[8]—(Wh. Ep.) interest in the urgency of fellowship and understanding between the races dates back to World War # 1. She saw so many raw experiences of prejudices and intolerance, particularly ~~in her~~ with reference to Negroes while she was with the Red Cross in France that she became alive to the tragic results for the first time. When she returned to the U.S. continued her interest. She is a member of Grace Cathedral but chooses to work and belong here because it offers a full opportunity to achieve in some active sense true X-tian fellowship.

Mr. Britton[9] not very much of a Churchman but became interested in this fine venture through me. Became my unofficial observer and is gradually seeing the point. Would like to see the church develop into a real center of intercultural and interracial activities—rather secular minded but with real possibilities.

Mrs. Jones—wandered around trying to find a church that was generally friendly and at the same time with a form of worship inspiring and instructive. At last she has come to this church and finds it is what she seeks.

Mr. Thwaites? was very enthusiastic at first because he was sure that this was the real thing. He's been out of church for 20 years. At present his enthusiasm is dead. We are to talk.

Mr. Harter likes the fellowship here and the thing that was being established. Became interested because he felt that this kind of church was the <u>right</u> kind <u>and is normal</u>.

I felt that these people were trying to answer objectively [for] the first time why they were here. It was a very salutary experience.

There was no tension present as had been the impression I had received about previous meetings—what the future holds I do not know. The spirit was good!

Next, I introduced a comment about our negotiation for the new church building. I was unable to give them all the facts because things are still in process. There was general comment of approval.

Next. The Membership Commitment. Sue and I had prepared the statement with Alfred's ok. It was presented as a statement from the co-pastors. On the whole there was approval of the idea. A few suggestions were made but after consideration were finally eliminated. It was formally approved with the authorization to print it and seek to get members on that basis. At first there was suggestion that we work on it further but when it was clear that it could be changed when we wanted it then the approval was enthusiastic.

It was announced that I would present during August on the Commitment so that the group would get a good orientation to the ideas. The first of September we plan to have a formal service of dedication for all those who have accepted the pledge.

On the whole we enjoyed the meeting.

The first sermon I preached was July 23. I used Phil 1:9–11 as text developing the idea of the tragic sense of life—the phrase taken from a page I read from Lewis Mumford's[10] *Herman Melville*.[11] The tragic sense of life arises from the fact that man's higher dreams are always undergirded by the possibility of the lack of attainment. What we see we are not quite able to achieve. The margin of error never disappears.

Next I developed the necessity for love's making for a conscience of the mind as well as a conscience of the heart. The conscience of the heart finds wisdom for the conscience of the mind. Apostles of sensitiveness must do that—be wisdom for the planners and designers and operators of society.

The general reception was whole and supportive. July 30 Alfred preached on The Prayer and The Will of God. Raised the problem of God's providence and purpose as over against man's desires but did very little with it.

In the afternoon we had the Fisks for dinner and then a small surprise reception. Mrs. Roberts played the piano. It was a very homey and delightful occasion. They were [*presented*?] with [*illegible*] for the entire family. Good clean fun and fellowship—a foretaste of what I hope will be increasingly true here.

Oh yes, July 23 I performed ceremony with Buell Gallagher for Roy Nichols.[12] Beautiful.

AD.

Notes

1. Although Thurman dates the beginning of the journal "15 July," it was most likely 16 July, which was a Sunday.

2. *The Merry Widow* (*Die lustige Witwe*) was a popular Viennese operetta composed in 1905 by Franz Lehár (1870–1948).

3. The incorrect numbering is in the original.

4. This is an important statement of Thurman's conception of the political dimension of the church and its relation to pacifism. From the beginning, Thurman wanted to keep

the church free from any official ideology (even one, such as pacifism, in which he deeply believed). But Thurman also identified his personal pacifism as not being "absolutist" and as nonprescriptive. He saw himself as living a pacifist life without telling others how to behave. (This allowed him to find a way to support those who chose to serve in the military without supporting the war effort as such.)

5. M. C. Otto opened *The Human Enterprise: An Attempt to Relate Philosophy to Daily Life* (New York: F. S. Crofts, 1940), 1–2, with a "meditation" in which the author climbed a hill with oak trees on a warm September afternoon and experienced a reverie of a "feeling with which we are all acquainted when everything seems strangely of one piece. It was a plain man's perception of a unity within and through the rolling expanse spread out from hill to horizon and beyond. For in experience of the plain man it is heightened awareness, not forgetfulness, of the world and its abundant life which lifts him out of provinciality into perspective." Otto had preached at Rankin Chapel in November 1943.

6. This was Anna A. Anderson, who by early 1945 was treasurer of the Fellowship Church.

7. Association for the Study of Negro Life and History. See *PHWT*, 2:6.

8. Bertha June Richardson Lucas.

9. George Britton.

10. Lewis Mumford (1895–1990) was a polymathic American author of numerous books on sociology, urban planning and cities, literary criticism, and the history of technology.

11. Lewis Mumford, in his study *Herman Melville*, 361, wrote that Moby-Dick "expresses that tragic sense of life which has always attended the highest triumphs of the race, at the moments of completest mastery and fulfillment. Where that sense is lacking, life shrivels into small prudences and weak pleasures and petty gains, and those great feats of thought and imagination which transform the very character of the universe and relieve human purpose from the scant sufficiency of toiling and eating and sleeping, in a meaningless, reiterative round, shrivel away, too."

12. The occasion was Rev. Roy Nichols's marriage at South Berkeley Community Church, a congregation he copastored with Buell Gallagher ("Berkeley, California," *Chicago Defender,* 5 August 1944).

🐦 FROM EARL FREDERICK ADAMS
7 AUGUST 1944
NEW YORK, N.Y.

Earl Frederick "Bud" Adams, a classmate of Thurman at Rochester Theological Seminary, outlines the careful strategy he is planning to obtain help for the Fellowship Church from the American Baptist Home Mission Society.

Dr. Howard Thurman
The Fellowship Church
Post Street at Octavia
San Francisco 15, California

Dear Howdy:

I have just received your good letter of August 4 and am delighted to hear of the progress being made in the Fellowship Church project in San Francisco.

San Francisco _______ Sunday — July 15
/1544

This is our first Sunday here. I wonder what
it will be like finally. The week has been very
full.

We arrived Wednesday morning, tired and
quite weary. We were met at the Ferry
by Alfred Fisk, copastor and Faye Britten, good
friends of ours. Faye was glad to be with us
and stole away from his business in order to give
us a personal welcome. He invited me & Sue to
go to the "Merry Widow" on Tuesday night.

Alfred Fisk is a highstrung, intense
individual with a deep sense of mission
and a profound sincerity. He is just dead to
stifle his imagination. As an example — we
were met about 11:15 o'clock. We were
carried immediately to see the proposed
church and then the present structure and
then to a conference with Dr. Clyde Smith, and
this conference lasted for nearly two hours —
after which we went to lunch for
another long conference with Rev. Simpson.

First page of Thurman's San Francisco journal. From the Howard Thurman
Collection, Howard Gotlieb Archival Research Center, Boston University.

I was terribly sorry to miss you when you were in New York, but Forest Ashbrook[1] has told me of your conversation with him.

Please rest assured of my very real interest in the Fellowship Church project. I will do anything possible to give it a boost. You understand of course that my own particular job is that of raising money for approved budget projects rather than the determination of what projects shall be included. Any funds appropriated will have to come from the Board of the American Baptist Home Mission Society. I will certainly put in a good word for the project with Dr. Beers[2] and John Thomas. I know that they will be very much interested, but I cannot of course prejudge what their decision may be with respect to a financial appropriation for this year. Their budgets are already pretty well allocated.

I expect to see Dr. Beers and John Thomas the latter part of August at our Northern Baptist Assembly grounds at Green Lake, Wisconsin. I think it would be better strategy for me to see them there face to face rather than try to hurry any approach in this regard. These things usually take a bit of time, and an effort to get an immediate answer usually results in a negative reply.

This letter brings you my heartiest greetings and my every good wish. Will hope to see you some day when my travels bring me to San Francisco. Meanwhile I will certainly do anything I can to be of help. Blessings on you.
As ever,
[*signed*] Bud
EFA:n
                                                                                     TLS.

NOTES

1. M. Forest Ashbrook (1897–1968), a 1924 graduate of Rochester Theological Seminary, was the longtime director of the Ministers and Missionaries Benefit Board of the American Baptist Convention.

2. George Pitt Beers, a graduate of Rochester Theological Seminary, was the executive secretary of the American Baptist Home Mission Society from 1932 to 1953.

 ALBERT B. CLEAGE, JR., "FELLOWSHIP CHURCH: ADVENTURE IN INTERRACIAL UNDERSTANDING"
OCTOBER 1944

This is the earliest known article about the Fellowship Church by one of its ministers and the only contemporary article on the church by Albert Cleage, Jr. By the time this article appeared in NOW[1] *in October 1944, Cleage had been living in Los Angeles for several months and studying film at the University of Southern California. The article offers a strong defense of the Fellowship Church and of the idea of an interracial church. Cleage would repeat this defense the following year,*

*writing to Thurman, "I am sincerely interested in the inter-racial church idea,
and feel that its extension during these critical days is a most significant contribution to the building of a more Christian world."*[2]

*If the article is on its surface complimentary to Alfred Fisk, its latter portions
offer a polite though sharp critique of Fisk's conception of the church. Cleage
demands that the church be open and avowed in its political commitments and
asserts that interracialism is not an end in itself but only a means to changing
the "socio-economic framework" of Negro oppression. In insisting that the church
work with "the friends of human freedom no matter what the banner beneath
which they march," Cleage was probably making a veiled reference to his bitter disagreement with Fisk over whether to invite Communists to speak at the
church. In this article Cleage's political commitments are those of a war-time
left-progressive and not the "Negro nationalist" he was sometimes called at the
time, much less the black nationalist he would become in the 1960s.*

"FELLOWSHIP CHURCH: ADVENTURE IN INTERRACIAL UNDERSTANDING" CRITICAL ANALYSIS OF FIRST SIX MONTHS OF SAN FRANCISCO'S INTERRACIAL FELLOWSHIP CHURCH— CO-PASTORED BY ONE WHITE AND ONE NEGRO MINISTER BY REV. ALBERT B. CLEAGE, JR.

San Francisco's interracial Fellowship Church is now approaching the close of
its first year of existence. Having weathered the storm of birth, infancy and
growth, it is now firmly established with two of America's outstanding preachers, an expanding community program and a growing congregation.

From the beginning Fellowship Church has tried to de-emphasize its interracial character, preferring to be known as a community church, incidentally interracial. In spite of this theoretical distinction, however, Fellowship
Church is nationally known as "San Francisco's interracial Church." The church
achieved national attention with the coming of Dr. Howard Thurman and his
wife Sue Bailey Thurman.

[The] Time magazine reporter sent to investigate the "project to which
Dr. Thurman was coming" explained his interest by stating, "Anything which
can drag Dr. Thurman across the country for a year must be important."[3]

Mrs. Franklin D. Roosevelt and Dr. Mordecai Johnson spoke at the testimonial meeting of church notables who gathered to wish Dr. and Mrs. Thurman
God-speed on their great Christian adventure.[4] Dr. Thurman spoke of Fellowship Church as "the most significant single step that institutional Christianity is
taking in the direction of a really new order for America."[5]

I arrived at Fellowship Church a few weeks after its organization.[6] All I knew of the project I had gleaned from the letters of Dr. Alfred Fisk, its organizer. He wrote: "We are organizing in San Francisco an interracial church to be known as 'Fellowship Church.'

"We do not want a church run by whites 'for' Negroes or one in which Negroes will merely be welcome to participate. We want to establish a church which will be of and by and for both groups. We are planning to have as co-pastors, with absolute equality of status, a Negro and a white person. The boards of the church, the choir, the Sunday School and its staff will be made up of both groups, and perhaps some Filipinos and others."[7]

I found the Church located in a very old residential neighborhood formerly occupied by the Japanese, but now termed the "Negro District." Negroes made up about 50 percent of the population. Twenty thousand Negroes were crowded into make-shift rooming houses and apartment houses which had accommodated about eight thousand Japanese.

The city was suffering from a bad case of riot-jitters. Everywhere people seemed to be waiting for the signal which was to begin the fire-works. Both Negroes and whites were frightened and angry in the presence of something they couldn't understand. Dr. Fisk, Fellowship Church's white co-pastor, wrote to Dr. Thurman, "Unless you come to San Francisco we perish!"[8]

San Francisco didn't like the "new Negro." They didn't like his independence, his war-boom pay-checks, and most of all they didn't like his increasing numbers. Very trivial things loomed large in their discussion of the "problem" ... "the way Negroes crowded onto the streetcars to get home from work" ... "the way Negro women entered the most exclusive shops in their work clothes."

Miss Venita Lewis of the Children's Bureau visited the city to oil the troubled waters. She lectured Negro leaders on the "disciplines of interracial living."

Policemen were being taught "sociology" by a rabid Negro and Jew hating priest who lectured at great length on the innate racial differences "about which we can do nothing."

In the midst of this bedlam I found Fellowship Church with 30 members and in [sic] infinity of good intentions. Dr. Fisk stated the problem well, "The challenge to a church in such a community is obvious. If ever the spirit of Christ were needed, it is here. To interpret that spirit as an effective force in the community is our task as we see it."

For the first six months of its existence Fellowship Church functioned without any formal membership. All persons who believed in the fellowship idea were welcome.

The nucleus of the congregation consisted of a group from the American Friend's Service Center which had been meeting for some months as the core group[9] (The Committee On Racial Equality). They were mature and sincere young people of both races interested in the ideal of human brotherhood. They earnestly worked to build this ideal into a militant, active church program. They brought a freshness of spirit and a sincerity of conviction which made of Fellowship something more than just another church, and which alone carried the experiment through the first trying months. Without them there could have been no Fellowship Church.[10]

To this vital nucleus other individuals were attracted. The Negro residents of the immediate community did not overfill the small auditorium as Dr. Fisk had apparently expected. As the congregation steadily grew, attendance remained almost evenly divided between Negroes and whites.

Fellowship Church, as any interracial venture, in the midst of the American community, faced the task of deciding just how far it wanted to go in its undertaking. Each individual faced the painful responsibility for his personal decision regarding the implications of his commitment to brotherhood and racial equality.

My months at Fellowship Church were devoted to hammering at one basic weakness. I saw clearly that the effectiveness and future of the church depended upon the building of a common social philosophy. People cannot work together to accomplish any program, however small, unless they agree in their interpretations of the total world in which they live.

A group of people cannot attack the "Negro problem" unless they understand the socio-economic framework out of which it has grown and upon which it depends. Only then can they decide whether or not they are willing to come to grips with the problem.

At the close of its first year Fellowship Church faces the crucial problem of undergirding its complete program with a common social philosophy. Its future development depends absolutely upon this decision. In this dilemma, of course, Fellowship Church is not alone. Liberal Christians everywhere cannot longer avoid their total responsibility to society by making pleasant and ineffective gestures in restricted and isolated areas of living.

To do something about the Negro problem implies also doing something about the Jewish problem, the Indian Problem, the African Problem, the Labor Problem, the Mexican, Chinese, and Japanese Problems.

A Christian church must be even more than a place where Negroes and whites can worship God together, or it will inevitably become less. It must function in every area of life as a united liberal force striking fearlessly out against all forms of oppression, bigotry and inequality. Its friends are the friends of human freedom no matter what the banner beneath which they march, and its foes are the oppressors of mankind, even though they march beneath the banner of Christ.

Now, First Half October 1944, 4.

NOTES

1. *NOW* was a Los Angeles bimonthly founded as the *War Worker* in July 1943 by an interracial couple, Bill and Elizabeth Cummings. Published until 1946, it was dedicated to demonstrating "that we of different races and colors and creeds can work in harmony; we say not only that it can happen, but that it is happening." See Kevin Allen Leonard, *The Battle for Los Angeles: Racial Ideology and World War II* (Albuquerque: University of New Mexico Press, 2006), 186.

2. From Albert Cleage, 24 April 1945.

3. For *Time* magazine's interview with Fisk and Cleage, see From Alfred G. Fisk, 8 June 1944, printed in the current volume.

4. The testimonial dinner was held on 30 May 1944.

5. To Alfred G. Fisk, 25 October 1943, printed in the current volume. Cleage evidently had access to the correspondence between Fisk and Thurman.

6. Cleage arrived in San Francisco at the beginning of February 1944, about a month and a half after the first service of the Fellowship Church on 12 December 1943.

7. This letter is not extant, but Fisk described his vision of the Fellowship Church in language similar to Thurman's from several months earlier. See From Alfred G. Fisk, 15 October 1943, printed in the current volume.

8. This is a paraphrase of Fisk's plea to Thurman in November 1943, "San Francisco, so it seems to me now, is doomed if you do not come!" (From Alfred G. Fisk, 6 November 1943, printed in the current volume).

9. That is, "the CORE group." The Committee of Racial Equality, organized in 1942, was a group within the Fellowship of Reconciliation. It became the Congress of Racial Equality the following year, when it became a separate organization. Bayard Rustin came to San Francisco in the fall of 1943 to organize a race relations workshop. It included Virginia Scardigli, a good friend of Thurman and a founding member of the Fellowship Church. See the biographical essay in the current volume.

10. Cleage's account of the origins of the Fellowship Church, which does not mention the Sakai Group, differs considerably from those of both Fisk and Thurman, who do not emphasize the role of CORE. Fisk does refer to the two main groups in the church as "the CORE group" and the "nucleus who were active starting the choice" (presumably the Sakai Group) (From Alfred G. Fisk, 26 January 1944). There was some overlap between the two groups. See the biographical essay in the current volume. Fisk also mentions the offer of the American Friends Service Committee to run the church summer school. The offer was rejected. See From Alfred G. Fisk, 26 January 1944; From Alfred G. Fisk, 17 February 1944, printed in the current volume.

❧ REVIEW OF DOUGLAS STEERE'S *ON BEGINNING FROM WITHIN*
OCTOBER 1944

Thurman's review of a book by his friend Douglas Steere[1] shows the continuing influence of Quaker spirituality on his religious thinking. Thurman is sympathetic to Steere's efforts to rethink the nature of spirituality and to analyze the "anatomy of the processes by which the saint effects social change."

In the midst of global war, vast armaments, armies numbering millions of men, tremendous external operations on a scale hitherto undreamed of by an age which has witnessed the full flowering of the industrial revolution made possible by the application of the scientific method to the mastery of nature, it is exceedingly important that our attention should be called to the deeper interior needs of modern man. That this need is unchanging and that the Christian religion addresses itself directly to this need is the heart of these essays grouped together under the title, On Beginning from Within.[2]

The thesis of the first four is that God cares for the individual, that there is a divine solicitation made manifest in Jesus Christ, giving to each individual an infinite value, and that each individual stands in immediate candidacy for responding to this divine solicitation. In the degree to which the individual responds to the divine solicitation he is a saint. For the saint is by definition "a man or woman who has become clear as to exactly what he wants of all there is in the world, and whom a love at the heart of things has so satisfied that he gaily reduces his cargo to make for that port."

Deep within every human being there is what Dr. Steere aptly calls the nerve center of inner consent, which is the point of contact for the individual with a wider and all-comprehensive nerve center of consent in the universe. The spiritual life of man consists primarily in maintaining a vital connection between these two centers. The vitality of this connection is the secret of the saint's power over the stubborn and recalcitrant aspects of his own personality as well as over the society and age in which he lives. It is the source of his joy; with his center pulsing in harmony with the divine rhythm, he discovers the secret of endurance with joy so that the "cross becomes a symbol of victory." Thus he is able to look out upon life with quiet eyes. Devotional exercises become the means for boring into the center to release the living spirit of the living God that lifts the whole level of the life of the individual and of society.

The chapter on "A New Set of Devotional Exercises" is very suggestive and helpful despite the fact that they are based in part upon the spiritual exercises of Ignatius of Loyola,[3] whose approach to life in some of its important aspects is hardly congenial to modern minds.

From the point of view of this reviewer, the most crucial issue raised by the essays is the analysis of the method or technique or anatomy of the processes by which the saint effects social change. That the saint has done so in the past, and continues to do so, seems to be the result of the exercise of skills of which he is scarcely aware. The terrible need of the moment is for a discovery of the precise methods, the concrete techniques by which the private good may be given social implementation to the end that the average individual may become a direct factor in the transformation of the age. This is, in the final analysis, the vindication of the thesis which these essays undertake to defend.

The style is simple, direct, warm, and inspiring. One looks forward with hunger to a further word from Dr. Steere as he explores the bearing of his central concern on the massive problems that confront our age.
Howard Thurman
Howard University

The Journal of Religion 24, no. 4 (1944): 284–85. © 1944 by the University of Chicago Press.

Notes

1. Douglas Van Steere (1901–95) taught at Haverford College from 1928 to 1964. His many works on Quaker religion and spirituality include *On Listening to Another* (New York: Harper, 1955) and *Dimensions of Prayer* (New York: Harper and Row, 1963).

2. Douglas Steere, *On Beginning from Within* (New York: Harper, 1943).

3. St. Ignatius Loyola (1491–1556), the founder of the Jesuit order, wrote his *Spiritual Exercises* from 1522 to 1524. They were first published in 1548.

☙ To Friends at Howard University
21 October 1944
San Francisco, Calif.

Howard and Sue Bailey Thurman write a general letter to their friends and acquaintances at Howard University about their activities at the Fellowship Church. They convey a sense of excitement at the cultural, political, and intellectual vitality of San Francisco.

Dear Friends at Howard,

You should have received some word from us before this time. But it has taken the three months we have been out here to establish things so that a letter like this, "covering all," could be written back to you. The blue enclosure will give you the salient facts about the church to date. We wish you might have been here for the inauguration of the Fellowship Church of All Peoples.[1] It was the first and only occasion of its kind ever held in this city. Perhaps that was due to the fact that the stately First Unitarian Church had not witnessed before on its platform, and in its audience, so many inter-relationships between groups. The Right Reverend Edward Parsons,[2] Bishop for many years of the Episcopal Diocese of California, Ira Condit Lee,[3] distinguished among Chinese laymen, Rabbi Elliot M. Burstein,[4] Chairman of the Board of Rabbis for Northern California, and Buell G. Gallagher,[5] former President of Talladega College and now co-pastor of the sister experiment in South Berkeley, played prominent parts in the dedication services. Joseph James,[6] baritone of the West, whose voice and interpretations remind us of Roland Hayes, was soloist. Several college men, including Lt. Edward Swain Hope,[7] were in the city at that very time waiting to sail for the Pacific War Zone. We felt close to Howard for some reason throughout the day. Perhaps it was because you were having your first Sunday Chapel for 1944–45, and then there were the telegrams which many of you were so gracious to send, coming through during the afternoon and evening.

Personal reports will inform you that Howard Thurman has just published, "The Greatest of These,"[8] a collection of prose-poems (read to many of you, and printed first in a series on the calendar of Rankin Chapel) which will be released by the Eucalyptus Press[9] of Oakland, California, in time for a Twilight Hour Reading in San Francisco on Sunday, October 29th. If you would like copies of the book, they may be secured after November 15th in the Office of the Dean of the Chapel, Howard University. A shipment will be sent also to Brentanos.[10]

We are participating considerably in organizations out here because it is necessary for doors to open for the 20,000 Negroes who have become an integral part of the city. H.T. is working with the Conference of Jews and Christians, the San Francisco Council of Churches, the Civil Liberties Union, and the Public Education Society, in addition to addressing numerous groups on a daily schedule. S.B.T. is working on the Board of Directors, as World Fellowship Chairman, of the Central YWCA of San Francisco (there is no colored branch here), on the executive committee of the Parent-Teacher Association of the practice school of the State College, and on the Board of Directors of the International Institute of San Francisco, the latter being particularly interested in the foreign communities in the city and especially now in the imminent return and rehabilitation of American-born Japanese to the state of California. Olive, our 17-year old, is attending San Francisco College, preparatory to entering Vassar, as a sophomore next fall, and Anne, the younger, is at Frederic Burk School.[11] Both of them have found their place of activity in the intercultural Junior Workshop of Fellowship Church.

It is not all work out here, however. When you come to visit us at Christmas or next spring, you will have a gay time in this queen of cities. There is Fisherman's Wharf, the like of which will not be found between San Francisco and Naples; Chinatown, informing and alluring; the numerous exciting restaurants with exotic cuisines which will give you the thrill of "eating around the world"; the Oriental garden in Golden Gate Park; the two famous bridges— "The San Francisco Bay" and "Golden Gate," with ships passing always, going out or coming into port; the finest lectures and concerts are here, and the most distinguished laboratories, conservatories, art galleries, libraries and museums. The San Francisco Museum of Art is exhibiting the paintings of the children who are in the Intercultural Junior Workshop of Fellowship Church at the beginning of the year and throughout the month of January, 1945.

We have been able to entertain many service men in our western home, among them the very special guests, Captain Walter Fisher[12] (formerly of the department of history), Major Shumato (M.D. from the School of Medicine), Lieutenant Brown (formerly in the School of Religion) and Sgt. Andrew Howard,[13] brilliant student leader during his undergraduate years at the University. We were very proud of them and their recent outstanding work as Howard men. Former "Coach" Harry Payne[14] is director of the Oakland USO which has been rated as one of the best on the west coast. "Dean" Thomas Earl Hawkins is out here working on his doctorate in Personnel Administration on the Berkeley campus. In addition, he conducts on Sunday evenings, an interracial discussion and recreation group for college and servicemen and women in the Bay region. Pauli Murray is pursuing a doctorate in Jurisprudence at "Cal"[15] and Jacqueline Myles is completing her work in Social Welfare at the same institution. Thurgood Marshal has spent days of valuable service here recently as an investigator for the N.A.A.C.P. Port Chicago trial.[16]

We would like to thank the 14 student organizations at Howard, who gave us the elegant silver service, and the members of the Faculty Wives Club, whose gift was the handsome dinner cloth, for making it possible for us to entertain so royally the various groups, especially the service men for whom it is often the last meal they will have in a "home" before going out to sea. In time your gift will have served men and women from practically every college and university in the east. There are occasions for the membership as well. Those should include you, but for the miles, for many Washingtonians have become "associate members" of Fellowship Church under provision #4 of the types of participation indicated on the blue folder. Mrs. Eleanor Roosevelt was one of the first of this group to "join" the Fellowship Church of All Peoples as an associate. She has requested copies of all materials, reports and studies made available for associates through the unfolding and developing program of the interracial-intercultural church.

Howard Thurman will see many of you when he returns to Washington for a few days in January. Meanwhile will come the holidays. Write a personal note on your Christmas cards this year. The affairs of your life, the kind of vacation you had, the various things you are doing this year, happenings at home with your children, mean more to us from this distance even than when we were there with you. We shall remember you at birthdays and fortunately we have many written in the Guest Book of beloved 605 Howard Place.

Sincerely yours,

THE HOWARD THURMANS

TLc.

NOTES

1. On Sunday, 8 October 1944. See HT, *Footprints*, 41–43.

2. Edward Lambe Parsons (1868–1960) graduated from the Episcopal Theological Seminary in Cambridge, Mass., in 1894, and thereafter attended Union Theological Seminary. He was a priest in a number of parishes in California before serving as Episcopal bishop of California from 1924 to 1941.

3. Ira Condit Lee was director of the Chinatown YMCA in San Francisco.

4. Elliot Maurice Burstein (1898–1975), a 1923 graduate of the Jewish Theological Seminary, was rabbi of Congregation Beth Israel in San Francisco from 1927 to 1969.

5. Buell Gordon Gallagher (1904–78), pastor of the South Berkeley Congregational Church, was a 1929 graduate of Union Theological Seminary, president of Talladega College (1933–43), assistant commissioner of education (1950–52) in the Truman administration, and president of the City College of New York (1952–69). He was the author of many books, among them *American Caste and the Negro College* (New York: Columbia University Press, 1938) and *Color and Conscience: The Irrepressible Conflict* (New York: Harper, 1946). He discussed the Fellowship Church in *Portrait of a Pilgrim: A Search for the Christian Way in Race Relations* (New York: Friendship Press, 1946), 140.

6. Joseph James was a native of Philadelphia. After singing in local churches, he worked as a professional singer before attending Boston University, where he received a degree in music, and thereafter combined a career as a concert recitalist with performances in all-black musicals and shows such as *Porgy and Bess* and *Green Pastures.* He relocated in 1939 to San Francisco, where he continued his musical career and became active in the black community. He found employment in the local shipyards, where he played an active role in the union campaign against racially discriminatory unions, and in 1944 he was elected president of the San Francisco branch of the NAACP. See Broussard, *Black San Francisco,* 159–65. He and his wife, Alberta Mayo James, a concert pianist, were active in the Fellowship Church, and she became the church's first choral director. James later resumed a career in musical theater, relocated to New York City, and appeared in the original Broadway production of *Lost in the Stars* (1949) and a Broadway revival of *Porgy and Bess* (1953). In 1962 he was elected president of the Committee for the Employment of Negro Performers. He was the author of "Race Relations on the West Coast: Profiles, San Francisco," *Journal of Educational Sociology* (November 1945): 156–78.

7. Edward Swain Hope (1901–91), the son of Morehouse president John Hope, had a B.S. and an M.S. from the Massachusetts Institute of Technology in civil engineering. He was the superintendent of facilities at Howard University (1932–44) and subsequently the first African American lieutenant commander in the U.S. Navy. He taught civil engineering at Howard from 1947 to 1951, when he became professor of civil engineering at American University in Beirut.

8. HT, *Greatest of These.*

9. A private press established at Mills College in 1930.

10. A chain of high-quality bookstores absorbed by Borders in 1995.

11. The Frederick Burke Elementary School was an experimental school associated with San Francisco State College.

12. James Walter Fisher, raised in Baltimore, received two degrees from Howard University (in 1936 and 1937) and taught history at Howard, Delaware State, and Morgan State College, where he also served as college librarian.

13. Andrew Howard was president of the Howard University Student Council (1942–43).

14. Harry Payne, a 1930 graduate of Howard, was a star quarterback on its football team and coached the football and track teams at Howard from 1936 to 1940.

15. Pauli Murray (1910–85) received law degrees from Howard University in 1944 and the University of California, Berkeley in 1945. In 1965, Murray was awarded a doctorate in law (J.S.D.) from Yale University, the first African American to be awarded the degree. She was a founder of the National Organization of Women in 1966, and in 1979 she became the first female African American priest ordained by the Episcopal Church. In 1944 Thurman successfully intervened on Murray's behalf after she launched a sit-in demonstration at

a Washington cafeteria and Mordecai Wyatt Johnson ordered her to desist. See Glenda Elizabeth Gilmore, *Defying Dixie: The Radical Roots of Civil Rights, 1919–1950* (New York: W. W. Norton, 2008), 392. The two remained friends. In a letter written after her return to Washington, D.C., she wrote to Thurman that "the East is depressing, the West is desolate, the North is hypocritical, the South is uncivilized—where does that leave us? (smile) Sometimes I think the planet is getting too uncomfortable for me . . . I promise to be less gloomy in my next letter" (From Pauli Murray, 30 April 1946).

16. On 17 July 1944 there was an enormous explosion at the U.S. Naval Magazine, a munitions storage facility at Port Chicago, California, north of San Francisco. Of the 320 casualties, 202 were African American naval personnel working in the dangerous job of munitions loading, a position that was largely limited to blacks. In August 1944 a number of the survivors of the segregated ordnance battalion that had suffered most of the casualties refused orders to load munitions at a nearby naval facility, claiming that nothing had been done to change the dangerous conditions that led to the Port Chicago explosion and also protesting the Jim Crow system of job assignments. In December 1944 fifty of the protesters were court-martialed and sentenced to long terms at hard labor. Their sentences were commuted in January 1946. The survivors were eventually pardoned by President Clinton in 1994. See Robert L. Allen, *The Port Chicago Mutiny: The Story of the Largest Mass Mutiny Trial in U.S. Naval History* (1989; repr., Berkeley, Calif.: Heyday Books, 2006).

From James Farmer
15 December 1944
New York, N.Y.

James Farmer's reclassification as I-A led to this note asking Thurman to write to Farmer's Washington draft board about restoring his conscientious-objector status.

Dr. Howard Thurman
1500 Post Street
San Francisco 15, Calif.

Dear Dr. Thurman:

This is an urgent note! I'm now having draft trouble!

This morning I received a card from my Draft Board classifying me I-A. This is a re-classification, because previously I have been 4-D. The re-classification came as a complete surprise, and I suspect some pressure has been put on the Board. Of course they know that I am a Conscientious Objector; I told them that before I was classified 4-D, but they arbitrarily gave me the ministerial deferment to avoid, I suppose, dealing with the C.O. matter.[1] I chose to let it remain so in order to continue in the work that I'm doing.

An immediate letter from you to the Draft Board would be most helpful, I'm sure. It is Local Board No. 12, 702 Florida Avenue, N.W., Washington {(1)}, D.C. Mr. Coleman was Chairman at the time I registered, filled in my questionnaire, and was classified 4-D. I suppose he is still chairman. Rev. Robert Moton

Williams of Asbury Methodist Church was at that time a member of the Draft Board (I think he was secretary), and perhaps he still is. {The card was signed by J. D. Pair, a Member of the Board.}

I do hope that you can write the Draft Board right away. I have until December 2{4th} for an appeal. Naturally, I do not relish going to prison, but the Army is out of the question. Like most people, I should want to remain in the work that I'm doing, but CPS[2] is the next alternative.

Cordially yours,

[*signed*] Jim

James Farmer

P.S.: I have finally completed my book, and am now seeking a publisher.[3]

j.
                                                                            TLS.

NOTES

1. In 1941 Farmer's local draft board refused to honor his decision to register as a conscientious objector and insisted that he accept instead a 4-D ministerial deferment, despite his being neither a minister nor a theological student. If he had been registered as a conscientious objector, as he indicates in this letter, he would have accepted placement in a Civilian Public Service camp. See James Farmer, *Lay Bare the Heart: An Autobiography of the Civil Rights Movement* (New York: New American Library, 1985), 78–83.

2. Civilian Public Service, alternative service for men who refused to serve in the military.

3. Farmer's manuscript "Religion and Racism," a revised version of his thesis that was supervised by Thurman, was never published. See Farmer, *Lay Bare the Heart,* 161.

To J. D. PAIR

18 DECEMBER 1944

[*San Francisco, Calif.*]

Thurman writes to Farmer's draft board about his reclassification to I-A status. The draft board later restored Farmer's ministerial deferment.[1]

Mr. J. D. Pair,[2] Secretary
Draft Board No. 12
702 Florida Ave., NW
Washington-1, DC

My dear Mr. Pair:

This is a letter on behalf of James Farmer whose classification has been changed from 4-D to 1-A.

I do not know the basis of this reclassification and it is not my purpose to raise a question at that point. I am sending this letter to confirm the fact that Mr. Farmer is engaged in the same work that occupied his full time when he was given the original classification. He is a graduate of the School of Religion of Howard University and is one of the secretaries of the Fellowship of Reconciliation.

If Mr. Farmer's classification remains 1-A would it be possible for him to be sent to a C.P.S. camp, inasmuch as during the time of his registration he certified the fact that he was a conscientious objector to war as well as a minister.

I hope that some adjustment can be made in this matter so that the individual's conscience can be respected within the limits of the Selective Service Act. I appreciate any consideration that you may give to Mr. Farmer. He was one of the most able students that I have had during my years of teaching at the University.
Sincerely yours,
Howard Thurman
Dean of the Chapel—On leave

TLc.

Notes

1. Thurman wrote to Farmer immediately after writing this letter: "A line to let you know that I have just sent an air mail special delivery letter to your draft board. I hope it will be of some help" (To James Farmer, 18 December 1944).

2. J. D. Pair (1872–?) was a black minister in the Washington, D.C., area who at age seventy became pastor of the First Baptist Church in North Brentwood, Maryland, where he served until 1957.

꩜ To Thomas B. Foster
21 December 1944
San Francisco, Calif.

As part of his contractual arrangement with the Board of National Missions of the Presbyterian Church, Thurman was required to file reports with Thomas B. Foster[1] at the denomination's national office. Each month Thurman described both new and ongoing activities, as well as gave an overall assessment of the work of the Fellowship Church. The report of December 1944 highlights the connections to San Francisco's Filipino community.

Dear Dr. Foster:

The two most important events for the past month were the Fellowship Dinner honoring the Filipino community and the December Twilight Hour.

The Fellowship Dinner was held at the old place—1500 Post Street.[2] We had an attendance {of} something more than 120 people. We served 122 meals. It was truly an interracial menu—both as to content and to preparation. I fried

120 pieces of chicken, a Filipino gentleman prepared the Filipino sauce in which the chicken was steeped and Miss Ishida, our temporary secretary, prepared the rice. The dessert was American cupcakes prepared commercially.

Our special guests of honor were the members of the Filipino Methodist Community Church.[3] Their Children's Choir sang some numbers, three men from the Church played Filipino music on string instruments and a very attractive Filipino lady gave the main address on "The Life of Women in the Philippines."

The decorations were made largely by our Monday Night Craft Group and they carried out a scheme suggestive of the Philippines. Certain members of the Special Committee cooperating with our church from the Presbytery were present. It was a thoroughly inspiring occasion—a suggestion of the possibilities in this area. It is our plan to feature other groups in subsequent monthly dinners. The meal was served for cost so that it was possible for a family to be present without wrecking the family budget.

The December Twilight Hour, as the program enclosed indicates, dealt basically with the fundamental universality of the Madonna–Child conception. Through the cooperation of the International Institute we were able to secure authentic racial types as listed in the program.

We had two frames about 4' x 4" elevated to a height of five feet so as to make for clear visibility in which the face of the particular subject was posed. They were on the right and left of the chancel. While the lights were focused on one the other was in preparation.

The attendance was a capacity one, something more than 200 people. It was truly an unforgettable experience. Photographs were taken of each individual and if you are interested in seeing them I think that can be arranged.

We have had the interior of the Church painted so that it looks much more habitable and worshipable.

We have a small Monday Night Craft Group, the directors of which have taken over the responsibility of special decorations for various events.

A Jewish sculptor of outstanding reputation has volunteered to teach seven of our children modeling as a part of our Saturday Intercultural Workshop. This begins with the new year.

There are several very important problems that must be thought through and I covet the opportunity to talk with you about them personally. I shall be in the east during the entire month of January. I am preaching at Yale, Vassar, Mt. Holyoke, Grinnell, Beloit, Denison and giving two lectures on worship at the Bonebrake Theological Seminary in Dayton.

In Boston and in Detroit special groups are being arranged to discuss the possibility of making financial contributions to our work here. When I am in

New York I shall call your office hoping to be able to see you. I cannot be more specific than this because of certain unknown quantities in my schedule.

I do hope for you an inspiring Christmas season.

Sincerely yours,

[*signed*] Howard Thurman

Howard Thurman

Dr. Thomas B. Foster

Board of National Missions

Presbyterian Church in the USA

New York, N.Y.

TLS. DH-PC

NOTES

1. Thomas B. Foster, a 1943 graduate of Union Theological Seminary, was an assistant to A. L. Roberts at the Board of National Missions War Services Unit, Presbyterian Church in the U.S.A., in Philadelphia.

2. The Fellowship Dinner was held on 24 December. The previous week the Fellowship Church *Bulletin* had called for the passage of HR 4826. The bill allowed for the naturalization of Filipinos in the United States, who were in danger of losing their status as American citizens if, as happened in 1946, the United States relinquished control of the Philippine Islands. See Fellowship Church *Bulletin*, 17 December 1944, 24 December 1944.

3. The Fellowship Church had recently exchanged sanctuaries with the Filipino Methodist Community Church.

"The Cultural and Spiritual[1] Prospect for a Nation Emerging from Total War"

1945

Probably delivered in the waning months of World War II, this is one of Thurman's most urgent talks on how America was being changed by conditions of "total war" and the tasks that awaited those who in the postwar period would seek to alter society for the better. Thurman sketches the growth of America from a religious to a frontier to an industrial society and then to the current state-centered, war-driven nation, when the "grim business of survival" had become all encompassing.[2] In response, small groups of individuals, here called "apostles of sensitiveness," would need to work from the ground up to ensure that America lived up to its political and spiritual potential. Racial minorities, those most "exposed to the effects of the breakdown of the democratic ideals," were in a "unique position" to become apostles of sensitiveness.

It is a simple observation that conditions of total war cause a profoundly radical shift in the generally prevailing culture pattern. When the Pilgrim Fathers ~~started~~ made in the new world a fresh start their culture pattern was integrated around certain definitely religious ideas. It is safe to say that here we had a religion-centered culture pattern. It was in the interest of religious freedom, the privilege of worshiping God after the urges of his own conscience, defining Him in terms suitable to his own needs and religious prerogatives, that the New World was founded. The touch stone of the common life was religion.

As the impersonal aspects of the world of nature more and more forced the pioneers to struggle against great odds for physical survival there began to appear certain alternatives in the culture determined by the fact of the frontier. As the forests were pushed back, a certain stripping of the veneers of settled life seemed mandatory. Men became hard because it was necessary to be hard to survive. Life was fluid because contact with nature was immediate, raw and elemental. The religion dominated culture pattern had to share honors with a frontier-centered culture pattern. The typical man of the new world was no longer the stern puritan with Bible in one hand and gun in other on his way to church but rather the frontiersman with all that fact and fancy have done to make him live in our minds.

As towns sprang up and whole communities developed aided and abetted by railroads and waterways time was ripe for still another ~~development~~ process. A development made possible by the ~~development~~ rise of modern science—the rise of industry. Factories appeared, more and more. The central figure, the dominant entity on the horizon was now the industrialist, a man of power whose accumulated wealth created cities, modern homes and a [*illegible*] and [*all?*] other things that are the common lot of American life. He made towns [*or?*] reduced them to deserted villages. Slums began sending forth their decaying rage into the bloodstream of the body politic. Our culture was now industry-centered.

The industry centered culture pattern became the great symbol of American life. The more cynical or realistic or prophetic individuals began referring to us as a people who worshipped the Almighty dollar. "Gold is God and the industrialist is his prophet"—from many pulpits, soap boxes and college halls came the thundering [*illegible*]. A new kind of social awakening began to make itself felt—men became concerned about hours of work, conditions of work, compensation etc. The individual must be cared for—there was increasingly a feeling that our salvation could come only if our culture pattern were dominated by a concern for the individual. Social service became a thrilling adventure for the zealous and a social gospel the battle cry for the zealot.

While this was working its way out into the by ways and corners of our national life, ominous clouds appeared on the European Horizon. Totalitarian states were ushered in by ~~the~~ swashbuckling dictators. Small fires appeared in Manchuko,[3] then Abysinnia,[4] then Austria, Checho-slovakia, Poland until at last all of Europe was rolling in billowing darkness. Then the Far East broke upon us with Pearl Harbor as its symbol—now the whole wide world is as midnight, the sky only lighted by bursting bombs; the grim silence of desolation, plague and hunger broken up by the Frankensteinian wail of [*dive?*] bombers. War is upon us— total, devastating, terrifying, [*ingenious?*]. The state taken over.

The culture pattern now is state-centered. All national life is now increasingly organized around the achieving of a vast national objective—victory for the United Nations.[5] Almost every detail of the common life is affected. Simple and complex routines are altered shifted with scarce notice. The clocks move up one hour by executive order.[6] New and unprecedented taxes are taken for granted.[7] The national debt takes on the character of pure mathematics.[8] The state decides who can buy what and under what conditions. Education is being reorganized, refitted to the common task defined by the state in terms of the national emergency.

The fact of <u>total</u> war in which it is declared that our very existence is at stake has forced a reversion to an earlier experience of the human race in that twilight moment when the mind was born. We do not know precisely when the mind was born but it does seem likely that such a miracle was not possible until man could function independently of his environment. As long as all the energies of human life were exhausted in the grim business of survival there was no surplus energy available for man to play around with his ~~environment~~ world. It was only out of surplus energy that imagination, art, culture, civilization could ~~be~~ come into being. In that far off time survival meant that which was primarily biological, physical, creaturely. Now we are once again at such a crossroads when increasingly all our energies are to be spent in surviving. But survival for us to-day means more than biology. It means the survival of certain ideas, ideals, ways of thinking, value qualities—vast [*overtones?*] making up the American way of life.

The profound question, therefore, is how can a nation engaged in total war provide for the internal survival of those values with which in its most lucid moments it identifies life itself? The cultural and spiritual prospect for such a nation is determined by the degree to which it is able to work out an answer to this question while it is still caught in the agonizing grip of total war.

In the first place, there must be present in the social mixture those who are willing to be Apostles of Sensitiveness for the whole nation. Those individuals who by their ability and skills will be at work in various ~~levels~~ areas of the national life, doing their jobs but who at the same time are ever on the alert to preserve those ideals and ideas of democracy which are being directly threatened at the points where they themselves have power or can exert [*illegible?*] influence.

They must never permit those sentiments that are genuinely democratic to become [*pocketed?*] or isolated under the guise that suspension must be the order of the day for the duration. They must resist [*even?*] ~~upon~~ every attempt to place false and misleading labels upon them such as <u>red</u>, <u>subversive</u>, divisive. This is a very clever device inspired by fear, [*often?*] bigotry, intolerance. The Apostles of Sensitiveness must stand guard first at their points of immediate and direct power.

In the second place—small groups that during more normal times have worked on behalf of tolerance, simple human service to others in need, a spiritual interpretation of life which ascribes to each individual a basic dignity and worth as a person—these must ~~be~~ intensify their concerns and their efforts that during this dark age, the flickering torch may be unquenched that it may light the way through the long post war dawn that is to come. A high place among such groups belongs to the National Conference under whose auspices we meet today. One of the dangers for all such groups is that they may seem to themselves to be wasting their time and energies as they look out upon the destruction of much for which they stand but it is important to note in passing that whatever the world of the future will be like depends in no small part upon the spear head that will be provided by those who ~~are~~ have worked out in a thousand social laboratories techniques and methods for implementing those ideals which are so seriously threatened at home and abroad. Yet, the solidity of such ideals can best be determined by the extent to which they can be believed and practiced at a time when they seem most irrational and fanciful. They will bear the scars of a thousand [*illegible*], they will be the [*really?*] fruitful veterans of total war, they will be present on the peace councils, they will establish the bounds and [*lay out?*] the city of friendly men beneath a friendly sky.

In the third place, minority groups are in a unique position to be apostles of sensitiveness keeping alive the true genius of the democratic challenge—mark the use of the word challenge. This is true because minorities are apt to be ~~the~~ most directly and immediately exposed to the effects of the breakdown of the democratic ideals in the body politic. The more stigmatized is the minority, the more tragic the plight the keener will be this awareness. They represent to the dominant majority the [*illegible*] for instance of the open sores in the ~~democratic~~ national life. One of the points at which the democratic ideal ~~begins~~ first shows signs of degradation is in the ~~life~~ treatment of the minorities.

There is an additional consideration. Those groups that suffer ~~for~~ most acutely from a betrayal of democratic ideals serve as a point of testing for the whole democratic process. Their responsibility then is to keep alive the growing edge of democratic life by insisting on the realization of national ideals of tolerance, courtesy, ~~freedom~~ the three freedoms etc. at the points of greatest testing. [*They?*] will be the minorities whether religious racial or what [*not?*] within our common life who will know first ~~whether we~~ if we win the war abroad and lose the war at home.

It is our common task to enlist all men of good will ~~in our national life~~ in the ranks of the Apostles of Sensitiveness who with rare courage and scintillating insight will dare to define practically and efficiently the American way of life so that it will not as now do violence to the democratic way of life. Such Apostles will be the sensitive nerve ends for the body politic and tomorrow and tomorrow and tomorrow will make a new track to the waters edge.[9]

AD.

Notes

1. Thurman crossed out "horizon of" after "spiritual."

2. "The Apostles of Sensitiveness" was one of Thurman's favorite catchphrases in the mid-1940s. It was the title of a sermon that he preached at the Fellowship Church on 11 February 1945, as well as a lecture that he gave at the Pacific School of Religion during the week of 6 May 1945, the week that the war in Europe ended. The sermon printed here was likely written shortly before or after the end of the war. Thurman used the phrase yet again for the title of a sermon in 1946, printed in the current volume, and in the title of a book that was published in 1947, *Meditations for the Apostles of Sensitiveness* (Mills College, Oakland, Calif.: Eucalyptus Press, 1947).

3. Manchukuo was the name given to Manchuria by the Japanese after their invasion in 1931.

4. Ethiopia.

5. The United States, Great Britain, the Soviet Union, and their allies.

6. Year-round daylight savings time, or what was commonly called "wartime," mandatory for all states, was in effect by an act of Congress (not, as Thurman writes, by an executive order), from 9 February 1942 to 30 September 1945.

7. From 1940 to 1944 the top federal income tax rate increased from 68 percent to 94 percent.

8. From 1 July 1941 to 1 July 1945 the national debt increased from $49 billion to $259 billion.

9. Reference to Olive Schreiner, "Three Dreams in a Desert," reprinted in HT, ed., *A Track to the Water's Edge: The Olive Schreiner Reader* (New York: Harper and Row, 1973), 56.

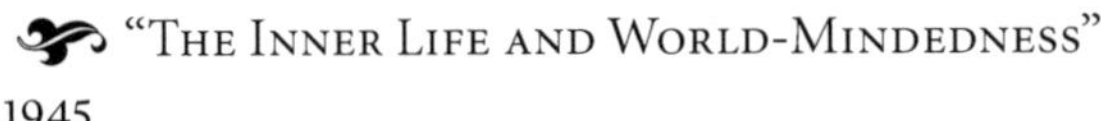 "The Inner Life and World-Mindedness"

1945

This essay appeared as part of a festschrift in honor of Conrad Henry Moehlman entitled Christian Leadership in a World Society. *Moehlman was professor of the history of Christianity from 1907 to 1944 at Rochester Theological Seminary and at its later incarnation as Colgate Rochester Divinity School. As Thurman later recalled of his teacher, Moehlman made the "great creedal battles of the church . . . seem contemporary, as very often they were."[1] The essay exists in two versions, one written before the end of the war in Europe and the other, the published version, changed to reflect the end of hostilities and the dropping of the atomic bomb.[2] The essay explores the disastrous separation of the modern church's "God of religion" from the "God of life."*

Man is a manifestation of life. It is this fact at least that he has in common with all other living things. We are so overwhelmed by the dramatic and external aspects of aliveness that each manifestation of life appears to be independent, complete and autonomous. Every tree, every animal seems to be essentially and uniquely alive without reference to a deeper level of aliveness. In the presence of the staggering mass of individual manifestations of life we are apt to overlook entirely the simple fact that life itself is alive. The essential aliveness of life is the ground of all the aliveness of the particular manifestations of which human beings are but one.

The term inner life suggests that there is present in the world of aliveness a self-conscious awareness of aliveness as aliveness. We do not know about other manifestations of life, but we do know that man is conscious of his being alive and is therefore conscious of life itself. This means that there is present in man a quality of detachment from varying aspects of his environment so that he is able to see himself as a private individual existence separate and distinct from other manifestations of life, but at the same time grounded in an essential aliveness which makes possible every other manifestation of life about him. The bearing of this observation on the fact of world-mindedness will be developed at another point in the discussion.

I

Man was doubtless able to become mind-conscious as a result of a long, difficult process. In his early stages of development it is reasonable to assume that the human animal was not mind-conscious. As long as all of the energies of the body were spent exhaustively in the hard task of keeping alive—escaping death from enemies on every hand, getting food, caring for the young—there was no surplus of energy available for the unique development of what we now recognize as the mind and the spirit of man. When it became possible to be protected from the constant and immediate threat of death, imagination that was not geared to the facts of survival made possible reflective thought. With the coming of reflective thought man could act to some extent independent of his environment— which means he could then see himself in relation to his environment.

The consciousness of mind is the thing that has made possible the development of the organized life of man in the world. It has given birth to religion, to art, to culture, in fine, to all that we mean by civilization. The unique thing about the awareness of mind is the fact that it is a self-awareness as distinguished from an awareness of something that is external to itself. The awareness of mind then is the clue to what we mean by the inner life of man. The mind turning in upon itself interprets its experience of itself in terms of a wider and more comprehensive Other which is its validation and gives it character. It follows then that there must be included in its consciousness not merely thought, ideas, concepts, but feeling tones, hopes, fears, yearnings and the whole range of value judgments which go to make up the inner life of the individual. The term, *inner life*, is more than mere formal discursive activity of the mind and must include what the term itself implies, the entire range of self-awareness of the individual.

Even the most cursory examination of the "range of self-awareness" reveals that there are at least three tremendous "driving forces in the life of the human race": that which makes for the perpetuation of the race in terms of reproduction and all the overtones that surround the experience of sex itself; that which makes for the physical survival of the individual; and that which yields to the individual a sense of meaning and significance that is not located in any particular aspect of the environment but suffuses all, giving richness and fullness to life. It is important to point out that it is the "joyous response" of the latter that the term religious covers most comprehensively. In the rest of our discussion the term "inner life" applies to the awareness of the individual responsiveness to realities that are transcendent in character, emanating from a core of Reality of which the individual is aware and of which the individual is also aware that he is a part.

The inner life, therefore, is activity that takes place within consciousness but does not originate there and is a part of a reality central to all of life and is at once the ground of all awareness, of all aliveness. It is here that man becomes conscious of his meaning and his destiny as a child, an offspring of God. To borrow a phrase from Eckhart, it is the "uncreated element" in the life of man. Here man hears his God speak to him, here he glimpses goals and objects of striving which have an implicit veracity for which he is willing to work, to suffer if needs be, to die in behalf of their realization in the world of manifestation in time and space. What he seeks in the world of activity is that of which he is already deeply aware in his inner life. The clue to the outer world of relations is found in the inner world of experience.

II

The concept of world-mindedness has to do with the development of the logic of the primary discoveries of the inner life in the external relationships between the multiple manifestations of life. Our concern is primarily with the relationships among human beings. It is not unreasonable to assume that our concern must be even more inclusive. The Prophet Isaiah saw a profound unity between man and the animal kingdom. He suggests that when men study war no more, then the lion and the lamb will lie down together. When the highest manifestations of life relax and uproot their fear of each other, then fear will disappear even among animals; for the knowledge of the Lord will cover the earth as the waters cover the sea. Therefore, the concept of world-mindedness is the outer expression among men of an awareness of the individual's sense of being a child of God, being rooted and grounded in the life of God.

The notion of world-mindedness does not necessarily imply sameness of cultural patterns including language and social habits; it does not imply oneness of religious expression or of political relations, but it does imply an overall awareness of the essential oneness of the human race. This essential awareness stands irrevocably opposed to all notions of the inherent superiority of one people as over against another or one nation over against another. It places at the center of all political, social, or economic arrangements among men a profound recognition of basic solidarity and concern for the guaranteeing of the right of each individual to have a climate in which his life may unfold in dignity, beauty, and fullness.

It is significant that in the development of the mind of man there has been historically the tendency to reduce the conglomerates of experience to manageable units of control, of understanding, of usefulness. This is most clearly manifest in man's relation to nature. Despite the fact that man is a part of nature he sees himself always as in one sense standing over against the world of nature. He has consistently broken nature down into units of understanding and utility. He has sought to understand its laws and how he may utilize them to his own ends. Curiously enough the advances in this regard have in a sense prepared the way for the working out of the concept of world-mindedness. I use the phrase "prepared the way" quite advisedly; for I do not mean that in the mastery of nature *per se* there is any guarantee that world-mindedness, in the sense in which it is here used, would of necessity follow. And indeed it has not.

The fact remains, however, that the scientific method, with its use of hypothesis, has made for the industrialization of natural resources and for the annihilation of space and time, significant and necessitous barriers between men. The advance in this particular has been more rapid than the adjustment that men have made to the new dimension into which they have been precipitated. *For the most part we are living in a new world and attempting to function with the habits and mentality of old world habitues.* We think in terms of continents and oceans and invisible culture barriers that separate the human race on this planet when the push of scientific advance has made the world into a neighborhood. This requires a kind of maturity for which we are quite unprepared. It follows then that our reactions are those of the immature and adolescent. This by no means make[s] them less deadly and destructive.

It is clear that with the new tools of destruction in our hands such as, the robot bombs that fly pilotless over the seas,[3] the B-29s that do precision bombing from miles above the earth, and finally the atomic bomb, in sheer self-defense something radical must take place in the basic interpretation which we give to the inclusive meaning of life. Obviously, no mere palliative measures are of any value. Nothing short of a profound revolution in the basic structure of our thought about human life and human destiny can be of any avail.

III

What then is the nature of this mandatory revolution? We must devise ways and means by which the large scale super power that is made possible by man's mastery of nature can have at its center an articulate ethical social responsibility. Perhaps the greatest problem of our age is how modern man can "get a living without losing all the other things that make life joyful and significant." The essential problem then is a spiritual one. It is deep within itself, at the core of his inner life, that man comes upon the tragic insistence that he was meant for joyful and significant living. But it is a joyful and significant life that cannot be content with a world of men and things. What one seeks for one's self must be held as valid for one's neighbors. The seeds of death are inherent in any form of private fulfillment which by its very realizability destroys the unfolding of the life of one's neighbor. This has been implicit in all high ethical religion and is the corner stone of the great Judeo-Christian tradition which has appeared like a fleeting ghost in the vast rooms of the massive palaces of western civilization. In the past, before power became so vast and our resources in nature so activated, we could run the risk of ignoring it and yet expect some measure of survival. But today this is no longer possible. Nothing short of a concept of world-mindedness that is deeply and directly rooted in the inner life of man can yield either the will or the courage to save us from utter and devastating desolation.

Of course this is not easy to accomplish. To take only one instance of the use of large scale power—economic imperialism. Suppose a great world economic power that has built its prestige, honor, and culture upon the fact that it has been sustained and guaranteed by the careful and scientific exploitation of the resources of other peoples and other lands, decided to relax its imperialistic will. Such a determination requires an entirely radical reorientation of its entire life down to the most insignificant detail. But if it placed at the disposal of its new purpose the vast creative resources of its own ingenuity, then ways and means would be devised by which such a consummation could be achieved.

The point is that the power that has been made possible by the achievements of scientific advance has not been regarded as amenable to any concerns that are not directly related to its own perpetuation. Fundamental to this is the additional fact that the whole intellectual process of the mind of modern man has been permitted to develop without any formal recognition of social responsibility. Much has been made of the dedication of the heart of men to goodness, to righteousness, while the mind has been dedicated to truth, interpreted almost entirely in terms of the descriptive accuracy of a particular mental process. Truth has not been interpreted as including values that transcend the narrow limits of a definite field of knowledge in operation. We have made all manner of divisions between scientific truth, ethical truth, religious truth, etc. The God of religion is regarded basically, where He is admitted at all, in contradistinction to the God of life. So true is this fatal dichotomy in our thought that value reference for the individual is commonly regarded as having little to do with the practical living of life.

It follows then that the deep ethical criterion so needful as a corrective and a motivation for the creative working of mind in its mastery of nature has been almost entirely lacking. It is for this reason that precisely at the moment in human history when we have made our more radical scientific advances in the world we have remained almost stationary in our ethical and spiritual progress. It is the crime of Christianity that the teaching and the words of Jesus are still revolutionary and radical after 2000 years of human history. By some this may be regarded as a compliment to the tremendous stature and timelessness of Jesus, but to me it means that with infinitely more existential resources at our command than he had we have failed to make good on the vision which he held before us.

Justin Wroe Nixon and Winthrop Still Hudson, eds., *Christian Leadership in a World Society* (Rochester, N.Y.: Colgate-Rochester Divinity School, 1945), 185–95.

Notes

1. *WHAH,* 54.

2. Thurman delivered a lecture with the same title as this essay as the opening lecture of a three-lecture series at the Pacific School of Religion during the week of 6 May 1945; the other two lectures were titled "Apostles of Sensitiveness" and "What Shall I Do with my Life?"

3. Reference to the German V-2 rocket.

❧ From M. C. Merriweather
5 January 1945
APO, New York

M. C. Merriweather,[1] a chaplain with the all-black 366th Infantry Regiment,[2] tells of the fierce fighting his unit encountered in northern Italy and of the respect in which Thurman was held by his former Howard students who were in the armed forces.

Dr. Howard Thurman
1500 Post Street
San Francisco, California

Dear Doctor Thurman:

Your communication of the eighth instant came to me sometime ago, and I should like to congratulate you on the very significant experiment in which you are now engaged. I'm sure it will prove quite conclusively that Christianity can work as a social force to create an atmosphere of fellowship and good-will among different race groups regardless of previous commitments or levels of culture. To know that such work is being done gives hope and encouragement to those of us over here who live and move in an atmosphere of hate, darkness and death. For at times the future outlook seems so hopeless to us until one wishes it possible to sleep until this night of darkness and despair passes over.

Our entire regiment has been committed to battle and we are now at grips with the enemy, and it is most remarkable how well these men are doing. We are facing a most formidable enemy far well experienced in this business of death who apparently stops at nothing to achieve an end. They use church towers for observation posts, their soldiers dress often in the gab' of priests to infiltrate through. They disregard every rule of warfare known to man. The Red Cross seems only a target for them at times.

About seventy-five per cent of our officers are Howard men. All of whom have given a good account of themselves in battle. Some have given the last measure of their devotion in order that their children and those that return may live in a better world in the future. Most of my time is spent at the Aid Station and as many of the men are brought back from engagements with battered and bleeding bodies, suffering beyond words, one wonders at times what word can one speak at a time like this that will be of help. Yet seldom do they complain or show any sign of bitterness. Their greatest hope seem to be to get well and get back into the fight. I shall not burden you longer with such unpleasantness as war, such should be forgotten.

Colonel Chase joins me in regards to you and Mrs. Thurman. He is doing a great job with his battalion. Quite often we get together and discuss our past experiences at Howard and the various personalities, and, of course, you always come into the discussion. You can never know the extent to which you have influenced the thinking of the men who know you and have heard you speak, and the esteem in which you are held by them.

Very truly yours,

[*signed*] M C Merriweather

M. C. MERRIWEATHER
CH(Capt)., 366th Infantry

TLS.

NOTES

1. M. C. Merriweather was a minister in the Christian Methodist Episcopal (C.M.E.) Church and pastored congregations at the Featherstone Temple in Memphis and the Thirgood C.M.E. Church in Birmingham, where he taught at nearby Miles College. In 1964 he became editor of *The Christian Index,* the chief publication of the C.M.E Church.

2. The 366th Infantry Regiment, first activated in World War I, was reactivated in 1941 and went overseas in March 1944. Members of the 366th were stationed in North Africa before transferring in November 1944 to Italy, where they remained until the end of the war.

⇝ TO THOMAS B. FOSTER
13 FEBRUARY 1945
SAN FRANCISCO, CALIF.

Thurman reports to Foster that he spent the month of January 1945 in the East and offers to forgo his salary for the month.

Dr. Thomas B. Foster
Board of National Missions
Presbyterian Church in the U.S.A.
New York, N.Y.

Dear Dr. Foster,

During the entire month of January and a few days in February I was in the East fulfilling engagements which were a part of my regular college and university preaching. In addition I had three meetings about the Fellowship Church. Inasmuch as I was not here during the month of January, if you do not wish to have the monthly check forwarded, I shall understand.

The most important single event in the Church during that month was the Fellowship Dinner, as a gesture of welcome to the returning Japanese Americans.[1] There was a total number of one hundred and thirty people attending the dinner, twenty four of whom were Japanese Americans. I am very certain from all of the things that I have heard that it was an experience of brotherhood on one of its profoundest levels of meaning. We have received some beautiful letters of appreciation for what was done.

I am enclosing a program covering the experience. More and more our Church is becoming a growing edge having in its fellowship an increasing number of the strands that go to make up American life.
Sincerely yours,
[*signed*] Howard Thurman
Howard Thurman

                                                                    TLS. DH-PC

NOTE

1. On Friday, 26 January.

᠅ TO THOMAS B. FOSTER
28 FEBRUARY 1945
SAN FRANCISCO, CALIF.

Thurman informs Foster of a number of new programs. He also mentions his decision to ask Howard University for another year's leave of absence to continue the work at the Fellowship Church.

Dear Dr. Foster:

There are three significant developments that are worthy of report:

1.

The Committee on Community Relations and Services is presenting two series of Sunday evening lecture-discussions. The first is a series on religion which I am taking for the four Sunday nights in March. Samples of the announcement are enclosed.

The second series will begin the first Sunday night after Easter, and will consist of three presentations on the issues that are being worked out in the conference of the United Nations to be held in San Francisco in late April. The idea is to guarantee as far as possible that those persons who attend will become informed on these important matters against the time when a public opinion in America will be called upon to give specific directions to our representatives.

2.

As an expression of appreciation for a regular Saturday morning religious service in Temple Emanu-El[1] in which I took the sermon{,}[2] the Rabbi on behalf of certain members of his congregation{,} made a gift of $1500 toward the work of the Fellowship Church. This is of profoundest significance because it shows not only the measure of concern this congregation has for the things about which the Fellowship Church has concern, but it also reveals an amazing measure of appreciation for the contribution which is being made increasingly to the community. Seeing my cramped quarters, Rabbi Reichert[3] offered to put at my disposal a room in the Synagogue which I might use as a place of study and retreat at my discretion.

3.

Last Monday evening at a full meeting of our Board a decision was made that will increase enormously the responsibility of the Board for the development of the Church. During the past six months practically all of the important representations, struggles, and decisions have been made by Dr. Fisk and me.

To some extent this has been inevitable. If the Church is to have a future, the membership itself must share completely in all matters having to do with the life and development of this idea. The question of organic denominational affiliation was discussed. The partial check of membership showed that the largest representation is Episcopal, next Methodist, next Baptist, then Presbyterian, and finally Congregational. There are two or three Roman Catholics. We do not know what the final checking will reveal. The consensus of opinion at the Board was that inasmuch as we are already interdenominational, and thoroughly so, the logic of our development would lead to some kind of interdenominational structure. A subcommittee of the Board is continuing the study and analysis.

A subcommittee was also appointed to study the financial situation to see what are the prospects of our becoming self-sustaining.

Another committee was appointed to find decent living quarters for the Thurman family. They expressed a desire to have me petition Howard University for an extension of my leave for another year. This I have consented to do.

Plans for a summer program cannot be made until we know whether there will be any space for carrying on such a program.

Sincerely yours,

[*signed*] Howard Thurman

Howard Thurman

Encl.

{NB I am sorry that the person who copied this used letterhead for the additional paper. HT}

Dr. Thomas B. Foster

Board of National Missions

Presbyterian Church in the U.S.A.

New York, N.Y.

TLS. DH-PC

Notes

1. Established in 1850, Temple Emanu-El (now Congregation Emanu-El) in San Francisco is the oldest Jewish congregation west of the Mississippi River.

2. On 10 February 1945.

3. Irving Reichert (1895–1968), a graduate of Hebrew Union College, received his rabbinical ordination in 1921. After leading several congregations in the New York City area, he was named rabbi of Temple Emanu-El in 1930. He was active in many liberal and progressive causes and was an outspoken opponent of Japanese internment during the war. Dismayed when Reform Judaism abandoned its traditional opposition to Jewish nationalism, he became a leader of the anti-Zionist American Council for Judaism (ACJ) in the 1940s, and this involvement led to his forced resignation from Emanu-El in 1948. He was executive director of the ACJ's West Coast division until his resignation from the organization in 1956.

☙ To George Thomas

17 MARCH 1945
[*San Francisco, Calif.*]

*George L. Thomas, who probably was Thurman's student at Howard, had
recently returned to his hometown. At the time of this letter, he was working for
the Portland Council of Churches; by 1947 he would be president of the Portland
chapter of the NAACP. Thomas had written to Thurman on 2 March telling
him of his "confused state of mind" and complaining that the local chapter of
the Urban League was "complacent" and "composed of reactionary Negroes and
white big business men." Thomas was involved in trying to set up various interracial activities in Portland and had been asked to start a new black church in that
city but was unsure of what to do, being "alert to anything that smells of segregation."[1] In this letter Thurman gives him some advice on how to proceed and
cautions him on the different set of difficulties he will probably face from whites
and blacks as he pursues his interracial goals.*

Dear George,

I am sorry that I cannot write you a long letter covering the various phases
of your letter to me, but I am up against it for time and energy. I shall go down
the list. You must realize that you are working in one of the most difficult areas
of human life. Fundamentally, your additional task is as difficult among white
people as among Negroes. I am afraid that many of the people who were most
insistent that you come felt that you would work miracles and take from their
shoulders the responsibility which is rightly theirs. You must understand this
with objectivity and do your job carefully and well, but keep the responsibility
on the local community. If your advice is sought relative to the Urban League,
insist that the ordinary man be represented on the Board. Have a specific recommendation in mind to make.

I cannot give you a specific date when I can come to Portland, but if it does
not involve a Sunday, I may be able to come up sometime after April 15th.[2] If
one or two things could be arranged so that in addition to my expenses there
would be some honorarium attached, I would appreciate that very much, because my expenses are very heavy and my income is seriously limited. If this
cannot be done I would consider coming up to do this one thing for you, just
for my expenses.

It is quite likely that you will go into the ministry while you are there, but I
want to talk the thing through with you before you make a commitment.

Your "Courtesy Month" plan is a good one. I would suggest further that you
get the Men's Group of that church[3] to have a mass meeting for Negroes only at

which their leaders would talk with them about civic responsibility and public behavior, civic responsibility and saving money, civic responsibility and home ownership. This would be a good thing to do.

I am very sorry, George, to know of the passing of your father. You have the great satisfaction of knowing that in you he always found a devoted and sensitive son. It was inevitable that the end would come, and I am glad that it did not come until you were engaged in the kind of work that gives to you a new sense of strength and dignity.

Give my love to everybody when you write.

Sincerely,

Howard Thurman

HT:am

Mr. George Thomas

305 YMCA Building

Portland 4, Oregon

TLc.

NOTES

    1. From George Thomas, 2 March 1945.

    2. Thurman would spend the week of 14 May to 18 May in Portland as a guest of George Thomas (To George Thomas, 7 April 1945).

    3. Bethel A.M.E.

To Thomas B. Foster

22 March 1945

[San Francisco, Calif.]

Thurman reports to Foster that the two congregations that made special efforts to support the work of the Fellowship Church are non-Christian. He also informs Foster of an upcoming meeting with the local Presbytery regarding the future relationship between the church and the denomination and expresses optimism that the relationship will be maintained.

Dear Dr. Foster:

    1.

The Sunday evening Lecture Discussion series concerning which I reported last month is now two-thirds over.[1] These have been well received with an average attendance of 55 and good thoughtful discussion. Some persons have attended the series who were not even acquainted with the other activities of the church, so that out of the series, per se, there will come new people. We are still working on the plans for the second series, but it is extremely difficult to get the kind of leadership what we need. Perhaps in my next monthly letter a definitive word will be available.

2.

The monthly inter-cultural dinner was built around India and her peoples. I am enclosing a sample of the program used. The dinner itself was held in the First Presbyterian Church because we have outgrown our present facilities. This was a gracious gesture on the part of that church. What we shall do for the remaining two dinners, I do not know.

3.

You may be interested to know that my volume of prose poems[2] which was published by Mills College is now in its second edition. The royalties from the sale of this religious poetry are being banked in a fund for establishing an inter-cultural, inter-racial reading room if and when we have proper quarters for it. The response has been most inspiring.

4.

Last Sunday, March 18th, the Buddhist Temple[3] had a special service in honor of the Fellowship Church of all Peoples. A sample program is enclosed. It is important to point out that this gesture of encouragement was the first of its kind that our church has experienced. It is a matter of great significance to me personally that the two ministers in San Francisco who have gone out of their way to extend courtesies of various kinds to me in connection with the work have been [a] Jewish Rabbi and a Buddhist priest. I make this statement without comment; for no comment is necessary.

5.

I am happy to announce that at last we have a secretary.[4] I have nearly lost my mind during the past seven or eight months trying to work things out under irrational and impossible handicaps. It is a matter of immeasurable relief to me to have a competent young lady to take secretarial responsibility in the church and at the same time to have a personal concern for the development of this whole idea.

6.

At the request of the church, I have sent a formal petition to Howard University asking them to extend my leave for another 12 months beginning July, 1945. This decision was reached by me and Mrs. Thurman after great searchings of heart, because the need at Howard University is greater than it has ever been, and yet it seems tragic to pull out from the Fellowship Church before the foundations are laid and the direction for the future is seen more clearly.

7.

Two articles have been written by me pointing out the development of the work here. The first one appeared in "Social Action" published by the Congregational

Board and the other one appears in the spring issue of "Common Ground."[5] A copy of the latter is included in my report.

    8.

Monday evening, April 2nd, there is scheduled a joint meeting between the Board of the Fellowship Church and the Committee of the Presbytery, at which time I hope that the relationship for the future will be worked out with sympathy and intelligent understanding. It is to the timeless credit of the Presbyterian Church of America that it has sponsored the Fellowship Church. It is my own desire that we shall be able to work out a plan for continuing this sponsorship.[6]

On the whole the work is developing in a healthy manner and I have every devoted wish that it shall continue.

Sincerely,

Howard Thurman

Enclosures
c.c: Dr. Clyde Smith[7]
228 McAllister Street
San Francisco, California

Dr. Thomas B. Foster
Board of National Missions
Presbyterian Church in the U.S.A.
New York, N.Y.

TLc. FC

NOTES

1. These lectures were primarily about the nature of community, as in Thurman's lecture on 25 March 1945, "The Church: Institution or Spirit?," Fellowship Church *Bulletin*, 25 March 1945.

2. HT, *Greatest of These*.

3. Probably the Buddhist Church of San Francisco, led by Frank Boden Udale.

4. Ayoko Murota.

5. For details on both articles, see HT, "The Fellowship Church of All Peoples" (Spring 1945), printed in the current volume.

6. The sincerity of Thurman's statement to Foster is clear but there were already tensions between Thurman and Fisk over their connection to the Presbyterian Church and worries about Thurman by Presbyterian authorities, as indicated in a letter to Foster from Presbyterian official Jacob A. Long, written on 3 January 1945: "In the light of the apparent difficulty between Fisk and Thurman's approach and a conference I had with Dr. Clyde W. Smith when he was in the East, I am quite anxious to sit down with Dr. Thurman when he is in the East" (Department of History, Presbyterian Church, U.S.A., Archives).

7. W. Clyde Smith was the executive secretary of the San Francisco Presbytery.

❧ To James Russell Brown
22 March 1945
[*San Francisco, Calif.*]

James Russell Brown,[1] the first African American chaplain in the U.S. Navy and a former student of Thurman's at Howard, wrote to him on 7 March telling of his experiences at the U.S. Naval Center at Great Lakes, Illinois: "There are times here when I wish that I might have a little more of what you have to offer. The problems here are numerous and varied, and sometimes extremely difficult. Sometimes the men need to be helped; at other times they need a good whipping." He congratulated Thurman for his work with the Fellowship Church: "I am sure that history's comment will have to be 'Well done, thou good and faithful servant.'"[2] In his response, Thurman congratulates Brown for his pathbreaking work.

Dear Russell,

I had wondered what had happened to the Lieutenant and whether he was in this country or abroad. I hope that your work will bring you to San Francisco, and you will have a chance to worship in our experiment out here, and I will have a chance to visit with you. The enclosed material explains what we are trying to do.

You have undertaken a very difficult assignment and it will require, as you know already, a maximum of understanding and devotion to the tasks to which your hands are set. I am glad that it is a man like you who is the first Negro Chaplain in the United States Navy. After you, will come many others in the course of the years and what happens to them will in some measure be a reflection of the magnificent job that you yourself are doing. Sign the commitment and return it please. Have you read Doug Steere's "On Beginning From Within"? I am sending you under separate cover an autographed copy of my little volume of poems prose.

Please remember me to Mrs. Brown.
Sincerely,
Howard Thurman

HT:am
Encl.
James Russell Brown
Lt. (jg) ChC, USNR
U.S. Naval Training Center
Great Lakes Illinois

TLc.

NOTES

1. James Russell Brown (1909–87) was born in Guthrie, Oklahoma, and earned a B.A. from Friends University in 1932 and an M.Div. from Howard University in 1935. He taught and served as dean of the Bishop Williams School of Religion at Western University in Quandaro, Kansas, a historically black college that closed in 1943. He became the first African American chaplain in the U.S. Navy in April 1944 and served until April 1946. After his chaplaincy, Brown pastored A.M.E. congregations in Kansas City, Kansas; Denver; Oakland; and Berkeley.

2. From James Russell Brown, 7 March 1945.

᭒ To Walter White

22 MARCH 1945
[*San Francisco, Calif.*]

Thurman writes a letter to Walter White, the executive secretary of the NAACP, recommending Channing Tobias for the Spingarn Medal.[1] *Tobias received the award in 1948.*

Dear Mr. White,

This is a letter on behalf of the nomination of Dr. Channing H. Tobias for the Spingarn Medal for this year.

I have been associated with Dr. Tobias since 1917 when I was a first year high school student in Florida. It is my considered judgment that over a period of more than twenty years, no single individual in our race has made a more consistent contribution to the development of American youth and manhood along lines of social understanding, intelligent, courageous character than Dr. Tobias. For years he has shuttled back and forth between the two worlds in which we live, carrying understanding, doing battle when that is indicated, making formal and informal representation among all classes of Americans whether they be officially something or not. Usually a man tends to become conservative and reactionary as his arteries begin to harden. This has not been true with Dr. Tobias. As the years have ripened and deepened his experiences he has seen to it that at the center of his system there would be a growing courageous liberalism that puts him in the front rank of those who are the living for instances of the meaning of democracy. A casual glance at his broad portfolio will give you some indication of the kind of interracial, inter-cultural leadership which he is at the moment exercising. This leadership is the climax of a long development over the years.

It would be a salutary thing at this critical moment in the world's history for the Spingarn Medal to be given to this man for his amazing leadership in the field of human relations and the direct contribution that he has made and is making in that regard. It is with enthusiasm and without reservation that I endorse his nomination.

Sincerely yours,

Howard Thurman

HT: am

TLc. FC

NOTE

1. Beginning in 1915 the Spingarn Medal was awarded annually by the NAACP to an outstanding African American. For many decades it was the most prestigious award in black America. It was named for and endowed by Joel E. Spingarn, professor of comparative literature at Columbia University and chairman of the board of the NAACP from 1913 until his death in 1939.

☙ "THE FELLOWSHIP CHURCH OF ALL PEOPLES"
SPRING 1945

One of the main purposes of the Fellowship Church was to generate publicity about its goals, and to this end Thurman wrote extensively about the church, publishing this article in Common Ground[1] *and a shorter article in* Social Action,[2] *both published in the spring of 1945.*

San Francisco is a "thousand cities within a city." There are rich international units from all over the earth nestled in the midst of its hills. In a very real sense it is the crossroads of the world and particularly of the Pacific Basin with which the destiny of America will be increasingly involved. No better spot could have been selected for a bold experiment in the genius of democratic living within the framework of religious faith.

The Fellowship Church of All Peoples in San Francisco was originally projected as a neighborhood venture in interracial religious fellowship. The plan for its organization and development was proposed a little more than a year ago by Dr. Alfred G. Fisk, Professor of Philosophy at San Francisco State College. The church as such came into being the second Sunday in December 1943, and its first name was the Neighborhood Church. Support for the venture was given by the Presbyterian Church, U.S.A., in whose fellowship Dr. Fisk is an active clergyman.

The idea of an interracial church has been part of the thinking of many groups in this country, and it is a dream which has haunted me for ten years. The first contemporary effort toward establishing such a church was made in Philadelphia in 1936, when an interracial committee of the American Friends Service Committee launched a Fellowship Church there.[3] It held monthly meetings during the winter months, at alternating Negro and white churches.

All those sharing responsibilities for the particular service were taken from the Negro and white groups. Usually Negro and white local pastors took the worship and the responsibility of presiding. The guest preacher was either Negro or white. The idea was not to establish a regular church in the community but rather to give a genuine testimony in the field of group relations. From Philadelphia, the idea has spread to other cities in the East.

The original idea of the Fellowship Church in San Francisco was different at one major point from the eastern movement: it was projected as a permanent full-time church located in a building, with a Negro and a white clergyman serving as co-pastors. Dr. Fisk has been the white co-pastor since the beginning. I came West in July of 1944 to join him. The plan for a Neighborhood Church was somewhat broadened and the name Fellowship Church of All Peoples established instead. The Church is a creative experiment in interracial and intercultural communion, deriving its inspiration from a spiritual interpretation of the meaning of life and the dignity of man. In faith and genius it is specifically Christian. Its membership commitment recognizes and undertakes to implement the conviction that the God of life and the God of religion are one and the same and that the normal relationship between men, therefore, is one of fellowship, understanding, and confidence rather than distrust, prejudice, and strife. The membership is open to any person willing to accept the commitment, to participate in its program, and to share in its responsibilities.

There are four kinds of membership: those who join bringing with them a letter from some other church, those who have never been a part of a church fellowship before, those who wish to be associated in this venture while maintaining their membership in their own church, and those living out of the city who wish to become national affiliates.

We think it important that an experiment of this kind should take place within the framework of historical Protestantism rather than as a movement outside the stream of the church. In this sense it may be regarded as a direct challenge to the policy of separatism and segregation in which all the historical Protestant denominations are involved.

The Fellowship Church is dedicated to seeking the answer to several crucial questions for Christianity and democracy. First, is it possible to establish islands of community or fellowship in a sea of religious and social strife, with any hope of their resolving the strife? Second, is it possible for an authentic interracial and intercultural church to develop—a church that will not be largely dominated by one particular group with some other group on the fringes? Third, is it possible for a Negro and white minister to share the leadership of such a church on the basis of their respective gifts rather than on the basis of their group affiliations? In other words, in any given venture of this sort will the Negroes tend to gravitate toward the Negro pastor for leadership and counsel, and white people gravitate toward the white pastor for these same services? Fourth, how fundamental, and of what kind, will be the opposition to the development of the idea in practice, both from ecclesiastical interests and other interests of the community?[4] What steps will be taken to neutralize its effect and to defeat its purpose? The work of the Church is too new yet for any conclusions to be valid. I can only indicate the kind of things we have been doing.

For about eight weeks during the summer of 1944, the Church conducted a Fellowship Camp. The program of participation was built around "adventures in friendship." Our purpose was to deepen the interests of the children in other nationalities and races, and feed this interest with authentic factual materials calculated to give them personal experience in appreciating some of the art, music, folkways, and group contributions of other cultures. The peoples studied included the American Indian, and Mexican, Filipino, Russian, Negro, Japanese, Jewish, and Chinese Americans. As far as our skills permitted, songs, stories, handicrafts, and worship materials were built entirely around the peoples studied. There were exhibits of large photographs of scenery and persons, posters, costumes, dolls in native dress. Once, during the period each particular group was studied, a flesh-and-blood member of that group visited the camp and talked intimately with the children about his cultural heritage. The most creative result of the weeks was the production of a series of watercolor drawings using as subjects those things the children had learned about the people. In the drawing class one day, several little Mexican, Anglo-Saxon, and Negro boys were looking at a large poster of Russian children. Presently one said, "There's a boy who looks like me." This remark was followed by the same expression from each boy present despite the fact that all the children in the picture were Russian.

There were occasional excursions to various parts of the city of special interest from the point of view of intercultural emphasis. For many of the children the far-famed Chinatown of San Francisco was visited for the first time. They were most excited to see the Chinese Post Office and Telephone Exchange. It was good also to see Bufano's statue of Sun Yat Sen,[5] who they had been told was a figure like the American George Washington.[6]

Another of our activities is a series of monthly Fellowship Dinners extending through the winter. The November dinner, first in the series, was designed primarily to point up the fellowship within the Church itself. Persons from three racial groups, in the preparations for the dinner, became much better acquainted as individuals. The after-dinner program that night featured a distinguished Chinese American soloist. The December dinner was in honor of the Filipino American community, with the program provided by the Filipino Community Church, whose members came as special guests. The *piece de resistance* of the meal was Filipino, and there was authentic music by gifted musicians and an illuminating lecture by a Filipino woman on the life of women in the Philippines. The Monday night adult craft group of the Church had prepared the decorations, which gave those attending some feel of life in the Islands themselves. The January dinner had as its special point of emphasis the home-coming of the Japanese Americans to San Francisco, with those who had returned by that time guests of honor. The dinners are conceived as a psychological attack on the barriers that tend to separate Americans from each other.

A new development in religious experience has been the monthly Twilight Hours, projected as a means for inspiring group worship through art appreciation. Thus far, music, poetry, and drama have been employed. The Christmas Twilight Hour presented a series of Living Madonna Types in tableaux.[7] The representatives included persons of American Indian, Anglo-Saxon, Negro, Filipino, Mexican, Korean, Chinese, Russian, Italian, Armenian, and Japanese American extraction. Light for each scene was focused on the particular "Madonna face," draped in "native" materials, in most instances using authentic headpieces representing the cultural backgrounds. Appropriate music created an international atmosphere. The result was not only beautiful but made for awareness that the Madonna conception is universal, as wide as the family of man.

The development of such an intercultural-interracial fellowship program is still only in process. We are experimenting with standing committees to give each person in the membership opportunity to express himself at those points which will give him fullest and most satisfactory participation. A reading room is being established in which there will be available the significant journals of opinion and other publications issued by various cultural and racial groups in the country. The national membership includes service men who are located all over the world, many persons from academic circles, churchmen, and several persons carrying major responsibilities in government.

It is too early to evaluate the significance of the venture. If in every community in the United States an experiment such as ours could be undertaken, the Church itself would once again set in motion those spiritual processes which gave to it its original impetus and power. The ideal may develop in various ways that are indigenous to the community in which it is unfolded. To those of us who have dreamed of it for years, it represents an authentic growing edge for far-reaching social change in making possible communities of friendly men in a world grown gray with suffering and hate.

Common Ground 5 (Spring 1945): 29–31.

NOTES

1. *Common Ground,* published from 1940 to 1949 and edited by Louis Adamic (1898–1951), was dedicated to promoting ethnic and racial diversity and equality.

2. HT, "Interracial Church in San Francisco," *Social Action* 11, no. 2 (February 1945): 27–28. Thurman's article was part of a special issue devoted to "Significant Intercultural

and Interracial Experiments," published by the Council for Social Action of the Congregational Christian Churches.

3. For Fellowship Church in Philadelphia, see the biographical essay in the current volume.

4. For a similar set of questions, see To Paul Robeson, 21 April 1944, printed in the current volume.

5. Beniamino Benvenuto Bufano (1898–1970) was a famous sculptor and activist. Although he was known for his statues of St. Francis of Assisi, his sculpture in St. Mary's Square of the Chinese revolutionary Sun Yat-Sen is a San Francisco landmark.

6. Alfred Fisk would also write about the intercultural workshop at the Fellowship Church in *Common Ground,* though somewhat more elliptically and without mentioning it by name. See Fisk, "Stereotypes in Intercultural Education."

7. This was a continuation of a practice that Thurman had started at Howard University. See *PHWT,* 2:xxxiii–xxxiv; HT, *Footprints,* 26–28.

❧ To Thomas B. Foster

25 May 1945
[*San Francisco, Calif.*]

From 25 April to 26 June 1945 San Francisco hosted delegations from fifty nations and many nongovernmental organizations at the United Nations Conference on International Organizations (UNCIO), the founding conference of the United Nations. The Thurmans basked in the attention that the conference gave their city and church. Sue Bailey Thurman was the certified press representative to the conference from the Aframerican Woman's Journal *and wrote a series of articles about the conference for the* Chicago Defender.[1] *The Fellowship Church was able to sponsor talks by visiting dignitaries,[2] including W. E. B. Du Bois, Mordecai Wyatt Johnson, and Rayford Logan,[3] and held a dinner for the Negro press covering the conference.*

Dear Dr. Foster:

1.

Two very important offers were made by the Fellowship Church to the community of San Francisco. At our regular Sunday morning service, President Mordecai W. Johnson was the guest preacher before the largest congregation that we have ever had. This was on April 29. In the afternoon of May 6, at 3:30 we presented Dr. W.E.B. DuBois in a Public Lecture on "World Peace and the Darker Peoples." This lecture was presented through the facilities of the First Congregational Church at Post and Mason Streets. There were in attendance more than 700 people. We prepared for special distribution at that time a new prospectus of the Fellowship Church. We are enclosing several. The cost of presenting Dr. DuBois was defrayed by the special fund given to the Fellowship Church by the Congregation Emmanuel sometime ago.[4]

2.

The other important item was a dinner in honor of the Negro Press who are covering the Conference for their reading public. This dinner was held on May 11 in the Dining Hall of the Westside Christian Church. There were more than 125 people present. The press representatives were from the Afro-American published in Baltimore, the Pittsburgh Courier in Pittsburgh, the Chicago Defender in Chicago, and the Kansas Call of Kansas City. This was an experience of great significance, because it [several words are *illegible*] an opportunity to become directly acquainted with some of the persons whose pens are doing a great deal toward molding the public opinions of one-tenth of our population.[5]

3.

I have been able to secure a gift of $900 from a friend in the East[6] toward the salary of a young lady[7] whose work will be of an intercultural-religious nature among the children of the community. She has worked with us as a volunteer for a year and now that she has completed her formal training, is available for full-time employment. I am asking a local Foundation[8] to match the $900 so that we can start her on a salary of $1,600 with a margin of $200 for equipment. This means that if we are able to get a place in which to work some basic things may begin happening among the children, both in their religious education and in their intercultural development.

I expect to leave for my vacation on June 10th, returning by July 10th. This means that I shall not have a formal report to make for the month of June. For that reason I am enclosing the two vouchers for May and June.
Sincerely yours,
Howard Thurman

Dr. Thomas B. Foster
Board of National Missions
Presbyterian Church in the U.S.A.
New York, N.Y.
cc: Dr. Clyde Smith
P. S.-We are out of vouchers at the present time, so only one can be enclosed.

TLc. FC

NOTES

1. Sue Bailey Thurman's articles in the *Chicago Defender* include "'Dress Circle' Affords Best View of Conference," 19 May 1945; "View of Confab's 'Dress Circle' Big Peace Factor," 26 May 1945; "Feminine Personalities Brighten Frisco Parley," 2 June 1945; and "'Dress Circle' Affairs Highlighted Parley," 16 June 1945. The articles were meant to provide a "women's view" of the conference focused on the nongovernmental organizations seated in the Dress Circle (the top balcony) of the War Memorial Opera House, including the various African American delegations.

2. Clarence Lorenzo Simpson (1896–1961), vice president of Liberia, 1944–1952 (and later Liberian ambassador to the United States and the United Kingdom), gave the Sunday sermon at the Fellowship Church on 27 May 1945. African American lawyer Hugh Macbeth (1884–1956), who had been a stalwart defender of Japanese Americans during the war, spoke on 3 June 1945.

3. Thurman's good friend Rayford Logan, of the Howard University Department of History, who was covering the conference for the *Pittsburgh Courier,* spoke at the Booker T. Washington Center on 20 May 1945 on "Race Minorities and the United Nations."

4. Du Bois gave the Fellowship Church a plug in a subsequent column on interracial churches on the West Coast: "In San Francisco Howard Thurman is co-pastor of a church which holds meetings of a high order of intelligence and is well-attended" (W. E. B. Du Bois, "The Winds of Time," *Chicago Defender,* 8 June 1946).

5. The meeting with the Negro press led to some favorable publicity for the Fellowship Church, as in this article by Ralph Mathews, "Watching the Big Parade," *Baltimore Afro-American,* 2 June 1945: "Dr. Thurman, working with a white pastor, is operating a church in which the race question has been abolished. The important thing is that the members are not cultists or fanatics, or screwballs—just plain everyday substantial citizens from all walks of life who believe in cooperation and practical Christianity. There are no mystic rites. Nobody thinks he's God, there are no angels and nobody pretends to be blessed with eternal life. This takes the stigma off of interracial mixing. The divisionists have cleverly perpetuated the idea in America that if white and colored work together politically, economically, or in religion they are members of the lunatic fringe. This keeps a lot of decent people in the same old rut. Dr. Thurman has proved that people can work together and still be both sane and respectable. I hope the idea spreads."

6. Mrs. Adele Levy, who gave Thurman nine hundred dollars from the Adele R. Levy Fund (From Adele R. Levy, 15 May 1945).

7. Heather Whitton.

8. Rosenberg Foundation.

❧ To Henry A. Myers

28 May 1945
[*San Francisco, Calif.*]

On 19 April 1945 Prof. Henry A. Myers[1] sent Thurman a copy of his latest book, Are Men Equal? An Inquiry into the Meaning of American Democracy.[2] *Myers's book set out a contrast between the egalitarian ideals of Jefferson and those of his many critics who believed that equality—between individuals, nations, or races—is an unworkable idea. The flood tide of the modern rejection of equality culminated in the totalitarian regimes of Europe and was still thriving in the American South. Thurman told Myers that his book was "the most stimulating and creative interpretation of democracy that I have ever read." Surely Myers's commitment to equality as the most fundamental tenet of democracy and his lambasting the racism of the white South contributed to that judgment. But*

Myers, coming from his lifelong interest in tragedy, also saw equality in a personal and experiential way that no doubt appealed to Thurman: "Only through loneliness and comradeship can one learn to accept others as his equals in ultimate value. Only after sharing sorrow and joy with others can one arrive at a tragic understanding that all men are subject to a common fate."[3]

Dear Dr. Myers,

There is an old saying that people erect their temples to their dead Gods because if the God is living they were so involved in trying to reproduce his life in themselves that there is very little time left for piling stone upon stone.[4] The analogy is not too apt in my case but it is true that since your volume came to me I have been so busy making the widest possible use of it that I have neglected to send a note of appreciation to you for sending it.

It is the most stimulating and creative interpretation of democracy that I have ever read. I am sure that my talking about it so much will have a direct result in the increase of sales. This is important, but secondary, in terms of the more significant fact that many people will read it if they buy it. I recommended it to Study Groups and to individuals. When I return in the late summer I shall get several copies to put on sale at the Church. You have done all of us a tremendous service at a critical moment in our history. Please accept my personal appreciation for the job that you have done as well as for your thoughtfulness in sending me a copy.

Indeed I do remember your visit to Howard University and the stimulating results of it.

I have taken the liberty to send a copy of a small volume of prose poems which I have recently published. You may be interested in the enclosed materials about the Church.

Thank you for your letter and the book.

Sincerely,

Howard Thurman

HT: am

Encl.

Dr. Henry Myers

Cornell University

Ithaca, New York

TLc. FC

NOTES

1. Henry Alonzo Myers (1906–55) was a professor of English and American studies at Cornell University. He was educated at Niagara University (B.A., 1929) and Cornell University

(Ph.D., 1933). Myers wrote several works of a philosophical bent, including *The Spinoza-Hegel Paradox: A Study of the Choice between Traditional Idealism and Systematic Pluralism* (Ithaca, N.Y.: Cornell University Press, 1944) and the posthumously published *Tragedy: A View of Life* (Ithaca, N.Y.: Cornell University Press, 1956), the culmination of a career-long effort to formulate a theory of tragedy.

2. Henry A. Myers, *Are Men Equal? An Inquiry into the Meaning of American Democracy* (New York: Putnam, 1945). Myers wrote in his note to Thurman: "In March 1941 [9 March] I came down to Howard University from Ithaca to speak on the subject of equality and found myself somewhat nervous at the last minute at the prospect of speaking in the Chapel. I often think of your kindness on that occasion . . . my talk has grown into a book . . . and I am hastening to send you a copy in remembrance of our meeting" (From Henry A. Myers, 19 April 1945).

3. Myers, *Are Men Equal?*, 61.

4. Thurman articulated this thought much earlier, in 1928. See *PHWT*, 1:141.

ॐ From Carl Murphy

28 June 1945
Baltimore, Md.

Carl Murphy,[1] editor of the Afro-American *newspapers,[2] asks Thurman if he thinks there is much that Americans can do for Africa, or if her advancement will come ultimately from a class of Africans leaving the continent to get education and then returning to help uplift the masses.*

Dr. Howard Thurman,
Howard University,
Washington, D.C.

Dear Dr. Thurman:

I am interested to know whether you think there is a great deal the average American can do for Africa? Of course we send experts like T. M. Campbell—agriculturists and scientists.

Isn't the main thing, however, that Africa has to send her young men abroad for education in the things she needs; that these people must go back, and, through elementary and grammar school education, lift the masses to the point where they will want and demand new and better products, better homes, better jobs, more money, better education, shoes and sandals?

Africans are, perhaps, the most retarded of the slow peoples, which I would rate in this order—Chinese, East Indians and then the Africans.

The Russians used to belong in that backward group but they have pulled themselves out. Perhaps as a result of this war, the Chinese may emerge. That will leave only the East Indians and the Africans to fight their way to a place in the sun.

How long do you think it will take?

Very truly yours,

[*signed*] Carl Murphy

Carl Murphy,

President.

cm/m

TLS. FC

NOTES

1. Carl Murphy (1889–1967) was an educator and a journalist. Born in Baltimore, Maryland, he earned degrees from Howard University (1911) and Harvard University (1913), and he attended the University of Jena in Berlin (1913). Between 1913 and 1918 he served as professor of German at Howard University. He joined the staff of the *Afro-American* in 1918 and became editor and publisher following his father's death in 1922.

2. The history of the *Afro-American* newspapers traces to 1893, when John Murphy, a former enslaved person, merged his one-page church publication with two other religious newspapers in Baltimore. By the time of his death in 1922, the *Afro-American* published five local editions, all along the Eastern Seaboard, and one national edition. The newspapers were among the widest circulated African American publications.

☙ To George M. Houser

17 July 1945

[*San Francisco, Calif.*]

Thurman sends a note to George Houser,[1] *executive secretary of the Congress of Racial Equality (CORE), stating his willingness to serve on the organization's advisory committee.*

Dear Mr. Houser,

I am sending this note to say that I shall be happy to serve as a member of the Advisory Committee of CORE. I have so many commitments that it will be impossible for me to attend meetings, but I shall be happy to help in any ways that are at my disposal. I think that the fundamental program to which CORE is dedicated is of primary importance, both for democracy and for Christianity.

Sincerely yours,

Howard Thurman

HT: am

Mr. George M. Houser

Executive Secretary
Congress of Racial Equality
7100 Kinsman Road
Cleveland 4, Ohio

                                                               TLc. FC

Note

   1. George M. Houser (1916–) is the son of Methodist missionaries. He spent his early years in the Philippine Islands, where he studied at Ling Nan University. He also attended the University of the Pacific and the University of Denver. Houser began his ministerial training at Union Theological Seminary, and while he was there he became a member of the Fellowship of Reconciliation and the War Resisters' League. In 1940 he became one of eight Union Theological Seminary students arrested and imprisoned for refusing to register for the draft. After his release, Houser moved to Chicago, where he and others, including James Farmer and Bernice Fischer, formed CORE.

✌ To Carl Murphy
17 July 1945
[*San Francisco, Calif.*]

Thurman responds to Murphy's query, outlining several steps that he believes Americans could take to help Africa.

Dear Mr. Murphy,

   Your letter[1] was forwarded to me from Howard University. As you may know, I am on the Coast for two years leave of absence from Howard, sharing in the establishing of an interracial, intercultural Church. You may be interested in the enclosed literature.

   I think there are several things that an average American can do for Africa.

   1. Accurate and informative material concerning Africa should be given the widest possible circulation, not only in the public press but through books and pamphlets, etc.
   2. Courses of study in colleges and high schools should be offered in the same way that courses are now given covering the social, political, and economic history of Europe.
   3. An inter-change of travelers and observers from this country to Africa.
   4. Scholarships for African students given on the precise conditions that the recipients will return to their particular country to give the widest possible range to their leadership in their own land.

These are some of the things that I think.
Sincerely yours,
Howard Thurman

HT: am

Mr. Carl Murphy

TLc. FC

Note

1. From Carl Murphy, 28 June 1945, printed in the current volume.

🖎 To Thomas B. Foster
18 July 1945
[*San Francisco, Calif.*]

Thurman sends a letter of resignation to Foster severing his official ties with the Board of National Missions. Prior to sending this letter, Thurman had two meetings with a Presbyterian official, Jacob A. Long, in which the incompatibility of Thurman's vision for the Fellowship Church with the vision of the Presbyterian Board of Missions was discussed extensively. Although for the time being the Fellowship Church would retain its Presbyterian affiliation, Thurman's "own sense of integrity" dictated that he stop drawing a salary from the Presbyterian Church.

My dear Dr. Foster,

I am sorry that I missed you in New York the other day. I was under the impression that you would be in the office during the entire month of June. I realize that I should have made a specific appointment, but my own schedule was too uncertain.

There are many things in connection with the Church and its development about which I wanted to talk with you. I am sorry that this was not possible.

The purpose of this letter is to give to you formally my resignation as an employee of the Board of National Missions of the Presbyterian Church, U.S.A. I would like this to be effective August 1st, or if it simplifies the matter of bookkeeping, July 1st. I have served in this relationship for one year, for I began my work in the Church July 15th. My relationship with your office and the persons there has been a rather happy experience. I am perfectly willing to continue sending a monthly letter to you about the development of the Church as I see it, but I do not wish for my salary to be carried as an item in the budget there.

Please know that this action on my part is a matter which has to do with my own sense of integrity, but should not be interpreted as having any bearing

either on the present or future relationship of the Fellowship Church and the
National Board of Missions of the Presbyterian Church. I am acting in my ca-
pacity as an individual, and I hope that this action of mine will not threaten in
any way the future of the Church here.
Sincerely,
Howard Thurman

HT:am
Dr. Thomas B. Foster
Board of National Missions
Presbyterian Church, U.S.A.
156 Fifth Avenue
New York 10, New York

                                                                    TLc. FC

🐎 From Jacob A. Long
10 August 1945
San Francisco, Calif.

*Jacob A. Long,[1] secretary of the Unit of City and Industrial Work of the Presbyte-
rian Church, U.S.A., explains how the denomination's vision for the Fellowship
Church differs from the experiment that Thurman and the congregation have
undertaken. While Long recognizes the interracial character of San Francisco, he
had assumed that it would be a neighborhood church for a community impacted
by an influx of new residents working in war industries. Before writing this letter,
Long met twice with Thurman; during their meetings the men concluded that
their visions for the Fellowship Church were incompatible and irreconcilable.[2]
Long was a vigorous proponent of a new, revitalized urban outreach in light of
the changing demographics of the nation's cities, including the burgeoning African American population. But the core of this strategy—neighborhood churches
serving local communities—clashed with Thurman's vision of the Fellowship
Church; he felt that the Presbyterians would turn the church into a less than
fully equal "mission church" and one that would shortly become overwhelmingly
African American. Long told Thurman that "it was our impression that while
this work [of the Fellowship Church] was to be interracial in character that the
primary function was to serve the immediate community in which the project was
located." This had never been Thurman's understanding of the church's mission,
and it was a position with which he strenuously disagreed. The same day that
Long wrote this letter to Thurman, he also wrote to another Presbyterian official,*

Thomas B. Foster, telling him that Thurman's salary subvention from the Presbyterian Church ended in June and that Fisk's was to end on 1 September.[3]

Dr. Howard Thurman,
1500 Post Street,
San Francisco, 9, California.

My dear Dr. Thurman:

Let me reply to your letter in which you request me to "write a memorandum to the church setting forth the purpose for which funds from the War Fund may be used" —

The portion of the Presbyterian War Time Service Funds appropriated to the Board of National Missions for administration is granted for varying projects in communities directly affected by the development of war industries. Included in this general category are the following types of projects for which grants have been made:

1. To strengthen the program of existing churches in communities affected by the influx of large numbers of people engaged in war industries.
2. For providing in new communities allocated to our denomination by comity agreement a Christian ministry including visitation, Christian Education, and provision for the public worship of God.
3. Cooperative efforts largely in government housing centers in which we work with one or more other denominations in accordance with a previously executed comity agreement.
4. For the support of industrial chaplains serving in war industry communities.
5. For a continuing ministry to displaced peoples (primarily Japanese and Japanese Americans).
6. Grants toward the erection of or purchase of buildings where needed as result of the influx of war workers.
7. Appropriations to the proper committees of the Home Missions Council and the Federal Council of Churches in America in connection with our interdenominational home mission work among war industry peoples.

It should be recalled that when the original appropriation was made for an interracial service in San Francisco including the appropriations made for the purchase of the Lutheran Church property on Geary Street, it was our impression that while this work was to be interracial in character that the primary function was to serve the immediate community in which the project was located. This would take in peoples of varying racial backgrounds although we realize that due to recent changes that community is today predominately Negro. Unfortunately your objective in the establishment of the Fellowship Church and that envisioned by the Board of Church Extension of the Presbytery of San Francisco, Dr. Smith its Executive, and myself as a National Board representative were not one and the same objective.

From all reports both from yourself and from other sources it would seem that little impression has been made upon the immediate community within whose bounds the work of Fellowship Church has been located. You will see therefore that it would be impossible if we are to maintain a clear conscience to continue to support the work of Fellowship Church out of War Industry Funds. Even were our Board able to make any further grants to this work it would have to come from sources other than War Industry Funds.

As indicated to you verbally, you will realize of course that if Fellowship Church is to be a completely independent organization we could not be justified in using Presbyterian National Missions Funds for that work. This is not to be construed as narrow denominationalism. Were we to support any one of the almost innumerable independent religious projects that have sprung up all over this county we would be establishing a precedent that we would be simply unable to follow. I regret that in the development of Fellowship Church it could not have been so organized that it would retain its community character and yet have affiliation with some one of the larger denominations. Or, if this could not be worked out satisfactorily an organization under the direction of the Home Missions Council might have been effected. This latter, of course, on the assumption that said Council would be interested in sponsoring the experiment.

I trust that this too lengthy letter may be helpful to you and will serve to give you in writing a sufficiently adequate statement of our position. I shall, of course, in accordance with your request addressed to our Mr. Foster, see that the grant toward your salary is quit.

I shall be glad to hear from time to time of the progress of the experiment in which many of us are most interested.

Cordially yours,

[*signed*] Jacob A. Long

Jacob A. Long, Secretary,

Unit of City & Industrial Work,

Board of National Missions,

Presbyterian Church, U. S. A.

JAL: mms

TLS.

Notes

1. Jacob A. Long (1896–1970), a Philadelphia native, was a building contractor before his call to the ministry and his study at Princeton Theological Seminary. After serving a con-

gregation in suburban Philadelphia, he worked on the staff of the Presbytery of Northern Philadelphia and in 1942 became secretary of the Unit of City and Industrial Work of the Presbyterian National Board of Missions. In 1944 he founded the Presbyterian Institute of Industrial Relations, with branches in Chicago and San Francisco. In 1949 Long became professor of Christian ethics at the San Francisco Theological Seminary in San Anselmo. For Long's innovative work with the Institute of Industrial Relations, see Richard P. Poethig, "Marshall Logan Scott and the Presbyterian Institute of Industrial Relations," *Journal of Presbyterian History* 83, no. 1 (Spring/Summer 2005): 5–23.

2. Jacob A. Long to Thomas B. Foster, 10 August 1945, Department of History, Presbyterian Church, U.S.A., Philadelphia.

3. Ibid.

To Jacob A. Long
21 August 1945
[*San Francisco, Calif.*]

In this letter Thurman tells Long that the Fellowship Church intends to become an independent church and to end its affiliation with the Presbyterians. Given that the Presbyterian Church's salary subvention for Thurman had terminated in June and was set to end for Fisk on 1 September, as well as the disagreement between Thurman and the Presbyterians regarding the mission of the Fellowship Church, this letter severing ties appears to have been a mere formality. Thurman tells Long that when the interracial character of the Fellowship Church has been firmly established, he intends for it to become more of a local community church.

Dear Dr. Long,

I am sending this formal letter on behalf of the Fellowship Church to express our very deep appreciation to the Board of National Missions, the Presbyterian Church, to you, and to all the other persons who made possible the opportunities for our coming into being and for the sustaining support that has been given. It is difficult for any of us to measure the significance of this account of faith and prompting of the opportunity that made possible the birth of Fellowship Church. I want you to know that our appreciation is concrete and enthusiastic.

By formal vote of the congregation, it was decided that we should try to work out a plan of organization and a program in keeping with the trend that has developed with our experimentation. At the present time this means that we shall try to become self-supporting and clarify our sense of direction and program. When this is accomplished it is our desire to seek cooperation with the Presbyterian Church and other Denominations at the points where this is possible on the basis of our program, our activities, and our organizational structure.

As I stated to you in my conversation, I shall be happy to continue sending the monthly letter, giving an account of our development and our progress. I am sure that it is the will of the congregation, as it certainly is my own desire, that in all future publicity we give full credit and recognition to the Presbyterian Church for sponsoring and pioneering us.

One further word needs to be said. In time, we shall do a specifically community job. This will come when internally the interracial and intercultural core of our Church is so well established that we can do a community job without our becoming a racial Church.

I want you to know personally that the magnificent and prophetic spirit with which God has blessed you will continue to be a source of inspiration to us all.

Sincerely yours,

Howard Thurman

HT: am

Dr. Jacob Long
Board of National Missions
of Presbyterian Church, USA
156 Fifth Avenue
New York 10, New York

Cc Dr. Chester Green
      228 McAllister Street
      San Francisco 2, California

TLc. FC

🖎 To Madaline Johnson
27 August 1945
[*San Francisco, Calif.*]

Thurman writes a playful note to his sister[1] encouraging her to stay in touch with his daughter Olive, who was beginning her college career at Vassar.

Dear Madeline,

Why in the world don't you write somebody sometime, about anything? Olive left for Vassar last night and because of our financial situation it was not possible for her to come by Washington. Drop her a note and let her know when you can come up to Poughkeepsie to see her or when you can meet her in New York. She will be desperately lonely and will need your comfort.

We have been forced to buy a home out here in order to have a decent place to live. We move September 1st and our new address will be 2660 California

Street. It may be that you will receive a letter from us in the Poorhouse or the County Jail because we are not able to pay our debts. Until that time you can relax. When have you written Mama? Am I or am I not to look forward to having a niece or nephew? Tell that doggone stork I don't want any foolishness out of him. Monk Watson[2] is out here.

Everybody sends love.
Hastily,
Howard Thurman

Mrs. Madeline Johnson
1234 Girard Street SE
Washington, D.C.

NOTES

1. Madaline Thurman Johnson (1907?–84) studied music at Oberlin College and the Oberlin Conservatory of Music (A.B., 1929; A.M., 1932). She accompanied the Thurmans to Europe in 1935 and stayed with the Thurman children in Geneva, Switzerland, while their parents toured India. Madaline studied eurythmics at the Dalcroze School in Geneva, studied at the Dalcroze School in New York City in the mid-1940s, and worked as a music teacher. She later moved to California, where she would remain for the rest of her life. Madaline suffered from major depression as an adult, a condition that required periodic hospitalization. A brief marriage to John B. Johnson ended in separation or divorce. Thurman wrote of her that "my relationship with Madaline was very close" (*WHAH*, 253). She and her family (such as Thurman in his autobiography) usually (but not invariably) spelled her first name as "Madaline" and the editors have used this spelling throughout, except in direct quotations.

2. Melvin H. Watson was fondly called "Monk."

᠀ FROM GEORGE E. HAYNES
19 SEPTEMBER 1945
PORTLAND, ORE.

In September 1945 George Edmund Haynes,[1] who had been the executive secretary for the Department of Race Relations for the Federal Council of Churches of Christ in America for over two decades, had recently returned from a trip to northern California, which he hailed in a press release as "An Interracial Experiment Station." After describing a number of interracial projects, he wrote that "probably the outstanding event . . . in the Bay Area, is the Church for the Fellowship of All Peoples," and he praised its impact on a wide range of ethnic and racial communities and on "church leaders, for whom this is a living challenge to their past policies and practices."[2] However, Haynes, a moderate to conservative in his religious views, is uncomfortable with the deemphasis of the divinity of Jesus in the latest version of the Commitment.

Dear Howard:

I hope this statement you so kindly lent me gets back in time. I am venturing one comment: Your former statement of the Commitment seems to me to have one point where the change is not an improvement—"Jesus of Nazareth"—from "Jesus Christ" or "the Christ." There are doubtless many points on both sides, but since you started with that, I wonder whether the change will not be a disadvantage when all the pros and cons are weighed. Your adventure has tremendous possibilities and may God's blessing attend you and Sue and all who are joining with your undertaking.

Yours faithfully

[signed] George Edmund

ALS.

NOTES

1. George Edmund Haynes (1880–1960) was an economist, an educator, and a social worker. Born in Pine Bluff, Arkansas, Haynes earned a B.A. from Fisk University in 1903 and an M.A. from Yale University in 1904. From 1910 to 1917 he was the first executive secretary of the National Urban League. In 1912 he became the first African American to receive a Ph.D. from Columbia University; his doctorate was in economics. After four years on the faculty of Fisk, in 1921 he became the first executive secretary of the Department of Race Relations for the Federal Council of the Churches of Christ in America, and he retained that position until 1946.

2. George Edmund Haynes, "An Interracial Experiment Station." This was a press release of a column dated 5 October 1945 and was part of a series entitled "Along the Interracial Front." The series was reprinted in a number of black newspapers, including the *New York Age.*

🦢 To A. L. ROBERTS

19 SEPTEMBER 1945

[*San Francisco, Calif.*]

Although Thurman had not met Albert Cleage (and would never do so), he had heard many opinions of his personality and capabilities, and he knew well of his ability to stir up controversy. Asked by A. L. Roberts,[1] a Presbyterian official, to offer some comments about Cleage, Thurman offers a cautious summary of what he has heard.

Dear Mr. Roberts,

Please pardon my delay in replying to the inquiry concerning Mr. Cleage. Unfortunately, I do not know Mr. Cleage personally. He had left the Fellowship

Church before I arrived. Mrs. Thurman had met him when she came out to visit the Church in April before we were on the job in July. Sifting through all of the various things that have come to my attention about Mr. Cleage's work here, the following items seem to be accurate:

1. He is an able, keenly intelligent and brilliant preacher.
2. He is a deeply religious man with a full social problem orientation. He believes, it seems, in making this fact clearly known at all times. He is critical of the way in which the Church has given its approval again and again to race and social discrimination within its fellowship and the silence which is obtained in the presence of some of the gross injustices in the social order.
3. It is not my impression that he does not believe profoundly in the Church and its mission, but rather that it should fulfill its mission more specifically in areas of social conflict.
4. Because of these things it is easy to see that the persons who come in contact with him will feel very strongly one way or the other about him.

I am sending this letter with impressions gathered in the absence of any personal contact with the man himself.

I hope that it covers the questions involved.

Sincerely yours,

Howard Thurman

HT: am

Rev. A. L. Roberts

156 Fifth Avenue

New York 10, New York

TLc. FC

NOTE

1. Alcwyn Lloyd Roberts, a 1931 graduate of Ohio Wesleyan University, joined the staff of the Board of National Missions of the Presbyterian Church in the United States in 1934 and remained until 1953, when he became general director of the Commission on General Christian Education of the National Council of Churches in the U.S.A.

To Frank T. Wilson

27 November 1945

[*San Francisco, Calif.*]

Thurman, still feeling that he "must go back to Howard, for next year," tries to arrange for his old friend Frank Wilson to take over the copastorship of the Fellowship Church during the time he plans to be in Washington, D.C. Nothing

*came of this plan, and within a few months Thurman would, reluctantly, resign
his position as Howard's dean of chapel.*

Dear Frank,

I have wanted to write you many times but complications out here have been
of such that almost no time has been available for correspondence. Our Church has
formally completed its permanent organization and a re-statement of purpose and
position. This is a fascinating story all by itself which I shall tell you in January.

When the Board meets next month I shall present to them the proposition
about which I talked with you last summer. In short, I shall propose your name
to them with the suggestion that you be invited to become the co-pastor of Fellowship Church for a period of six months or a year while I am back East. There
is the slim possibility that the Church and the University might agree to some
division of my time each year. All of this will be discussed at the meeting next
month. Then the proposal will be made to the University. In any event I feel that
I must go back to Howard, for next year. We have a home out here so that you
and the family would be assured of a nice place in which to live.

The Eucalyptus Press is publishing a small volume of 35 to 40 pages dealing
with meditations of certain Negro spirituals.[1] I shall send you a copy if it is off
the press before I come East. I have not done Stuart's[2] chapter yet but hope to
get it worked out in short order.[3] I'm working on another chapter for the Pacific
Coast Theological Society on "The Christian Ethic and the New Fascism."[4]

I think of you often and trust that the exigencies of this year will not take
a too heavy toll on you spiritually and physically. You must know that you are
constantly buoyed up both by my affection and my prayers. There is no greater
inspiration to me than the strength that comes from your own friendship.

Love to everybody.
Sincerely,
Howard Thurman

Dean Frank T. Wilson
Lincoln University
Chester County, Pennsylvania

TLc.

Notes

1. HT, *Deep River.*

2. William Stuart Nelson.

3. HT, "Judgment and Hope in the Christian Message," in *The Christian Way in Race
Relations,* edited by William Stuart Nelson (New York: Harper, 1948), 229–35, printed in the
current volume.

4. Published as HT, "The Fascist Masquerade," printed in the current volume.

⁊ "The Fascist Masquerade"
1946

On 11 August 1945, Thurman received a letter from Randolph Crump Miller asking him to contribute an essay on the role of "human relations" (which primarily meant race relations) for a volume on "The Christian rediscovery of resistance and resource."[1] Thurman agreed to write the essay[2] but rather than the broad and sweeping essay on global race relations that Miller wanted, he structured it around a single topical and controversial political theme, called in the essay "the basis of fascism as it has developed in America during the past decade." Its overtly political nature marks a striking departure from almost everything Thurman had written to that point, as he recognized. "I have just completed an essay on the 'Fascist Masquerade' which marks my venturing into a brand new field of creative expression," Thurman wrote his friend, Ruth Smith, in April 1946. "I shall let you know what becomes of it."[3]

The essay speaks to the critical importance of political questions for Thurman in the months after the jarring end of World War II. Like many liberals and progressives such as former vice president Henry A. Wallace,[4] Thurman was deeply worried about a revived American fascism, and whether the postwar era would usher in a new period of reaction and racial retreat, as happened after World War I.[5] And like most of his peers, he thought that if there were to be a new American fascism, it would arise, and be nurtured, in the South. (His friend, William Stuart Nelson, would later write in 1948 that "the totalitarian political mind of the South is accompanied by an explicit fascism toward the Negro."[6])

Thurman's essay ultimately transcends its specific political context, making an argument about the general failings of the church. Antisemitism has flourished, he argues, because hatred of Jews has been sanctioned by, and is part of official doctrine in, most established Christian denominations. The traditional notions of salvation, making invidious distinctions between the "saved" and the "unsaved" provide the underlying theological basis for all racism. If the revolutionary implications of the Christian ethic are not carried out, Thurman argues, the pseudo-revolutionary allure of fascism will appeal to many malleable minds. As long as the authentic message of Christianity is ignored, pseudo-revolutionary quasi-fascists will use Christian trappings to lure the unwary. Only by returning Christianity to its true meaning can the fascist masquerade be exposed for the fraud that it is. Like few other of his writings it demonstrates Thurman's deep immersion in the political battles of his time, and his recognition that the Church's ultimate success or failure as an ongoing spiritual enterprise in large part rested on its ability to defeat the challenge posed by "The Fascist Masquerade."

The purpose of this chapter is to analyze the basis of fascism as it has developed in America during the last decade and to delineate the challenge which it presents to the Church in its commitment to an ethic which is at once revolutionary and compelling. Special attention will be given to the aspect of fascism which lends itself to the release of unrestrained passions in human nature, causing the focusing of hatreds on individuals because of race, class or religion.

1. DEFINITION OF THE TERM

There is a medley of confusion as to what fascism is and how it operates in modern life. The indiscriminate use of the term reveals that it is a "catchall" to describe individuals or movements with whom we are in disagreement or concerning whom we wish to express contempt and disapproval. It is of critical importance to define our terms as accurately as possible not only so as to make clear what it is with which we are dealing, but also, so as better to discriminate between the doctrine itself and its concomitants, as we point up the true basis of the challenge which it represents.

Mussolini[7] states:

> The foundation of Fascism is the conception of the State, its character, its duty, and its aim. Fascism conceives of the State as an absolute, in comparison with which all individuals or groups are relative, only to be conceived of in their relation to the State.... The Fascist State is itself conscious, and has itself a will and a personality—thus it may be called the "ethic State."*[8]

Further he says:

> The State is a spiritual and moral force in itself, since its political, juridical, and economic organization of the nation is a concrete thing.†

Concerning liberty under fascism, Mussolini affirms:

> The Fascist State organizes the nation, but leaves a sufficient margin of liberty to the individual; the latter is deprived of all *useless* and possibly

---

*Benito Mussolini, *The Political and Social Doctrine of Fascism* (New York: Carnegie Endowment for International Peace, 1935), p. 13.

†Ibid., p.13.

harmful freedom, but retains what is essential; the deciding power in this question cannot be the individual, but the State alone!*

As to the place of religion under the fascist state, he avers:

> Fascism respects the God of the ascetics, the saints, the heroes, and equally, God as he is perceived and worshipped by simple people.[†]

Ralph Robey[9] writing in *Newsweek*, July 30, 1945, on "One Way to Identify a Fascist" defines fascism strictly in terms of economic theory.

> The distinguishing characteristic of Fascism is complete government control and direction of all production and marketing, but this is accomplished, not through government ownership of the factors of production, but within the framework of a system of private property. And such complete government control and direction of what private owners shall do with their property is the only distinguishable characteristic of Fascism. It has no ideological relation to whether it persecutes the Jews, any more than Communism is philosophically related to the liquidation of the Kukoa[10] or the denial of the freedom of religion. In other words both Communism and Fascism in their basic concepts, are strictly economic, and the curious quirks and antisocial traits that those who run the system may develop have no necessary relation to the underlying philosophy of such systems. To be specific, a person may be arrogantly intolerant and simply unspeakable in his attitude toward other races, and still not be a Fascist.

The War Department in a statement issued to members of the armed services under date of March 24, 1945, defines fascism more inclusively than as that which has to do only with the economic life:

> Fascism is government by the few and for the few. The objective is seizure and control of the economic, political, social and cultural life of the state. Why? The democratic way of life interferes with their methods and desire for: (1) conducting business; (2) living with their fellow-men; (3) having the final say in matters concerning others as well as themselves. The basic principles of democracy stand in the way of their desires; hence—democracy must go! Anyone who is not a member of their inner gang has to do what he's told. They permit no civil liberties, no equality before law. . . . They maintain themselves in power by use of force combined with propaganda based on primitive ideas of "blood" and "race," by skillful manipulation of fear and hate and by false promise of security.[‡11]

---

*Ibid., p. 14. Italics mine.
[†]Ibid., p. 16.
[‡]Quoted in *Time Bomb*, by E.A. Piller (New York: Arco Publishing Company, 1945), p. 12 ff.

Further, in the statement the War Department gives "Three Ways to Spot U.S. Fascists":

> Fascists in America may differ slightly from fascists in other countries but there are a number of attitudes and practices that they have in common. Following are three. Every person who has one of them is not necessarily fascist. But he is in a mental state that lends itself to the acceptance of fascist aims.
>
> 1. Pitting of religious, racial, and economic groups against one another in order to break down national unity is a device of the "divide and conquer" technique used by Hitler to gain power in Germany and in other countries. With slight variations, to suit local conditions, fascists everywhere have used this Hitler method. In many countries, anti-Semitism (hatred of Jews) is a dominant device of fascism. In the United States, native fascists have often been anti-Catholic, anti-Jew, anti-Negro, anti-labor, anti-foreign-born. In South America, the native fascists use the same scapegoats except that they substitute anti-Protestantism for anti-Catholicism.
>
> Interwoven with the "master race" theory of fascism is a well-planned "hate campaign" against minority races, religions, and other groups. To suit their particular needs and aims, fascists will use any one or a combination of such groups as a convenient scapegoat.
>
> 2. Fascism cannot tolerate such religious and ethical concepts as the "brotherhood of man." Fascists deny the need for international cooperation. These ideas contradict the fascist theory of the "master race." The brotherhood of man implies that all people—regardless of color, race, creed, or nationality—have rights. International cooperation, as expressed in the Dumbarton Oaks proposals, runs counter to the fascist program of war and world domination. . . . Right now our native fascists are spreading anti-British, anti-Soviet, anti-French, and anti-United Nations propaganda. . . .
>
> 3. It is accurate to call a member of a communist party a "communist." For short, he is often called a "Red." Indiscriminate pinning of the label "Red" on people and proposals which one opposes is a common political device. It is a favorite trick of native as well as foreign fascists. Many fascists make the spurious claim that the world has but two choices—either fascism or communism, and they label as "communist" everyone who refuses to support them. By attacking our free enterprise, capitalist democracy, and by denying the effectiveness of our way of life they hope to trap many people.*

The basic concept

The three definitions have certain elements in common. In the first place, they agree that under fascism the State is not only central but supreme in its com-

---

*Ibid.

plete control and direction of the economic life. In the second place, the individual is always and in all circumstances subordinate to the State, and, what is more important, the significance of the individual is defined by the State. In the third place, the State is epitomized by that individual or those individuals who are able to speak on behalf of, or themselves to *personify,* the State. This means that the fate of the average citizen is in the hands of those who have taken onto themselves, or have had delegated to them, the power of the State. The peculiar character of such power or powers is that social responsibility that extends beyond the defined categories is reduced to zero. Such power has its own ethic, etiquette and ritual. Its major function is to keep itself fat and strong. To those who "belong," who satisfy the demands of the etiquette, there is given a priority in terms of privilege, security and status. This fact becomes the basis of a generalization as to equality and inequality. Therefore, it seems clear to the writer that fascism in the very nature of the case has to be committed to a fundamental inequality among men. This theory of inequality, a derivative from the basic fascist doctrine of the State, becomes a doctrine of inequality from which there flows a bloody stream of racism and terror. As Jacques Maritain says, writing in *Commonweal,* January 4, 1943, "Racist law is nothing but a secondary ideological process which aims at justifying a primitive criminal passion and freeing it of all restraint."[12]

This concomitant of fascism, namely, racism is significant because it gives to any current doctrine of racial inequality or superiority a new dimension of dignity and respectability. Obviously, this particular concomitant of fascism is not new; it merely provides a fresh banner under which the same old warriors may parade. American soil is particularly fertile for this new facade. Already in solution in American mores and folkways there is the compound that recognizes, for all practical purposes, the basic "inequality" among men. This is evident in many of our statutes, our customs and in our social structure. It is not meant to ignore the ideal of equality as set forth in the Declaration of Independence or in the Constitution, for that matter; nevertheless, in Church and State any notion of equality that extends into the realm of rights has been constantly most bitterly fought and challenged. In Jefferson's original draft of the Declaration of Independence he makes the connection between equality and private rights unmistakable: "We hold these truths to be sacred and undeniable: that all men are created equal and independent; that from that equal creation they derive *rights* inherent and *inalienable.* . . ." In a further revision he says, "We hold these truths to be self-evident; that all men are created equal; that they are endowed by their creator with equal rights, some of which are inalienable and inherent. . . ." We draw the line at equality of rights.[13]

We must hold steadily in mind the fact that an important part of the menace of fascism as defined here is its property as a catalyst. It crystallizes moods, attitudes and fears that are already in solution. Our country has a long and ig-noble record in the Vigilante tradition. It is true, therefore, that in a wide variety of instances hate organizations spring up, flourish for a season, disappear, and reappear in another form without any formal ideological recognition of the existence of classical fascism, either as a political or economic doctrine.

2. American Examples

It is now in order to examine a sampling of certain contemporary movements in American life in the light of our discussion up to this point. To get one's hands on facts relative to the so-called fascist movements in American life re-quires far more time and skill than were available to the writer. There is an abundance of materials on the various movements and individuals who were operating under the general classification of fifth columnists[14] and whose re-cords are now a part of public property. But these activities were largely directed against the government to hinder the successful prosecution of the war. For the most part they did not represent a direct challenge to the Church. But there are other movements that draw largely upon the church-going people and whose leadership defines their position within the framework of Christianity despite the fact that their appeal is to criminal passion, freed of all restraints. Again it is difficult to know accurately the numerical strength of these move-ments because of the inaccessibility of records and the potent tendency to exag-gerate their strength and power.

I have chosen three organizations because they represent three different lines of attack: one is avowedly political in intent; one is definitely antilabor; one is woven into the social fabric of American life, walking upright under its own name and title. They present the challenge most clearly, and they crystallize attitudes that are ever present in American life, in the homes, the churches and the schools. They make the obvious appeal at the level of the average American's fear and mistrust of minorities, and do this in the name of authentic Christian-ity, patriotism or Americanism.

Christian American[15]

The headquarters of the Christian American is Houston, Texas. The choice of the name is very significant. To call itself Christian is to announce to the un-wary that the organization is not in opposition to, or is not to be contrasted with, the Church and that for which the Church stands. It is to symbolize in the popular mind the highest form of idealism and righteousness of which millions can conceive. It is a magic password. To be American is to appeal to pride of country, and, what is more important, pride of section that gives to the average individual a certain sense of separateness, making for a special category of dis-tinctiveness owing to the accident of national origin. To be a Christian Ameri-can is to be but a little less than an angel.

The Christian American came into national prominence by its sponsorship of the "Right to Work" Amendment.[16] According to E. A. Piller in *Time Bomb* this group was actively at work on behalf of such an amendment in the State of Arkansas during 1943. On March 4, 1943, in the State Legislature of Arkansas there was a bitter debate on this particular amendment which resulted in its passage of the House by a vote of 62 to 29. This bill seeks to destroy unionism by abolishing the closed shop. Coupled with this is the "anti-violence in strikes" law which places a heavy penalty on any union that is accused of threatening to use violence against any individual in its effort to keep a man from going to work to break a strike. The Legislature of Louisiana passed the following resolution relative to the Christian Americans:

> WHEREAS Hitler has boasted and emphatically stated that it will be a simple matter in our country to set capital against labor, Negro against white, Catholic against Protestant, and Christian against Jew,
>
> WHEREAS recently in the Heidelberg Hotel, a public headquarters was announced for an association known as Christian American, which association is domiciled and located without the state of Louisiana, and has boasted and advertised the fact that they have come into the state of Louisiana for the purpose of seeing that our legislature would enact laws, which laws would create animosity, antagonism and unrest among the employers and employees of this state and interfere with the harmonious relations of capital and labor in this state,
>
> BE IT RESOLVED that the legislature of Louisiana do request the FBI and the Dies Committee to investigate the source of revenue, general activities, and personnel and the objectives of The Christian American Association of Houston, Texas, to ascertain and determine whether or not said association is conducting subversive activities in the United States.*

The *New Republic* for July 20, 1942, quotes a spokesman for the Christian American as saying:

> White men and women have been forced into unions with black African apes whom they must call "brother" or lose their cards and their jobs.[17]

The sinister aspect of this movement is in the fact that it is backed by a group of skillful men who are adequately financed and who recognize that under the guise of their basic theory of inequality they can appeal to the fears and the frustrations of the rank and file of Americans without restraint. One of the sponsors of the Christian Americans, according to Harold Preece in a signed article in the August, 1946, issue of *NOW*,[18] is the man who started the "Eleanor

*Ibid., p. 54.

Club"[19] rumor about secret revolutionary organizations of Negroes, sponsored by Mrs. Roosevelt. The organization is fascist because it is concerned with the control of production by a select few in whom all powers are resident and who in turn can determine arbitrarily the priority of privilege. This is the basis of the attack on collective bargaining; the appeal to racial and religious prejudice is the masquerade.

The Nationalists

During the summer of 1945, Eugene Segal, Scripps-Howard Staff Writer, published for his paper a series of articles under the general title, "The Nationalists Unmasked."[20] Mr. Segal begins his first article, appearing in the San Francisco *News* under date of July 16 with these significant words:

> Capitalizing on prejudice and discontent, the Nationalists party of former U.S. Senator Robert R. Reynolds[21] is seeking to weld the dissident groups of the country into an organization which he hopes will become a dominant force in American politics.

Mr. Segal states that the methods used are those employed by Hitler in his rise to power.

> They have started a campaign of infiltrating the ranks of groups which may have a real or fancied grievance against the federal administration and its policies.
> They have taken over a Midwest farmers' organization. Their henchmen are moving into key spots in labor unions. They have formed two veterans organizations. . . .
> They have started a youth movement. . . . The Nationalists have won the affiliation of certain church groups and have the backing of the president of an old established theological seminary, who preaches a hate creed in the school's official publication.
> The Nationalists are anti-Negro, anti-Semitic, and anti-Catholic, and anti-foreigner as situations demand, but apparently they will accept any convenient alliance.

Mr. Segal lists Robert Reynolds as leader of the movement, and sharing his leadership "is Gerald L. K. Smith,[22] rabble rouser, founder of the 'American First Party'[23] and idol of various 'mothers' groups."[24] Continuing the listing of personnel the reporter says:

> Around Reynolds and Smith moves a circle of satellites, such as Carl Mote, of Indianapolis, part owner of two small public utilities and president of the National Farmers Guild;[25] Mrs. Lyrl Clark Van Hyning of Chicago, head of We, the Mothers Mobilize for America, Inc.;[26] the Rev. Gerald

Winrod, popularly known as the "Jay-hawk Nazi" of Wichita, Kansas;[27] and the Rev. Harvey Springer, a Denver rabble-rouser who is called the Cowboy Preacher.[28]

In the article under date of July 20, 1945, there is an account of a convention held at the Englewood Baptist Tabernacle, Englewood, Colorado, January 6, 1944. There were 350 young people and pastors present, representing churches in seven Midwestern states. At that time an organization was formed of the "Christian Youth of America," with national headquarters in Englewood. Segal says, "A call was issued to 'all Christian youth organizations in America to join us in a united front against the flood of communism in the land.' One Kenneth Goff was named Chairman of the Youth Movement."

Writing about Goff, Segal says, "He formerly was on the advisory staff of the American Youth Congress and a member of the National Executive Committee of the Young Communists League. . . ." After coming into the Nationalist camp he wrote for Gerald L. K. Smith's *The Cross and Flag.*[29]

The movement, crystallized at Englewood, has taken in the youth group of the "Rev. Bob Parr's Church in Detroit and organizations in Buffalo, Los Angeles, and other cities." They distribute tracts among high school students and servicemen.

The Ku Klux Clan

The story of the Klan is familiar to any person conversant with the history of the country. The modern Klan[30] presents a critical challenge to the Church because, as do the other organizations mentioned, it bases its position within the framework of Protestant Christianity. Occasionally one is reminded through a news item or the public press that the organization, often in new dress, is a potent factor in American life. To set before us clearly how sharply defined is the issue which the Klan represents I quote at some length from the stated ideals of the organization:[31]

1. This is a White Man's Organization, exalting the Caucasian Race and teaching the doctrine of White Supremacy. . . .
2. This is a Gentile Organization, and as such has as its mission the interpretation of the highest ideals of the White, Gentile peoples. . . .
3. It is an American Organization, and we do restrict membership to native-born American citizens. . . .
4. It is a Protestant Organization. Membership is restricted to those who accept the tenets of true Christianity, which is essentially Protestant. We maintain and contend that it is the inalienable right of Protestants to have their own distinctive organization. We can say to the world without apology, and say truly, that our forefathers founded this as a Protestant country and

that it is our purpose to re-establish and maintain it as such. While we will energetically maintain and proclaim the principles of Protestantism, we will also maintain the principles of religious liberty as essential to the life and progress of this nation, and we will vigorously oppose all efforts to rob the American people of this right.

RACIAL IDEALS

1. We stand for White Supremacy. Distinction among the races is not accidental but designed. This is clearly brought out in the one book that tells authoritatively of the origin of the races. This distinction is not incidental, but is of the vastest import and indicates the wisdom of the divine mind. It is not temporary but is as abiding as the ages that have not yet ceased to roll. The supremacy of the White Race must be maintained, or be overwhelmed by the rising tide of color.

2. We must keep this a White Man's Country. Only by doing this can we be faithful to the foundations laid by our forefathers.

   a. This Republic was established by White Men.

   b. It was established for White Men.

   c. Our forefathers never intended that it should fall into the hands of an inferior race.

   d. Every effort to wrest from White Men the management of its affairs in order to transfer it to the control of blacks or any other color, or to permit them to share in its control, is an invasion of our sacred constitutional prerogatives and a violation of divinely established laws.

   e. We would not rob the colored population of their rights, but we demand that they respect the rights of the White Race in whose country they are permitted to reside.

   f. Purity of the white blood must be maintained.

CHRISTIAN IDEALS

1. We magnify the Bible—as the basis of our Constitution, the foundation of our government, the source of our laws, the sheet-anchor of our liberties, the most practical guide of right living, and the source of all true wisdom.

2. We teach the worship of God. For we have in mind the divine command, "Thou shalt worship the Lord thy God."

3. We honor the Christ, as the Klansman's only criterion of character. And we seek at His hands that cleansing from sin and impurity, which only He can give.

4. We believe that the highest expression of life is in service and in sacrifice for that which is right, that selfishness can have no place in a true Klansman's life and character; but that he must be moved by unselfish motives,

such as characterized our Lord the Christ and moved Him to the highest service and the supreme sacrifice for that which was right.*

There are many other groups following the same general line to be found in various parts of the country. In the winter of 1945 Allan L. Swim,[32] Scripps-Howard Staff Writer, published a series which he called "Merchants of Hate." One may find them in the morgue of any Scripps-Howard newspaper. The point of the series is to make clear that hate is a commodity for which there seems to be a ready market in American life. And one of the best counters is patriotism and religion—as witness the well-known activities of Father Coughlin[33] and Father Terminiello.[34]

There is something ominous about the totalitarian notion, whether it is in a small, loosely thought-out hate organization, a large powerful organization like the Roman Catholic Church or an institution of higher learning. The matters of dedication, motivation and intent are in a sense irrelevant. The point is that given the acceptance of totalitarian theory, there is no other-than-self reference by which character may be determined. At any particular moment the organization may have social weal as its aim universally extended, but it stands ever in candidacy to be manipulated in terms of all that stands against social weal. As a case in point let us give a passing glance to technocracy.[35]

William Russell writing in the *Annals of the American Academy of Political and Social Science* for July, 1935,[36] says:

> The present situation is different from any that has gone before, because modern business enterprise for the first time is able to bring under one central control all necessary raw materials and fuel resources, the mechanism of transports and communication, the mechanism of fabrication and assembly of parts to produce the completed article of consumption.
>
> But say the technocrats, we can save this society. We can give everybody an equal treatment. We will provide everybody . . . with everything he could buy if they had an income of $20,000 a year (Howard Scott) or $4,000 (Goodwin Watson).[37] . . . We will determine, by techniques, that we have mastered, the capacity for consumption of the American people, and we will plan production to match it. . . . We will tell people what work they are to do, and provide everybody with everything that is good for them to have. . . . There will be no depressions etc. . . .

Totalitarianism is a threat to, and the enemy of, liberty ever—it makes no difference whether the totalitarianism is benign or wicked, its power works inevitably towards the absolute and it cannot survive with any competitor. Watch for the signs in your community, whatever may be the banner or the masquerade.

*From a photostatic copy appearing in *NOW* (semi-monthly) First half, August, 1945.

3. The Challenge to the Church

The appeal of fascism

The appeal of the organizations outlined and similar ones that are functioning sectionally and nationally, is in the fact that they meet a need in the lives of the people that is not being met by the Church. They provide three very important things for their followers:

1. Integrated action. There is a crisis dramatized which calls for action on the part of the individual. A sense of urgency is communicated and an assignment made well within the ability of the devotee. This was exemplified, for instance, in Father Coughlin's platoon scheme of organization. Each person was urged to gather around him twenty-five others to read *Social Justice,* to listen to the weekly radio address, to contact congressmen, etc. A job needs to be done; the job is defined within the ability of even the simplest person; there is a short distance from center to circumference. The strategy of this appeal is that when a person acts on an idea, he secures his stake in it.

2. They inspire a willingness to sacrifice. Here again, the extent of sacrifice is carefully charted. In most instances, it means a willingness to be counted on the "right" side even at the expense of separating one's self from former friends and even relatives. I have seen the Klan in western New York separate families, set brother against brother—in one instance it actually caused men who "belonged" to walk down a certain side of the street so as not to pass by the door of a particular shop owner who opposed the organization.[38] In their most fanatical demands, even life may be forfeited. Here the symbol of the State as being the Highest Loyalty and the individual having his status defined only in reference to it, is on the point.

3. A sense of collective destiny that gives to the individual a validity and a profound sense of significance. The individual counts. He may be poor, ignorant, hungry or unemployed, but he is caught up in a movement that promises his redemption from these things if he joins with others in removing the obstacles which are the obvious enemies of his security.

Further, these organizations exploit the active and latent prejudices that the average American has against non-white races on the one hand and against Jewish people on the other. They make it possible for a creative rationalization to provide a cloak for group hatreds which can be objectified as true Christianity or true Americanism. In other words, they provide for a legitimatizing of sadistic and demoniacal impulses of which, under normal circumstances, they might be ashamed. To appeal to anti-Negro sentiment in many sections, communities and among many groups is a "natural" for the would-be demagogue. It is sure fire.

The Failings of the Church

The fact that these appeals are made in the name of Christianity is itself most revealing. It is no answer to the fact to say that it is a false interpretation of Christianity. Such a reply merely etches more clearly than ever that the Church has done a wretched job in making clear what the Teaching is, either about God or man. It is to the utter condemnation of the Church that large groups of believers all over the United States have stood, and, at present, stand on the side of a theory of inequality among men that causes the Church to practice in its own body some of the most vicious forms of racial prejudice. It often affirms separateness solely on the basis of race, which separateness it insists upon in worship, in organization and even in its graveyards. I remember hearing a Mohammedan say in an address before a young people's society in a Christian church, "Allah laughs aloud in his Mohammedan heaven when he beholds the Christian spectacle of the First Baptist Church White and the First Baptist Church Colored."

The bitter truth is that the Church has permitted the various hate-inspired groups in our common life to establish squatter's rights in the minds of believers because there has been no adequate teaching of the meaning of the faith in terms of human dignity and human worth. The same default is evident in the effectiveness of the appeal to anti-Semitism. The responsibility of the Church to teach Christianity and at the same time not to aid and abet anti-Semitism seems to the writer to be morally inescapable. The roots of anti-Semitism are much deeper than this statement would indicate. In essence, anti-Semitism is a form of protest arising from the fundamental rejection in our culture of the ground of Christian Ethics which is to be found in the prophets of Israel. The presence of the Jew becomes the unconscious symbol of that rejection and the attack on him is the measure of the rejection of the ethic. Anti-Semitism is the result of the battle against the ethic.

The crux of the issue for the Church is this: The Church is irrevocably committed to a revolutionary ethic, but it tends to implement the ethic by means that are short of that which is revolutionary. The dilemma is to try to implement a revolutionary ethic without resorting to revolutionary means. The appeal of the fascist is in terms of that which is revolutionary by the standards to which the appeal is made. This was certainly true of fascism in Italy, in Germany, and is implicit in our own varieties. It was on the basis of the revolutionary character of fascism that it was the object of concern, observation and in some instances, indictment on the part of the federal government during the war that has just ended. The Church must be as revolutionary in practice as it is in the genius of the ethic to which it is dedicated.

One of the things that weakens the positive stand of the Church with reference to the position of inequality of men in fascism is the curious social result of the doctrine of salvation. The very categories of "the saved" and "the sinners" load the scales on the side of inequality in intrinsic worth. For whatever reasons, whether by election or by self-surrender, a man comes into "the fold" he at once is seen by himself as being in a basic category of superiority. This is the psychological fact—there is a desert and a sea that separates him from his fellows who do not "belong." There is just a step between this and the straight practice of the doctrine of superiority due to the fact of special grouping or racial origin. If I am saved by grace, it is without merit, ultimately, on my part, but the operation of a divine Power whose purposes are beyond my apprehension or understanding. Unless that state is for all and enjoyed by all potentially, there is no fundamental difference between the spiritual arrogance arising from my state of grace and the spiritual arrogance arising from the incident of race. The issue is softened, somewhat, if my state of grace is on the basis of some measure of personal merit and achievement.

If it be true that God is the source of life, then it follows that each individual is grounded in God in a direct and primary manner. There can be no valid distinction between the God of religion on the one hand and the God of life on the other. The task of the Church then must include the conquest of the world, and in the fulfillment of that task it can rely upon the guarantee of God in whom life and all of the great potentials of mind and spirit are grounded. Such a position establishes the infinite worth of all individuals and denies that for which fascism stands in its regard for persons. The degree to which the Church stands for less marks the measure of its tacit support of such theories of life as fascism affirms. This places a great teaching responsibility upon the Church to give a growing, dynamic and intelligent content to the faith which it inspires men to have in Jesus Christ as Master and Lord.

Further Reading

Bryson, Lyman. *Which Way America? Communism—Fascism—Democracy.* New York: The Macmillan Company, 1939.

Dennis, Lawrence. *The Coming American Fascism.* New York: Harper & Brothers, 1936.

Mussolini, Benito. *The Political and Social Doctrine of Fascism.* New York: Carnegie Endowment for International Peace, 1935.

Piller, E. A. *Time Bomb.* New York: Arco Publishing Company, 1945.

Swing, Raymond Gram. *Forerunners of American Fascism.* New York: J. Messner Inc., 1935.

Thomas, Norman M. *After the New Deal, What?* New York: The Macmillan Company, 1936.

NOTES

1. From Randolph Crump Miller, 11 August 1945. Randolph Crump Miller (1910–2002), a native of California, received his Ph.D. from Yale in 1935. After teaching at the Church Divinity School of the Pacific, in Berkeley, in 1952 he joined the faculty of the Yale Divinity School, eventually becoming the Horace Bushnell Professor of Christian Nurture. His many books include *The Clue to Christian Education* (New York: Scribners, 1950).

2. To Randolph Crump Miller, 14 August 1945.

3. To Ruth Smith, 17 April 1946

4. In 1944 Vice President Henry Wallace defined a fascist as "one whose lust for money or power is combined with such an intolerance toward those of other parties, races, classes, religions, cultures, regions or nations as to make him ruthless in his use of deceit or violence to attain his ends." With "several million Fascists in the United States," Wallace claimed that one of the great challenges facing the United States after the war would be the fight against fascism "within the United States itself." Henry A. Wallace, "Wallace Defines 'American Fascism,'" *New York Times Magazine*, 9 April 1944. For liberal and progressive fear of domestic fascism in the 1940s, see Leo P. Ribuffo, *The Old Christian Right: The Protestant Far Right from the Great Depression to the Cold War* (Philadelphia: Temple University Press, 1983), 178–224.

5. See Thurman's reflections on African Americans and World War I in "A 'Native Son' Speaks," in *PHWT*, 2:246–252.

6. William Stuart Nelson, "Critical Issues in America's Race Relations Today," in *The Christian Way in Race Relations*, edited by William Stuart Nelson (New York: Harper, 1948), 11.

7. Benito Mussolini and Beniamino de Ruti, *The Political and Social Doctrine of Fascism* (Worcester, Mass.: Carnegie Endowment for International Peace, 1935), 13. Mussolini's contribution to this volume consisted of an authorized translation of his article on "Fascism" from the 1932 edition of the *Encyclopedia Italiana*. Benito Mussolini (1883–1945) became premier of Italy in 1922 as the leader of the National Fascist Party of Italy. He transformed his position into a dictatorship dedicated to the principles of fascism. He initiated anti-Semitic measures in the late 1930s and created a formal alliance with Nazi Germany in 1939. Deposed in 1943, he led a Nazi-backed puppet state in the north of Italy until his capture and execution in 1945.

8. Thurman's footnotes are reproduced from the text.

9. Ralph Robey (1899–1972) was an economist and journalist, a conservative critic of the New Deal, and the author of *Roosevelt versus Recovery* (New York: Harper, 1934). From 1941 to 1953 he was chief economist of the National Association of Manufacturers. His definition of fascism implicitly labeled the New Deal and its continuation under President Harry Truman a fascist economic system.

10. Thurman probably meant Kulaks.

11. As Thurman's footnote indicates, this quotation is from E. A. Piller, *Time Bomb* (New York: Arco Press, 1945). Emanuel A. Piller (1907–85) was a popular journalist who also wrote *World Aflame: The Russian-American War of 1950* (New York: Dial Press, 1947).

12. Jacques Maritain, "Racist Law and the True Meaning of Racism," *Commonweal* 38 (4 June 1943): 181–88. (Thurman gave an incorrect date.) Jacques Maritain (1882–1973) was the leading Roman Catholic philosopher of the twentieth century and a prime figure in the revival of the reputation of the medieval scholastic philosopher St. Thomas Aquinas. Maritain spent World War II in the United States, in exile from his native France. He was an

outspoken critic of anti-Semitism and the role of the Roman Catholic Church in perpetuating it. His condemnation of racism included strictures against racially discriminatory practices in the United States.

13. Thomas Jefferson's first completed draft of the Declaration of Independence, known as the "Rough Draft," was finished in late June 1776. The first version cited by Thurman is the original wording of the Rough Draft, and the second version cited is the corrected version. However, the corrected version has its own corrections and cross outs. It reads, "they are endowed by their creator with ~~equal rights, some of which are~~ inherent and inalienable rights." In the final version, adopted on 4 July 1776, this became "they are endowed by their creator with certain unalienable rights."

14. "Fifth column" is a term that dates to the Spanish Civil War, when Emilio Mola, a loyalist general, said that "there are four columns marching on Madrid, and the fifth shall arise from within the city." An extensive pro-Nazi and profascist "fifth column" in the United States was widely believed to exist in the war years, its presence touted in a number of sensational, but exaggerated, accounts such as John Roy Carlson, *Under Cover: My Four Years in the Nazi Underground of America* (New York: Dutton, 1943), and numerous spy films on Nazi saboteurs. Although there were Nazi spies in the United States, especially in the period before the Japanese attack on Pearl Harbor, there was no organized "fifth column."

15. Almost all of the information on the Christian American was taken from the account in Piller, *Time Bomb.*

16. "Right to work" laws prohibited a closed shop in which all persons employed by a business were required to join a union and pay union dues. There was agitation for "right to work" legislation after the passage of the Wagner Act in 1935. The Taft-Hartley Act of 1947 made the passage of "right to work" laws much easier, and they were adopted in most southern states.

17. B. Herndon, "Pappy's Dixie Fascists," *New Republic,* 20 July 1942. The "Pappy" in the title was Wilbert Lee "Pappy" O'Daniel (1890–1969), the dominant political force behind the creation of the Christian American. O'Daniel was a colorful figure who turned his promotional talents as a radio personality into a political career. He was elected governor of Texas in 1938 and 1940, and served in the U.S. Senate from 1941 to 1949, after defeating the up-and-coming congressman Lyndon Baines Johnson in a famously close and controversial election. O'Daniel was increasingly reactionary in his later years.

18. For *NOW* see Cleage, "Fellowship Church: Adventure in Racial Understanding," n. 1, in the current volume.

19. During World War II a rumor started, primarily among white southerners, that black women had organized "Eleanor Clubs" to rally against whites, taking their inspiration from the strong civil rights agenda of First Lady Eleanor Roosevelt. There is no evidence that any Eleanor Clubs were ever founded. With the supposed slogan of "a white woman in every kitchen by 1943" or some variant thereof, the Eleanor Club rumor speaks to the increasing vocational mobility of southern black women during the war years and their growing inclination to reject domestic work as overly servile. See Howard Odum, *Race and Rumors of Race: Challenge to the American Crisis* (Chapel Hill: University of North Carolina Press, 1943), 73–89. Contrary to Thurman's suggestion here, it seems unlikely that the Eleanor Club rumor had a single progenitor.

20. Eugene Segal was a longtime newspaper reporter in Cleveland.

21. Robert Reynolds (1884–1963), a U.S. senator from North Carolina (1932–45), announced the formation of the Nationalist Party, with an isolationist and segregationist

ideology, in early January 1945 ("A 'Nationalist' Party Launched by Reynolds," *Chicago Tribune*, 8 January 1945). Reynolds claimed that he was no longer a Democrat because that party had been "taken over by the Communists, reds, and pinks." For the Nationalist Party, see Piller, *Time Bomb*, 102–8.

22. Gerald Lyman Kenneth Smith (1898–1976) was a Disciples of Christ minister and a prominent follower of Huey Long. After Long's assassination, Smith took up leadership of one of the strands of Long's Share Our Wealth movement, turning it in a strongly segregationist and anti-Semitic direction, and he would be one of the country's most prominent far-right agitators for several decades after World War II.

23. The America First Party, not connected to the isolationist America First Committee that had opposed American preparedness before the attack on Pearl Harbor, was founded by Smith in 1944. As the party's presidential candidate, Smith received fewer than two thousand votes. See Ribuffo, *Old Christian Right*, 174–75.

24. There were a number of isolationist and anti-Semitic groups formed during World War II that claimed to represent the interests of mothers opposed to their sons fighting in a sanguinary Jewish-inspired war, among them: We, the Mothers; National Blue Star Mothers; and Mothers and Daughters United. See Piller, "The 'Mom' Menace," in Piller, *Time Bomb*, 109–20; and Glen Jeansonne, *Women of the Far Right: The Mother's Movement in World War II* (Chicago: University of Chicago Press, 1996).

25. Carl Henry Mote (1884–1946) was the editor of the anti-Semitic and isolationist magazine *America Preferred* and the author of *The New Deal Goose Step* (New York: D. Ryerson, 1939). See Piller, *Time Bomb*, 81, 135.

26. See Piller, *Time Bomb*, 117–18. Lyrl Clark Van Hyning (1892–1973) founded We, the Mothers Mobilize for America in 1941. It was probably the largest of the far-right, isolationist, anti-Semitic women's organizations founded during World War II.

27. Gerald Burton Winrod (1900–1957) was a fundamentalist preacher whose magazine disseminated his isolationist, anti–New Deal, and anti-Semitic ideals. He came close to winning the Republican nomination for the U.S. Senate from Kansas in 1938.

28. Harvey Springer (1907–66) was a conservative fundamentalist minister who preached in cowboy attire.

29. *The Cross and the Flag* was published from 1942, when it was founded by Smith, until 1977, one year after Smith's death.

30. Thurman was writing here of the second incarnation of the Ku Klux Klan, which was founded in 1915 and had its heyday in the 1920s but rapidly declined thereafter. In response to the growth of the civil rights movement, there would be a second revival of the Klan in the postwar decades, especially in the southern states. The Klan, especially in this third phase, was not a single organization but a group of loosely connected organizations sharing a common ideology.

31. This is reprinted from *NOW*, first half of August 1945.

32. Allan LaVerne Swim (1911–81) was a Scripps-Howard reporter who in 1947 became publicity director for the CIO and editor of the *CIO News;* he helped to take the CIO in a more anticommunist direction. After 1951 he spent the rest of his career as a publicist and publication director for overseas U.S. agencies.

33. Charles Coughlin (1898–1976), an ordained Roman Catholic priest, became one of the most popular radio preachers of his day. At first a supporter of Franklin Roosevelt, by the mid-1930s he was a strong opponent of the New Deal and increasingly prone to making anti-Semitic statements. The Detroit diocese forced him to abandon his radio broadcasts in 1942.

34. Arthur Terminiello (1908–?) was a Roman Catholic priest and an associate of both Charles Coughlin and Gerald L. K. Smith. He is best known for an incident in Chicago on 7 February 1946, when he was arrested after a fracas caused by an anti-Semitic and racist speech he had just delivered. He was indicted by Chicago authorities for inciting a riot, and the case eventually reached the U.S. Supreme Court, where in the important First Amendment case *Terminiello v. Chicago*, 337 US 1 (1949), the court ruled in Terminiello's favor. See Ribuffo, *Old Christian Right,* 216–24.

35. Technocracy was a movement founded by Howard Scott (1890–1970) that maintained that rule by engineers in a scientifically organized society is a superior form of organization to either capitalism or communism. At the height of its popularity in the mid-1930s, its advocacy of highly centralized control and its skepticism of democracy led some of its critics to compare it to fascism.

36. William F. Russell, "So Conceived and So Dedicated," *Annals of the American Academy of Political and Social Science* 180 (July 1935): 168–75.

37. Goodwin Watson (1899–1976) was a psychologist who in 1936 founded the Society for the Psychological Study of Social Issues. During the mid-1930s he had connections to technocracy.

38. For Thurman's experiences with the Klan while a student at Rochester Theological Seminary, see *WHAH*, 49–50.

To Friends at Howard
JANUARY 1946
SAN FRANCISCO, CALIF.

Thurman uses the occasion of a letter on the Feast of the Epiphany—always a happy and joyous time in the Thurman household[1]—to update his friends at Howard on the Fellowship Church. He provides information on some of the members of the church and relates some of the busy doings at the church during the United Nations conference in San Francisco.

Dear Friends at Howard,

We are grateful for the tradition that the Wise Men did not reach Bethlehem until 12 nights after Christmas. For this gives us opportunity this year to survive the most hectic holiday of an entire lifetime, and still get off a communication to our friends far away, calculated to reach them by midnight of January 6th. So, in the old spirit we send you our warmest greeting for the "Twelfth Night," and offer with it a second brief account of life for us in San Francisco, relating the most recent developments at the Church for the Fellowship of All Peoples.

The church in philosophy and practice, moves into a second year of widening influence in the total life of the community. Being no longer an "experiment" or a "venture," it has become a growing spiritual and intellectual experience in interracial and intercultural communion for the city. In the last report to you, we spoke at length of the program of worship, and intercultural education, having less to say about the personnel of local membership initiating it. If the church has affected the society of the metropolis of the west coast in any vital ways, it is because of the subtle and overt performance of men and women here, in various occupations and positions who have devoted their energies to the propagation of the "Fellowship Church Ideal."

Sunday evening, December 30th, we had a farewell reception for the Chairman of the Church Board, a Canadian, who leaves the city soon for another assignment, after having served here in the Far Eastern Division of the British Consulate. He was 20 years in China and Japan and so could make a remarkable contribution with his brilliant use of the languages and sympathetic knowledge and understanding of the peoples.[2] The international import of his contribution has not been more far-reaching than that of the Chairman of the Intercultural Committee of Fellowship Church, who during the entire war period was script traffic director in the broadcast-division of the Office of War Information. With her previous background as an art Gallery director, she has been the spearhead for the development of a comprehensive intercultural program for 1945–46.[3]

In the field of social work, the influence of the Church increases. Perhaps our most distinguished member, the Director of the International Institute of San Francisco, received the Annual Koshland Award (1945), for an outstanding contribution to the Field of Social Work in the state of California. Several members of her staff are members, as well as the Editor of San Francisco Teachers' Journal—the official organ of teacher[s] of the city system. The former president of the P.T.A. of the State College Practice School and Chairman of its program committee is Chairman of the Women's Department of Fellowship Church;[4] likewise the Principal of the Adult Education and Americanization School for this district, and the two teachers in charge of the Girl Scout program of the most heterogeneous school in the city, are among our most creative and active members. In the world of civic affairs, the regional secretary of the NAACP[5] as well as the local president of the same organization,[6] are here, together with the president of the San Francisco Japanese American Citizen's League,[7] the former and latter serving on the Church Board of Directors.

Others in various walks of life—shipyard workers, clerks, advertising engineers, day laborers, tradesmen, a mortician, who has worked with considerable success at putting his ideals into practice in one of the most exclusive mortuaries in the city, and a public health officer employed in a Shipyard Housing project, who drives away at the ideal of having the diverse racial groups there, share life harmoniously and completely in living facilities in work and in recreation. This is an earnest of the spirit of the membership.

Taking a backward glance at last spring, the UNCIO[8] brought out several of our most interested and devoted national associate members. President and

Mrs. Johnson were here and Mrs. Harper Sibley, wife of the former President of the U.S. Chamber of Commerce, who was chosen most distinguished "mother" in the U.S. in 1945 and is the current President of the National Council of Church Women. Mrs. Mary McLeod Bethune also worshipped with us during this time. President Johnson addressed a warm and enthusiastic Fellowship Church audience, made up of friends and well wishers of the University of the West.[9]

We presented Dr. Dubois at an afternoon Vesper during the Conference,[10] and His Excellency, Vice President Simpson of Liberia who spoke at an 11 o'clock Service. Also a special dinner was tendered the members of the National Negro Press assigned to the U.N.C.I.O. Rayford Logan was among them, as Adviser to the "Pittsburg Courier" on Foreign Affairs.[11]

A description of the Summer Intercultural Junior Workshop is included. Dean Watson[12] came out from Howard to visit us during that time and joined the director in conducting the children around to study the international statues in the city's parks. Camille Nickerson came lately to present a recital of Creole Music, the first of our Intercultural concerts for the 1945–46 season.[13] She made a tremendous impression. We do not know of an artist receiving such generous criticism from the San Francisco and Stanford University Press, for such a distinctive cultural contribution. Miss Nickerson was followed in December by Professor Chang Shu-Chi, the distinguished artist from Chungking, who painted the famous "Two Hundred Doves of Peace," presented by his government to the White House, a few years ago.[14] There will be recitals of American Negro and Scandinavian songs, in February, and in March.

And now for us. H.T. has brought "Deep River" off the press, the second volume the Eucalyptus Press of Mills College has published for him since he has been out here.[15] He comes to Howard for the Week in Prayer in January. He preaches at Vassar, the University of Chicago, at Yale, and the Cathedral of St. John the Divine, in New York, during the trip East.

S.B.T. begins the second year as member of the Board of Directors chairing the first World Fellowship Committee that the Central YWCA has had. San Francisco's 65 nationality and all-inclusive racial groups are here to be drawn into the All-Association Program. She was elected delegate for 1946 from the Board of the International Institute to the Social and Recreation Council of the Community Chest, and will continue as Co- chairman of the program committee of the P.T.A. of the State College Practice School (program enclosed) until the end of this year. A report of this program was presented in Washington, at a joint Conference of the Children's Bureau and the National Congress of Parents and Teachers. She will begin editing "Fellowship Trails,"[16] a new quarterly of Fellowship Church activities, due off the press, January 30th.

Our older daughter, Olive was granted a scholarship for study in the Drama Department at Vassar. If you ever see her down Washington, give her an extra handclasp for her parents. Especially those of you who have shown such kindness through the years in your continuing interest in the well being of all the children of the University community.

Anne has been admitted to the San Francisco Conservatory of Music, and such has been her state of health out here that she is growing tall like the Californians!

We hope the Wise Men will leave their richest gifts for you—Joy . . . Peace—and a New Year bringing the Fulfillment of your dreams.
Sincerely yours,
The Howard Thurmans
2660 California Street
San Francisco 15
California

TL.

Notes

1. See To Reinhold Niebuhr, 28 December 1934, in *PHWT,* 1:229–30.

2. Hugh MacMillan (1892–) was a longtime missionary in Taiwan and the author of *Till Now in Formosa* (Taipei: English and Canadian Presbyterian Mission, 1953) and other works on his missionary years. He first met Thurman at a retreat in Pawling, New York, in 1925 (HT, *Footprints,* 51).

3. See Bailey, "One World in Embryo."

4. The director of the intercultural workshop was Heather Whitton.

5. Probably Noah Webster Griffin (1896–1974), a Florida native and a 1923 graduate of Fisk University. He served as the principal of high schools in Tallahassee and St. Petersburg before becoming executive secretary of the Florida State Teachers Association. After losing a fight (and his job) in an effort to equalize the salaries of black and white teachers in Florida, he became a field secretary for the NAACP, serving in San Francisco from 1944 to 1950.

6. Joseph James.

7. Dave Tatsuno (1913–2006) was born Masaharu Tatsuno and was raised in San Francisco; he was a 1936 graduate of the University of California at Berkeley. Ambitions of becoming a Presbyterian minister were derailed by his entering a family business, a Japanese-oriented department store. During World War II he was interned in the Topaz Relocation Center, near Salt Lake City. The haunting home movies he took during the war (in a smuggled camera) were later compiled into a much acclaimed film, *Topaz* (1945).

8. The United National Conference on International Organizations, the founding conference of the United Nations.

9. That is, Howard graduates on the West Coast.

10. Du Bois would later write of the Fellowship Church that "Howard Thurman is co-pastor of a church which holds meetings of a high order of intelligence and is well attended" (W. E. B. Du Bois, "The Winds of Time," *Chicago Defender,* 8 June 1946).

11. For Logan's role at the San Francisco conference, see Kenneth Robert Janken, *Rayford W. Logan and the Dilemma of the African-American Intellectual* (Amherst: University of Massachusetts Press, 1993), 175–80.

12. Melvin Watson.

13. Camille Nickerson (1888–1982), a native of New Orleans, graduated from the Oberlin Conservatory and had a career as a performer, collector, and composer of Louisiana Creole music. She taught at Howard University from 1923 to 1962.

14. Chang Shu-chi (1900–1957), a watercolorist best known for his pictures of flowers and birds, came to California during the war years as part of a goodwill mission on the part of Chiang Kai-shek. He was the father of the historian Gordon Chang.

15. HT, *Deep River*.

16. This evidently did not materialize, but in 1949 the Fellowship Church started to publish a magazine, the *Growing Edge*, at first monthly and subsequently quarterly.

❧ From John Scott Everton

9 January 1946
Grinnell, Iowa

John Scott Everton,[1] dean of chapel at Grinnell College, writes to Thurman for suggestions of potential black candidates for enrollment at Grinnell, which had been without any black students for several years. The dearth of blacks at Grinnell reflected the fact that through the end of World War II, many private northern colleges had few black students. This included even those, such as Grinnell, that purported to support liberal and progressive views. Grinnell had admitted its first black student in 1863 and had its first black graduate in 1879. The factors that acted against matriculation of blacks at Grinnell were common to liberal arts colleges elsewhere: an underlying ambivalence toward black students on the part of some of the faculty and student body; location in an area that had a minuscule African American population; and the reluctance of blacks to attend a school where few, if any, blacks were enrolled. Thurman took Everton's overtures seriously. He wrote to his old teacher and financial adviser Lorimer Milton on 12 March 1946 suggesting that a prospective applicant consider Grinnell College for her education.[2] An exchange program with Hampton Institute was started in 1947. Until it was disbanded in 1954, seventeen Hampton students each spent a semester at Grinnell.[3]

Dean Howard Thurman
Howard University
Washington, D.C.

Dear Dean Thurman:

Since returning to Grinnell from India, I have heard many expressions of appreciation for your visit here last year. I know that both students and faculty will welcome the opportunity of hearing you again, and I am wondering whether

1946 Fellowship Church tea dinner honoring Camille Nickerson, an interpreter of New Orleans Creole music and a Howard University faculty member (from left: Samantha Lee, Virginia Scardigli, Nona Moffatt, Annie Clo Watson, Mari Ogaski, Sue Bailey Thurman, Camille Nickerson, Mrs. Clyde Bonner). From the Bailey Thurman Family Papers; Manuscript, Archives, and Rare Book Library, Emory University.

there would be any possibility of your coming to us in the school year 1946–47. If you do have available dates in that year, either for a college church service on a Sunday or for a convocation during the week, I would be very glad to hear from you and to make definite arrangements.

Grinnell College has not had any Negro students for the past several years. There are some of us here who are concerned about this and who believe that we should have both Negro and white students at Grinnell. It is recognized that after this lapse of some years it would be very important to have the very best representatives of the Negro race on campus if there is to be a completely satisfactory adjustment between the Negro and the white students. One of the women's houses have indicated that they would be glad to have Negro women students living in their house, and there is considerable interest on the part of the students at the present moment in this possibility.

One of the difficulties which has confronted the administration in securing Negro students has been to find students of the caliber that would be successful

Intercultural Workshop of the Fellowship Church. From the Howard Thurman Collection, Howard Gotlieb Archival Research Center, Boston University.

here at Grinnell and who would adjust both academically and socially to a situation in a college where they would be a very small minority group. A further qualification for such students would be their willingness to enter into what would be in effect an inter-racial experiment.

I am writing to you to inquire as to whether you could suggest the names of two or more able Negro students who might be interested in coming to Grinnell College for the continuation of their college work. I believe it would be desirable to have students who were more mature than those on the freshman level, at least until we had re-established the principal of having Negro students here at Grinnell. Do you know of any students who would be interested in transferring to this college? Our second semester this year begins on February 4, so that perhaps it is too late for us to do anything about it this year. However, if you do have any suggestions I would be very glad to have them and to pass them on to the administration office. If there are no students that you could recommend just now, we would appreciate it if you would keep in mind our desire to do something about this matter and possibly you could suggest during the spring some students who might wish to come here in the fall of 1946.

Heather Whitton, director of the Intercultural Workshop of the Fellowship Church,
leads participants in an arts and crafts project. From the Howard Thurman Collection, Howard Gotlieb Archival Research Center, Boston University.

It is only fair to say that there are some students and some members of the faculty who are not enthusiastic about the idea of having Negro students at Grinnell,
but I believe that the majority would welcome them warmly and would make every
effort to help them have a satisfying and enriching experience here at the College.
You should also know that in the community of Grinnell there is only one Negro
family so that the opportunities for social relationships in the community would be
more limited than in a community where there were more Negroes. However, I am
sure that we are never going to solve our racial problems unless we begin to learn
to live together, and I see no better place to begin this than in the college community as the college group should be the group that is most free from prejudice and
which offers the best possibility for the operation of democratic principles.

I will appreciate any suggestions which you may have concerning this matter, and I also hope you will give some consideration to my suggestion that you
return to Grinnell to speak in 1946–47.

Every good wish to you for the year just beginning.

Sincerely yours,

[*signed*] John Scott Everton

John Scott Everton

JSE:bj

TLS.

Notes

1. John Scott Everton (1908–2003) was a graduate of Redlands University (1930) and Colgate-Rochester Divinity School (1931) and obtained his Ph.D. at Yale (1934). An ordained Baptist minister, he was dean of chapel at Grinnell College before becoming president of Kalamazoo College (1949–53), an official of the Ford Foundation in Burma, U.S. ambassador to Burma (1961–63), and president of Robert College in Istanbul, Turkey (1968–71).

2. To Lorimer Milton, 12 March 1946.

3. Stuart A. Yeager, "The Black Experience at Grinnell College through Collected Oral Histories and Documents, 1863–1954," in the "Student Papers" collection at Grinnell College Libraries Special Collections, Grinnell, Iowa.

"Apostles of Sensitiveness"
10 February 1946
New York, N.Y.

Thurman delivered this sermon in New York City's Cathedral of St. John the Divine in February 1946; it was published as a pamphlet by the Interracial Fellowship of Greater New York,[1] which sponsored his visit. It was the most extended presentation he ever made of one of his most popular phrases, the "apostles of sensitiveness."

Thurman defined "sensitiveness" similarly to one definition of the Oxford English Dictionary: a "keen susceptibility to outward impressions." In common usage this definition has largely been supplanted by the somewhat pejorative sense of "one who is morbidly self-aware" or "the emotional state of one who is too delicate to fully live in the real world." Thurman's is a robust sensitiveness, belonging to those who have what he calls here "a highly developed sense of fact" and are eager to enter into deep empathetic knowledge of the experiences of others. Although he had spoken of a similar concept as early as "College and Color" (1924),[2] the phrase entered his vocabulary during the war years. He probably first used it in "The Cultural and Spiritual Prospect for a Nation Emerging from Total War,"[3] which he delivered in 1945; and in the title of his 1947 book, Meditations for Apostles of Sensitiveness.[4] *In the sermon he argues that the apostles of sensitiveness abhor all forms of chauvinism—toward one's church, one's race, one's nation—and try, through the extension of empathy, to root it out in others. Thurman also argues that apostles of sensitiveness realize that none of the apparent contradictions in life is final, including the contradictions of racial inequality. "[E]ven the most stubborn and recalcitrant aspects of life," Thurman argues, "shall take shape in accordance with the imperious demands of one's focused dedication." "Apostles of Sensitiveness" is another example of how Thurman en-couraged his listeners to adopt a commitment to nonviolence and a Gandhi-like tenacity of spirit in confronting the problems of segregation and inequality.*

My prayer to God is that your love may grow more and more rich in knowledge and in all manner of insight, that you may have a sense of what is vital—Thus speaks the Apostle Paul to the church at Phillipi.[5] A sense of what is vital—a basic and underlying aliveness to life and its vast potentialities at every level of experience—this is to be an Apostle of Sensitiveness.

T. S. Eliot, in an essay on literary criticism, suggests that the literary critic must have, above all else, a highly developed sense of fact with reference to many different areas of fact.[6] It is a most searching observation, for it applies equally as well to any person who undertakes really to be alive to life—to be an Apostle of Sensitiveness.

Each of us may have a highly developed sense of fact with reference to some particular area of fact and experience. It is this quality of modern life that is responsible for such amazing developments in particular fields of interests, in-quiry and living. But it is at once a revelation of the profoundest peril of our age. Specialists abound in the professions, in the crafts, in all the many-sided activities of our common life. This is well. The point is that the mountain peaks of specialization are not to be scaled down but the valleys are to be raised.

A man may be said to have prejudice with reference to persons or activities or a particular set of relationships, if he has a highly developed sense of fact covering a very narrow area. If he has a highly developed sense of fact with ref-erence to his particular church with an almost inevitable blindness or ignorance with reference to other churches and faiths, he is a religious bigot. Or, if he has a highly developed sense of fact with reference to his particular race, with an almost inevitable blindness or ignorance with reference to other races, he is a racial bigot. If he has a highly developed sense of fact with reference to his par-ticular country, with an almost inevitable blindness or ignorance with reference to other nations, he is a political bigot.

The Apostle of Sensitiveness must have a highly developed sense of fact with reference to other people. By the use of a disciplined imagination issuing in self-projection, which may be called a sense of fancy, he becomes increasingly aware of their hopes, their fears, their dreams and their livingness. He enters into their experience, even though he may not become a part of their experi-ences, as he remains himself. There can be no love among men even on the most intimate levels of their experience, if they are not alive to each other, if they are unable to have a sense of what is vital to, and within, another. This is the authentic basis of respect for personality. In essence, it means meeting people where they are, <u>and treating them there</u> as if they were where they ought to be.

By so doing, one places a crown over their heads that for the rest of their lives they are trying to grow tall enough to wear. To have a highly developed sense of fact with regard to other people is the searching demand of our faith, if we are to be in the spot which we occupy—Apostles of Sensitiveness.

There is a second prerequisite for the man who would be an Apostle of Sensitiveness. He must have a keen sense of alternatives. The sense of alternative is what is meant, basically, by freedom. Where there is no sense of alternative, there cannot possibly be freedom. The sense of alternative is guaranteed in human life, by the fact of death. Suppose you could not die. It would mean, for instance, that with reference to any given situation to which you were subjected, you would have no choice but to endure, forever and ever. But death gives you an alternative. What a blessing this alternative has been in the long march of mankind from the slimy oozes of some primeval ocean bed to the finest flowering of personality that expired on a cross outside a city wall!

The sense of alternative is always present. However hard it may be to find it, it is a primary fact of life. When Napoleon was at the height of his power, sealing his tyrannical will in Europe with the blood of countless human lives, Abraham Lincoln was born in a log cabin in Kentucky. The Interracial Fellowship of Greater New York is an insistence upon the exercise of another alternative to segregation within the Christian Church and the institution it controls. When according to the <u>New York Times</u>, Mayor O'Dwyer[7] ordered the tax commissioner to conduct an investigation designed to enforce State laws against discrimination, it is the exercise of alternatives.[8] It is easy to say that human nature, being what it is, or the social order being what it is, we must accept things as they are—to say: "It is unfortunate, but in the course of time, things will improve but for the present we cannot do anything about them." The Apostle of Sensitiveness <u>knows</u> that something can always be done, for he knows that the sense of alternative is the true incentive to social change and the sound basis of building a society of friendly men underneath a friendly sky.

Of course, if it be true that life is in essence, finished, completed, fixed, frozen, then it is ridiculous to talk in terms of alternatives. But on the other hand, if it be true, as I think it is, that life is dynamic, malleable, fluid, unfinished, then however barren may be the manner or the circumstance, the growing edge is implicit in the fact of existence and it becomes not only reasonable but also mandatory for the human spirit, brooding creatively over any aspect of experience, so to hold one's consummate, articulate, desire at dead center until at last even the most stubborn and recalcitrant aspects of life shall take shape in accordance with the imperious demands of one's focused dedication. To be overcome with paralysis, fear and indecision in the presence of crusted intolerance, and injustice however deeply entrenched, is to say "No" to life and affirm that the contradictions of one's experiences are in themselves ultimate. This is to deny the sense of alternative, to reject the Holy Spirit of God, to turn one's back upon life. The Apostle of Sensitiveness is profoundly aware of what is vital, quickening and alive and becomes the very point at which God breathes into circumstance, the breath of life.

There can be no sense of alternative that is not conditioned by one's sense of the future—hence the Apostle of Sensitiveness has a sense of the future. One final comment at this point. That which is already fulfilled has no future, only a past. It is for this reason that men of all ages have turned with such hopefulness to their youth—because they are on the make. The guardians of the status quo, the defenders of faith once for all delivered to the saints, all these deny the future. In effect, they say that the present exhausts the possibilities of life and is a dead-end street—in them there is no sense of the future and therefore no outlet for God. A sense of fact with reference to many different areas of fact, constantly illumined by a sense of fancy, a sense of alternatives with reference to any situation, however apparently impossible, a sense of the future with reference to the past, and the present, however glorious—this is the equipment of the Apostle of Sensitiveness who in every age is God's creative, growing edge announcing the divine dream for the men of earth— Now my prayer to God is that your love may grow more and more rich in knowledge and all manner of insights, that you may have a sense of what is vital.

TD.

Notes

1. *The Apostles of Sensitiveness* (New York: Interracial Fellowship of Greater New York, 1945). The Interracial Fellowship of Greater New York was organized in 1943; it was one of the many interracial religious organizations that sprang up during World War II. Its most visible activity was a monthly church service, held alternately in a white church and a black church. Besides Thurman, some of those who preached at the fellowship's services were Channing Tobias, William Stuart Nelson, and William Lloyd Imes.

2. Printed in *PHWT*, 1:36–41.

3. Printed in the current volume.

4. HT, *Meditations for Apostles of Sensitiveness.*

5. Philippians 1:9, "And this is my prayer: that your love may abound more and more in knowledge and depth of insight." (New International Version)

6. T. S. Eliot, "The Function of Criticism" (1923) in T. S. Eliot, *Selected Essays* (New York: Harcourt, Brace, 1950), 18. Thurman began his 1939 lecture series "Mysticism and Social Change," printed in *PHWT*, 2:190–191, 194–222, with the same reference.

7. William O'Dwyer (1890–1964) was mayor of New York City from 1946 to 1949, when shortly after his reelection he was forced to resign in a corruption scandal.

8. Mayor O'Dwyer called upon his tax commissioner to investigate ways of rescinding the tax-exempt status of New York City private colleges that discriminated against or maintained quotas for Jewish, Roman Catholic, and African American students—this following

a Mayor's Commission on Unity's report showing discriminatory practices by almost all private colleges in New York City ("Tax-Free Colleges Face City Scrutiny," *New York Times*, 31 January 1946). For more on the report of the Mayor's Commission, see Benjamin Fine, "Bias in Colleges against City Youth Charged in Report," *New York Times*, 23 January 1946. In 1946 a campaign by organizations including the American Jewish Congress and the NAACP was under way for vigorous enforcement of the statutes prohibiting discrimination in the state (Tod M. Ottman, "Government That Has Both a Heart and a Head: The Growth of New York State Government during the World War II Era, 1930–1950" [Ph.D. diss., State University of New York at Albany, 2001]).

☙ To Charles Gilkey
19 February 1946
San Francisco, Calif.

Writing to his friend and fellow dean of chapel Charles Gilkey,[1] Thurman outlines the options he faces in deciding whether to remain at the Fellowship Church or return to Howard. Uncertain about what to do, Thurman also mentions the possibility of a position at the School of Religion of the University of Iowa.

Office: 2142 Pierce Street
San Francisco 15

Dear Charlie,

I am sending this note to let you know how deeply grateful I am for the thoughts you expressed in your letter under date of February 4th. It is most strengthening to me to know that you are joining me in the soul searching that is necessary in order to find what is the will of God with reference to my own decision. My experiences on this trip have not made the decision easier, because there was an almost staggering response to the messages that were channeled through me as I moved from campus to campus. Tomorrow night we are having our first preliminary discussion with the Board of the Church; perhaps something will emerge there that will be helpful in determining the next step. The Church is growing and it is requiring a more and more penetrating kind of leadership and understanding as the days unfold.

The alternatives before me seem to be as follows:

1. To remain here as permanent base of operation, giving 8 or 9 months to the work of the Church and living a normal and established family life, and devoting 2 or 3 months out of the year to work in the country at-large.
2. To devote 6 months of each year here and a semester on a college campus in the East, preferably, Howard University, but if that cannot be, then on

some other campus. During the period in the East I would be free to circulate to some extent among the colleges and schools.

3. To give up the work here completely and return to Howard University on full-time permanent basis. One of the serious difficulties in that decision is the fact that Howard University does not take kindly to the idea of my being available to preach at other colleges and universities as I have done in the past. If I return therefore, it means a greatly circumscribed ministry as compared to the sort of thing I enjoyed before my leave to come to the Coast.

4. I have been approached informally and confidentially by the School of Religion of the University of Iowa about the possibility of coming there as a professor. There are hurdles to be made in the event that the appointment comes through, a hurdle as to race and as to my not having a PhD. At any rate, I have been invited to be a visiting professor there this summer beginning June 11 and going through August 9. I think that I shall accept this invitation if it can be worked out in the light of the rather chaotic state of my long-time plans.

These are the major factors under consideration. I may add that Mrs. Thurman is willing to cooperate in any one of these points and joins me in my deep concern for maintaining some measure of constant contact with our students. I do not wish to burden you with my own problems but it is a very singular thing that when I was facing the first really great crisis of my life and career back in 1931 I read a book of yours, which more than anything else caused me to find my bearing.[2]

With very deep feeling,

Howard Thurman

HT:am

Dr. Charles Gilkey

Rockefeller Memorial Chapel

The University of Chicago

Chicago 37, Illinois

TLc.

NOTES

1. Charles Gilkey (1882–1968), a graduate of Harvard University (1903) and Union Theological Seminary (1908), was pastor of the Hyde Park Baptist Church in Chicago from 1910 to 1928 and was dean of chapel at the University of Chicago from 1928 to 1947.

2. Thurman's first wife, Katie Kelley, died in late 1930, plunging him into a deep depression. We do not know which of Gilkey's books made such a profound impression on Thurman. Those available by 1931 include *Jesus and Our Generation* (Chicago: University of Chicago Press, 1925) and *Present Day Dilemmas in Religion* (Nashville: Cokesbury, 1928).

꩜ To Melvin Watson
2 March 1946
San Francisco, Calif.

In this letter to his protégé Melvin Watson, Thurman expresses uncertainty about his future but still seems to be hoping to find a way to split his time between San Francisco and Washington, D.C. Watson, then at Howard University, heeded Thurman's call and over the next two years, while completing his doctorate at the Pacific School of Religion in Berkeley,[1] would spend much time with the Thurmans and preaching at the Fellowship Church. For much of spring 1947, when Thurman was teaching at the University of Iowa, Watson in effect served as the interim minister at the Fellowship Church. As a jocular Thurman wrote to him on 11 December 1946, "You are hereby commanded to be the minister in charge during this total period, presiding each Sunday, for which you will be compensated unless I change my mind about the compensation. If you have any questions, see my lawyer!"[2]

1725 Washington Street
Office: 2142 Pierce Street
San Francisco 15

Dear Monk,

I'm sorry that I did not have the chance to meet the apple of your eye. I received a message to telephone her but it was too late for me to do so before getting on the train.

I'm back home struggling with my decision. Thus far, I have decided to accept an invitation to be Visiting Professor at the Summer School of the University of Iowa beginning June 9th and going through the first week of August. I hope to know by the 1st of April what my plans for next year are going to be. I'm sending another letter to the President[3] seeing if he will ask the Board to permit me to work out a 6 months - 6 months plan between the Church and the University. If this goes through I will be willing to come to the University in September and remain through the Winter quarter. I do not think he will agree to it but I'm trying.

I wonder if you would think through the idea of coming out here, living at the house with your bride and taking my responsibilities in the Church while I am away in Summer School. This is contingent upon a final confirmation from Iowa. I do not think there is any question about it. If this were done as far as your coming is concerned you and the young lady might come out here and be married before I leave for Iowa about the 6th of June. You would remain here until the middle of August. I feel very certain that the Church will be in a position to pay you $40 or $50 a week for your time. Think it through and as my plans freeze I will get in touch with you. It would be a fine opportunity to combine a good vacation and not take it on the cuff either.

You will doubtless see Sue when she is in Washington for a day or two.

Please know how grateful I am for all of the expressions of your love to me. Sincerely yours,

Howard Thurman

Mr. Melvin Watson
Howard University
Washington, D.C.

TLc.

Notes

1. Melvin H. Watson, "An Examination of Karl Marx's Theory of the Proletariat," Th.D. diss., Pacific School of Religion, 1948.

2. To Melvin H. Watson, 11 December 1946.

3. Presumably, To Mordecai Wyatt Johnson, 4 March 1946, printed in the current volume.

To Mordecai Wyatt Johnson
4 March 1946
San Francisco, Calif.

Thurman in this letter expresses an interest in finding a way to split his time between the Fellowship Church and Howard University. Thurman argues that if he returns to Howard, he should be able to continue to visit northeastern colleges on a regular basis, and he states that his speaking engagements had proved profitable for Howard. He strenuously defends himself against the insinuations, presumably from Johnson, that his frequent travels had diminished his usefulness to the broader Howard community and argues that when on campus, the dean of chapel position is a seven-day-a-week responsibility. Thurman also mentions his intention to devote all of his time in the future to spreading the Fellowship Church idea "in various parts of America."

Office: 2142 Pierce Street
San Francisco 15

Dear President Johnson,

I regret very much that the visit in Washington was so brief that I did not have opportunity to talk with you at length about the development of Fellowship

Church and the plans that are being made for its future. You have been the one person in the country in the field of religion who has seemed to hover over the Fellowship Church creation with a spirit of warmth and understanding needful for so significant a venture. Therefore, I wanted to talk with you as much about the direction that Fellowship Church will be taking as much as my future relationship either to it or to Howard University. The interest that Howard University people over the country, including faculty, student body, trustees and alumni has had a salutary effect upon the people in the San Francisco community. Not a week passes but that letters come in with small checks from students or alumni scattered around the country or in Washington. And often important visitors to the city come to the morning service, having been urged to do so by some trustee or friend of a trustee to Howard University. For the above reasons I had hoped that Howard University would have a continued relationship to the Church for the Fellowship of All Peoples.

When I secured my leave from Howard I did not feel that my work there had been completed. All during the period of the war I tried to give continuous spiritual guidance to students in the armed forces and I felt all along that I should be present to meet the returning veterans where they are in their present frustration and to help them to develop a deeper sense of religious experience which Negro students need, particularly at this time. My experience during the Week of Prayer was certainly a testimony to the heights and depths of this need. It was for these reasons that I raised the question of the possibility of effecting some arrangements by which I might have a continuing relationship with the University and with Fellowship Church, for the next two or three years. Ultimately, I hope to give all my time to developing the ideas of Fellowship Church in various parts of America.

The request that I am making to the Trustees through you is that I be permitted to work out with you for the next two years an arrangement by which I would be in residence at Howard from September to April and return to Fellowship Church when the University year is nearing its close and the work of the Church for the spring and summer is getting under way.

With reference to my being away from the campus so often, a matter which has come up several times, I have never given to you my interpretation of its significance. I need not attempt to make a case for the development of the religious life and the ministry of the Chapel during the years of my connection with the University. The work speaks for itself. One need only to recall precisely what the status of the informal and formal religious life was among the students 12 years ago. In the first place, except when I was off campus, I worked 7 days a week and often 7 nights as well. Other administrative officers and faculty had week-ends free, but I could not ever do this. In the second place all of my off-campus activities were in connection with some aspect of the religious life usually in a college, school, or university campus, rarely ever at other churches, forum, and the like. This meant a constant cross fertilization of Howard's religious life with other campuses and the accompanying enrichment of both. Further, this was the method by which the student exchanges with Vassar, Penn State, Columbia, Connecticut Wesleyan, Smith, Bucknell were developed and continued to so fine a point. Many times other institutions have invited me as a result of the personal interest of certain Howard University trustees who wanted to share with other schools the religious leadership of Rankin Chapel. From all of these activities it is Howard University that has profited and instead of my work suffering, it has been enormously enriched thereby.

I hope Mrs. Thurman gets to Washington. She is attending the YWCA Convention in Atlantic City, and I hope she has a chance to see you.

My warmest personal greetings to the family.

Sincerely,

Howard Thurman

President Mordecai Johnson
Howard University
Washington 1, D.C.

TLc.

🕊 To Eleanor Roosevelt
4 March 1946
San Francisco, Calif.

Thurman writes to former First Lady Eleanor Roosevelt updating her on the work of the Fellowship Church and inviting her to visit the church.

Office: 2142 Pierce Street
San Francisco 15

Dear Mrs. Roosevelt,

On behalf of The Church for the Fellowship of All Peoples, I am writing to give you some latest information concerning developments in the church and to express the wish of the congregation that you permit us to present you to a city-wide audience addressing yourself to a subject of your own choosing.

We are well into the last half of my two years' leave from Howard University to work in developing the Fellowship Church. My original leave was for one year but this has been extended because the development here is so significant and so full of promise for the future that I was moved to remain longer than my original intent. The Church has developed from a group of 35 persons, largely white and Negro who greeted us on the 1st Sunday morning in July, 1944 to an average Sunday morning attendance of 150, well balanced between white and non-white. We are organized now on a permanent basis as an Interdenominational, interracial, as well as intercultural Church.

Largely through the generosity and social vision of Mrs. Levy[1] of New York City (whom you know) we have been able to secure the services of a very competent young lady on a full time basis as the Director of our Intercultural Workshop for Children.[2] See enclosures.

It is clear to us that despite the difficulties inherent in the American environment it is possible for men and women of varying national and racial heritage to worship together with important carryovers into various aspects of their community life. This is of the profoundest significance both for Democracy and for Christianity.

As a part of our varied important offerings to the community of San Francisco, we are anxious to have the high privilege of presenting you in a public appearance. If you can give us a date under what arrangements would it be possible?

Our oldest daughter, Olive, is quite near you at Vassar College.

Sincerely,

Howard Thurman

Mrs. Eleanor Roosevelt
Hyde Park
New York

                                                                        TLc.

Notes

1. Mrs. Adele Rosenwald Levy.
2. Heather Whitton.

 From John Haynes Holmes
19 March 1946
New York, N.Y.

John Haynes Holmes[1] writes to Thurman about the Commitment of the Fellowship Church, in its second iteration, which affirmed "a vital interpretation of God as revealed in Jesus of Nazareth whose fellowship with God was the foundation of his fellowship with men."[2] Holmes thought that this was "disastrously limiting" to the church by singling out Jesus as a figure for religious emulation. Thurman did not care for the letter and wrote to a friend the following month that "Dr. Holmes was quite pontifical and gave me the impression of the kind of arrogance that I did not associate with him and his attitude."[3] *However, Holmes's letter and the associated sentiments must have made an impact on the church, since in 1949 the Commitment was changed to "a vital experience of God as revealed in Jesus of Nazareth and other great religious spirits."*

Dear Mr. Thurman:

I have your letter of the 14th, and have read the enclosed material about your Fellowship Church of All Peoples with real interest and sympathy. I appreciate the fine spirit of your undertaking, but must do this with definite reservations.

I cannot myself sign your Commitment nor become one of the members at large of your church, since you interpret religion "as revealed in Jesus of Nazareth." I cannot thus confine religion, which I believe has been revealed equally in Buddha, Zoroaster, and such modern saints and prophets as Gandhi and Kagawa. Religion is universal—its revelation is everywhere, in every great prophet, and in every human heart. I should be faithless to my own spiritual convictions if I attempted to bind them in any way to a distinctively "Christian fellowship."

But there is a second and much more important aspect of this matter. Putting aside all questions of personal opinion, there remains the fact that your Commitment, as identifying religion exclusively with Jesus of Nazareth, is inconsistent with any church which undertakes to represent a "fellowship of all peoples." All peoples should include not only Christians but Jews, and Mohammedans, and members of all other faiths the world around. A "fellowship of all peoples" means what it says or it means nothing. From this point of view I feel that you are rather disastrously limiting and thus defeating yourselves at the very start.

I have more and more come to feel in my ministry that we must organize men spiritually around nothing less than religion itself. Just as I abhor sectarian divisions of Protestantism, so I abhor the larger divisions of religion itself. We should refuse to recognize any divisions anywhere. There is one God, and all men of every diverse faith are children of that God, and therefore brothers one of another. I hope it may be possible for you to take your fine idea, which is obviously so genuine in your own hearts, and universalize it in the way which I am suggesting.

Very sincerely yours,

[*signed*] John Haynes Holmes

John Haynes Holmes

Rev. Howard Thurman,

The Fellowship Church of All Peoples,

2142 Pierce Street,

San Francisco 15, Cal.

                                                                          TLS.

Notes

1. John Haynes Holmes (1879–1964) was one of the most prominent liberal ministers of the first half of the twentieth century in the United States. Raised as a Unitarian and ordained as a Unitarian minister, he was called to the pulpit of the Church of the Messiah in Manhattan in 1907. He was active in a vast number of political causes and was a founding member of both the NAACP and the American Civil Liberties Union. In addition he was an uncompromising pacifist during World War I. His pacifism led to his break with the Unitarians in 1919 and the reorganization of his church as the nondenominational and unaffiliated Community Church of New York, where he remained minister until 1949.

2. HT, *Footprints*, 52.

3. To Ruth Smith, 17 April 1946.

To Agnes Robinson

12 April 1946

[*San Francisco, Calif.*]

Thurman writes to his former secretary, Agnes Robinson, telling her that if he returns to Howard University (which at the time of this letter looked increasingly unlikely), he wanted her to return as his personal secretary. Although this did not occur, Robinson's connection to Thurman remained close, especially after her marriage in 1949 to Thurman's protégé Melvin Watson.

Dear Agnes,[1]

I'm ashamed of myself that I have not written you, but you can imagine how hectic the days are when I say to you that I am busier here than I was in Washington. Sue went East to attend the convention of the YWCA and had a visit with Olive, and spent two days in Washington. I was East for January and a large part of February. From June 8–August 8, I shall be a Visiting Professor at the University of Iowa. I hope that Monk will come out here to preach at the Church while I am gone. Olive is doing very well at Vassar. Ann is in her first year at high school, is as large as her mother, and wears lipstick five days a week. She feels she is quite a young woman, despite the fact that she is only 12. She is about to run me crazy trying to figure out how to help with her Algebra every night.

I have asked the University Trustees to authorize the President to work out an arrangement with me by which I can spend seven months out here and four or five months at Howard. I shall know what their decision is when the Board meets. There does not seem to be much of a disposition to encourage this kind of an arrangement so that I am not at all clear as to where I shall be next winter. As soon as I know I shall let you know. Of course, if I return to Howard there is no question about the fact that I would want you to come back as my secretary.

You know that without asking. I wish that I could be more definitive in the matter, but such is the case. I have a new little [book] on Negro spirituals[2] which was published the first of February—Several other things on the pot boiling.

Because I do not have time to write is no indication at all that my affection for you is any less than it was. Sue and I talk about you very often, and express the great desire to see you and your family and little Billy.[3] If you have an extra snapshot of him, please send it around.

Take care of yourself and let me hear again soon.
Sincerely,
Howard Thurman

Mrs. Agnes Robinson
Alcorn College
Alcorn, Mississippi
                                                                                      TLc.

Notes

1. Agnes Regina (née Butler) Watson (1918–2003), a native of Washington, D.C., attended Howard University and later worked as an assistant secretary to Mordecai Wyatt Johnson and as a secretary to Howard Thurman. She married Melvin Watson in 1949 and subsequently moved to Atlanta, where her husband was the longtime minister of Liberty Baptist Church. She worked in the business office of Morehouse College for over thirty years until her retirement in 1984. Among Robinson's proudest accomplishments was typing the final version of Martin Luther King, Jr.'s doctoral dissertation.

2. HT, *Deep River*.

3. William P. Robinson, Jr. (1942–2006), Agnes Robinson's son from her marriage to William P. Robinson, Sr., was a graduate of Morehouse College (1964) and of Harvard Law School (1967) and worked as an attorney in Norfolk, Virginia. In 1981 he was elected to Virginia's House of Delegates, succeeding his father, Norfolk State College political scientist William P. Robinson, Sr. (1911–81), who served in the Virginia legislature from 1969 until his death. Robinson Jr. served in the House of Delegates until 2001.

⌁ From Mordecai Wyatt Johnson
26 April 1946
Washington, D.C.

Mordecai Wyatt Johnson writes to Thurman that if he wants a continuing relationship with Howard University, it will have to be on a full-time basis.

Dear Dean Thurman:

At their annual meeting on Tuesday, April 9th the Trustees of Howard University unanimously voted the following action affecting all teachers now on leave of absence, except those in the Armed Services:

That all war time leaves of absence to members of the teaching staff be brought to an end as of June 30, 1946 with the exception of those teachers in the military service, and that all teachers on such leaves of absence be required to return to their duties at the University on or before September 1, 1946.

In view of the steadily increasing enrollment of the University and the urgent necessity of placing at the disposal of the students the fullest possible services of all our ablest personnel, it has not been considered possible to make any exception in the application of this regulation.

I assure you that in your case this is due to no lack of high consideration for the value of what you are doing now and for what you have indicated it is your purpose to do ultimately in the field of developing fellowship churches in various parts of America. It is due solely to the strong sense of the duty which we owe to the responsible work with which we are here charged and which we know now stands in need of the full-time attention of all the ablest personnel we can secure.

I hope that your plans will permit you to return and to give us your full-time attention during the school year 1946–47.

Please give my greetings and good wishes to the members of your family.
Sincerely yours,
[*signed*] Mordecai W. Johnson
Mordecai W. Johnson
President

Dr. Howard Thurman
2142 Pierce Street
San Francisco 15, California

                                                                TLS.

Published courtesy of the Moorland-Spingarn Research Center, Howard University Archives.

To Mordecai Wyatt Johnson

30 April 1946
[*San Francisco, Calif.*]

Thurman, clearly frustrated, writes to Johnson asking for some clarification of his status at Howard.

Dear President Johnson,

Once again I'm writing to see if I can get some word from you. I received no acknowledgement of my long letter with my request in it to the Board of Trustees. Ten days ago I sent an airmail, because I had received no communication since

the meeting of the Board, and now I am writing again. All of my plans must of necessity be in a state of confusion until I know what is the final disposition of my request to the Board. Not to get any word, favorable or unfavorable, is most difficult to understand. I know that the demands made upon your time are limitless and that decisions involving one man and his future may not be as important as some of the other great issues to which you are giving your time. On the other hand, there is nothing more important to a man than his life and how he shall spend it. Will you please let me hear something from you so that I will know how to act in the light of the decision. It is very embarrassing to me personally to write this kind of letter to you, but I don't want to give up trying to hear without exhausting all possible resources.
Sincerely yours,
Howard Thurman

President Mordecai W. Johnson
Howard University
Washington 1, D.C.

TLc.

To William Herbert King
30 April 1946
[*San Francisco, Calif.*]

For many years Herbert King was Thurman's closest friend and confidant. They often traveled together—as in the summer of 1931 when they went to Europe after the death of Thurman's first wife the previous winter—and their correspondence hints at the depth of their friendship. The crisis concerning King's traumatic ouster from his position as a national associate secretary of the YMCA in June 1943 was a turning point in their friendship, and in its aftermath their correspondence became less frequent, for reasons that are not entirely clear. By 1949 Thurman was writing a mutual acquaintance that "I have not heard from Herb in more than three years."[1] Their friendship did resume thereafter. King became pastor of the Grace Congregational Church in Harlem in 1946, and in 1958 he joined the faculty at McCormick Theological Seminary in Chicago, where he remained until his death in 1966. A posthumous tribute to King written by his seminary colleagues remembered King as a person "of many qualities and moods, contradictions, and paradoxes," a "many-sided, enigmatic man." The tribute continued, "Herb was made for solitude rather than society. Even against those nearest him he defended the inner citadel."[2]

Dear Herb,

I have been greatly lost not being in touch with you. I thought that it was the thing that you wanted. I'm writing to find out whether you are willing to drop me a note and let me know how you are doing and what your plans are for the future. We are staying out here at least until the Fall and the possibilities are for much, much longer time. I have not received any official word from Howard about their end of my future. When I hear from you I will write in great detail about many things.

Sue and Ann join me in love to you and the family.
Sincerely,
Howard Thurman

Mr. William Herbert King
106-6 32nd Avenue
Corona, Long Island
New York

                                                                   TLc.

NOTES

   1. To Sam Rosenberg, 29 July 1949.
   2. "Editorial," *McCormick Quarterly* 20, no. 1 (November 1966): 3.

"GOD AND THE RACE QUESTION"
MAY 1946

In November 1942 Thurman received a letter from Glenn Clark,[1] a prominent lay religious figure, inviting him to join a select group of about twelve Christian leaders in Washington, D.C. for the first two days of 1943, for a period of collective prayer and discussion.[2] Among those invited to attend known to Thurman were Rufus Jones, E. Stanley Jones, Congressman Walter Judd, and the only other African American invited, George Washington Carver.[3] The organizers of the meeting, who asked Thurman to keep the invitation confidential, envisioned the gathering as a new Pentecost, where by praying together they would find common objectives and then apply them "in our homes, our daily work, and the great political, economic and social problems that confront us."[4] Thurman wrote back that he looked forward to attending the 1943 meeting "with high hopes."[5]

The group called itself the Fellowship and was connected to (in ways that are not entirely clear) the organization known as the Fellowship (later known as the Family), a loosely structured politically conservative evangelical organization best known for its congressional and presidential prayer breakfasts. The founder of the

Fellowship, Abraham Vereide, was one of the participants in the prayer group, and his notion of "Spiritual Cells,"[6] the title of his contribution to the endeavor, provided a framework for the enterprise.[7] Rufus Jones would write in the volume's introduction to the book written by the group that "we are distinctly averse to the promotion of a new organization. . . . We want to be a contagious cell, working like the capillary oozing of sap, not by officials and motions and votes and propaganda."[8] But if the Fellowship used language untypical for Thurman, for instance claiming that its participants "all look to Christ as Lord and Saviour," not all of the participants, among them Thurman, Rufus Jones, and E. Stanley Jones, were conservative evangelicals. The Fellowship issued no joint statement or platform. The world crisis formed an obvious backdrop to its deliberations. The group met at least three times, in the earliest days of 1943, 1944, and 1945.

At the 1944 meeting, Rufus Jones stated that "the next twelve months hold more portent for the future of mankind than any year since the birth of Christ," and E. Stanley Jones, a prominent Indian missionary, observed that "the next great conflict—if it comes—will be between the white and colored races." Thurman is recorded as agreeing with these sentiments, and all agreed on the need for deep thinking and profound prayer about the future course of humanity.[9] At the 1945 meeting (with Thurman, already in San Francisco, not in attendance), the group decided to write a book, with each member of the prayer group contributing a chapter. The book was published in 1946 under the title Together.

Thurman's short essay "God and the Race Question" closes the volume.[10] It is one of his strongest and most succinct statements on the incompatibility of racial inequality with genuine Christianity. "Racial and class prejudice," states Thurman, "is directly a denial of the existence of God the Father." Those who deny the unity of humanity deny the unity of God and must be "a polytheist, or worship a God who is without moral character." The very "structure of the universe is radically opposed" to the idea of racial or class prejudice. Until this principle is recognized and guides people in their "worship, their economic, political, and social arrangements under which they live," we are condemned to "war, strife, chaos" and "making life on this planet a shambles and a desecration."

GOD AND THE RACE QUESTION

"Our Father, Who art in heaven"—It is within these words that the spirit of Jesus takes flight into the holy of holies where his Father dwells in fullness and completeness. It is the magic formula crowding into its content all that man and God mean to each other. It is an expression of the oneness of life and the inextricable kinship between God and man. The things that divide men from each other so that their life on earth is a denial of the affirmation "Our Father" are not only sinful, immoral, but more explicitly, atheistic. They are, in essence, the denial of the existence of God who is the Father of life.

Racial and class prejudice is directly a denial of the existence of God the Father. It causes men to assume that God is not the Father of mankind. Quite logically, then, the dilemma is a cruel one—if my God is not the Father of all men, then it follows that he is merely my Father, and of those who are of my color, class, background, culture, and so on. Then men who are of a different color, class, background, or culture must of necessity have some other God who is *their* father or, what is worse, they are cosmic bastards, cast upon the sea of life without mooring, course, or anchor. Either my God is the Father of all mankind or he is not. If he is not, then I must provide in my thinking for the presence in the universe of other gods who are worthy of the name of Creator because their creatures exist in the world along with me. A religious man who holds racial prejudice must be a polytheist, or worship a God who is without moral character. There is no greater immorality—or amorality—than a religious man or institution that draws an arbitrary line among men on the basis of race or color.

When we reflect upon this, the conclusion is inescapable that, in practice, Christianity has made a specious distinction between the God of life, on the one hand, and the God of religion, on the other. The God of life is regarded as the Creator of the world. He is without moral character in any sense—he is not good or evil. He is impersonal—like a generative force manifesting itself in the life urge and its rich variety. The God of religion, however, is supreme in a rather narrowly circumscribed area having to do with piety, devotion, and prayer, but he is quite incapable of influencing the forces of life that create the great struggles for mankind. The simple form that this takes is the characteristic notion that matters of religious ideals and ethics are not really germane to the ordinary lives of individuals. The idea may be stated thus: "Religion is not practical; the distinction must be kept in mind constantly between what is practical and what is idealistic." Hence, ideals of brotherhood are fine as religious ideals and preachments, but they are not really practical in the world of men and institutions.

We hear men say that men are brothers in Christ, by which some may mean that brotherhood is a fiction, except in the rather highly restricted area under the control of the God of religion. It is for this reason that a widespread racial exclusiveness appears in the Church and often among religious people generally. It is the only rational basis for interpreting the phenomenon of the separate or segregated Church. Think of it: First Baptist Church (Colored), First Baptist Church (White); St. Mary's Episcopal Church (Colored), St. Mary's Episcopal

Church (White), and so on. Even cemeteries must be separate because there must be no confusion, no mixing, of races when the climax of human history comes and the graves give up their dead. This curious, malignant growth in Christianity stems basically from the notion that there is either more than one God, or there is a basic distinction between the God of life and the God of religion, or there is but one true God (mine) and other Gods are false. This is contrary to the message of the prophets of Israel and the life and teachings of Jesus Christ.

But if it be true, as the opening words of the Lord's Prayer would indicate, that the God of life and the God of religion are one and the same, then the categories of separateness, even in the matter of worship and all of its derivatives, must be regarded as antireligious, anti-God, anti-Christian, which would make them a blasphemy and a great infidelity. To deny brotherhood is to deny "Our Father," and to deny "Our Father" is to practice atheism. It is to say, in effect: There is no God, no sin, no future life—nothing but the survival of the fittest, and every race for itself.

I submit that the structure of the universe is radically opposed to that sentiment and practice. It is literally true that "of one blood" are all men created. The human lungs, heart, liver, and so forth, are all the same. The blood types are the same. The air we breathe and the food we eat serve the purpose in every human body. Physical death and birth are the same for all mankind. For better or for worse we must live together on this planet. Any man who denies this for any reason whatsoever cannot enjoy the fullness of life. Until this central fact becomes the common possession of men, guiding their practice, their worship, their economic, political, and social arrangements under which they live, there can be neither peace, prosperity, nor joy among the sons of men. Instead there shall persist war, strife, chaos, and a great and stark desolation making life on this planet a shambles and a desecration.

"God and the Race Question," in *Together,* edited by Glenn Clark (New York: Abingdon-Cokesbury, 1946), 118–20.

NOTES

1. Glenn Clark (1882–1956) was for many years a professor of literature at Macalester College in St. Paul, Minnesota. In 1930 he started a summer camp and retreat that became the kernel of the Camp Farthest Out movement, and this rapidly grew to a large network of summer camps. After 1942 Clark devoted himself full-time to the Camp Farthest Out movement.

2. From Glenn Clark, 12 November 1942.

3. Rufus M. Jones, "Introduction," in *Together,* edited by Glenn Clark (New York: Abingdon-Cokesbury, 1946), 7–11. George Washington Carver (1863–1943), who died on 5 January 1943, was too ill to attend.

4. From Glenn Clark, 12 November 1942.

5. To Glenn Clark, 29 December 1943.

6. Abraham Vereide, "Spiritual Cells," in *Together*, edited by Clark, 96–104.

7. For the connection between *Together* and the Fellowship, see Stephen W. Angell, "Howard Thurman and Quakers," *Quaker Theology* 9, no. 1 (Fall–Winter 2009), available at http://quest.quaker.org/issue16-contents.htm (accessed 12 November 2012). Abraham Vereide (1886–1969) founded the Fellowship, later known as the Family, in 1935. For more on this organization, see the popular account by Jeff Sharlet, *The Family: The Secret Fundamentalism at the Heart of American Power* (New York: HarperCollins, 2008).

8. Jones, "Introduction," in *Together*, edited by Clark, 11.

9. Glenn Harding, "The Leadership of Youth," in *Together*, edited by Clark, 105–6.

10. HT, "God and the Race Question," in *Together*, edited by Clark, 118–20.

To George Buttrick

3 May 1946

[*San Francisco, Calif.*]

George Buttrick[1] was one of the leading preachers and liberal Protestant figures of his time, best known as the general editor of the twelve-volume commentary The Interpreter's Bible *(1951–57), which was intended to "bridge the gap between exegetes and the rank and file teachers and preachers."[2] Buttrick and Thurman were friends and admirers of each other's work. Thurman had used George Buttrick's* The Parables of Jesus[3] *as one of the main texts in a study group at the Fellowship Church,[4] and during the years that Thurman was in Boston and Buttrick was at Harvard, the two would often exchange pulpits. Thurman was the only African American annotator for* The Interpreter's Bible *and wrote the commentary for the books of Zephaniah and Habakkuk. In this letter Thurman tells Buttrick that it was "a matter of genuine satisfaction to have some share in so important an enterprise."[5] Thurman was also asked to comment on other sections of* The Interpreter's Bible.

Dear Dr. Buttrick,

I have comments on Numbers 1, 4, and 5 as follows:

With reference to Number 1, the choice of title seems to me to be most happy, because it is in itself descriptive of the purpose of the new Commentary.

With reference to Number 4, I think that an article should be included treating the Pharisees. This seems to me to be very important because they have figured largely in the usual interpretations of the teachings of Jesus, and in my judgment, such interpretations have been for a long time a fruitful source of Anti-Semitism within the Christian tradition.[6]

With reference to Number 5, the unity of the introduction, exegesis, and exposition is good. I wish more attention could have been given to the question dealing with the bearing of the revolutionary ethic implicit in Paul's Christianity on the problem which faced the slave, Onesimus. The counsel of the ethic to the man who is not a slave is one thing, but what it says to one who is a slave with reference to his predicament may be another thing.[7]

The exposition seems to me to be explicit to the point of becoming a crutch. The point of the exposition ought to be to stimulate creative thinking based upon the basic facts, textual and historical of the text. The exegesis ought to guarantee a highly developed sense of fact in the mind of the preacher, with reference to the materials, textual and historical; while the exposition ought to stimulate a highly developed sense of fancy with reference to the materials concerning which the preacher already has a sense of fact. The topical arrangement is excellent and extremely suggestive, but the development of the topics on the basis of the text seems to me to make for laziness and dependence upon the outline.

Since being out on the Coast I have heard very excellent things concerning Dr. John Wick Bowman, Professor of the New Testament, San Francisco Theological Seminary, San Anselmo, California.[8] I have seen nothing of his work but pass the suggestion on to you for what it is worth.

It is a matter of genuine satisfaction to have some share in so important an enterprise.

Sincerely,

Howard Thurman

Dr. George Buttrick
The Interpreter's Bible
608 West 122nd Street
New York, New York

                                                                          TLc. FC

NOTES

1. George Arthur Buttrick (1892–1980), born and educated in England, was a graduate of the Lancashire Independent Seminary in Manchester but spent his entire career in the United States. He was minister at the First Union Congregationalist Church, Quincy, Illinois (1915–18); at the First Congregationalist Church, Rutland, Vermont (1918–21); and at the First Presbyterian Church, Buffalo, New York (1921–27) before being called to the pulpit of the prestigious Madison Avenue Presbyterian Church in New York City, where he remained until 1954. In that year he was named minister to the Memorial Chapel and Plummer Professor of Christian Ethics at Harvard University, where he remained until his retirement in 1960. One of the outstanding preachers of his era and the author of numerous books, he is probably best known as the general editor of the twelve-volume *Interpreter's Bible* (New York: Abingdon-Cokesbury, 1951–57).

2. Patrick J. Willson, "The New Interpreter's Bible (Vol. 1): General and Old Testament Articles; Genesis, Exodus, Leviticus," *The Christian Century* 112, no. 34 (November 22, 1995): 1112.

3. George Buttrick, *The Parables of Jesus* (New York: Harper, 1928).

4. *WHAH,* 149.

5. Thurman's commentary on Habakkuk will be published in *PHWT,* vol. 4, forthcoming.

6. Thurman, like many Protestant modernists of his time, was concerned with revising the standard Christian view of the Pharisees as narrow-minded bigots whose crabbed conception of Judaism provoked the reaction of Jesus. Thurman used Louis Finkelstein's *The Pharisees: The Sociological Background of Their Faith* (Philadelphia: Jewish Publication Society, 1938) in a study group at the Fellowship Church (*WHAH,* 149). Finkelstein's interpretation of the Pharisees emphasized that their religious ideals came out of their position as an economic underclass in Judea, congruent with Thurman's interpretation of the religion of Jesus in *Jesus and the Disinherited.* Thurman's most extended discussion of the Pharisees (which was perhaps not as distant from the traditional Christian view as he imagined) was in "The Significance of Jesus I: Jesus the Man of Insight," printed in *PHWT,* 2:44-54.

7. Paul's Epistle to Philemon, the shortest of the Pauline epistles, largely concerns the fate of Onesimus, who is generally seen as a fugitive slave, the property of Philemon. Paul counsels Philemon to take back Onesimus, who was "no longer as a slave but more than a slave, a beloved brother" (Philem. 1:16). Whether this was indeed a call to manumit Onesimus (and whether this is an authentic Pauline epistle) has been much debated. In this letter Thurman argues that the "revolutionary ethic" that is "implicit" in Pauline Christianity has a very different meaning for those who are enslaved and those who are not. Thurman would make a similar argument central to his 1949 book, *Jesus and the Disinherited.*

8. John Wick Bowman (1894–?) was the author of *The Religion of Maturity* (Nashville: Abingdon-Cokesbury, 1948) and *Which Jesus?* (Philadelphia: Westminster Press, 1970).

꩜ To George Thomas
4 May 1946
[*San Francisco, Calif.*]

Thurman indicates that faced with Mordecai Wyatt Johnson's ultimatum, he has largely made up his mind not to return to Howard. Thurman sees the Fellowship Church as a national movement and wants to devote the remainder of his career to fostering its growth in cities across the United States.

Dear George,

I have about made up my mind to resign from Howard University. I received a letter from the President this week saying that all persons must return by September 1. It seems clear to me that for the next 10 or 15 years I should give my life to the Fellowship Church Movement in this country. All of this is to say that if the group in Portland with your leadership and men like Dr. Morgan and others wish to organize an interracial Church I shall be very glad to cooperate in any way that I can, even to the extent of coming up for a week-end periodically, until the Church gets on the way. Will you talk with the interested people, including your new Executive Secretary to see what the chances are for its development?

I have gotten several good notes from various people up there about the Easter experience. Thank you for everything.

Sincerely,

Howard Thurman

Mr. George Thomas
2854 S.E. Tibbetts Street
Portland, Oregon

TLc.

❧ To Mordecai Wyatt Johnson

13 May 1946
[*San Francisco, Calif.*]

After receiving Mordecai Wyatt Johnson's letter informing him that he must return to full-time status at Howard by the fall of 1946 or forfeit his appointment, Thurman offers his resignation; his anger at the decision of Johnson and Howard's board of trustees is apparent here. The letter marks a definitive end of one phase of Thurman's career, which until coming to the Fellowship Church had been spent—as student, minister, and teacher—within the institutions of the black church and historically black colleges. This letter marks as well a watershed in Thurman's relation with his former mentor, the man who inspired him to pursue both the ministry and an academic career, Mordecai Wyatt Johnson.

My dear President Johnson,

I received your letter May 3rd, stating the decision of the Board of Trustees at their April meeting, concerning the status of persons now on leave from the University. I regret that they did not find it advisable to act with favor on my request to them through you that, for the present you and I be permitted to work out an arrangement whereby I would be able to spend a part of each year on the job at Fellowship Church. I have weighed this matter very carefully and have reached the conclusion that the right thing for me to do at this time is not to return to the University. In arriving at this decision, I recognize that since there can be no exception made in the above ruling, the University has no choice but to insist upon my resignation as Dean of the Chapel and Professor of Christian Theology in the School of Religion. I herewith submit that resignation.

For 14 years I have been a part of the official family of Howard University and have given a large share of the most productive part of my life to the work there. It is with emotional lacerations and a deep sense of personal loss therefore, that I make the fateful decision which is herewith set forth. I had hoped that it will be possible for me to continue a relationship to the University in some provisional manner, making it unnecessary for me to be separated completely from its total life. The ruling of the Trustees makes this impossible however, so I must be true to what seems to be the right thing for me sub specie aeternatis.[1]

I wish to express my appreciation to you personally for the privilege which has been mine to be associated with you with some measure of intimacy over the last 10 or 12 years. I love Howard University; the students and faculty are a part of the very fiber of my life. I feel however, a wider call that I must answer, and I do so with the same high hopes with which I came to Howard University in 1932. Within the next week I shall send a letter expressing personal appreciation to the Trustees for the generous cooperation which they have manifested in my work in connection with this venture here. I shall try to have my personal effects out of the house at 605 Howard Place by July 1. If at any time I can be of some particular service to the University, I hope you will feel free to command me.

May I say again in closing that I regret that circumstances provide no means by which I may continue the development of the Church here and serve Howard University for a part of the year, but since this is the will of the Trustees, I make my choice on behalf of this remarkable development within the framework of organized religion.
Sincerely yours,
Howard Thurman

President Mordecai Johnson
Howard University
Washington, 1, D.C.

TLc.

NOTE

1. Latin for "under the aspect of eternity."

To WILLIAM STUART NELSON
16 MAY 1946
[*San Francisco, Calif.*]

Thurman writes to William Stuart Nelson, chairman of Howard University's School of Religion, and explains his resignation from Howard. Thurman writes that he had wanted to use Howard to help develop potential candidates to minister at the Fellowship Church and similar institutions elsewhere.

Dear Stuart,

The enclosure explains itself. It goes without saying that the decision was a most difficult one for me to make, but I feel a deep urgency and an exhilaration in the choice. I trust that during the period that I am East in the winter, it will be possible for me to have some continual contact with the men in the School of Religion. I had hoped that it would not have been necessary for a complete separation from the University because there is no theological institution anywhere in the United States preparing men for leadership in this new development within the Christian church. It seemed like a "natural" for Howard University to do that. I could see myself combining perhaps a quarter's lecturing at Howard University with week-end preaching in the East each winter, and eventually using our Church here as an important laboratory for a year's internship for white and Negro or any other kind of men who are looking forward to a career as leaders in this field but as this did not turn out I shall have to do something else with the time. I hope that when I come East in June or July from Iowa you and I can have a long quiet afternoon in which to talk.

I am planning to make my course on Mysticism and Ethics into a volume[1] at the end of the summer session at Iowa. [I will be teach]ing only one course with plenty of opportunity for writing. The campus Methodist Church has asked me to take their pulpit for the period, but I shall only do it four or five times.

The work here is growing steadily and with new promise everyday. My best to you in all the things to which your hands are set.

Sincerely,

Howard Thurman

Dr. Stuart Nelson
Howard University
Washington 1, D.C.

                                                                              TLc.

NOTE

1. This volume was never published.

❧ TO EMILY CROSBY

20 MAY 1946

[*San Francisco, Calif.*]

In this letter to his friend Emily Crosby,[1] Thurman describes his intent to leave Howard as "the most crucial decision of my life."

Dear Em,

I'm sending this hurried note to let you know that the decision has been made. When President Johnson replied he simply restated what he had said to me in January. Therefore, in the light of his letter I had no alternative if I wanted to work at the Church, save resign. This, I have done. I'm enclosing a copy of my letter to Mordecai. I [would] like for you and Art to read it and return it to me. It goes without saying that this was the most crucial decision of my life, because it means burning bridges behind and sailing forth in the open independence of the sea. There is a deep sense of quiet confidence that has come over me now, and I think that the days ahead, however difficult, will assure me of the rightness of my decision. I want you to know how grateful I am for the thoughts and anxiety with which you and Art have followed my life during these eventful days. You have no idea how much that has meant in providing a cushion of absorption.

As our plans stand now, I will leave here about the 6th or 7th of June and shall go directly to Iowa City. Lest I forget, my address there will be School of Religion, University of Iowa, Iowa City. If we can swing it, Sue will come East to see me receive the degree and she and Olive will go on down to Washington to dispose of our household goods. They will return to San Francisco about the 6th or 7th of July. Does that mean that they will miss you? My very special friend, Virginia Scardigli, has been designated by me to take special charge of the Crosbys while they are here. She is the Chairman of the Intercultural Committee of the Church and is a really alive and vital person who knows San Francisco thoroughly and well. This is all that I can say now, but I wanted to get this to you at once.
Sincerely yours,
Howard Thurman

TLc.

NOTE

1. Emily Crosby (1903–79), née Emily Brinley Morgan, married the Philadelphia businessman Arthur U. Crosby in 1924.

To Edwin C. Berry

22 MAY 1946
[*San Francisco, Calif.*]

Criticizing a pamphlet sent him from an official of the Portland, Oregon, Urban League,[1] Thurman affirms his opposition to any theory holding that the races are essentially distinct, with intrinsic differences, and to the use of the biblical texts (what Thurman here calls "biblicism") as a means of determining social and political relations.

Dear Bill,

Your letter and book reached me while I was under the hammer with an attack of the flu. I'm making haste now that I am out to send you a note. I have read the material which you suggested. From my point of view there are several things to be said. The attempt to account for the origin of the Negro race by an appeal to Scripture is unsound and extremely dangerous, because it fits into the kind of Biblicism that can very easily be the basis of racial discrimination and notions of white supremacy. I have always been unqualifiedly opposed to such proceedings, both from the point of view of scholarship and psychology. When on Page 76 the author says that God has stamped Negroes with characteristics which forever distinguish them from other races, of which characteristic color is only one, he is seeking to give Divine sanction to error and prejudice of the most vicious kind. His answer to the question on Page 79 is patronizing and "holier than Thou" in tone, and despite the affirmation that God is no respector of person it does not make a clear definitive case for simple brotherhood, which after all is the point.

On the whole then, Bill, I think that this sort of thing is dangerous and unwholesome and the fact that it masquerades under the banner of Christianity makes it the most deadliest kind of in-fighting. If anything can be done to limit its circulation, I think it would be quite worthy.

Thank you for your letter and it was good to see you.

Sincerely,

Howard Thurman

Mr. Edwin C. Berry[2]
Urban League of Portland

TLc.

NOTES

1. The title of the pamphlet is not known.

2. Edwin C. "Bill" Berry (1910–87), a native of Oberlin, Ohio, attended Oberlin College, Duquesne College, and the University of Pittsburgh, training as a social worker. He started working for the Urban League in Pittsburgh in 1937 and in 1946 became the first director of the Urban League branch in Portland. From 1956 to 1972 he was director of the Chicago Urban League. He played major roles in Martin Luther King, Jr.'s Chicago campaign in 1966 and in Harold Washington's 1983 successful run for the Chicago mayoralty.

To Irving R. Reichert

29 May 1946

[*San Francisco, Calif.*]

Thurman writes to the rabbi of Congregation Emanu-El in San Francisco praising the temple's religious service.

Dear Rabbi Reichert,

Please accept my personal appreciation for the inspiring experience which was mine in the Temple two weeks ago.[1] I do not see how a person could experience the ritual of your service without a profound stirring of mind and heart towards God. Mrs. Thurman and I felt that the whole experience was a benediction breathing peace.

The Guild luncheon was very instructive to us because in it we were able to see how deep are the roots of the faith of Israel in the possibilities of human life. We were so happy that you invited us and we were profoundly impressed by the quality of authentic fellowship which the group shared with us.

I have sent a letter of appreciation to Mr. Zellerbach[2] stating to him that his contribution will be used towards our Intercultural activities. It will mark the first contribution towards the fund that we are raising for the salary of our Intercultural Director for another year. I'm constantly amazed over the fact that with so little money so much can be accomplished, and yet sometimes it is an agonizing task to get the so little money. Before I leave for the University of Iowa a week from Thursday, perhaps it will be possible for you and me to have an hour's talk about several things.

Thank you again for your own spirit.
Sincerely yours,
Howard Thurman

Rabbi Irving F. Reichert
Congregation Emanu-El
Arguello Blvd. and Lake Street
San Francisco, California

                                                                              TLc.

Notes

  1. Thurman preached at Congregation Emanu-El on Saturday morning, 18 May.

  2. Harold Lionel Zellerbach (1894–1978) was the longtime president of Crown-Zellerbach, one of the world's largest paper products companies.

➦ From Alfred G. Fisk
27 August 1946
Big Basin, Calif.

In this letter, Alfred Fisk, although couching his words as a possibility warrant-
ing further discussion, indicates his desire to relinquish his role as copastor, with
Thurman, of the Fellowship Church. The ostensive reason for Fisk's decision was
the lack of an adequate Sunday school for his son, but as he describes it, even
this issue touched on Fisk's deep misgivings about the direction of the church
and its lack of a public ceremony of Commitment to the Fellowship Church and

to Christianity. For over two years it had become increasingly clear that Fisk's conception of Christianity was more traditional than those of Thurman and many other members of the church. He had been on the losing side of most of the important church controversies, especially the decision to end the affiliation with the Presbyterians. At the time of the decision, Fisk wrote to Presbyterian officials, "how regretful I am over this, and that it means that my relation to this work will terminate in the near future."[1] Still, Fisk waited a year to act on this resolution, lowering his profile in the church and making a conscious decision to keep controversial opinions to himself. He had "studiously refrained from trying to make Fellowship Church the kind of church" he and his wife sought for their children, a situation he no doubt felt was untenable in the long term. There was no sense of personal hostility between Fisk and Thurman, but the friendship and association between the two men was largely exhausted. Fisk would have nothing to do with the Fellowship Church following his departure, and the two men rarely interacted thereafter. Left unsaid was perhaps the most basic reason for Fisk's resignation: Thurman had become the dominant spiritual authority in the church, and it was time to bring the copastorate to an end.

Dear Howard,

I wish that you could join us here and enjoy the beauty and inspiration of these grand old trees, the tame deer that wander into our camp—and perhaps even the chattering of the blue-jays, though when they open their convention at 6 a.m. in the trees above our bed it is a bit annoying.

We are sleeping out under the trees and have a small tent to dress in. Getting meals on the camp stove and trying to keep things clean amid all the dirt and dust of this camp has made us appreciate the comforts of home, so that it will seem wonderful to get back. A vacation which accomplishes this is certainly fulfilling one of the valid functions of such a period!

Our vacation has been interrupted several times by necessary returns to the city, and I have brought my typewriter with me so that I could do some necessary work growing out of the College Workshop and other matters. We do not plan to return to the city now until late September 1st or on the 2nd. So I will not be present at next Sunday's services.

Eleanor and I have been trying to think through the problem of our continued relationship to Fellowship Church. To be quite frank with you, we do not feel that Fellowship Church is at all satisfactory to us personally as a family church. It has no Sunday School, no Sunday evening youth program for junior or senior High School students, and no training program for young people in preparation to joining the church.

David is now 14. He should join the church. And I should like to have it mean something quite significant to him. (And this is a problem that involves others than David. When largely through my influence George Sugihara became a Christian, it was a tremendous thing for him—coming from a Buddhist background and an atheistic position. He signed a commitment and is a member of Fellowship Church, coming twice a month regularly from San Leandro to attend. But Fellowship Church makes nothing of "joining the church" or becoming a Christian. I would think that there should be at least as significant recognition at such a moment as when a person becomes a citizen of the United States—a very impressive ceremony, if you have witnessed it.)

While Eleanor and I are very critical of "churchianity" we nevertheless feel a great debt to the organized church, and feel also that the church represents a potentially great strength for influencing society. We regret being a part of an institution which is cut off from the organized churches of the nation.

Eleanor and I feel strongly that we cannot further neglect what we feel to be the spiritual welfare and spiritual development of our children. This means arranging for them some other church home than Fellowship Church. But it is important, too, for us as a family to be together in the same church. In other words, we feel that we ought to leave Fellowship Church.

Of course originally we hoped that Fellowship Church would become the kind of church which would make a church home for our children. That we do not feel it to be so, is not necessarily a reflection upon the church—but perhaps more so upon ourselves! Nevertheless we are what we are, and seek for our children the kind of church which we, not someone else, approves of. (And since Mrs. Bachels a year ago seriously condemned me for trying to impose my ideas upon a church which did not want them, I have studiously refrained from trying to make Fellowship Church the kind of church which Mrs. Fisk and I seek for our children.)

As you know, the reason I have remained at Fellowship Church the past year has been my earnest commitment to the interracial brotherhood for which it stands, and my hesitation to do anything which might be interpreted by some as harming the idea for which Fellowship Church stands. This same factor still holds in my thinking. It is the old ethical problem of the conflict of values. But {after} a year in which I have been the battleground of such conflict I long to resolve it and find some way to relax the tension.

I have not found it. Should the Fisks as a whole family leave Fellowship Church and make some other church home? Could some compromise be worked out whereby Mrs. Fisk and the children attend a church near enough to Fellowship Church (First Methodist or First Presbyterian) where I could pick them up after morning service and we go out to Sunday dinner together? Though this would preserve the technicality of the co-pastorate and avoid any adverse comment in national publicity regarding Fellowship Church, it would be very unsatisfactory locally—not only to the Fisks, but to members of Fellowship Church who would naturally think it strange for Mrs. Fisk and the children to attend church elsewhere.

Before resuming my work at Fellowship Church I want to talk the matter over with you. I trust that you will appreciate my frank sharing with you of my personal problem. You will realize that I would not come to you with it unless I felt a warmth of understanding and appreciation in you. I do feel that, and I hope that you and I may always keep that closeness of relationship.

{I hope that you yourself have had a restful and otherwise satisfactory vacation—and the same for Sue. It is a matter of real regret to us that we did not see more of Olive while she was West—our fault.}
{Cordial greetings to you all,}
[*signed*] Alfred.

NOTE

1. Fisk to Friends [War Services Unit, Presbyterian National Board of Missions], 15 September 1945, Collections of the Department of History, Presbyterian Church (U.S.A.).

✎ BOOK REVIEW: *RELIGION IN HIGHER EDUCATION AMONG NEGROES*, BY RICHARD I. MCKINNEY
SEPTEMBER 1946

Richard I. McKinney[1] was a student of Thurman's at Morehouse College in the late 1920s and early 1930s and thereafter studied at Newton Theological Seminary and Yale. McKinney's 1945 book, a version of his 1942 dissertation with the same name, was on a subject of long interest to Thurman, and this review contains some of Thurman's most trenchant observations on blacks' higher education.

Religion in Higher Education Among Negroes.[2] By Richard I. Mckinney. Yale University
   Press, 1945. pp. xiv–165. $3.00.

Dr. McKinney in his study, *Religion in Higher Education Among Negroes,* has made available a valuable contribution to that phase of Negro education that has been deeply neglected in most general surveys of the field. He traces the influence of religion in the founding of American colleges and high lights the motivation that it generated in the founding of colleges for Negroes. Here is a somewhat detailed analysis of the relation of religion to the basic problems in the lives of Negro students due to the peculiarities of the social setting in which they move and think and function. He has not neglected a consideration of the attitudes of the persons responsible for shaping the broad policies governing the schools and of those other individuals on whose shoulders rests the responsibility for implementing these policies. There is a classification of church-related and state-controlled colleges in terms of the relevancy of religion, formally considered. The role and the status of the religious worker on the campus is examined. A discussion of the course offerings is outlined in comparison with and in contrast to the voluntary student religious organizations. There is a statement of the financial expenditures for religion in the various colleges with a breakdown in terms of salaries of teachers of religion, amounts spent for voluntary religious activities such as the Y.M.C.A. and Y.W.C.A., and the contribution that the students themselves make to over-all national student religious movements. The chapter before the final "Findings and Recommendations" is a discussion of the sampling of opinion of upperclassmen regarding the students' attitudes toward religion (rather loosely defined), toward compulsory chapel, and toward the religious sincerity of the college administration and staff. In this significant chapter the author utilizes his years of teaching and administrative experience on several college campuses and seems able to deal with the issues from the inside.

In the final chapter concerning "Findings and Recommendations," the most significant item has to do with the first recommendation. It says in part that "the College for Negroes, if it is to be effective, must take account of the various environmental factors which help to condition the life of the student before, during, as well as after his college experience. This means, among other things, that the college administrators will be interested . . . in the personality growth and adjustment of each student." It is obvious that what Dr. McKinney says about Negro education in particular applies to education for any other group in our common life. One would wish that a clearer and more definitive distinction could have been made between the issues facing the average student coming out of the average American college and those facing the average Negro student coming out of the average Negro college. It seems to me that the unique role of religion is best revealed in an analysis of these relative issues.

One of the functions of American education is to guarantee and to perpetuate the established patterns of American life. The presupposition is that the persons who are being educated are to function in the social order on the side of those who make the policies that determine the destiny of the country. The very fact that it is one of the common judgments of public-school education that it is well within the range of possibility of the most ordinary male student in the class to become President of the United States, is a case in point. This means that the degree to which American education is effective in the lives of the students marks the measure of the level of privilege and control for those who are exposed to it. When a Negro boy comes through that same system, whether it be in Cambridge, Massachusetts, or Daytona, Florida, he is to some extent imbued with the same social estimate of his possibilities. When he is through with his education, however, he is faced with the problem that in broad outlook, there is no ceiling to his effective aspirations—he has the techniques and the philosophy that belong to the typical American—but he functions in society as a member of a minority. This fact is apt to issue in the profoundest kind of frustration affecting his total outlook. In addition, if he has been educated in a segregated school, it means that the very conditions under which his education takes place are a constant denial of the basic assumptions by which his education is motivated. Therefore, the only possible justification for a segregated school in our country is the demand that in that kind of restricted environment, educators and students should test out techniques and methods which, when released in society, will be so revolutionary in their effect that they will destroy the very segregated institutions that made it possible to develop these techniques and methods. The Christian religion with its revolutionary ethic would be most reassuring and stimulating to the Negro student in such a dedication. It should mean that the revolutionary ethic of Christianity would be provided with a revolutionary technique. Unless religion in higher education among Negroes performs this function, it will not be able to challenge and inspire the loyalty and devotion of the most thoughtful administrators, faculty, and students on the various campuses.

Dr. McKinney has done a distinguished service in clearing away the underbrush and, by implication, high lighting the unique contribution of religion to the evolving pattern of higher education among Negroes.

Religion in Life 15, no. 4 (Autumn 1946): 619–20.

NOTES

1. Richard Ishmael McKinney (1906–2005) was born in Live Oak, Florida, and graduated from Morehouse College (1931) and Newton Theological Seminary (1934), where his B.D. thesis was "The Problem of Evil and Its Relation to the Ministry to an Underprivileged Minority." After receiving an M.Div. from Newton Theological Seminary in 1937, he attended Yale Divinity School, where he received his Ph.D. in 1942. He taught at Virginia Union (1935–42); Storer College in Harpers Ferry, West Virginia (1944–51), where he was the college's first black president; and Morgan State (1951–78). His other books include *History of Black Baptists of Florida, 1850–1985* (Miami: Florida Memorial College Press, 1987), which he coauthored with George Patterson McKinney; and *Mordecai—The Man and His Message: The Story of Mordecai Wyatt Johnson* (Washington, D.C.: Howard University Press, 1997).

2. Richard I. McKinney, *Religion in Higher Education among Negroes* (New Haven, Conn.: Yale University Press, 1945).

⤳ To George Houser

14 October 1946

[*San Francisco, Calif.*]

Thurman's letter to Houser concerns the plans of the Fellowship of Reconciliation (FOR) and CORE to sponsor a "Journey of Reconciliation" involving an interracial team of individuals who volunteered to test the 1946 U.S. Supreme Court decision in Morgan v. Commonwealth of Virginia, *which outlawed discrimination on interstate buses.[1] The Journey of Reconciliation was co-led by FOR national secretaries George Houser and Bayard Rustin and went through the upper South states of Virginia, North Carolina, Tennessee, and Kentucky. Traveling in April 1946, the volunteers stopped in fifteen cities, with over thirty speaking engagements at churches and other venues. The Journey was quite controversial among mainstream civil rights groups and was opposed by Walter White and Thurgood Marshall of the NAACP, on the grounds that it would likely provoke a blood bath and not advance the cause of the fight against Jim Crow. However, it proved less violent than its critics feared.[2] The Journey of Reconciliation was perhaps the most significant effort of FOR and CORE to date to publicize their principles of radical nonviolent action. They had pioneered these principles during World War II, using a small interracial group of volunteers who were schooled in the principles of nonviolence and willing to risk arrest and physical harm to publicize their opposition to Jim Crow. Thurman thoroughly approved of the action, and here he suggests that the Journey of Reconciliation specifically reach out to white southerners—especially to sympathetic white ministers—and help them to form "islands of refuge" that would endure after the Journey had moved on.*

Dear George Houser:

Thank you very much for your letter under date of September 30 enclosing your memo on Bus Travel. I endorse the proposal very heartily and am certain that it will provide a much needed rallying point for those people in the South who are personally and collectively dedicated to good will.

I have one suggestion that I am sure you have thought through already. It would be a very effective thing to include as many audiences of white people as possible in the speaking itinerary on the return trip. It would be wonderful if the group could appear before Negro and white Ministerial Associations which appearance conceivably may result in a formation of a series of small committees officially appointed by the Ministerial Alliances. These committees could be little Boards of Strategies and islands of refuge for those persons who would try to carry on after our group has left. It would strengthen the effort

enormously to let the religious units spearhead the attack wherever possible. It would keep the challenge in the one completely unanswerable area.
Sincerely,
Howard Thurman

Mr. George M. Houser
Racial and Industrial Secretary
Fellowship of Reconciliation
2929 Broadway
New York, 25, New York.

                                                                                TLc.

NOTES

1. *Morgan v. Commonwealth of Virginia,* 328 U.S. 373 (1946). The narrow decision was limited to buses, the scope of the decision was unclear, and there were no provisions for enforcement. The decision notwithstanding, interstate bus travel in the South remained segregated until the 1960s, with the more famous reprise of the Journey of Reconciliation, the Freedom Riders. See Raymond Arsenault, *Freedom Riders: 1961 and the Struggle for Racial Justice* (New York: Oxford University Press, 2006), 11–55.

2. Arsenault, *Freedom Riders,* 18–22. See also Derek Charles Catsam, *Freedom's Main Line: The Journey of Reconciliation and the Freedom Rides* (Lexington: University Press of Kentucky, 2009).

❧ FROM BENJAMIN E. MAYS
22 OCTOBER 1946
[*Atlanta, Ga.*]

Mays writes to Thurman of his surprise that Thurman is leaving Howard. He tells Thurman of the big expansion in the postwar enrollment at Morehouse.

Doctor Howard Thurman
The Fellowship Church of All Peoples
2142 Pierce Street
San Francisco 15, California

Dear Howard:

I was very glad to get your letter of September 26. I was surprised and somewhat shocked to know that you had severed your connections with Howard University for good. I am sure you will be greatly missed there.

Things are moving along very well here at the college. We have 860 men. We had planned 500 men as the maximum, but had conceded the necessity of taking possibly as many as 600 men this year. We found ourselves taking 260 men more than we had planned to take and 360 more than the normal enrollment which we hoped to settle on. But we could not refuse a Morehouse man who was drafted from the college and who has spent from two to four years in the armed services. We could not say to those men that they could not come back to Morehouse. It seems that every Morehouse man who left to go to the army wanted to return to Morehouse.

As you would expect we have had to increase our staff considerably and we have had to provide new classrooms and new housing facilities. We have done a pretty good job and yet we need to do still more.

Please remember me kindly to Sue and to Anne when you write her and to Anne.

With kindest regards and best wishes, I am

Yours truly,

Bennie

BEM:ch

TLc. MSR-H

From Ellsworth M. Smith
24 October 1946
Detroit, Mich.

Ellsworth M. Smith[1] of the Church of All Peoples in Detroit, another fledgling inter-racial church effort, gives Thurman an enthusiastic report on the church's progress.

Dr. Howard Thurman
2142 Pierce Street
San Francisco 15, California

Dear Dr. Thurman:

We are zooming along with our Church of All Peoples.[2] I became the first full-time paid minister the first of September, and we are holding our own financially so far. The other members of the Staff are co-equals with me—the only difference being that I give full time to the direction of program and get paid for it.

The Y.W.C.A. gives us a small office for ten dollars a month; our attendance is slowly growing at the Vesper Hour services; we have forty applications for membership, most of whom will follow through; we have the outstanding colored musician in Detroit as choir director, for free; and a splendid organist, white, for free. Our Social Action Committee has missed only one week in its meetings since early Spring, and recently eighteen to twenty have attended; we have thirty people trained and ready to meet with groups of all sorts in segregated churches and can make up a variety of "teams" to present our message in different ways.

We are now trying to schedule a few Sunday afternoon mass meetings like the one you addressed last June.[3] We have written for Carey McWilliams[4] in the near future, and Muriel Lester in the Spring.

Can you jot down the names, and, so far as possible, the addresses of a dozen or more leaders of both races whom you would recommend for these special meetings, leaders you would be glad to have at your own meetings. I just don't know the field as well as I should and would greatly value your suggestions. Since this is a new venture, we need to pay undue attention to how well-known our speakers are.

To get more time and space, and to clear St. John's for the reestablishment of their own Vesper Service, we had to seek a new church "home." We have been unanimously invited by the Vestry of St. Andrew's Memorial Episcopal Church to use their entire plant Sunday afternoons and evenings. It is the loveliest small church I have ever seen.

This is the most deeply satisfying work I have ever done. Our people join me in sending cordial greetings to you and to your people. Let's get together whenever possible!

Sincerely,

[*signed*] Ellsworth M. Smith

Ellsworth M. Smith

EMS:vb

TLS.

NOTES

1. Ellsworth M. Smith, director of the Detroit Council of Churches, was a Unitarian minister who taught at Berea College and pastored congregations in Cincinnati and Detroit before becoming executive director of the Midwest Unitarian Universalist Conference.

2. The Church of All Peoples was organized in Detroit in July 1945 under the auspices of the Detroit Council of Churches. At the end of 1946 it had a full-time minister, Ellsworth M. Smith, and 140 members, who met weekly at St. Andrew's Memorial Episcopal Church on Sunday afternoons (to permit its members to attend other congregations on Sunday mornings). See Jack, "Emergence of the Interracial Church," 34. In April 1945, after Albert Cleage sought a letter of reference, Thurman wrote to the Detroit Council of Churches recommending Cleage, though this did not lead to Cleage's appointment (From Albert Cleage, 24 April 1945; To Thorburn T. Brumbaugh, 30 April 1945). Among the volunteer ministers associated with the church were Thorburn Brumbaugh and the prominent black minister Charles A. Hill. The subsequent history of the congregation is not known, but it does not appear to have had a long life.

3. On 30 June 1945.

4. Carey McWilliams (1905–80), a liberal journalist, is best known for his works on California, including the state's racial minorities. One of his most well-known works is *Factories in the Field: The Story of Migratory Farm Labor in California* (Boston: Little, Brown, 1939). From 1955 to 1975 he was editor of the *Nation*.

❧ To Mrs. Ralph Eckert

5 December 1946

[*San Francisco, Calif.*]

In this appeal to Elizabeth Eckert[1] for funds, Thurman lays out the church's organizational and financial needs. With the resignation of Alfred Fisk, Thurman has taken over the full responsibility of running the church and is currently looking for a white copastor who would give the church additional institutional stability. Thurman wrote many similar letters at this time to other potential supporters of the Fellowship Church.

Dear Tumsie:

I am sorry that the letter is so long getting to you but here it is. Our Church is not subsidized by any organization or denomination. We are solely dependent upon contributions from members and concerned individuals for our continuation as far as budget is concerned. Our problem is acute because the standard that we maintain, and that we are maintaining, is as high as imagination, intelligence and consecration can make it. It would be most unfortunate if we did not do this because instead of our presenting a challenge to the community and the nation we would be an object of compassion and pity. Our operating expenses total roughly $800 a month. Our membership in San Francisco is about 170 and they contribute an average of $425 a month towards this budget.[2] An additional $100 or $150 comes in from National Associates or occasional contributions. The operational deficit has been met each month from a backlog of funds that individuals have given me during the past two years. This fund is about exhausted. In order to maintain ourselves we must get from some source approximately $3600 for 1947. Our membership is growing slowly which means that the average monthly income will increase. We do not contemplate a growth sufficient to absorb the $3600. This amount represents one important need.

We were given a $300 grant from an individual to get an Interracial Choir started. This we have done by securing the services of a very able teacher of voice. All of our soloists and our Fellowship Church Quartette are volunteers even though one of our soloists, who is also a member of the Quartette, earns his living by singing professionally.[3] We have easily the finest Choir of its size in the city. So convinced is the Director of her sense of mission, that a good part of the meager $75 a month paid her is put back into the Choir in the form of new music that we are unable to buy.[4] We need $1800 to finance the Choir for 1947. In addition to singing at our regular services both the Choir and the Quartette render a tremendously significant service by appearing at a variety of meetings in which their music and their interracial constituency make a most important contribution. Early in the New Year we expect to have an established Choral Vesper program on the radio. This is another need.

At the present time I am taking the full responsibility as a single Minister since there has been a change in Dr. Fisk's plans. We are greatly in need of another Minister, a Caucasian, who will not only carry out the co-pastorate plan of our structure, but such a person would supplement my own work by building a framework of our organization in ways that it is impossible for me to do. The demands placed upon my leadership in the city of San Francisco and the country give me a unique opportunity, not only to publicize this revolutionary experiment in which we are engaged, but also on the ground here to attract a wide variety of people of good will and consecration. We need someone to channel them, or in the language of the Church, to put them to work on behalf of our ideal. It will cost us a minimum of $3500 to get that kind of man. This is another urgent need.

With reference to the Intercultural Workshop, I shall not know for another ten days whether our $1000 grant will be forthcoming from the Rosenberg Foundation. If this does not come through our Workshop must close January 1st, for our funds for that purpose are exhausted as of that date.[5]

As you know, we have no building nor do we own any property upon which a building may be placed. For the past two and a half years we have been working quietly here and are exercising an influence in the city far in excess of our age and numerical strength. We have friends here who will help us secure a property—that is, this is my faith. What we need most urgently is to secure the services of a good public relations person who can capitalize on our program, activities and development in order to secure the funds we need to house and establish our work. If January 1st we could secure the services of such a person, in six months time, with our wide contacts in San Francisco and the country, we ought to be able to raise the $250,00 [*sic*] necessary.

This is the story, Tumpsie, and I hope that in your conversation with Mrs. Smith,[6] her spirit may be moved to back this tremendously significant undertaking. If necessary, I should be very glad to come down to Los Angeles to talk the matter over with her if there are questions that must be cleared up in her mind before she can make a commitment.

It was good to see you and Ralph and the children.

Hurriedly,

Howard Thurman

Mrs. Ralph Eckert
1700 Wayne Ave.
South Pasadena, Calif.

                                                                            TLc.

Notes

1. Elizabeth Flournoy Eckert (1908–88), the daughter of Richard Orme Flinn, longtime minister of the North Avenue Presbyterian Church in Atlanta, married Ralph Eckert, a prominent Los Angeles–area psychologist, in 1935.

2. In the beginning of August, Virginia Scardigli, the acting secretary of the church, estimated the membership of the church at 250, of whom 115 were national members not living in the immediate vicinity (Virginia Scardigli to John G. Poon, 1 August 1946).

3. The members of the Fellowship Quartette in 1946 were Joseph Van Pelt, first tenor; William Van Seiden, second tenor; Raymond K. Fong, baritone; and Emery Mellen, bass. When joined by the quartet's director, Corrine Williams, soprano, the group became a quintet. Van Seiden was later replaced as second tenor by Rokee Acevedo.

4. The choir director was Corrine Williams.

5. The grant was not renewed, and the formal program lapsed at the end of 1946. Although aspects of the intercultural workshop were retained, these were on a more modest scale.

6. Eleanor Lloyd Smith, a prominent Los Angeles philanthropist. She was the matriarch of a family that provided considerable financial support to Thurman and his endeavors. See To Carleton E. Byrne, 26 April 1952, to be printed in *PHWT*, Vol. 4. The dedication of Thurman's *Meditations of the Heart* (New York: Harper and Brothers, 1953) was "To Eleanor Lloyd Smith, in whom the inner and the outer are one."

⤔ From James E. Sams
15 December 1946
Daytona Beach, Fla.

Sams writes to Thurman about the division of property with Alice Sams, Thurman's mother. Sams's writing style is difficult to understand, but he is apparently reconciled to the separation from Alice Sams. However, he evidently wants Thurman to give him a vacant lot, jointly owned by him and Thurman's mother, on which he would build his own house.

Peace Wonderful Peace
Daytona Bch Fla
12–15th 46[1]

Dear Rev Thurman

Receive Very happy To hear from You Now listen Rev Yours & Your belove Sister Little more then Two years ago Came to me unaware For devideing of the Home but at ~~time~~ That time I was Not ready to do. Or carry on with The intire family Knowing as I did Know that the intire Family had hatered And Malice and strife Instore against me For many Years Against me so When You all Made the request Two Years ago Revend it was at The right place but Not the right Time because I thought Within Myself that I had not paid of in Full but at this Writeing I that the Old account is settle ~~whd~~ what I Name and interpet Growing hatered In Your intermediate Family as I am now And him so bourden Down in heart in Mind for so long and espeially sister and We Were closely Allied in friendship Listen rev the first Thing ~~thad~~ that You put In you trunk is {the}Part That you take out This is like unto {a} heart Felt sorrow to a Regenerated soul. Truly born of God. No rev all I am asking for is the one Little house on the vacate Lot[2] that would give You all the big house and two small Houses Yes all Fates is jam up For 46 Bal due on Loan $402.91

Monthly payments $12\oo I hope to build a home on The lot and live the small House until New one is Finish Your mother can Live on her rent and all Family can come and live At home in Peace amen {over}[3] it will cost about $12\oo For Saviors Service my cincere love To You and Family & Church at large Respt Yours
For That Peace That Passes all Human Understanding
[*signed*] JE Sams

ALS. FC

NOTES

1. This letter was not postmarked until 10 January 1947.
2. "(The is Vacant)" is written in the left margin.
3. Meaning to turn the page over.

❧ FROM TODD DUNCAN
31 DECEMBER 1946
WASHINGTON, D.C.

Todd Duncan,[1] Thurman's good friend and former colleague at Howard University, indicates that he can continue to support the music programs of Fellowship Church, though not at the level of the previous year.

My dear Howard,

I would like to write you a long letter and tell you what I think about you, your work, and your wife but "beins" I'm a singer, ain't no speaker and dare not try to write the kind of letter you put out I will just say that I am wishing that 1947 will give you the realization of many of your dreams.

About our music project I am not in position to do what I did last year due to the fact that I have already committed myself to the extent of about $600 for a cause which is in fact a conviction with me. But I do not mean that I have left you and so I am proposing that Gladys and I be responsible for $100 for the year 1947. I hope this small amount and a very big understanding heart will please you. Love to you and Sue.
[*signed*] Todd
Todd

Dr. Howard Thurman
2142 Pierce Street
San Francisco 15, California

                                                                              TLS.

Published courtesy of the Todd Duncan Papers, Bentley Historical Library, University of
    Michigan, Ann Arbor.

NOTE

1. Todd Duncan (1903–98) was born in Kentucky, and after earning an undergraduate degree at Butler University in Indianapolis (1925) and a master's degree at Columbia's
Teachers College (1930), he joined the music faculty at Howard. A trained operatic baritone
who sang with African American opera companies, he is best remembered for creating the
role of Porgy in George Gershwin's *Porgy and Bess* on Broadway in 1935, a role he sang with
distinction in its original production and at Broadway revivals in 1937 and 1942. In 1945
Duncan sang the role of Tonio in Leoncavallo's *Pagliacci* with the New York City Opera,
becoming the first African American to sing with a major American opera company. He
later sang as Escamillo in Bizet's *Carmen* and had the title role in Verdi's *Rigoletto* with the
company. In 1949 he created the role of Stephen Kumalo in Kurt Weill's *Lost in the Stars*,
based on Alan Paton's novel of South Africa, *Cry, the Beloved Country*. He left Howard in
1945 to pursue his singing career, and after his stage and recital career ended, he was a vocal
teacher into his nineties.

THE CHURCH FOR THE FELLOWSHIP OF ALL PEOPLES (PAMPHLET)
1947

*In 1947 the Fellowship Church published a sixteen-page pamphlet,[1] its most
ambitious publicity effort during Thurman's tenure. The pamphlet included information about many aspects of the church's operations, including its finances,[2]
its various clubs and activities, its music program, its political involvements,[3] and
its guiding principles. The opening two sections, reprinted here, are programmatic
statements by Thurman and Fisk on their understandings of the meaning and
purpose of the Fellowship Church. Thurman's piece, "The Historical Perspective," is his first full statement of his involvement in the creation of the church,
the kernel of what he would a decade later elaborate in his book-length account,*
Footprints of a Dream. *The article contains Thurman's first published account,
some eleven years after the event, of his "Khyber Pass experience" that set him on
a path toward the Fellowship Church. Fisk probably wrote "World Community
Begins at Home" in 1945. By the time it appeared in this pamphlet he had left the
church. It remains his only published account of the reasons for his involvement
in the Fellowship Church and emphasizes that those who talk of international
justice need to make sure that their own houses and neighborhoods are in order.[4]*

The Historical Perspective

Again and again I have been asked by many people over the country, "How did Fellowship Church get started? Was it organized before you went to San Francisco? Why would you leave a position with life tenure at Howard University to go out to California to devote your full time to something that runs counter to the social pattern of American life both within and outside the church? Moreover, a development that may collapse any time?"

It is in reply to questions such as these, and also for the purpose of clarification that the following account is written.

The story has its roots far back into the past. We were seated, Mrs. Thurman and I, in an automobile on our way up to Khyber Pass and the border of Afghanistan in the winter of 1936.[5] The end of our journey to India was now in sight and our minds were full of thoughts about the meaning of what we had observed in that fabulous land. After our minds shuttled between India and America as we saw missionaries at work, business men functioning, colleges and universities fulfilling their appointed tasks, it was clear to us that there was a fundamental contradiction that lay like a malignant growth at the heart of the Christian movement as it had expressed itself in our own country. This 'will to separateness' within the Church on the basis of race made the Church one of the strongest bulwarks in American life defending and exemplifying racial prejudice and the discrimination resulting therefrom. Indian students, Christian and Hindu, constantly reminded us of this fact. A certain Hindu felt it so strongly that he said he regarded me as a traitor to all the darker peoples of the earth because I was abroad in India standing within that tradition.[6]

Earlier in the month we had received a press account of the first meeting of what was called an interracial church in Philadelphia—a movement started by Miss Marjorie Penny,[7] who at the time was one of the secretaries of the American Friends Service Committee. But this was not a church in the sense that it had a ministry and regular religious function and a location. It was rather a movement calling together people once a month for religious service under interracial leadership. It marked a significant step and as soon as I returned to the country I identified myself with it, sharing in the leadership on several occasions. But this did not seem to meet the situation that was at the heart of the problem.

Accordingly, when we returned to America it was clear to us that somewhere we must give our lives to establishing a church that would test whether or not there was enough vitality in religious experience to inspire men and women to normal natural brotherly relations. We knew the east, our roots were there, and it was natural for us to think in terms of that section for our venture. There were many informal discussions with several persons in the field of religion, notably Dr. Channing Tobias[8] of New York City with whom many younger men had shared their dreams through the years.

During the intervening years at Howard University we experimented with a wide variety of creative approaches to religion and religious experience, calling into them at the level of participation, as wide a spread of racial and cultural contributions as possible. Not only were we concerned about enriching the life of the University through these various functions, but we were testing as well, the growing conviction that if the Ideal is big enough and the commitment of implementation sufficiently profound, differences of race or color become superficial and trivial. What bigger ideal could there be than the deepening of an experience of the living God through intercredal, interracial and intercultural worship and the practical influence of this experience in the stream of life?

It was against this background of my thinking that I received, one day in the Fall of 1943, a letter from A. J. Muste of New York City, telling me about a proposal to establish an interracial church in San Francisco. He suggested that if I knew a young Negro minister who could be interested in such an enterprise to send the name, with a letter, to Dr. Alfred Fisk of the San Francisco State College. Soon after that I received a letter from Dr. Fisk myself, making essentially the same request and stating that he had resigned the Presbyterian Church of which he was a minister and expected to become a co-pastor of this new enterprise which he was initiating.

The first formal meeting of the group for worship was in December 1943. The young man sharing the co-pastorate with Dr. Fisk was Rev. Manley Johnson, a senior in the Berkeley Baptist Divinity School. Dr. Fisk continued as a full professor at San Francisco State College, and, in the nature of the case, gave only a part of his time to the Church. Early in 1944, Rev. Albert Cleage, a graduate of the Oberlin Divinity School, succeeded Mr. Johnson, and remained with the Church until June 1944.

Our connection with the Church began in July of that year. When we came to San Francisco there was no formal organization of the Church as such. There was a temporary Board made up of men and women, Negro and white, and the co-pastor arrangement. The first name which the group had selected during the early weeks of its beginning was "The Neighborhood Church" which seemed to them expressive of their intent. Dr. Fisk was convinced that despite this limitation of scope, if the Church fulfilled itself it would be of tremendous significance. A little later the name was changed from Neighborhood Church to Fellowship Church for All Peoples. This was the title as it appeared on the sign in the yard of 1500 Post Street when we arrived here.

The first task was to establish some formal basis of membership through the channel of an acceptable commitment of faith. Such a thing had been proposed in the early stages of the development but without success. At my first meeting with the temporary Board it was very interesting to hear the testimony of the various people as to why they were interested in the development of this venture. By the end of July I had prepared a commitment with Dr. Fisk's sanction, which commitment was presented to the Board for its approval, with the understanding that during the month of August, while Dr. Fisk was away on vacation, I would preach each Sunday morning on a section of this Commitment so as to provide an opportunity for those interested to understand the basis upon which we were planning to go forward. This was done. It seemed absolutely necessary to work carefully at this point before any formal attempt was made to secure members. It was not until September 1944 that we had members of the Church as such. The group that had worked on this from the beginning with Dr. Fisk gave to our joint leadership an enthusiastic, cooperative response, heightened by the fact that the work was becoming stabilized.

From the very beginning of the venture, the Board of National Missions and Church Extension of the Presbyterian Church, U.S.A., under the leadership of their Executive Secretary in this area, the late Dr. Clyde Smith, gave not only a financial contribution of $3600 a year and the rent-free use of a property for meeting, etc., but they also provided counsel and encouragement. If this important historic denomination had not stood hard by the Church in those crucial months the sheer physical basis so essential for continuation would have made survival well nigh impossible, if not altogether so.

At once certain things seemed clear to me in the light of all of the thinking and planning that we had done over the years against the background of our life in America. First, the location of the Church itself was very significant. One of the simple devices by which the pattern of segregation spreads in American life is by the placing of institutions whose commitment is opposed to segregation into relatively segregated communities or neighborhoods and given in those neighborhoods a community assignment. The degree to which this assignment is carried out the church becomes like the neighborhood. It was important, therefore, for us to be located so as not to be identified with a particular neighborhood.

Second, *at least in the early days,* we should not become involved in community settlement activities, for this would merely make of the church a kind of 'dumping ground' for uplift and sacrificial helpfulness that often is terribly degrading to the personalities of all the people involved. This emphasis on our part has made for much misunderstanding but the validity of the position has justified itself.

Third, the problem of maintaining an authentic interracial character in an environment that is not under control had no ready solution. From our observation we knew of no single institution that had been able to do this without introducing certain artificial controls such as, for instance, a mechanical equalization of participation from various groups. The miracle of Fellowship Church today is that it has maintained an authentic interracial character as a natural response to the ideal.

Fourth, while we wanted to develop the church within the framework of historical Christianity we did not see how such a thing could be accomplished and at the same time the church not become denominational. It was the daring dream that some historic denomination would be able to see in us the growing edge of a radical implementation of the Christian ideal in human relations, which implementation at the moment was not possible within the framework of the denomination as it has been developed in this country. Such a denomination would brood over our development giving it all of the spiritual and moral and economic support that its resources could yield, to the end that we would serve both as a challenge and as a leaven within the Church itself. This could not be worked out and therefore, it was necessary for us to go on our way as a church, independent in affiliation and organizational financial support, but interdenominational in character, with a provision made in our structure for the closest kind of cooperation and fellowship with historic Churches. This, of course, illustrates in a dynamic dimension the historic dilemma of the Protestant branch of the Christian movement in history.

Fifth, the basis of our appeal should be as broad as the varieties that go to make up American life. To project the church merely on the Negro-white basis as it was originally conceived would in the end defeat its purpose. We began thinking of and introducing in our plans the inter-cultural motif from the beginning of our work in July, 1944. This was done through a radical alteration in the program content of the first summer activity for children. The group studied the various peoples who go to make up American life. They memorialized their impressions through more than 65 water colors which were exhibited in the San Francisco Museum of Art under the billing of Fellowship Church. The program content of the various dinners held by the church carried this same emphasis. And, finally a two-year experiment in an Intercultural Workshop for Children. The purpose of this activity, the financial basis of which has been made possible by a joint grant from the Rosenberg Foundation of San Francisco and Mrs. David Levy of New York City, was to answer two important questions:

a) Can the church undertake the broadening of the horizons of children with reference to their knowledge and interpretation of other peoples in America without the negative aspects of the missionary enterprise?
b) Is it possible to develop simple techniques, methods, and useful materials to this end, that can be made available to any person of normal intelligence and imagination who wants to do this thing in his community wherever it is located?

It is our judgment that the answer to both of these is a positive one, and at the end of our experiment the entire story will be written up and made available. In addition to this intercultural motif it was necessary to seek to interest people of varying cultural backgrounds in active membership in the Church. For many reasons this development is slow but authentic.

Sixth, would it be possible to develop a choir, interracial and intercultural in character that would be not only a singing unit, but also a psychological unit whose core would be a logical expression of the genius of the church? This is showing every possible indication of high fulfillment and is novel in American church life. The beginning of such a choral development was made possible by a gift of $300 from the celebrated Negro baritone, Todd Duncan of Washington, D.C.

Seventh, our church, born essentially in the womb of a social issue, would have great difficulty in maintaining a spiritual center of integration. Dr. Fisk recognized this at once for he insisted even in the earliest days that the basis of the church should be worship. However the social issue is so acute that it required tremendous care to vouchsafe the religious genius. In an effort in this direction since July, 1944, we have conducted seven religious study groups, three-fourths of them have had to do with an understanding of mystical religion as the dynamic for such action. In addition, much of the content of the preaching has been in terms of deepening the spiritual life of the people. The response at this point has been both encouraging and inspiring.

Eighth, our church will have to be a growing edge for the entire community and to that extent prophetic for America as a whole. In order to do this we will have to combine social awareness, spiritual motivation, and creative fellowship in a single unifying experience. This, we have sought to do not only through Sunday morning worship but through the medium of a monthly Coffee Hour coming immediately after Morning Service at which time there is much personal small talk and the formal introduction to the group of some community agency dedicated to the same basic ends that we seek. Further, an occasional tea for the whole congregation at our home at which time some person of a different culture or background is enjoyed with all of the overtones of understanding and thickening of relationships resulting therefrom.

Ninth, whatever is done for children in religious education should spring from the basic core of the church itself. Accordingly, this Fall we are working with children on Sundays from this point of view for the first time. Suffice it to say that the parents of the small children who share in this are the sponsoring committee of the activity itself.[9]

Tenth, the work with the young adults is being undertaken this year in the light of the fundamental commitment of the church. The plan which they are using was arrived at by a group process in which there was full participation. There are four scheduled meetings a month, two of which are discussions, one a dinner in some restaurant preparing food not native to America, and one meeting given completely as a contribution in terms of a job to be done, to various community organizations working in the same general direction of the Church.[10]

To summarize, the basis of the Church is no longer Negro-white only, as it was in the beginning. It is no longer conceived as a neighborhood church. It is achieving an authentic fellowship across denominational, class, cultural, and racial lines. Its membership is both local and national with a provision made for those persons who wish to remain in their own church and be members of Fellowship Church. The financial support of the church stems from the local membership, from its national associates, and from a variety of friends whose concern for the ideal to which we are dedicated is greater than the tendency to separateness and exclusiveness that is the curse of America and so often the disgrace of Christianity.

While our growth is not spectacular it is definite and significant, manifesting an increasing faith in the fulfillment of God's dream that we are all one.

World Community Begins at Home

The United States cannot take to the peoples of the world what we do not practice at home. Democracy and brotherhood may be inherently excellent, and we may extol them to the skies, but if we do not live by them, we cannot teach other peoples to do so. World community begins at home.

As individuals we are apt to criticize the foreign ministers of the big powers and denounce the mistakes that have been made in international relations. That gets us nowhere. Writing letters to Congress, making speeches (if we can), attending meetings—these things we will continue to do, and I do not decry them. But they do not bring in the Kingdom of God. Most of us can work more effectively for world peace by beginning right where we are. Quietly, unobtrusively we can set to work first upon ourselves. To make of ourselves gracious and kindly personalities, sensitive to other peoples' hurts and frustrations; to be heedless of our own welfare and benefit and of things that mean aggrandizement of self—this is no small task. Even to live without exploiting another human being is not easy. To go through twenty-four hours, one day, without taking advantage of anyone else, without living "on their backs" so to speak, profiting by their inadequately requited labor or their exploited service—this would be for most of us to enter a new kind of life. But it is the life of the Kingdom of God, and we can begin it today without waiting for peace treaties to be signed or war to be outlawed by the nations.

We begin, then, on ourselves. For most of us, that is a job so big that we will be working on it the rest of our lives. Meanwhile, too, we will set to work on conditions nearest to us, the community relationships which we touch. How eager we are to bring democracy to Germany or the Four Freedoms to the Balkans! But that is not our assignment. Rather we should begin with the needs of our own community. Is it nothing to us that a Filipino serviceman is refused entrance to first class restaurants in San Francisco? that a Japanese-American or a Negro cannot buy a home in most of the respectable sections of our city?

We pride ourselves on San Francisco as a melting pot of all peoples, a cosmopolitan city. We take pride, for instance, in our Chinatown. We think of it as a "glamorous" spot. We like to show it to our friends. But Chinatown is our shame! It is the worst slum west of the Mississippi, and the tuberculosis rate there is several times what it is in the rest of the city.

San Francisco is the world in little, and to build democracy and brotherhood here is much more our responsibility than to say what Britain should do in India, or what Russia should do in Rumania. Even the problem of making San Francisco what it ought to be, is too vast a task for most of us. But we can begin in some little corner. We can begin building a bridge between two people, so that where there was separation before there is community now. Soon it will grow from two to twenty. And suddenly that will be our world. We will no longer live in a world of hate and exploitation and strife, but in a world of the familyhood of God, our world.

We will be under no illusions as to achieving "greatness." But we will not despair because the world afar off contains much evil. When we walk in the light, darkness holds no terror; indeed it does not touch us, the light alone is real.

That what takes place in the intimate relations of neighborhoods *is* important, is shown by the fact that in the Detroit riot of two years ago,[11] though there was much looting and havoc in the sections of the city where occupancy was completely Negro, and similar damage in nearby sections that were completely white, no looting occurred in those areas where Negroes and whites were intermingled in non-segregated living. As one of the whites told a news reporter, "You wouldn't damage the property of your neighbors when you know them and are friends with them." So important was this community feeling in preventing rioting, that it has been cited again and again as an illustration of how to prevent race friction. Similar instances have occurred in certain Federal Housing projects, and the fellowship among the interracial crew of the liberty ship, *Booker T. Washington,*[12] is a saga talked of round the world.

To some extent any of us can write another such chapter. We can create little islands of goodwill and fellowship in the seeming sea of hatred. The islands will grow and become linked together until a veritable continent is born. The tiniest island is important. It may be but a couple of neighborhood children taken to the Zoo together. But if a sense of oneness grows up between those two, it is an achievement on a small scale of the very thing we long for, in bringing the nations together.

World order and world justice, then, like charity, begins at home. Most of us and our neighbors are not completely free from thoughts of vengeance toward our erstwhile enemies. Most of us and our neighbors believe in force, in building more tanks, more planes, more rocket bombs—which will make other nations hurry to build more tanks, and more planes, and more rocket bombs. Most of us and our neighbors believe in maintaining our nation's "uncompromised sovereignty" (whatever that is); and securing far-flung bases so that we can protect ourselves and make other nations behave. Most of us and our neighbors want our nation to be the "greatest" and most powerful, and with the highest standard of living of any. Most of us and our neighbors want our particular kind of people (race or class or select group) to be the "leaders" in our society, directing affairs, and reaping the rewards of such direction. Most of us and our neighbors need a great deal of interior overhauling and of spiritual redemption before the Kingdom of God has a chance where we are. Yes, world peace, like charity, can begin at home, with us.

The Church for the Fellowship of All Peoples (San Francisco: Church for the Fellowship of All Peoples, 1947), 3-7.

PD.

Notes

1. The pamphlet is undated, but evidence makes clear that it could not have appeared before May 1947 and probably appeared shortly thereafter. However, some of its sections were likely written considerably before that date.

2. The pamphlet reported an annual operating budget of $11,800, enough to pay Thurman's salary, rent to the Theater Arts Colony for the Sunday worship space, and other expenses, balanced against revenue of $11,800 raised from pledges ($3,450), Sunday collections ($2,800), and special gifts and grants ($5,550).

3. The Community Relations Committee was involved in such causes as the creation of a California Fair Employment Practices Commission, working to eliminate discriminatory anti-Japanese land legislation, and the fight against restrictive covenants.

4. Fisk would subsequently publish another article that drew on his experiences at the Fellowship Church but did not explicitly mention the church: Fisk, "Stereotypes in Intercultural Education."

5. For background, see Dixie and Eisenstadt, *Visions of a Better World,* 84–116.

6. Ibid., xi–xxv.

7. On Marjorie Penney, see *PHWT,* 2:318–20.

8. See *PHWT,* 1:3.

9. The Fellowship Church did not start a Sunday school until there were enough members with young children to make this practical. It began at the church in January 1947 with six children and increased to twenty students by April. Elsewhere in the pamphlet, the purpose of the school is described as giving the pupils an "opportunity to discover a sound spiritual basis for everyday living; that whatever they were taught should be so basic that nothing need be unlearned later, but that all would contribute to building dependable foundations for lifelong growth."

"The Arrival of the Magi," a Fellowship Church Christmas tableaux, 1946 (back row, from left: Jean McEwan, Kaye Dunham, Raymond Fong, Hansel Harter, Jean McHenry, two unidentified, Anne Thurman; front row: Noah Griffin Sr., Dave Tatsuno). From the Howard Thurman Collection, Howard Gotlieb Archival Research Center, Boston University.

10. This was the Young Adult Group, started in the fall of 1944 by Thomas Hawkins, Thurman's protégé and the dean of men at Howard University, when he was studying at the University of California at Berkeley. It is described in the pamphlet as attracting "young men and women from a rich cross-section of social backgrounds—all races and creeds."

11. The riot took place on 20–21 June 1943.

12. The SS *Booker T. Washington* was a liberty ship, a cargo ship built to support the war effort. Commissioned in 1942, it was captained by Hugh Mulzac (1886–1971), the first African American captain in the U.S. Merchant Marine, who insisted on an interracial crew.

❧ To C. Durham Grandy
17 March 1947
[*San Francisco, Calif.*]

Thurman responds enthusiastically to news of an interracial church in North Carolina. His comments reflect his own understanding of his role as the unofficial leader of a small yet significant movement toward interracialism in Christian churches. As a result of his pastoral duties, many of his customary preaching engagements around the country could not be accommodated by his schedule. Thurman informs Grandy that it will be a year or longer before he can get to Durham to preach.

Dear Dr. Grandy:

I am deeply moved by the contents of your letter under date of March 5th. I found it in San Francisco when I returned on the 14th.

It is a matter of excitement that in Durham, North Carolina there is the beginning of a prophetic Christian Church. I am interested to know about the development and the experience itself. If you have any descriptive material will you please let me have it.

I am sorry it will not be possible for me to preach for you this year, but I hope that sometime within the next twelve or fourteen months I can arrange to do so.

I am enclosing one of our membership forms so that you will get some idea about what our basis of membership is. I want you to know how happy I am that something of this sort is beginning in North Carolina.
Sincerely yours,
Howard W. Thurman

Dr. C. D. Grandy
613 Mobile Avenue
Durham, North Carolina
                                                                    TLc.

 ✺ FROM GEORGE THOMAS
18 APRIL 1947
CAMBRIDGE, MASS.

The Ingersoll Lecture on Immortality, which Thurman delivered at Harvard University on 14 April, was the most prominent lecture or sermon he had yet delivered. As his former Howard University student notes in this letter, somewhat overenthusiastically, it was well received. Thurman too was impressed by his reception, writing friends shortly afterward that "the response was overwhelming in many ways" and that giving the lecture had been "a tremendous experience for me."[1] In many ways the Ingersoll lecture, which became the basis of Thurman's first book to be issued by a major, commercial publisher, marked his transition from someone known primarily by his circle of admirers to a preacher with a national reputation.[2]

Thurman would give the lecture again, in San Francisco on 18 May at Temple Emanu-El; twelve hundred people attended, and several hundred had to be turned away.[3] His choice of venue was partly in recompense to the congregation for making possible the writing of the lecture. As he would write in his autobiography, "Much of the preparation for the lecture was done under extreme pressure. During the early years at Fellowship Church, the congregation met in a small building with no room for an office. Our family lived in a crowded, congested apartment. I had no place to work, to write, or to think. I was offered the use of the facilities of Temple Emanu-El, which included a library, a quiet lounge, and the assistance of a secretary. I completed almost all of the writing of The Negro Spiritual Speaks of Life and Death *in the library and lounge of the temple."*[4]

The Negro spirituals were among Thurman's favorite subjects for sermons; they were the topic of a series of lectures he had given as early as 1928 and one that he had often returned to in the intervening years. He had recently published a short book of sermons on selected spirituals.[5] *Still, he hesitated in making the spirituals the subject of his Ingersoll lecture, which would be delivered to a predominantly white audience, because of his sensitivity "to the pervasive notion that black scholars were incapable of reflective thought on any matters other than those that bore directly on their own struggle for survival in American society . . . I chose to examine the Negro spirituals again in spite of this prevailing opinion and not because of it."*[6]

The charge to the Ingersoll lecturer—to speak on "the Immortality of Man"— was also a challenge to Thurman, since it was a subject he rarely if ever spoke on, and he probably was not a believer in personal immortality. But "he felt challenged by the possibility of discovering my own thought on immortality." Thurman concluded that the spirituals spoke less about individual immortality than about "the immortality of life itself."[7] *When the lecture was reprinted in 1975, Thurman wrote of blacks and whites in America as "two ugly monoliths" that are "ruthless, bitter, destructive, blind to good," without a past and with "only a blurred future." The message of spirituals, he wrote, was that "hope was built into the fabric of the struggle."*[8]

Dear Rev. Thurman,

I waited a few days before writing on the chance that you might be back in California when this gets there. Of course I am assuming that you went home from Cambridge.

I just learned that you were coming to Harvard when I read an article in the Boston Globe date[d] February 19. It was on the upper corner of page 13 and was titled "Negro Spiritualists Topic for Ingersoll Lecture."[9] The first sentence said: "The idea of Immortality in Negro Spirituals will be the subject of the Annual Ingersoll lecture on the "Immortality of Man" at Harvard University this Spring." It went on to talk about you. I cut the article out of the paper and put it on my desk. On the Sunday preceding the lecture I was down in the South Station. I had left my books to get some air and mail a letter home. While I was there the Senator[10] arrived from New York and you were on it. I believe that you were wearing a gray top coat and a gray hat. You stopped at the information booth before leaving the station. I started to speak to you but I looked so bad in my study clothes and my army field coat that I decided not to shame you.

You really "knocked them out" at your lecture. You really impressed Harvard and, believe me, Harvard is hard to impress. But the most important thing of all is the fact that you recognized me after all these years. I have been walking on air ever since I was that proud. When I left the chapel I walked with a Professor of History at Pomona College. He is retiring this year. He told me that he was on his way to Maine but when he learned that you were to be at Harvard he had to stop off and hear you.

The New York Tribune certainly gave you a big write-up, didn't they? They quoted great hunks of the lecture verbatim. Did you give them a copy or did they have a reporter present. They had you at the top of the article. As I understand it, yours was the second—not the first lecture to be given so that shows how you rate. I'm sure that you have a dozen copies of the article. If you haven't, I'll loan you mine to make a copy if you wish.

Well, I've got to get back into my books. Please give the Charming Lady my best regards. If this little note seems incoherent and illegible just realize that it is the effort of a tired graduate student suffering from a slight case of writer's cramps.

Now the poem I want is the one that goes "Star light, star bright, Lay this body ~~down~~ down."[11] But if you care to send more than one do so because I am something of a spiritual friend.

Sincerely,

[*signed*] George P. Thomas

                                                                        ALS.

Notes

    1. To Coleman Jennings, 21 May 1947; To John Darr, 12 May 1947.

    2. HT, *The Negro Spiritual Speaks of Life and Death* (New York: Harper, 1947). It had previously been printed, with the same title, in the *Harvard Divinity School Bulletin* 13 (1947/48): 5–25.

    3. To Mr. and Mrs. Joseph James, 17 June 1947, printed in the current volume.

    4. *WHAH*, 217.

    5. "The Message of the Spirituals," *PHWT*, 1:126–37; HT, *Deep River*. Some of the material in this book drew on an earlier article, "Religious Ideas in Negro Spirituals," *Christendom* 4 (August 1939): 515–28.

    6. *WHAH*, 216.

    7. Ibid., 216, 217.

8. HT, *The Negro Spiritual Speaks of Life and Death* (Richmond, Ind.: Friends United Press, 1975), 3–4.

9. The Ingersoll Lecture on the Immortality of Man (now the Ingersoll Lecture on Human Immortality) was first delivered in 1896 at the Harvard Divinity School. William James (1897) and Josiah Royce (1899) were among the early lecturers. Thurman was the first African American to give the lecture. In recent years those giving the Ingersoll lecture have included Marian Wright Edelman (1993), Albert Raboteau (2010), and Toni Morrison (2012). In 1968 Thurman's student Walter N. Pahnke was the Ingersoll lecturer.

10. The *Senator* was a Pennsylvania Railroad train that traveled on the Northeast corridor from Washington, D.C., to Boston.

11. As quoted by Thurman in his Ingersoll lecture:

> I know moon-rise, I know star-rise,
>   I lay this body down.
> I walk in the moon-light. I walk in the star-light,
>   To lay this body down.
> I walk in the graveyard, I walk through the graveyard
>   To lay this body down.
> I lie in the grave and stretch out my arms,
>   To lay this body down.

For Thurman, this spiritual meant that man "is heir to all the buffetings of the fixed and immovable, yet he can lay the body down and stretch out his arms and be at one with moonrise and starlight" (HT, *Negro Spiritual Speaks of Life and Death*, 23).

✌ FROM MADALINE THURMAN
1 MAY 1947
[*New York, N.Y.*]

Madaline Thurman, then in New York City, writes of her involvement with the Dalcroze School of Music and responds to Thurman's scolding of her for not keeping in contact with him and the rest of the family. Madaline tells her brother that while physically exhausted, she is doing well emotionally.

My dearest Howard,

I certainly needed your letter which I just received to remind me of the fact that my personal life is <u>nil</u> and that I have been very selfish in my neglect of mama. I did send her a letter last Sat. night & plan to send her a dress as soon as I can. Also, I'll go down in July, cant leave before because of the unwinding of the tremendous climax which I am now approaching.

Eliz. was in Fla. week before last saw mama and told me how anxious she was about me. I am getting along very well on the inside, but physically—am so damn tired, suffering from a terrific cold, and moving into the last week of school which is the sort of strain I've never experienced before. Yesterday the 5 of us who are trying for certificates, drew our three subjects in movement which we must prepare to teach to members of the 2nd and 3rd yrs classes, before a jury next Wed. I drew 2 of the hardest & one of the easiest; The hard ones are centered around ideas in movement which I never heard of before 3 months ago. However, I've done a lot of thinking about and experiencing of them recently. In short, I must prepare lessons on Tempo (easy) Time & Space, Syncopation[1] (conflict). However, each of us has to teach only <u>one</u> of those lessons; we draw lots for that too. Then, we have the half hour oral on Thursday; & a party Fri for which I must complete an original choral & orchestral piece to be performed. I shall give your address to the secretary at school in case I collapse.

Back to the lessons: we must plan them with such care that the class will experience the subject <u>emotionally</u> from our exercises & improvisations, understand them intellectually from our explanation. Tomorrow morning I start preparing. Please think of me, all of you, Wed. morning. I'm not worried about failure if I fail, I fail; I simply want to do the best that I can. The clue is to think of the class & one's responsibility to the class. The difficulty is centered around the almost super human demonstrations of dedication & love of humanity shown by Miss Schuster[2] who is inch by inch killing herself for us & the democratic ideals of the Dalcroze Method[3] we want to come through now because we know that life will show us only a few more examples of dedications & probably no more—to an ideal of personal integration. (Fear not my feet are on the ground!)

This time next Sat. which seems eons away, I'll be free—over on Mr. Mendel's[4] roof at at a party for our class. Then I can write Ma each week, find a place to live for next year, finish details of work neglected now, collect pay for teaching at Jefferson School[5] & go to Fla.

Your book arrived this week. Thanks, I have read much already—only in small bits however. It is beautifully bound and beautifully written.

How are my little or big nieces. Tell them I love them & will write sometime soon—How is the church progressing? Is Mark still out there? Frances & the boys are fine, I hope.

It is now Sunday morning. I went to bed about 7 last night its now 7:30. I must bathe do a few other personal chores & get to work. Fortunately for me Eliz. left Fri night. Thus I can work in peace.

I shall write ma to night.

You have no idea how different I am now from what I was when you saw me last—much more calm and integrated. May God bless you.
Bye,
[*signed*] Madaline
P.S. Give my love to Sue when you write. I hope Mother Bailey will not suffer pain.
Bye

Thurman family, c. 1945 (from left: Olive Thurman, Howard Thurman, Sue Bailey Thurman, Anne Spencer Thurman). From the Howard Thurman Collection, Howard Gotlieb Archival Research Center, Boston University.

NOTES

1. Madaline writes "Syncopotion."

2. Hinda Schuster (1907–84), a disciple of Dalcroze, headed the Dalcroze Music School in New York City from 1944 to 1994.

3. Madaline Thurman had been interested in the Dalcroze Method—a combination of music, dance, and movement often known as eurythmics—since the 1930s, when she studied with its founder, the Swiss composer and pianist Émile Jaques-Dalcroze (1865–1950) in Geneva, Switzerland (in 1935–36). See *PHWT*, 1:261; *WHAH*, 110.

4. Arthur Mendel (1905–79) was a prominent conductor and musicologist who taught at the Dalcroze School in the late 1940s. A specialist in the music of Johann Sebastian Bach, he was among the first to advocate for authenticity in baroque performing practice.

5. Probably the Jefferson School of Social Science (1943–56), a large Communist-run school for adult education.

Madaline Thurman Johnson with unidentified woman, c. 1945. From the Bailey Thurman Family Papers; Manuscript, Archives, and Rare Book Library, Emory University.

To Mr. Ward
6 MAY 1947
[*San Francisco, Calif.*]

Thurman spoke at the prestigious Commonwealth Club of California[1] on 13 June 1947 on "The Genius of Democracy" and received, he noted proudly to a friend, a standing ovation.[2] It is unclear precisely what the Commonwealth Club originally asked him to speak about, though they probably requested a talk on an aspect of race relations. Thurman, as he often did, used the occasion to speak more on race broadly and place the question of black-white interactions in a larger and implicitly religious context. The talk at the Commonwealth Club was likely similar to one he had delivered a few weeks earlier, "Reflections Concerning the Democratic Dogma," in St. Louis on 16 April.[3]

Dear Mr. Ward:[4]

I was over in Marin County most of the day and was unable to telephone you, so that as a substitute, I am sending this note.

For the first time in my life I am completely stumped in the matter of trying to decide about an address. I have been stumped before but never completely stumped. My field of technical training is religion. It is also the area of my major concern. I share thoroughly the point of view of your committee namely that the matter of the race of the speaker is merely coincidental, but the important thing is what he has to say concerning the field of his competency. In the last analysis, this is the best argument against racial narrowness. I followed this policy for years making all of my public appearances on behalf of an interpretation of religion. Obviously, this is out for the Commonwealth Club.

As an American citizen, I am concerned about the survival of Democracy in the world. My thinking in the field is from the point of view of an American citizen rather than from the point of view of a Negro. It is for this reason that it is my judgment that a talk having to do with an analysis of Democracy and the problem that it faces for survival in the modern world is timely and very much to the point, so much has happened on this planet during the past ten years that there is grave danger that we lose our nerve and undermine our confidence in the integrity of our faith in democracy itself. I wish therefore that you and your committee would re-consider the possibility of having me speak on Democracy. If this can be done, I shall be happy to appear on Friday, June 13th.

Sincerely yours,

Howard Thurman

TLc.

NOTES

1. Founded in 1903, the Commonwealth Club of California is the oldest open forum on public affairs in the country.

2. To Mr. and Mrs. Joseph James, 17 June 1947, printed in the current volume.

3. Reba Schinault, "Democracy Keynote of Phyllis Wheatley Dinner," *Pittsburgh Courier*, 26 April 1947. Although his St. Louis talk was before a black audience, Thurman's comments in his letter to the Commonwealth Club indicate the similarity of theme and content between the two talks. In St. Louis he spoke on "his increasing concern lest all Americans lose their confidence in the idea of democracy." The integrity of democracy "was attacked in Germany during the rise of Hitlerism and in our own country when democratic practices were short-circuited during the war. This might suggest," Thurman added, "that democracy is not a valued concept if it cannot be used effectively in times of crisis." Thurman went on to discuss three elements that comprise "the genius of democracy." The first was "civic character which issues from civic responsibility." Drawing on the war, he continued, "Food rationing, work in defense plants, as well as active participation in the armed forces meant automatically a new dimension in civic character. Those possessing such character act as if they belong. The tension during the war between Negroes and whites was caused by the Negroes' participation in the war which gave them a greater sense of belonging and resulted in actions that violated stereotypes. That is why the vote is so important . . . it is the minimum level of reasonable civic participation." The second

element was "freedom, a sense of alternative or option in reference to worship and where one lives. That is why I am so concerned about restrictive covenants because the degree to which any individual is denied an alternative as to where he might live, just in so far the alternatives of all the people of the body politic are stifled." The third element in democracy "points to the future, I think God is sending America to school to teach all of its peoples of different cultural heritages and roots how to live together."

4. Stewart R. Ward was the executive secretary of the Commonwealth Club of California.

To James C. Baker
12 May 1947
[*San Francisco, Calif.*]

In this letter Thurman asks a local Methodist bishop to assign a young Methodist clergyman, John Yamashita,[1] to serve as an assistant pastor at Fellowship Church. (Thurman misspells Yamashita's name.) Although Bishop Baker[2] turned down Thurman's request, Reverend Yamashita did preach regularly at the church. Japanese Americans formed an important part of Fellowship Church from its inception; they were active in its membership and leadership, and the church, located in the former Japanese quarter of San Francisco, had a special involvement with Japanese Americans' war-time plight and their difficult postwar readjustment. The church had a dinner "honoring the returning Japanese Americans" on 26 January 1945.[3] Prominent Japanese American members of the church included Dave Tatsuno, president of the San Francisco chapter of the Japanese American Citizens League, who was an early member of the church's board of trustees; and the first church secretary, Ayako Murota.[4]

Dear Bishop Baker:

I regret very much that your crowded schedule has made it impossible for me to have the privilege of a conference with you.

The matter concerning which I wanted to confer with you has to do with the possibility of the Church for the Fellowship of All Peoples securing the full or part-time services of Rev. John Yashamito. As you know perhaps, our church is interracial, intercultural, and interdenominational in character. Our membership consists of persons who come from many of the Protestant branches of Christianity, white and Negro, Japanese-American, a few Chinese-Americans, a few Mexicans, two American Indians, etc. This in addition to the fact that among the white Americans are some who are first generation Europeans or Canadians. At last we are in a position to provide a dynamic Christian fellowship for peoples of widely diversified backgrounds.

Because of the general climate on the Pacific Coast that in some ways is not congenial to Japanese Americans, we are particularly anxious to provide an experience of complete integration within our religious fellowship for Japanese Americans on all levels of participation in what we are doing. It would be a very great thing if there were at least one church on the Pacific Coast in which these people shared the leadership and membership participation as a part of a fellowship of heterogeneous people. I need not say to you that they have sustained a profound injury both spiritually and psychologically from which it is extraordinarily difficult for them to emerge with some measure of vitality and health as American citizens. The proposal that we have in mind as a church is but a tiny step in the direction of atonement.

I am wondering therefore, Bishop Baker, if you would be willing to assign Reverend Yashamito to Fellowship Church for a year and further would it be possible for some part of his salary to be carried by the Methodist Church. This would give to him an invaluable experience against the time when some churches within the framework of Methodism on this coast might be able to work out an integrated program involving Japanese-Americans with Caucasians and others. I realize that it is possible to consider this request as being very presumptuous, but knowing somewhat of your deep personal and official concern I am taking the liberty to make this proposal.

There are many questions that you may raise about the practicality of this or concerning other aspects of the proposal itself. It will be a pleasure for me to confer with you at your convenience that we may talk together concerning this urgent and crucial matter.

Sincerely yours,
Howard Thurman

Bishop James C. Baker
83 McAllister Street
San Francisco, California

TLc.

NOTES

1. Hiroshi John Yamashita (1912–84), a Nisei born in California, was a Methodist minister for Japanese American Methodist congregations in San Francisco and Los Angeles.

2. James Chamberlain Baker (1879–1969) was a Methodist minister and denominational leader. He graduated in 1898 from Chaddock College, which later merged with Illinois Wesleyan University. He also was the first director of the first Wesley Foundation (at the University of Illinois), Methodism's ministry to college and university students. Baker was elected bishop in 1928 and was assigned to Korea and Japan. In 1932 he was moved to California, where he spent the remainder of his career.

3. Fellowship Church *Bulletin*, 21 January 1945.

4. Thurman wrote the following of Ayako Murota: "The day the bomb fell on Hiroshima, [she] sat in my office as the news came over the air. She had family there. We were both devastated by the announcement. She used my large handkerchief to absorb her tears.

No words were said. There was only the sound of the broadcast, with its lurid description of the carnage. We could establish no psychological distance between ourselves and the horror of the moment. The experience flowed together as a single moment in time. This was Fellowship Church, not in action but in *being*" (*WHAH*, 162).

To Benjamin E. Mays

23 May 1947
[San Francisco, Calif.]

In his autobiography Thurman called Rabbi Irving Reichert one of his "treasures of the spirit." Reichert was the influential rabbi of the oldest Jewish congregation west of the Rockies, Emanu-El; it was in his temple that Thurman preached his first sermon in a Jewish religious service. Reichert did not receive an honorary degree from Morehouse College; however, on 3 June 1947, eleven days after Thurman wrote to Mays, the rabbi stood behind the podium as the college's commencement speaker.

DR. BENJAMIN E. MAYS

IS IT POSSIBLE AT THIS LATE DATE TO CONSIDER GIVING REICHERT HONORARY DEGREE IN HUMANE LETTERS? HE IS ONE OF AMERICA'S GREATEST RABBIS WITH A VISION FAR BEYOND THE BORDERS OF ISRAEL. IT WOULD MEAN OUR FIRST RABBINICAL ALUMNUS AND PERHAPS THE FIRST ONE IN THE COUNTRY FROM ONE OF OUR SCHOOLS. IN ADDITION HE WOULD BE OUR ANCHOR MAN ON THE COAST AGAINST THE TIME WHEN WE DEVELOP THIS SECTION. HE LEAVES HERE MONDAY MORNING. MAY I HEAR.

HOWARD THURMAN

TLc. FC

From G. W. Evington

11 June 1947
[*San Francisco, Calif.*]

G. W. Evington responds to Thurman's complaint that public transportation employees are discriminating against African American patrons. Throughout his life Thurman consistently confronted all practices—even those that others viewed as minor slights—that he believed systematically dehumanized racial and ethnic minorities.

Dear Rev. Thurman:

It was good of you to write to us to bring to our attention the action of one of our crews in passing up some colored people and making derogatory remarks.

I wish to assure you that this matter will be placed before the Division Superintendent for disciplinary action of the crew involved.

Thank you for bringing this incident to our attention.

Cordially yours,

[*signed*] G. W. Evington

G. W. EVINGTON

Superintendent of Transportation

GWE: HCB

TLc.

✍ TO MR. AND MRS. JOSEPH JAMES

17 JUNE 1947

[*San Francisco, Calif.*]

Thurman's friends Joseph and Alberta Mayo James left San Francisco (and a deep involvement with the Fellowship Church) to return to New York City to pursue their acting and singing careers. Joseph James had recently appeared on Broadway (in small parts) in major revivals of Henry IV, Part I; Henry IV, Part II; *and* Oedipus Rex *and was embarking on an ambitious recital tour, performing song cycles of Debussy, Beethoven, Mussorgsky, and Ravel (with his wife as accompanist). In this letter Thurman tells them about his recent success in lecturing on Negro spirituals at Temple Emanu-El in San Francisco, updates the Jameses on recent developments in the Fellowship Church, and shares his perspective on black community politics in San Francisco.*

Dear Joe and Alberta:

You will pardon the sending of a formal letter this way, but my dear brother and sister, if you hear from me at all before August, it will be this way.

Thank you for your wonderful letters full of authentic flavor, the nearest and most accurate substitute for a face-to-face visit. I am glad that you have a nice apartment, and that at last you have come into the fulfillment of the aristocratic frame of reference for which you have been in candidacy for so long. Please describe me accurately to your butler so that next year when I come a-visiting, I will not be bounced.

Sue is in Arkansas with her mother and will be there for some days to come. She is now desperately trying to find someone to live with her and give to Mother Bailey the kind of care that her years and her situation require. I am saving your letters for her scrutiny when she returns.

You should have been here for the Ingersoll Lecture. There were twelve hundred people out at Temple Emanu-El, with several hundred turned away.

More than five hundred attended the reception. Last Friday, I gave a talk for the Commonwealth Club on "The Genius of Democracy." At the end there was a standing ovation. I mention these things because it means that the name Fellowship Church is becoming a part of the vocabulary of San Francisco. This is very much in order because the plans that we have call for a first mortgage on the city.

I am deeply aware of what you had to say about Carleton.[1] He is caught between his genuine desires to be a leader of the people (Why I do not know.), and an authentic interest in the scientific practice of medicine. I am very certain from several things that I have picked up, that he was black listed in the county medical society because of his so-called radical activities. I have counselled with him as much as possible, but the demands that are made upon me are so overwhelming that I cannot see him very often. I have not been by his office in three months. We chat occasionally over the telephone. About three weeks ago, he had the "liberal" wing of the Black Cabinet over to his home.[2] I was a little distressed that the group of fellows over there did not seem to know how to think. There is a tremendous need for the work of the Cabinet.

There is a move to establish a Jim Crow section of the California National Guard.[3] They are asking the ranking reserve Negro officer Morse to head it up. This is one of the matters discussed over at Carleton's the other night introduced by Morse himself. It seems clear that he is going to accept it, on the theory that if he doesn't, someone else will.

Back to Carleton, I think that he has been put on the staff of a hospital across the Bay and hopes to move into San Francisco from that vantage point, but I am not sure about the angles.[4] We have a new Negro newspaper, the Sun,[5] owned by a "philanthropic" white man down town, with all Negroes in the show case. I don't know how it is going to turn out, but it seems to be promising. This week a great National Baptist Negro Congress, six or seven thousand strong invades Oakland with a spill over in San Francisco.[6] It is rather acute because the Key System[7] is on strike and those who find themselves on this side stay, and those who find themselves on the other side stay unless they are willing to swim the Bay.

The Church is growing in a very encouraging manner. For the past six weeks, we have had a capacity congregation; this means about 230 exclusive of the choir. I think that by the first of August, we shall have a white minister[8] who will be serving an internship for a year. Heather's[9] work ends July 1st. It will seem very strange to her not being a part of what we are doing. I hope you will enjoy the new brochure.[10] It tells the story in a very good way.

Jacqueline Myles' brother is here studying for the Dental Board and is living with Mrs. Henderson. We think it is a good deal. I am glad you approve of the course that Mrs. Henderson is taking. It has been a good stimulus to her and she seems much happier.

Take care of yourselves, the two of you, and let me hear when you can.
Sincerely,
Howard Thurman

TLc.

Notes

1. Carleton Benjamin Goodlett (1914–97), a native of Florida, was a 1935 graduate of Howard University, where he was an usher in Thurman's first class of ushers at Rankin Chapel. He went on to receive a Ph.D. in psychology from the University of California at Berkeley in 1938 and a medical degree from Meharry Medical College in 1944. He thereafter established a private medical practice in San Francisco. Thurman was one of his patients. Goodlett also had a career as a newspaper publisher, acquiring the *Reporter* in 1945 and the *Sun* in 1948. He made the *San Francisco Sun-Reporter* into one of the most influential black newspapers on the West Coast. Active in numerous civil rights campaigns and in Democratic Party politics, Goodlett ran an unsuccessful campaign for governor in the Democratic primary in 1966 and played a significant role in furthering the careers of many black politicians, including Willie Brown, the first African American mayor of San Francisco. Brown was instrumental, in 1999, in renaming the majestic plaza in front of San Francisco City Hall the Carleton B. Goodlett Plaza. During the late 1940s and the 1950s Goodlett was close to leftist CIO unions and to organizations associated with the Communist Party, such as the California Labor School, in ways that apparently made Thurman uneasy.

2. The "black cabinet" in San Francisco borrowed its name from a group of black officials, primarily from the middle and lower echelons of the New Deal, that met regularly in Washington, D.C., in the late 1930s. Informally called the Black Cabinet, the group represented and promoted blacks' interests to the federal government. The most prominent members of San Francisco's Black Cabinet included Mary McLeod Bethune, chief of the Negro Division of the National Youth Administration and the group's only woman; and Robert C. Weaver of the Federal Housing Authority, who in 1966, as secretary of housing and urban development, became the first African American cabinet secretary. It is not clear who all the members of San Francisco's Black Cabinet were and what Thurman's objections were to their deliberations.

3. The California National Guard established on 1 January 1947 two all-Negro units, the Sixth Engineers Combat Group and the 719th Anti-Aircraft Artillery Battalion, over the objections of civil rights groups and the American Civil Liberties Union. Two other all-Negro units were created by July 1949, when the California National Guard was officially desegregated. As with the regular military, the desegregation order was implemented cautiously and slowly, and in 1950, when units of the California National Guard were mobilized for the Korean conflict, there were still two all-black units.

4. According to Thurman, by 1950 Goodlett had attending privileges at what was then called the Palo Alto–Stanford Hospital Center (*WHAH*, 156).

5. The *Sun* was acquired by Carleton Goodlett, supposedly in a poker game, and in 1948, after merging with the *Reporter*, became the *Sun-Reporter*.

6. The National Baptist Training Union and Sunday School Congress met in Oakland from 14 June to 22 June. On 20 June, on "Booker T. Washington Night," an annual highlight of the convention, Thurman was the featured speaker at Oakland Municipal Auditorium.

Joseph James, a defense worker, concert baritone, president of the NAACP chapter in San Francisco, and member of Fellowship Church. From the Bailey Thurman Family Papers; Manuscript, Archives, and Rare Book Library, Emory University.

7. The Key System was a privately owned network of streetcars and buses that operated in Oakland and other East Bay cities from 1903 to 1960.

8. Robert Meyners.

9. Heather Whitton.

10. Excerpts from the pamphlet *The Church for the Fellowship of All Peoples* are printed in the current volume.

✌ To Beulah S. Jenness

17 June 1947
[*San Francisco, Calif.*]

*Thurman writes to Beulah S. Jenness, who was upset by the controversy sur-
rounding the release in November 1946 of the Disney film* Song of the South.[1]
*The film was based on the Uncle Remus stories of Joel Chandler Harris.[2] The film
was widely condemned by African American organizations including the NAACP
and the National Negro Congress as stereotyped and giving a false view of race
relations under slavery and the post-Reconstruction South. Jenness thought that
the complaints smacked of "hysteria" and that "the picketing of the picture weakens the faith of whites in the leadership of the blacks." Uncle Remus in the film
"was a black man who portrayed wisdom and good judgment," while the leading
white characters displayed "selfishness and spite." Whites too, she argued, were
the victims of negative depictions in Hollywood films—drunken and promiscuous
women, dissipated aristocrats, violent and loutish gangsters, and so on. Moreover
protests over a film, a mere "fantasy," only took attention from the "many real
and present wrongs which need righting."[3] Thurman writes a careful and friendly
letter to Jenness applauding her frankness and sharing her concerns but strongly
defending the protests and their importance. Thurman argues that the film did
not question the hierarchy of caste that dominated southern race relations and
that whites as a whole were never judged by negative stereotypes, but racial and
ethnic minorities invariably were so judged.*

Dear Mrs. Jenness:

Your letter addressed to me under date of April 26th is at last being answered. I have been in and out of the city so much during the past six months
that most of my correspondence has suffered.

Your letter is very difficult to answer—I would much prefer talking the matter through with you. First of all, I appreciate profoundly the frankness and
directness with which you have written. I also find the quality of your concern
over this matter decidedly reassuring. To be sufficiently concerned over the realization of the most creative relationships possible between the races is deeply
moving.

I think that the mood and the point of view out of which the picketing arose
were far removed from hysteria. It arises, rightly or wrongly, out of the profound resentment of the perpetuation of the slavery stereotype. The fact that
Uncle Remus was wise and rich in humor and intelligence is from the point of
view of the people who picketed, completely irrelevant. They would say that the

setting provided for no overtones that would tend to cause the average white person who saw the picture to appreciate the Negro as a man whose most fundamental significance is in the fact that he is a man. The reasoning would continue, as long as the caste lines are held intact so that a Negro may be depicted as having great qualities and so forth, but qualities which express themselves in a frame of reference that is full of frozen personality differentials, then the status of the Negro as a man cannot move.

You refer to the fact that there is plenty of shame connected with the showing of your race in the film, but the conditions are not analogous, because the white man is temporarily in the ascendancy in the world. He is the prestige bearer of society, when movies are shown that reflect discreditably upon him, they are localized in the sense that they are not regarded as applying to all white people. In other words, the white man in America is not fighting the kind of stereotypes which he has inflicted upon the Negro. When I was in India, I saw Hollywood films that were quite terrible in what they showed about the American white man, and the American Negro. At no single time however, did I have to explain upon query that the pictures having to do with white people were exceptional; that they did not apply to all the white people in America. The Indians took for granted that this was true, but over and over I had to explain that what they saw in the movies [*illegible*] on Negro life did not apply to all the Negroes.[4]

I appreciate your letter very much and it is good to know that such a person as you care so much that she is willing to write so fully and graciously about it. Sincerely yours,
[Howard Thurman]

Mrs. J. F. Jenness
342 Oxford Avenue
Palo Alto, California

TLc.

Notes

1. *Song of the South* combined live action with animated sequences, and the African American actor James Baskett (1904–48) played the central role of the narrator, Uncle Remus.

2. Joel Chandler Harris (1842–1908), a white Georgian journalist, drew on African American folklore in his extremely popular Uncle Remus stories, which he published in nine volumes after 1880.

3. From Beulah S. Jenness, 26 April 1947.

4. For Thurman's concerns about stereotyping in the 1930s, see Dixie and Eisenstadt, *Visions of a Better World*, 185; and *PHWT*, 1:301.

❧ To Board of Fellowship Church
12 July 1947
[*San Francisco, Calif.*]

Thurman was involved in every aspect of planning for the Fellowship Church, and his concerns, as here, were often centered on enhancing its interracial and intercultural dimensions.

To: Board of Fellowship Church
From: Howard Thurman

The development of the Church has gone beyond the organizational structure which was projected two years ago. I would like to submit for your consideration the following revisions:

1. That the Board be enlarged so as to draw into the formal leadership of the Church a larger cross-section of the membership. As a tentative proposal, I suggest an increase of three or five—that would make thirteen or fifteen.
2. That we re-examine the plan of permanent standing committees chaired by representatives of the Board. The principle is sound, but it has not worked out. Either we should find out what is wrong with the application or devise a new technique.
3. A special committee should be set up for handling problems incident to the purchasing of a site for the church.
4. Careful thought should be given to a job analysis for the internee, co-pastors.

Arrangement is being considered whereby Rev. John Yamashita who is a Methodist clergyman in Oakland will supply the pulpit of Fellowship Church every fourth Sunday for the next several months. You will recall that it was he concerning whom I wrote Bishop Baker, but the Bishop could not see eye to eye with me in the matter.[1] John's coming will cause no additional burden to the budget. The plan is a very far-reaching one because it will mean a monthly exposure of the Congregation to the religious leadership of a Nisei and it will also mean for Rev. John Yamashita, the kind of opportunity to give wings to his thoughts and his spirit that in the very nature of the case, he cannot experience in a segregated church. It is my proposal that he begin the fourth Sunday in August, and each fourth Sunday until further notice. It is also possible that during the winter, he may have a study group of not more than four meetings. This is highly tentative.

You will recall my statement relative to Mr. Acevedo. It is my proposal that we invite Mr. Acevedo to be a part-time internee, beginning in the fall when his school opens. In my conversation with him, I have suggested that he spend a month attending as many activities of the church as possible so as to determine where he can best fit in and precisely what he would like to do within the frame work of our commitment.

With reference to vacation, arrangements were made with Mr. Watson to take charge during the month of August before the Meyners were in the offing. I suggest that the original Watson proposal remain with Mr. Meyner sharing the pulpit and perhaps preaching the third Sunday in August. The schedule of preaching that I am suggesting is as follows:

Monk Watson   August 5th and 10th
Bob Meyner   August 17th
John Yamashita   August 24th
Monk Watson   August 31st

September 28th, I shall have to go to Cleveland, Ohio to take a Memorial Service for a friend[2] who arranged for this in her will. It is my plan to be out of the pulpit for that weekend only.

The weekend of July 20th, Mrs. Thurman and I will be the house guest of Mrs. Smith hoping that out of that visit a part of our problem will be solved.

Rev. Gifford advises us that Dr. Fisk agreed to pay him $2.00 a month extra for the use of gas during the winter months. The interim-committee suggested offering him $11.00 flat each month and forget about the past. Mr. Gifford is unwilling to forget about the past. I therefore suggest that in order to keep our records straight, we pay him $8.00 and that we ask Mrs. Mobley to clear with Mr. Gifford about the use of gas for the winter. This can best be done when we know how much time Mrs. Mobley will be able to work this fall.

[*signed*] Howard Thurman

Howard Thurman

{Hansel—this is the material about which I told you. H.T.}

TLS.

Notes

1. To James C. Baker, 12 May 1947, printed in the current volume.

2. The friend was Jessie Wickwire Overholt (1892–1947), a Quaker, pacifist, feminist, and philanthropist. In Thurman's eulogy he said, "[H]er life dramatizes what can be done by the single person who is willing to become a lung through which God breathes in a fevered and disordered world" (HT, "Jessie Wickwire Overholt").

❧ To Eugene Blake

19 December 1947
[San Francisco, Calif.]

In accepting an invitation to preach at a church pastored by Eugene Carson Blake,[1] Thurman explains his commitment to the University of Iowa's School of Religion. He points out that the school has been doing "for twenty years theoretically what we are trying to do practically."

Dear Gene:

Thank you for your letter under date of December 6th. I would like very much to speak for the Chapel at your church on January 15th. It will mean making a special trip down to Pasadena to do it. Inasmuch as I do not use the plane, I shall have to come down by night train on Wednesday and return Thursday evening, so as to be back to work Friday morning. To do this puts me under tremendous pressure because beginning the second day of February I shall leave for the University of Iowa where I am teaching for the second semester. I shall commute about every fourth week between Iowa City and my church here. The School of Religion at the University of Iowa has been doing for twenty years theoretically what we are trying to do practically in a metropolitan center.

It is for this reason that I am going through the wear and tear of teaching there in the philosophy of religion and continuing my work here. This arrangement will be carried out only for a single semester which time I shall use also in securing commitments for building a permanent church home here and stabilizing our work. I am convinced that there is no more important validation of Christianity than the demonstration that it is possible for men of different origins to worship together and to share their fellowship in the common activities of daily life. It is to this that our church is dedicated and with God's help we shall secure what we need to make this possible.

If I came down, I would like to talk with you in greater detail about what we are doing. If you think that it is worth my time to make the extra trip down to do this for your group, please let me know by return mail.
Sincerely yours,
Howard Thurman

TLc.

NOTE

1. Eugene Carson Blake (1906–85) was a Presbyterian minister and ecumenical leader. He graduated cum laude from Princeton University and studied at the University of Edinburgh. Blake taught for one year (1928–29) at Forman Christian College in Lahore, India (now Pakistan) before going to Princeton Theological Seminary. He served several congregations over the years, including the First Presbyterian Church of Pasadena. In 1951 he was

elected clerk of the Presbyterian General Assembly, the highest position in the Presbyterian Church. He was president of the National Council of Churches from 1954 to 1957 and general secretary of the World Council of Churches from 1966 to 1974. An outspoken proponent of racial integration, he was a featured speaker at the 1963 March on Washington.

✨ "Judgment and Hope in the Christian Message"
1948

Howard University's Institute of Religion held its first annual conference in June 1943. A project of the School of Religion, it had as its main purpose exploring the social dimensions of Christianity and for the first few years had the theme of "Christian Imperative in Race Relations." It is not clear if Thurman participated in the first conference, but he was surely sympathetic to its objectives. "It is our judgment that race relations in America do not conform to the demand of the Christian ethic . . . [we] cannot give our endorsement to any proposals which seek merely to improve existing conditions while, at the same time, perpetuating the pattern of subordination and superordination. The Christian ethic admits no pattern of behavior which denies the essential dignity of personality."[1] He did participate in the second annual institute in mid-June 1944, presenting the paper "The Cosmic Guarantee in the Judeo-Christian Message."[2] This was one of Thurman's last appearances at Howard as dean of chapel before his move to San Francisco in early July. Thurman did not speak at the succeeding conferences, though the institute's director (and dean of Howard's School of Religion) William Stuart Nelson decided to prepare a volume of essays from the first several conferences. Thurman reworked "The Cosmic Guarantee in the Judeo-Christian Message," making it more politically pointed and eliminating some of its more obscure aspects, and published it as "Judgment and Hope in the Christian Message."

The volume was intended as more than a collection of random essays. After an opening essay by Nelson that systematically explored different social and political aspects of race relations and Christianity, and though the essays were all written individually, as Nelson noted in the preface, "the chapters may very properly be regarded as the product of a group enterprise."[3] Indeed most of the authors of the volume were Thurman's longtime friends and colleagues (which, in addition to Nelson, included Frank T. Wilson, Richard I. McKinney, Benjamin Mays, and Marion Cuthbert, among others), bringing together many of the most distinguished black Christian progressives in the country. Thurman's essay, "Judgment and Hope in the Christian Message," was one of two that closed the volume and offered more general reflections on the volume's theme.[4] Both versions of Thurman's essay center on the contrast between the "God of Religion," the God worshipped in church, and the "God of Life," the God who is everywhere else; or rather Thurman insists that they are one and the same and that "life is alive." This statement, Thurman acknowledges, "may seem utterly redundant" and "meaningless," but it was one of the foundations of his religious thought. "The guarantee of the ethical" is to be found "in the underlying vitality of the universe as expressed in the aliveness of life, which is in turn sustained by the God of life." Peoples and nations that neglect "to build their civilizations toward ends of high ethical responsibility" will ultimately suffer "the judgment of God." However, an individual who dedicates his or her life to realizing social justice "can depend on the God of life to sustain him even in his moment of greatest despair and frustration."

I

Implicit in the Christian message is a profoundly revolutionary ethic. This ethic appears as the binding relationship between men, conceived as children of a common Father, God. The ethic is revolutionary because the norms it establishes are in direct conflict with the relationship that obtains between men in the modern world. It is a patent fact that attitudes of fellowship and sympathetic understanding across lines of separateness such as race, class, and creed are not characteristic of our age. Whatever may be the concomitant reasons therefor, we are faced with the naked truth that twice within a quarter of a century our world has been involved in two wars and at the present moment most of the countries that have survived are themselves armed camps. This tragic picture indicates, at least, that we have not found a way by which to implement the insights of the Christian ethic or that the ethic itself has been rejected.

The religious implications of the ethic demand that the individual place at the center of his life a completely unswerving commitment to a God who is conceived in terms of supreme worthfulness. This conception of God finds its manifestation at many different levels of life. The far-reaching significance of this fact becomes at once the guarantor of whatever universal validity there is for the ethic itself. In the final analysis, life must sustain the ethic or it is a snare and a delusion. Practically stated, it raises the question and answers it in the affirmative as to whether or not a man who undertakes to live in the world on the basis of the Christian ethic can expect to be sustained and strengthened in his great endeavor.

The genius of the ethic is found in the great call of Israel, "Hear, O Israel, the Lord thy God is One, and thou shalt love the Lord thy God with all thy mind, heart, soul and strength; and thou shalt love thy neighbor as thyself."[5] In the mind of Jesus this was the creative summation of the Law and the prophets. Here we have the astounding insight that there is no distinction between the

God of life on the one hand, and the God of religion on the other. The insight is central and inescapable and may be regarded as an incisive statement of the character of the universe. God is one even as life is one; life is one because God is one. However it is stated, it adds up to the same thing.

God is the source of life. This is a basic assumption, a qualitative premise upon which all of the varied structures of meaning rest. This, of course, means that every creature is grounded in God in a direct and primary manner. It would follow, therefore, that all creature potentials, both positive and negative, are indirectly grounded in the same manner. The relationship of any particular form of life at any specific level, however highly differentiated, to the source of life is ultimately identical with life itself. That which sustains a rattlesnake cradles the turtledove; that which nourishes the strawberry makes the poison oak to thrive.

The kinship that exists between forms of life is not to be found merely in structural similarities or identities, important as these may be. But it is to be found primarily in a common ground of origin and sustenance. The struggle between forms of life, between higher and lower, between strong and weak, even when this struggle is on behalf of sheer physical survival in terms of food, must be regarded as fratricidal. The more highly developed the form, the more clearly discernible should be the facts of kinship both within the species and between the various species. This is the inevitable conclusion to be drawn from the assumption that there is but a single source of life, and that source is dynamic and creative.

The recognition of God as the source of life carries with it the judgment that life is alive. The statement that life is alive may seem utterly redundant and therefore meaningless. It is the insistence that inherent in the conception of life as a category is the same pulsing vitality which is quite apparent when we consider an individual or organism. It is easy for the term to be regarded as a metaphysical abstraction when applied to the ground of being. The character of life is essentially dynamic, carrying a certain seeming autonomy all its own. What is observed in the simplest creeping insect is but a picturesque expression of the activity which is the ground of all being. From this point of view mechanistic or materialistic interpretations of life seem singularly without meaning.

We are so overwhelmed by the dramatic and existential aspects of life, such as growth, orderly functions of organs, total behavior characteristics of various kinds of organisms, etc., that each living thing seems to be in itself quite autonomous and self-contained, having no reference to any sustaining factors beyond the environment in which it finds survival. There is something which seems quite automatic about all living things. One recalls that in the New Testament the reference is made to the earth as being automatic in its relation to life.[6] Every tree, every dog, every man seems to be essentially and uniquely alive without any contact with any deeper level or ground of vitality. And yet it is to be noted that trees die, animals die, men die, but trees remain, animals continue their existence, and men are fruitful and multiply. The gross vitality of all living things is the ground sustaining each particular one; human beings in this sense are but one variety of living things. A vital urgency maintains the process of fructification without regard to the disintegration of any particular expression of life.

The assumption that God is the source of life means that the aliveness of God is infinitely more significant than, and is basic to, the aliveness of life. It means further that the patterns of life manifestations as expressed in the manifold development of potentials are without ceiling terminus. They can be limited only by the aliveness of God. This is equivalent to saying that they are without limitations.

II

It is one of the curious paradoxes of religion that what it demands of man, conceivably the highest manifestation of life, is so overwhelmingly and obviously particularized that it tends to force a specious distinction between the secular and the sacred. This may be due to the evolution of the mind. The moment fine distinctions as over against gross distinctions became articulate for human beings, separate universes of discourse were possible. The technique of rationalization matured. The sacred came to be regarded as that which was, in some unique sense, the divine domain. Religious ceremonies, deeds of a certain kind, categories of particularized behavior, rituals, and the like all were interpreted as being a part of the religious frame of reference. It is to be noted that all experience remained one in essence, but the conditions under which experiences took place and the need which they met in the life of the individual became the clue to their definition. If it be true that structurally all experience is one, then to check one experience as being of God and the other as being of the devil is a question of value judgment rather than of experience itself. The moment a divine quality of uniqueness is given to a particular category of experience, the way is clear to make a false distinction between the God of life and the God of religion. The insistence that all life be lived with high ethical religiousness becomes the only valid basis for living. When men say that religion is not practical, they are really affirming that the God of life and the God of religion are separate and distinct. In other words, they mean that the God of religion is an illusion or a figment of the imagination or merely the cry of anguish in the presence of a world of imponderables.

It follows, then, that in the insistence of religion that God is one, there is precluded the possibility of a distinction between the God of life and the God of religion. God is one and man's relationship to God is automatically one of kinship through origin. This kinship implies an organic relatedness between God and creature. The awareness of this relationship expressed on the lowest level of life is in terms of gross responsiveness to sustenance; on the highest levels of life there is included not only gross responsiveness but a self-consciousness of mind. The unique thing about the awareness of mind is the fact that it is a self-awareness as distinguished from an awareness of something external. In fact, I am conscious of myself as a thinking organism. To the degree which this self-awareness becomes inclusive of other manifestations of life by which it is surrounded and of which it is a part, to that degree does it become mandatory for the individual thus aware to regard others as he regards himself. The higher, therefore, that one's self-estimate becomes, the higher of necessity will be the regard with which one evaluates one's relation to others. If God sustains and is the ground of the organic life of man, then, by the same token, he becomes the ground of those aspects of the life of man that are the distinct results of man's personality achievements. The realm of thought, feeling, desiring, dreaming is sustained by that which sustains man's physical body. It is reasonable then to affirm that he who undertakes to deal kindly with his fellow men or to walk with them in paths of justice and mercy may expect the same support that his environment gives to his physical body.

The question then is, Is it reasonable to assume that the universe is grounded in a limitless vitality that can sustain the revolutionary demands of the Christian ethic? When a man on a quite rational basis can justify his hatred of another man and can then reject this hatred as being unrighteous and therefore life-denying, will the universe leave him unaided and unsustained or may he expect the strength and the vitality needful for such an enterprise? It is my position that the guarantee of the ethical demand is to be found in the underlying vitality of the universe as expressed in the aliveness of life, which in turn is sustained by the God of life.

There is a sense in which the aliveness or the vitality of life may be regarded as being neutral. This would seem to be indicated in what Jesus has to say about God's causing the sun to shine upon the just and the unjust without discrimination.[7] It is true that he who demands an ultimate resource will become the channel through which that resource moves and in his experience will become powerful, apparently omnipotent, whether he be benevolent or demoniacal. The seeds of continuity are the ethical or unethical quality of the goals that are sought. It is reasonable to me to place well within the range of the mind and power and love of God not only the releasing of infinite energies on demand but the screening of the ends to which these energies are directed. If the end be rejected because it is life-denying and destructive, there can be no ultimate sustenance for such an individual or nation. The judgment of God appears again and again in the process of history, dramatized in the rise and fall of peoples who have neglected to build their civilizations toward ends of high ethical responsibility. If a man be selfish, hardened as to sympathies, insensitive to the needs of others, in the end he destroys himself because life denies him at the last its blessing, and the qualities that he manifests he becomes. This does not mean that the wicked do not prosper, but it does mean that the diabolical character of the enterprise itself destroys the vehicle so that finally energies are scattered and dissipated. He who places his life completely at the disposal of the highest ethical end, God, to him will not be denied the wine of creative livingness.

The bearing of all of this upon the intricate relationships between Negroes and white people in the United States is not far to seek. If it be true that the normal relationship between men is activated kinship, grounded in a common dynamic origin, then attitudes of mistrust, of fear, of prejudice, whatever may be the extenuating justification for them, are a repudiation of the ethical meaning of life. He who undertakes to approach his fellow as a brother and will with courage, intelligence, and integrity fashion his life on the basis of such an imperious demand can depend on the God of life to sustain him even in his moment of greatest despair and frustration. The hardest task is to be found not in affirming this kind of conviction but rather in discovering techniques of implementation that will make so great a commitment a common part of the daily round of experience. Our hope is in a devotion to life in this dimension and our judgment is in the barrenness which we sustain in not living this religion.

"Judgment and Hope in the Christian Message," in *The Christian Way in Race Relations,* edited by William Stuart Nelson (New York: Harper & Brothers, 1948), 229–35.

Notes

1. "Howard University Holds Institute of Race Relations," *Chicago Defender,* 26 June 1943.

2. "Religious Seminar Held at Howard U.," *Chicago Defender,* 3 June 1944.

3. William Stuart Nelson, ed., *The Christian Way in Race Relations* (New York: Harper Brothers, 1948), vii.

4. The other concluding essay was the similarly titled "Judgment and Hope in the Nature of Man and Society," by Thurman's onetime student at Morehouse and good friend Richard I. McKinney (in Nelson, ed., *Christian Way,* 236–56).

5. Mark 12:30, quoting Deut. 6:4 and Lev. 19:18.

6. Probably Matt. 6:28.

7. Matt. 4:45.

🎗 "Standing on Tip Toe"
4 January 1948
The Fellowship Church
San Francisco, Calif.

In this powerful New Year's sermon, Thurman explores the seeming contra-dictions of life and the important lessons, for him, that no dichotomy, however experienced, is ultimately final and that "standing on tip toe" suggests a sense of integrity and openness to the ambiguities and contingencies of existence.

(Dr. Thurman opened with two paragraphs about an oak tree that rises seventy or eighty feet in the air.)[1]

I want you to think for a little while this first Sunday in the New Year about the very simple proposition that the essence of the meaning of life is found when we discover how to make a life of significance within the daily round of our common life; and I have chosen a phrase borrowed from the Apostle Paul. "Standing on tip toe" is a phrase he uses describing man's attitude or his outlook, describing the future with reference to those things that are behind and those things that are to come.[2] Another phrase that could be used is in the Epistle that bears the name of John: "I rejoice that I have found you walking in the truth."[3] Very interesting! Both phrases suggest the possibility of reaching up out of one's own context, reaching forward from within the meaning of one's present and past, walking in the Truth as contrasted with trying to find the Truth in places where you don't walk. Now that's the idea and that is really all that I have to say for this first Sunday in the New Year, but I am not going to sit down.

Three Areas of Contrast

There are three areas to which I will call your attention, which seem to me to illustrate this essential fact: that it is within the stream of life that we get the meaning of life. For some reason that I do not quite understand, we seem always to be harassed by contrast, by "either-or" necessity, by a doublesome, and it has done a very vicious thing to our minds because so much of life is contrasted in that way—light-darkness, day-night, male-female—that we tend to interpret all of life in terms of "either or," and we get into very critical difficulties.

1) Past vs. Present

For instance, we make an artificial and what seems to me an essentially unwar-ranted distinction between the past and the present, as if the past were some-thing which in itself is completely final, completely finished, completely written off, like a bad debt; and the present we tend to think of as something that <u>is</u>, is now merely, is all one, of one piece; that which is before us now, a part of our immediate experience. We say, for instance, to a person when we are going away, "Goodbye, I'll see you again"; and, when three weeks are gone, you come back, and you meet the person, and you do see him again, you do meet him again. But in a sense you don't ever see anybody again, you don't ever meet him again, because something has happened between the first time and the next time, that has, in a very profound sense, altered the very mixture of one's life; and yet something of one's former self remains, always intact. I never renounce the past; I cannot ever escape the fact that I am a part of my past, that my experience of another period of life has entered intimately into the making of the present unit that I call myself. So, to some extent I am bound by the past, and to ignore the past as if the past has no existence, is to be very careless of one's mind.

So, it seems to me that, whatever we do in the present, and whatever we do in the future, we must think of the future as something that is in a sense always becoming the past, and the thing that we call the present is merely the point at which the future and the past meet and tarry.

(At this point Dr. Thurman used an illustration from the behavior of ants.)

The present is a moment when the past and the future meet and greet each other. The present is a very satisfying thing, but it is never an isolated thing; therefore, whatever I do with the present, whatever I may look forward to doing in the future, must take into account the past. Now, there is much more that could be said about that, because there are many problems in it. Am I imprisoned by the past so that I can't shake it off? Can anything of tremendous significance happen to me, to my past, that will move into the centre of all my values in life, and so transform me that tomorrow and tomorrow I shall be something different?

Of course that is possible, and it happens again and again, but it always happens against the background of what I have been. If I ignore that, I am not where I ought to be. So that standing on tip toe with reference to the past and the present is merely standing within the stream that has created us, with which we are familiar, and using all our accumulated wisdom, experience, knowledge, and insight; using all of that as shoulders upon which you stand to look, and to reach into the future. I can't stand on tip toe by getting out of the stream, and I can't do it. No, I have to accept my little solution. As Stephen Benet makes Abraham Lincoln say, "You could have made a better looking man, but you didn't, so I will have to do with what I have and use it to the limit of its potential, and not waste time trying to borrow somebody else's potential, for they are busy as can be using it up."[4] No, I can't do that.

2) *Right vs. Wrong*

The second aspect has to do with right and wrong. Life would be very simple if at every point you knew exactly: <u>This</u> is right and <u>this</u> is wrong. It would be wonderful, and there are many people who are sure that they do know it that way—that <u>this</u> is right and <u>this</u> is wrong, because their authority has told them so, and of course they assume that they have understood their authority correctly. But, even though my authority is clear as I see it, when I apply this knowledge that comes from my authority to the problem with which I am dealing, then I become the sole interpreter between this and this. If I am a man of integrity, if I am a person of authentic honesty, then with reference to my authority, I shall try to be as intelligent as possible, so that moving from the insight to the application, I shall not muddy the insight. If it happens that I am always trying to locate from within my context the grounds of my authority, then my problem is much more acute because the scene shifts, the picture changes, and I find that, because of some new experience that I have had, things do not seem to be quite as clearly divided as before. Grant the fundamental insight of rightness, which I find inescapable, and the fundamental insight of rightness as contrasted with wrongness, and grant that one can't escape one's training, the way in which it influences one's conduct shifts.

If I may be personal a moment—I had a grandmother who always insisted that we children should do nothing on Sunday morning but have our morning prayers and have breakfast and go to Sunday School. She also insisted—and this was a great trial in my early life—that my shoes should be shiny on Sunday morning. I always enjoyed playing on Saturday, when there wasn't any school. I didn't have any sense of nightfall, and then I went to sleep and Sunday was another day. Of course I had neglected my shoes, but she wouldn't let me shine my shoes on Sunday. I couldn't even dust them off. She had a very strong conscience about the observance of the Sabbath. Now, I don't have that sort of conscience, and when I polish my shoes on Sunday morning, I don't think I am doing anything wrong; but some little thing shoots through me, warning that all is not well.

In this notion is the whole paradoxical relationship between that which is right and that which is wrong. There must always be the awareness of the fact that, whatever be my interpretation of the meaning of right and wrong, I have come to my conclusions on the basis of what my authentic experience is and has been.

Now it means that, if I stand on tip toe, I do it from within the stream of my own moral experience and moral teaching and moral living. It means, too, that if I approach life the way it reads in my heart, I must realize this awful truth: that I always can be mistaken. Someone has said that a man may live all his life sure that he has done his duty, only to discover just before he dies that his life has been a mistake. Those of you who were present at the Christmas Vesper Service will remember the thing that I read about the Worshipers in the Art. There are problems tied up with that. If you cling to the worshipers of the art, if you cling to the meaning of right and wrong within you, there is no escaping that, in the last analysis, you must say yes or no, no one can say it for you.

3) *Ideal vs. Real*

There is one other aspect of this, not only with reference to right and wrong, but with reference to the ideal and the real. There are some who are listening this morning who congratulate themselves that they are realists; more would insist that they are practical and set the theoretical over against the practical. I remember the first course[5] I took in a strange land, still the United States, but a strange land. I was waiting for the teacher to say something that had relevance to my own needs—but he never did. I read everything prescribed and I took the examination, but he still didn't do it. So, after the course was over, I went to see him, and I said "You didn't do anything practical." And he said that, if I thought Philosophy was practical, I should become a bond salesman. He made a strange impression on me. We have done a comparable thing in our religion, in that if anyone worships God at all, he worships the God of religion on Sunday.

There is another God who lives downtown on the street, in the school, where the checkbook is. Now he is the God of life, and we say to ourselves without realizing it, "This ideal which you talk about must be measured in terms of the authentic meaning or significance of life. We are really practical because this is a practical world." The inference is that the God of religion is at a disadvantage in life and that, when he looks out into the arena, he is at the mercy of the God of life. So I shift my allegiance so that I'll always be on the safe side; I become pious in here, and I go without religion out there. The result is that I tend to be ethical and religious as I move away from the area that involves my own security, but I tend to be irreligious and unethical as I move toward the centre of my security. For instance, if a person tells you a lie "out of whole cloth," (I don't know what that means exactly) you may feel that he lied and that he didn't have to. But, if he is really in a jam, right up against it, and he springs a fabrication that is just breathless to look at, you admire his technique, because we have settled for that distinction between the theoretical and the practical. We apply it to all world situations. We don't want any theoretical idealists to take over the control or the running of the situation, the control or demonstration of those formal or informal agreements under which we live. But I ask you to look at it. The world has been run by practical, hard-headed people who know what the score is. And what has happened? Two world wars in twenty-five years, hunger everywhere, madness everywhere, fear everywhere. It is the practical man who has created that kind of impasse. It may be a fairly decent idea to give another sort of man a try at it; he can't do anything worse than have another world war, nor make more mistakes than have been made.

Conclusion

Walking in the Truth, standing on tip toe, in this year 1948 means for us, I hope, finding a little of significance within the daily round of our common living. Therefore our prayer can be summarized in this that I would like to share at the end: Give me the courage to live, really live, and not merely to exist.

TD.

Notes

1. From Otto, *Human Enterprise,* 66–68. See also HT, San Francisco journal:

I think of a black oak I have long admired. It rises seventy or eighty feet into the air, a thing of rugged beauty every day of the year and every hour of the day. Whether seen in the searching light of noon or in the mellow colors of sunset, whether barely visible as a dim mass on a dripping, sultry night or clearly etched against the sky at dawn—each recurring presence arouses a fresh sense of the oak tree's greatness as an achievement of life and intimates something of that unfathomable mystery we call nature, that complexity into which every living thing sends its roots.

But it is not the impressiveness of this oak which just now brings it to mind, not its strength or dignity or beauty. It is its behavior in autumn and winter—if a tree may be said to behave. Unlike the maples and hickories in the same grove, it refuses to give up its leaves. Rains, snows, winds have no effect. The tug of the elements is powerless to bring them down. They change from green to red then to the color of the marshes when the winter's snows are first gone. They wrinkle, dry up, and rustle in the breeze, but do not release their grip. They linger through the winter as memories of departed days haunt the mind of a man whom a change of fortune has retired from active life.

Then comes spring. In March the leaves appear to be thinning out and before April ends they are gone. What rains, snows, winds, blustering from without, could not do, the quiet prod of life, working from within, does with ease. As the sun climbs higher in the Zodiac, and the responsive sap ascends the tree trunk and ramifies into branches and twigs, the clinging leaves drop away. For new leaves do not come because the old leaves have fallen, the old leaves fall because new leaves are coming; or, to speak more accurately, because the life cycle of the tree turns from sustaining old leaves to developing new ones. It is true of the oak tree and of the Tree of Life. Everywhere the passing away of the old and the coming of the new are inseparable phases of a larger process active in both.

2. "On tiptoe" is an unusual translation for the obscure Greek term in Rom. 8:19 translated as "earnest anticipation" in the King James Version and as "eager longing" in the New Revised Standard Version. "On tiptoe" is used in J. B. Phillips, *Letters to Young Churches: A New Translation of the New Testament Epistles* (New York: Macmillan, 1947).

3. 2 John 1:4.

4. "You could have made a better-looking dog / From the same raw material, no doubt / But, since you didn't, this will have to do" (Stephen Vincent Benét, *John Brown's Body* [Garden City, N.Y.: Doubleday, Doran, 1928], 217).

5. This was probably "An Introduction to Reflexive Thinking," one of the two philosophy courses that Thurman took at Columbia University in the summer of 1922. See *PHWT,* 1:lvi–lvii.

✍ To Charles C. Perrin
10 January 1948
[*San Francisco, Calif.*]

In this letter to a financial supporter of the Fellowship Church, Thurman describes the growth of the church and the interracial ordination ceremony for Thurman's copastor Robert Meyners.

Dear Mr. Perrin:[1]

I too have missed seeing you during the visits to the Crosbys. Each time I inquired of you Art said that you were away. During the spring, I shall be in Philadelphia two or three times and I hope we shall see each other on one of the visits.

Please accept my sincere thanks for your check for the work of the church. It is a matter of immense satisfaction to me to be able to report that the church is developing in a very sound and inspiring manner. Our membership is growing slowly, but steadily, and an increasingly wide cross-section of the people is being attracted to what we are doing. Our plan for the internee, co-minister, a young white fellow and his wife, a graduate of the University of Chicago, is proving significant and profoundly useful.[2] Already one national denomination has applied to have us consider a man from their church when the present internee leaves. The plan is to have young men from various denominations serve with us for a period and then return to their own church having had an exposure to the unique work that we are undertaking. It is a good plan, and it is sound in its educational theory not to speak of its significance for prophetic religion. In addition we have a part-time, young Mexican working somewhat in the same capacity while he is completing his graduate work in one of the schools in the Bay Area.[3]

Next Sunday, we are having the ordination ceremonial of the young white minister at our morning service. He is Congregational, and is being ordained into the Congregational ministry, but the service itself is under the sponsorship of our church which is nonsectarian. The sermon is being preached by a Methodist clergyman from Chicago, the ordination is given by a Congregational minister, the charge to the church by a Presbyterian, etc. The laying on of hands will be shared in by Methodists, Presbyterians, Congregationalists, Baptists, a Jewish Rabbi, from one of the local temples, and a woman. The service is simple without dramatics, but the whole experience is a fleeting glimpse of what we hope some day to be the regular expression of formal religious life.

I am sending you under separate cover a copy of my Ingersoll Lecture on Immortality which I gave at Harvard last April. I hope you will enjoy reading it.

Best wishes for a good New Year.

Sincerely,
Howard Thurman

Mr. Charles C. Perrin
12 South 12th Street
Philadelphia 7, Pennsylvania

                                                        TLc.

Notes

1. Charles C. Perrin (1883–1968) was chairman of Towers, Perrin, Foster, and Crosby, Inc., a Philadelphia reinsurance and management consultant firm, from 1934 to 1949. He was a business partner of Thurman's good friend Arthur U. Crosby.

2. Robert Meyners (1922–) was an assistant pastor at the Fellowship Church from 1947 to 1949. He is a graduate of the University of Chicago. After leaving Fellowship Church, he spent several years in Europe and subsequently received his Ph.D. from Union Theological Seminary (1958); his dissertation was titled "An Investigation of the Basis for Christian Resistance to Civil Authority." He later taught at Chicago Theological Seminary before deciding to change careers, and after training as a sex therapist and educator, he became the assistant director of the Masters and Johnson Institute of Research into Human Sexuality in St. Louis. His books include (both with Claire Wooster) *Sexual Style: Facing and Making Choices about Sex* (New York: Harcourt, Brace, 1970) and *Solomon's Sword: Clarifying Values in the Church* (Nashville: Abingdon, 1977).

3. George Acevedo.

⮞ To Alice Sams
31 January 1948
[*San Francisco, Calif.*]

Thurman writes to his mother about a maturing life insurance policy, giving careful instructions (without mentioning names) for Alice not to tell her husband, James Sams, about this sudden windfall.

Dear Mama,

Once again I must send this typewritten letter, because I am leaving for Iowa in two days and I want to get this note of information to you.

Your Metropolitan policy which I pay out here has matured. It was an endowment, age eighty, which means that as far as the Metropolitan Life Insurance Company is concerned, you are eighty-years old.[1] What the facts are however, I have no notion. The policy has been lost, and in order to clear the record, I have asked the company here to have the Metropolitan agent there come out to the house and get your signature on a blank which says that the policy has been lost or destroyed. When the man comes, merely sign your name and he will witness the signature. This is all that you have to do. It is unnecessary for you to discuss the policy with him, simply say that you gave it to your son, years ago, and he has lost it. I do not know who the beneficiary is in the policy, but in the course of a few weeks, after the signature has been sent to New York, they will send you the check to the amount of $680.00, I think. And if the check is made out to you, endorse it, and send it to me, and I will take care of it for you.

Please do not discuss this with anybody because if you do it may make for difficulties. I am enclosing several stamped envelopes with my Iowa address on them. All you need to do is to put your letters in them, and send them along. Before they are out, I will send you another set.
Take care of yourself, all of our love,
Your son,
[Howard Thurman]

                                                                                       TLc.

NOTE

  1. Born in 1872, Alice was seventy-five or seventy-six at the time of this letter.

"MAHATMA GANDHI"
1 FEBRUARY 1948
THE FELLOWSHIP CHURCH
[*San Francisco, Calif.*]

In this sermon Thurman offers an informal eulogy for Mohandas "Mahatma" Gandhi, who was assassinated on 30 January 1948, some six months after the declaration of Indian independence on 15 August 1947. In the sermon Thurman recounts his meeting with Gandhi twelve years earlier and goes on to discuss the universal religious significance of Gandhi's career, while emphasizing the importance of viewing Gandhi within a specifically Hindu religious tradition. The editors have tried to reconstruct gaps in the sermon from an incomplete transcript.

After the news was announced concerning the passing of Mahatma Gandhi, I changed my plan to follow up another dimension of our discussion of last Sunday on the Moral Struggle, and instead to think with you for a little while about some aspects of the meaning of this little man whose life has affected more human beings directly than perhaps any other single figure in our time.

It is very difficult to talk about it. I think all human beings soon or late, make a profound accommodation to the fact of death. For we know that one by one, the duties end and one by one, the lights go out. But nevertheless, when death comes to anyone who is close to us, the mind once again begins going through old bureau drawers, looking up old documents. Death always gives to those who live, a refresher course in the meaning of life. Mahatma Gandhi's death is no exception.

I shall never forget, and you will pardon this personal reference, there will be two or three of them in the course of our thinking. I shall never forget the time some ten or twelve years ago, when it was our privilege to see Mr. Gandhi, and to talk with him for several hours.[1] It was all very strange, and it is symbolic of the kind of man he was. When our journey in India was announced, he sent a note inviting us to spend the Christmas holidays as his guest in his Ashram,[2] but because of low blood pressure[3] from which he was suffering, it was impossible for us or for him to have any guests, and then it was decided that he would meet us in New Delhi when we were there on the evening of the opening of the National Assembly, but his illness had kept up, and his doctors forbade him to come to New Delhi. Two weeks before we were sailing, one morning in Bombay, I got up and decided that it would be impossible for us to come back to America without seeing Mr. Gandhi, and so I went down stairs on the first floor to send a telegram to him to find out if his physical condition was such that it might be possible for us to see him.[4] As I walked out of the door on my way to the Post Office, I met a Gandhi follower, and I noticed him because he had the Gandhi cap, made out of cotton cloth, and he looked at me, and I looked at him, and he said, "Are you Mr. Thurman," and I said, "I am." "I have a letter for you," and it was a letter from Mr. Gandhi saying that he had been advised that in two weeks we would be sailing from India, and he was very anxious that the delegation and he would have the opportunity to sit down and think through some things together—and then this is the illustration of the quality of the man—"I am resting at a little town in the native state of Dharampur about four hours from Bombay.[5] If your schedule is so ironclad that it is impossible for you to take any time out now, I would suggest that at the end of your schedule, and before you set sail, you come to Wardha[6] to the Ashram, and we may have a visit there. If that be impossible, then I will, with my two physicians who are accompanying me on this trip, come to Bombay and sit down and talk with you and the delegation, because I feel that there are some things which we ought to say to each other." Well, of course you know what I did, I stopped everything, and that night at 7:45, when the train left for the nearest stop to this Bardoli I was on it together with Mrs. Thurman and Mr. Carroll.[7]

We were met at a little station at three o'clock in the morning, and I was the official waker upper for everybody, and at this little station, Mr. Gandhi's secretary[8] met us in an old Model T Ford, and we were driven to a mango grove on the edge of town in the midst of which was a bungalow tent . . . a tent that had five rooms, and Mrs. Thurman went into sleep until morning, and I sat under one of those trees talking with Mr. Gandhi's secretary about Mr. Gandhi. At daybreak, we found ourselves in the Model T again, and over hard, rough road, we came to the little town of Bardoli on the edge of which was a clearing and in that clearing there was a tent and a flag pole, and flying from that flag pole was the India National Congress flag, and as the Ford rattled to a precipitous stop, this little man walked out from the tent with a shawl around his shoulders and gave the greeting to us, and gave Mrs. Thurman a hand out of the car. We sat on the floor of his tent. (He offered to get two chairs from a neighbor down the road if we were so made that it wasn't quite a reasonable thing to expect us to sit in comfort on the floor.) He put in front of him, an old-fashioned, silver-plated watch, and he apologized for it, saying, "We have only three and a half hours, and we have many things to talk about. We must do it by the watch."

Then he proceeded asking all sorts of questions about America, particularly about American Negroes and their history and at the end when there was only fifteen or twenty minutes left, he said, "I am very sorry that I have used all the time asking questions about America; perhaps you have some questions you would like to ask me, but before you do, will you do something very special for me? Will you sing a spiritual for me. . . . 'Were You There When They Crucified My Lord?'" He said, "I think it is one of the great timeless insights of religion." Of course you can imagine what happened. It was done with love, that is all I can say. Then there were two questions that we had to raise, one which I will mention to you.

We wanted to know from him why was it his campaign of non-violence and non-cooperation, his campaign of satyagraha, why was it that campaign had failed of its objectives.[9] He said, and this is the first point in my thought about him, he said, "A great creative spiritual and ethical ideal such as ahimsa, if it is to be effective over a time-interval of sufficient duration, must become the private position of a great multitude of people. The masses in India were unable to sustain so creative an ideal for a time interval of sufficient duration to be effective because," he said, "they do not have the vitality. They do not have the vitality because," said he, "the masses of the people in India are hungry," and for a few minutes he sketched in deft outline, but in dynamic quality, the poverty of India, and how many millions of people who live from childhood to maturity to die and to be burned on the burning ghat[10] without once ever in their entire lives having the physical satisfaction of a stomach full of food, be-cause the masses of the people are hungry, and are therefore unable to provide the physical aspect of vitality. "I withdrew from politics," said he, "and began the work of the spinning wheel because I feel that if the village cottage industry as symbolized by the spinning wheel can be re-established, then that will provide one important link in the guaranteeing of the elemental physical basis upon which moral and spiritual vitality may be built."

The second reason for the low vitality was what he called a lack of self re-spect, and I thought he was going to say that there was a lack of self respect because of the presence of the conqueror in their land, but before I could get the query half stated, the remark half stated, he held up his hand to say no, "They have lost their self respect because of untouchability in Hinduism," and then he talked about it. "The thing that happens to the soul of a man when for any reason whatsoever, he is led to a position that causes him to look with contempt upon his fellow men, so I began working on that," and this reveals another interesting thing about the quality of the man's mind and spirit. "I attack it in two ways, in the first place, I am a caste Hindu, so I adopted into my family an untouchable, little girl, and I announced to all caste Hindus, 'This is what I mean, for if you are unwilling to have an untouchable as an intimate primary part of your own household, then your faith about the redemption of the untouchable is unsound.' And the second thing, that I did," said he, "was to change the name, to change my reference at any rate from untouchable or Pariah to Harijan, and the word Harijan is a combination Hindu word which means 'Child of God,' and now," said Gandhi, with sort of a boyish radiance and chuckle in his face, the sort that made you want to pinch him—just a little. He said, "If a caste Hindu calls an untouchable, Harijan 'Child of God,' then this constant, repetitious utterance will create in the spirit of the caste Hindu the kind of moral frustration that will not be removed or absorbed or adjusted until he changes his attitude toward the untouchable, so," he said, "I attacked the attitude of the caste Hindu toward the untouchable by using the only weapon that I know, and that is the Spirit of Truth," with the result that within two years after his campaign, the attitude towards millions of caste Hindus shifted from that which was negative to that which was positive as touching the untouchable so much so that in the city of Trivandrum which is the capital of Travencore, when we were there three months before this conversation, no untouchable was permitted to cross the street on which was located a Hindu Temple lest his shadow would contaminate it. And if an untouchable saw a caste Hindu on the road, he would have to drop prostrate on the ground, until the caste Hindu passed lest his shadow would profane. Thirteen months after Gandhi started his campaign, The Maharaji at Travencore, this native state, by royal decree opened all Hindu Temples to untouchables.[11]

Now Gandhi is dead, and he was killed by a Hindu, according to the press, a Hindu who belonged to, according to accounts, an extremely bitter, nationalistic group.[12] One of the inevitable results of oppression, always is to create among certain sensitive human spirits the kind of dynamic despair, that makes them count their individual lives as of no consequence if by the giving of their lives the cause for which they work and live can be salvaged, or redeemed, or saved. Every time in human history men have oppressed each other, there has been squeezed out of that pressure the fanatic, the man who relaxes all confidence in any particular(?)[13] other than violence and bloodshed because under times of great pressure, violence and bloodshed seem to be the effective, efficient, quick, sudden way by which men are forced to relax their strangle hold on other men. The theory is that if by violence you make a man who is choking you so conscious of the threat that is being put upon his life at some other point in his great anxiety to save his own life, he will relax his strangle hold on you

in order that he may build defenses. It was true and it has been true throughout the years, and this man was sure, I think, I don't know of course, but this
man was sure that the great enemy to the genius and the great fulfillment as a
national state was the man who constantly talked compromise, as the political
manipulator interpreted it.

Now this brings me to the next aspect of our consideration—the approach
of the religious man as touching social change, and the approach of the politician or the economist, and the sociologist are apt to be fundamentally different
approaches. The ends that are sought are the same. Let us assume that, but the
religious man is never willing to make a distinction between means and ends, if
the religious man interprets the end as merely an extension of the means, and
the means as merely an extension of the end, it is like taking a zero, and pushing
it out and out and the longer you push it, the longer the line becomes, but the
line is an extension of the zero. I mean of the spot, of the period . . . Now the religious man approaches social change from that point of view. It is illustrated in
the life of Mahatma Gandhi again and again when he was ready to break the Salt
Tax Law, which he felt was so terrible and so symbolic of the last act of arrogant
oppression on the part of the British. He advised the Viceroy as to his intention,
letting him know when he was going to start on his march and where he would
stop all along the way, and as precisely as he could determine it, when he would
walk out into the bay, and dip up the salt water, and take it to the shore, and put
it under heat, so as to distill the salt from it, so that there would be no question
in the mind of Viceroy as to the integrity of the thing that Gandhi was doing
and the reasons for it.[14]

Now, the political reformer and the social reformer whose motivation is basically non-spiritual, is apt and I speak with caution because there is a world of
disagreement here, is apt to use any means to achieve his ends. Ethic insights are
determined by the bearing that any particular act has upon the end. So morality
becomes narrowly defined, because it is defined exclusively in terms of end, and
the bearing of any act upon the end. It is for this reason then that Mahatma
Gandhi, Jawaharlal Nehru, even though to Jawaharlal after his father's death,[15]
Mahatma Gandhi was Bapu,[16] and when Nehru's father died, it was Mahatma
Gandhi who was there, and who took over and who saw to it that Nehru would
have all the things that was in keeping with his dream of his father, and when
Gandhi was shot, it happened that Nehru was there, the head of a great state on
his way to prayer meeting with a saint.

Now there is one other thing . . . Gandhi was not a Christian, and there are
people all over the world, who felt that he would have been really a great man
if he had become a Christian. When the Indian National, the Reform Act of
1935 was passed by Parliament, and became the Act of India for the reorganization for the government with the larger participation on the part of Hindus,

and Moslems, etc., representation in the India National Assembly was based upon numerical strength of the various religious communities, and inasmuch as about sixty-four Indians out of about one hundred in India are Hindus, and maybe twenty-five to twenty-six are Moslems, so forth, it meant that the Hindu had the largest political representation in the National Assembly.[17] Eighty million of these Hindus are untouchables, and they were led by Dr. Ambedkar,[18] who was professor at the Law School at the University of Bombay, and who spent ten years living in New York City. Now, Ambedkar realizing that he was in a strong position with eighty million political votes, as it were, it became very necessary that there be some forces at work to try to get this block of votes, and the thing on which Gandhi had been working on from one point of view, turns up again in the empirical and elemental forces that were driving the Hindu in the direction of which Mahatma Gandhi with his spiritual insights saw that it was [the] inevitable direction of the Hindu people if they were to survive, and that is to change their attitude toward the untouchables, but at any rate, various religious leaders came to Dr. Ambedkar to try to get him to deliver this block of untouchables into their particular fold, and that would increase automatically their representation, and when the Christian, whose name I will not call, talked with Dr. Ambedkar about this, Dr. Ambedkar was quoted to me by an Indian as saying, "No, I lived ten years in New York City, in a Christian land. I traveled pretty much over the country, and I am afraid to trust the untouchables to the Christian."[19] Now after I say that, I recognize this that one of the important aspects of the whole missionary emphasis in India as far as it talked about the individual worth of the human spirit and demonstrated in terms of living, of service, the genius of the Christian spirit to that degree would the Christian spirit also work towards the release and the redemption of the untouchable, but Gandhi was not a Christian, he had great reverence for Jesus. I asked him only one question about it. "What," said I, to Gandhi, "is the greatest handicap of Jesus Christ in India," and his immediate reply is this, "Christianity."[20]

Now whether there will be great bloodshed and great madness in India because of his immediate passing only God can tell, but there is this thing I would say in closing about him. He demonstrated to me what is possible for the individual human spirit to achieve in his life time, if he has enough integrity to place his life completely at the disposal of his deepest and profoundest insights. For when Mr. Gandhi was asked, "Don't you think you had better hurry." This was when he was sixty-five years old, "because you will be dead and India will not be free," and he said, "No, I don't think I should hurry. Time is on the side always of the man who devotes his life to truth. I can wait ten years, twenty years, fifty years, or one hundred years, but God cannot be defeated in India, despite all of the present indications to the contrary not withstanding." It is to love people when they are your enemy, to forgive people when they seek to destroy your life . . . This gives Mahatma Gandhi a place along side all of the great redeemers of the human race. There is a striking continuity between him and Jesus, and please hear what I am saying, and don't misquote me . . . There is a striking similarity between him and Jesus, and it is this: That Jesus believed that the only way by which his people could be released from Rome, was by loving the Romans. He projected this notion upon the ears of his hearers, and upon the minds of the people of his generation, and because he did this, and because others had done it strategically before in varying degrees, there was let loose on this planet, a faith in the possibility of love that provided a psychological and social climate in which Gandhi could do his work. For I believe that if Jesus had not lived in Palestine, and thought and then received the answer of his spiritual contention that he did, then Gandhi would have been eliminated by the British Government when he was in South Africa when he first initiated his revolutionary campaign, but because of what Jesus had thought and taught, but more important released in the climate of life, men had adjusted themselves to the notion of the possibility of Ahimsa.

Gandhi is dead! Once again violence wins a battle, but it is my confidence that only love will win the war!

TD.

NOTES

1. For background on the Negro Delegation's meeting with Gandhi, see Desai, "With Our Negro Guests," 332–39; and Dixie and Eisenstadt, *Visions of a Better World*, 65–116.

2. Thurman's account here differs in some particulars from what the editors have been able to ascertain. See Dixie and Eisenstadt, *Visions of a Better World*, 97–99.

3. On 9 January 1936 Gandhi's secretary, Mahadev Desai (1892–1943), announced that Gandhi was suffering from high blood pressure. Most of his engagements were canceled for the next several months.

4. Gandhi met with the Negro Delegation on 21 February 1936; the delegation embarked from Colombo to return to the United States on 8 March 1936.

5. Bardoli was a town in the native state of Dharampur.

6. Gandhi's main ashram.

7. Edward Carroll.

8. Mahadev Desai.

9. This question, and Gandhi's elaborate answer, has no counterpart in Mahadev Desai's "With Our Negro Guests," Desai's account of the conversation between Gandhi and the Negro Delegation published several weeks after the meeting.

10. A river-side funeral pyre.

11. The Negro Delegation visited Trivandrum (now Thiruvananthapurum) in the native state of Travencore (now in Kerala) in late November 1935. About a year later, on 12 November 1936, the maharaja of Travencore, Sri Chithira Thiurnal Balarama, declared the Hindu temples of Travencore open to untouchables.

12. Gandhi was assassinated by Nathuram Godse, a member of the paramilitary Rashtriya Svayamsevak Sangh, associated with the Hindu Mahasabha Party. The conspirators

felt that Gandhi had sold out Hindu interests by agreeing to the partition of India that created Pakistan, though Gandhi accepted the decision to partition India as a condition of Indian independence with the greatest reluctance. Godse and a coconspirator were hanged by the Indian government, and several other participants in the plot served long prison sentences.

13. The question mark is in the original transcript.

14. Gandhi began his salt march, protesting the tax that the British government imposed on every purchase of salt in India, on 12 March 1930. He reached the sea at Dandi, some two hundred miles away, on 6 April. Lord Irwin was the viceroy.

15. Motilal Nehru (1861–1931) was a wealthy lawyer and twice president of the Congress Party.

16. "Bapu" is Gujurati for "Father" and a common title of respect for Gandhi.

17. The Government of India Act of 1935 was the last attempt by the British government to provide for a framework for Indian self-government. Most of its provisions were never implemented. The constitution divided representation according to religious affiliation and reserved one-third of the seats in parliament and government for Muslims. There was a debate on whether to include the untouchables as Hindus or provide them with separate representation. Gandhi argued strongly that the untouchables should be included as Hindus. In the 1931 census of India, of a total population of 352,195,140 there were 239,195,140 Hindus and 77,677,545 Muslims, so approximately 68 percent of the population was Hindu and 22 percent was Muslim. The 1931 India census included the current nations of India, Pakistan, Bangladesh, Nepal, Bhutan, and Burma.

18. Bhimrao Ramji Ambedkar (1891–1956) was the leader of India's Dalits (a term he preferred to Harijan, which he felt was condescending) and differed with Gandhi on whether the untouchables should have separate representation. In 1916 he received his Ph.D. in political science from Columbia University. He taught law for many years at the Government Law College at Bombay.

19. After having spoken for many years on the unsuitability of Hinduism for untouchables, in the last year of his life Ambedkar converted to Buddhism, along with an estimated twenty million of his followers, marking the first significant return of Buddhism to its birthplace in almost a millennium.

20. This exchange is not in Desai, "With Our Negro Guests."

❧ To T. W. Coggs

20 FEBRUARY 1948
[*San Francisco, Calif.*]

After the death of Thurman's mother-in-law, Susan E. Bailey, on 31 January 1948, Thurman consults the president of Arkansas Baptist College[1] about plans to establish an I. G. Bailey Memorial Library on campus. Sue Bailey and her mother, in the years before her death, had established a community library, which on Susan E. Bailey's death was to be transferred to Arkansas Baptist College and the Arkansas Agricultural, Mechanical, and Normal (AM & N) College at Pine Bluff (now University of Arkansas at Pine Bluff t.s. f).[2] The I. G. Bailey Memorial

*Library at Arkansas Baptist College was dedicated on 23 May 1948, though it is
not clear how long it remained open.*[3]

President T. W. Coggs[4]
Arkansas Baptist College
Little Rock, Arkansas

My dear President Coggs:

I am writing this letter on behalf of myself and Mrs. Thurman relative to an
arrangement and understanding which our mother, the deceased Mrs. S. E. Bailey, entered into with Dr. Clark while he was Chairman of the Board of Trustees
of the college. Several pieces of property valued at approximately $2,000 were
exchanged for a consideration, including the establishing of a library at the college to be designated as the Reverend I. G. Bailey Memorial Library. This library
would memorialize the life and the work of one of the first missionaries from
the college to the people of the state. It was Mrs. Bailey's understanding that the
library, to some extent, would be geared to the needs of rural ministry.

There are some books that are being sent to the college, concerning which
Mrs. Thurman talked with you when she was there some weeks ago. If the plans
of the agreement between the then Chairman of the Board of Trustees and
Mrs. Bailey are carried out we would like to add to the collection of books from
time to time and to seek to interest others in doing the same thing. Will you
please advise me at your earliest convenience as to the status of this matter and
what the formal mind of the Board of Trustees is concerning it?

I hope that sometime while I am in residence here it will be possible for
me to see you on the campus there. Thank you for your consideration in these
matters.

Sincerely yours,
Howard Thurman
HT:is

                                                                TLc.

NOTES

1. Arkansas Baptist College was founded as the Arkansas Baptist Institute in 1884 and
acquired its present name in 1887.

2. "NCNW [National Council of Negro Women] Establishes Award, Mother-Daughter
Citation," *Chicago Defender,* 26 June 1948.

3. Arkansas Baptist College did not have a formal library when Dr. Coggs became president in 1937. He set aside space on the second floor of the education building and also
established the Arkansas Baptist College Collection of Negro Literature. It was not until
1967 that the college opened a proper library, now known as the J. C. Oliver Library. The
status of the Reverend I. G. Bailey Memorial Library through these changes is not clear. In

1960 Thurman and Sue Bailey Thurman dedicated the I. G. Bailey International Room at Arkansas AM & N College at Pine Bluff. See "Boston Dean Off on 8-Month Trip," *Chicago Defender*, 9 January 1960.

4. Dr. Tandy W. Coggs (1887–1992) was the president of Arkansas Baptist College from 1937 to 1955.

❧ EASTER SERMON
28 MARCH 1948
THE FELLOWSHIP CHURCH
SAN FRANCISCO, CALIF.

Thurman's 1948 Easter sermon at the Fellowship Church discusses the Jewish roots of Easter in the Passover sacrifices at the Temple in Jerusalem and, more generally, the nature and meaning of sacrifice that are at the heart of Easter.

Whenever the ordinary routine of our common life is interrupted by experiences of high celebration, we are reminded once again that one of the great gifts that distinguishes man from some other expressions of creation is "a sense of history." It is a sense of history that marks man as a time-binder.[1] Easter is such a celebration in the history of our culture, our civilization and our religion. Not only with reference to ideas is it impossible to say that in essence the thinking of any individual is original, but it is particularly true in the group and collective experiences of the race. The roots of Easter are both pagan and Jewish. "Pagan," using that word in the sense that may be descriptive of civilizations and cultures that are not a part of our own, and "pagan" in that sense. Pagan because long before the Christian era, this celebration of spring time was a part of the common experience of the race.[2] And when we participate in it, we do but in essence first of all, underscore the fact that all life is one. "Jewish" in the sense that the paschal lamb, the Passover feast, was a moment in the history of Israel, when Israel was delivered from under the bondage of Egypt under the Pharaohs; and in the precipitation of that deliverance, Israel became a self-conscious people; and the interpretation of the meaning of the life of Israel, and tied up intimately with the God of Israel, was on its fateful and productive way. The Paschal Lamb, the Feast, this celebrated the deliverance in time, of the redemption of a people from bondage and from human slavery. Now it is a matter of very interesting significance to me, that in the continuation of the traditional feast, and in another dimension, in Christianity, the central figure of the drama, Jesus of Nazareth, is in orthodox theology regarded as the Paschal Lamb.[3] Even the phrase is lifted bodily out of Israel, so that instead of there being a Paschal Lamb involved in the moving ceremonial of the Jewish Passover, Jesus of Nazareth of Christian theology becomes the human Paschal Lamb and his function in the Christian dogma, viewed from that angle, is one of redemption so that the Jewish householder marking the redemption of Israel from slavery and the deliverance of Israel from the bondage of the Pharaohs, moved into the stream of the Christian development as an act once again by which God precipitates the redemption of man from their sins. It's an interesting thing, isn't it?

Now there is something else that is rather extraordinary about this. From the earliest days of the celebration of the Feast, long before the destruction of the temple in seventy,[4] it was an act of worship extending over a period of five to six days in which the Jewish devotees came from all parts of the world to celebrate the Passover in connection with the Temple at Jerusalem. Indeed some scholars tell us that during the period of the celebration, as many as 2,500,000 Jews gathered at Jerusalem to prepare themselves to participate in this great, moving dramatic expression of gratitude to God. It is small wonder then that during the last days of Jesus in Jerusalem that the political manipulators who had put their heads together with the Romans in order to bring about the destruction of Jesus because of his influence on the mass mind and the gripping power of his essential message of good tidings. It is small wonder that they did not, according to our own tradition, you see, that they did not want to arrest Jesus in the daytime because people were there from everywhere. People who had heard about this teacher, the mass move of the Israelites who had heard about Jesus, the new teacher in Israel. So they didn't want to have any mass crisis on their hands, so they said we can't arrest him in the daytime and in the nighttime we can't arrest him because we can't find him. In our record, every evening at sunset the little band of disciples went outside the walls of the city—why? To hide! So that no hired assassin could destroy them. So how will we arrest him so that the masses won't know about it until it is accomplished? We can't do it in the nighttime, you see, we can't arrest him in the nighttime unless we can find him.

Well, there was a man among his twelve[5] who felt that if somehow he could make Jesus see that there could be no deliverance of Israel from the domination of Rome, that there was no possibility of the change for which the devout Jew longed, as long as he, Jesus, was dillydallying with notions about loving your enemy and all kinds of teddlywinks that the Roman empire couldn't understand. So if I can do something that will really make him show his hand, or if not, if I can make the kind of a situation which will make God show his hand in the redemption of Israel . . . so . . . "I'll tell you where he is hiding." "How will we know him in the dark?" "I'll kiss him, the man I kiss, you grab." And so they caught him. Interesting.

The Feast of the Passover. The great moment when Israel paused to thank God for deliverance. Inevitably tied up with all the meaning of this drama in the development of the doctrine of redemption in Christianity. When the Jewish community after the destruction of the temple, began celebrating this in the home, this feast when wine is drunk as the symbol of something and unleavened bread is the symbol of something, etc. The Gentile world said, "Ah, those Jews are not trying to celebrate some Passover, those Jews are really drinking human blood, they are drinking the blood of Gentiles. So we had better get rid of them."[6] Criminals who had murdered often dragged the dead bodies of their victims into the Jewish community and left them for the authorities to find them; so that the authorities would know that this person who is dead in the Jewish community was a person who had been killed by the Jews so that blood might be sucked and it might become a part of the celebration. Hence this experience which is filled with the moving drama of the redemption of a people, become . . . (wire spliced) . . . can serve as the symbol, you see, of the Paschal Lamb, Jesus whose blood had redeemed, etc. etc. We celebrate it in a ceremonial of eating the bread, symbol of the body, drinking the wine, symbol of the blood. They celebrated it in their homes before there were churches, you see. And what happened? Precisely the same rumor that went around about the Jews that they drank blood during this time was circulated about the Christians, and the first great Christian persecution arose out of the fact that these Christians are not really worshipping this dead Jew but they are drinking human blood in this ceremonial that they had. And hence that was the battle cry for the Christian persecution, in the Roman Empire. Now this means one thing basically, that I can't take my little world of meaning and ceremonial and close the door and say that this is mine. I don't know anything and neither do you. Everything to which you lay claim, in the laying claim to it, even though it is intimate and precious and of the very essence of the meaning of life to you, in the laying claim to it you underscore your solidarity.

Now with that as a background, let me take the last few minutes to relate what I think Jesus contributes to your working paper.[7] And your statement about this may be even better than mine, but this is mine. He gave to the world the vision of a great ideal. And here again, you see, it was not the first time that a great ideal had been visited upon the sons of man. But he gave to the world a great ideal, an ideal that was creative and an ideal which said that the human race, that human beings are one family, and that there is no difference. He demonstrated this in all sorts of little ways. From the Jewish community for instance, as we look at his disciples we see that one disciple was a rather flaming nation[alist],[8] another disciple who was a tax collector[9] and therefore an outcast, one of those apostate sons of Israel who had betrayed it from the inside, he had one. One was a zealot[10] who thought that the only thing a Roman could understand was the shedding of his own blood, he had one, all of them were there. Even a man like Peter, just an ordinary fisherman who as a result of his long experience, had learned how to wait. But there he was. Just people . . . God's family. Nothing can destroy the worth of any human being. That's what he said;

all kinds, even little children belong. I imagine when he went from town to town teaching, there was always a group of children following him. Little children, women, even a woman who had been selling her body to gratify the lusts of men and to eke out some corner of economic security for herself at the price of everything that she had that was worthwhile. When she looked into his face, she said, "You know, I belong too." All belong . . . everybody. Everybody feels that. That was his dream. And there's nothing quite like it you know. Because that's all we're really trying to do, isn't it? We're trying to say that we belong . . . that we belong to a family and because we are unable to say that, we surround ourselves with a breastwork of fears of various kinds. Fear of old age, and poverty therefore I'll build me a bank account and annuities and X's and Y's, fear of my neighbors so I'll get me not just a lock but a good lock on my front door and all the windows and if I'm sleeping on the ground floor I'll get bars there. I want to be a member of the human race, but I can't. They won't let me. So build this to keep from being invaded. We'll have an Atlantic Pact,[11] and a circle of radar, one atomic bomb a week or a month or whatever it is. We want to be a member of the family, but we can't—but that was his dream. If I could just be a member of the family! Suppose once before you died, all of the barriers could be let down, and for one transcendent moment you could be a part of the family! That's what he's talking about.

And then the second thing is that he suggested ways, concrete ways, ordinary ways by which this could be done. Quite a realist, if I may put it that way. Simple ways, he called it love (that's the overall thing that we talked about in Christianity). And even that notion that he talked about—what is the meaning of the law and prophets what did Jesus say, he reached back to that crowing point of creative spiritual synthesis in Israel, "Hear, O Israel, the law of God is one." "Thou shalt love the Lord thy God with all thy mind, heart, soul and strength and thou shalt love thy neighbor as thyself."[12] Right out of Israel he picked it. Love and what is it, pushing, pushing the base of yourself out, out until it includes the not-self, the other person. So that when you look at the not-self, the other person, you don't know whether you're looking at the not-self, the other person, or you're looking at yourself. That's what it is, just being a part of the family again, you see. And how do you deal with people? You meet them where they are, and you treat them where they are, as if they were where they should be, that's all. And in so doing may lead them into the glory of their possibility as members of the family, so that no thing, no evil thing, that you ever do is quite a full and adequate representation of you. There is something of you that can't be intimately involved in the diabolical and the wicked and the terrifying and iniquitous . . . interesting, simple. And then he said, not only these techniques—you have your own and you know them as well as I—but all of these techniques.

But also he said there is a power, there is a power available to you. It'll give you what it takes to do it. And it's within reach of everybody . . . God . . . the father . . . the Father of us all . . . inside of you, outside of you. He cares for you, the sparrow that falls, for the grass that grows, for the lily. "Look at them," said he, "look how they grow, they don't work, they just lily their way through life." It is a part of the breathing, pulsing, life. It is He who is in the breath, that makes the breath vital. If it were lifted out of the breath, there would be no vitality in the breath, there would be no life in it. The aliveness would be taken out of life, if He withdrew. He's everywhere, he's in you . . . reach out—or be quiet. Speak to Him thou for he hearth and Spirit with spirit may meet. Closer is He than breathing, nearer than hands and feet. He's right here. You are his child. You're part of the family. God cares for you. He's real, He's near.

And then he said, finally, that He is love . . . that there is at the center of what men regard as impersonal order; blind, unconscious energy; or blind, mindless matter . . . that there is at the center of the very essence of existence not only order, not only logic, not only rationality, but kindness. And this to me is the most amazing emphasis that he gives to our working paper. That in a world like this, a world that seems to breed on brutality, where there is so much that depresses and so little that uplifts and inspires, that in your right mind you can say that at the heart of life there is love . . . that's what he said, that's what he talked about, that's what he demonstrated.

Why would he, does it make sense? Now there is only one way from my own experience that the thing makes sense. When I love you . . . when the self-regarding impulse with which I guarantee my own sense of the integrity of myself, when I take that impulse and apply it to you, and I say as I look in your face, I love you. When I say that, I know that there is only one limitation that I can experience as far as you are concerned, and that is the limitation of my power to fulfill. So, for love's sake, I will do for you with enthusiasm and glory and wonder <u>all</u>, even the most distasteful thing, the most embarrassing thing, the most revolting thing. But if you need it, for love's sake I will do that for you with wonder and awe and glory and beauty. When no power in heaven or hell or earth could <u>make</u> me do it if I didn't want to do it. I'd die first. Now you can kill me because after all death is a little thing. And I won't do that! But if I love you, I'd do it gladly. Almost everybody in this room has demonstrated that, and you've had it done to you. You've cared for the wounded, the sick, doing all those things with them and for them that left to yourself, in a thousand years you wouldn't have courage or nerve or will to do. But when the anguish of the loved one begins to pulse through you, all that there is in you moves out to redeem. And when that happens to you, something else happens. It seems that at last all the meaning of life has broken open in your mind. And without knowing, you understand, and without trying, you <u>are</u>. Now that's what he was talking about. It is the God in life that does that. The vision of the great creative ideal, the simple methods and techniques by which that ideal may be implemented and become a part of the warp and woof of human experience … a power, limitless in resource, and infinite in energy, available to all who reach out, or reach in. Making it possible for them to be a part of the human family and to experience the glory and the wonder of being a Child of God.

And so we salute him as one who, because he had learned how to live, knew how to die.

TD.

Notes

1. "Time-binder" was a phrase popularized by the Polish American writer Alfred Korzybski (1879–1950), the author of *Science and Sanity: An Introduction to non-Aristotelian Systems and General Semantics* (Lancaster, Penn.: International non-Aristotelian Publishing Co., 1933) and the founder of General Semantics, a popular philosophical movement that had a considerable vogue in the 1930s and 1940s. According to Korzybski, animals were space-binders, with the power of locomotion, while only humans were "time-binders," able to comprehend changes and the passage of time. Both "space-binder" and "time-binder" became common terms in Thurman's work in the late 1940s and 1950s, although there is no evidence that he had any particular interest in General Semantics.

2. Cf. "Spring with its bursting buds and blooming flowers must have made profound impressions upon primitive man" ("Virgin Birth," in *PHWT*, 1:33).

3. From John the Baptist's salutation to Jesus in John 1:29, "behold the Lamb of God who takes away the sin of the world."

4. 70 C.E.

5. Judas.

6. Although anti-Judaism was a part of Christian teachings and practice from the earliest days of the new religion, blood libels—accusations of Jews murdering Christians to use their blood in Passover rituals—do not date before the twelfth century. Since the destruction of the Second Temple, the paschal sacrifice has not been part of the Passover seder, and unlike the role of wine in the Christian communion service, wine in the Passover seder does not symbolize blood. For the evolution of the blood libel accusation, see Gavin I. Langmuir, *Toward a Definition of Antisemitism* (Berkeley: University of California Press, 1990).

7. Thurman was giving an ongoing sermon series at the Fellowship Church in the spring of 1948 on the general subject of "Your Life's Working Paper."

8. Judas.

9. Matthew.

10. Simon the Zealot.

11. This was the popular name for the North Atlantic Treaty, signed in Washington, D.C., on 4 April 1949 by representatives of twelve nations that created the North Atlantic Treaty Organization (NATO), a military alliance against the Soviet Union and its European allies.

12. Mark 12:29–31 and Matt. 22:34–40, quoting Deut. 6:4–5 and Lev. 19:18.

To Aubrey and Marigold Burns
23 April 1948
[*San Francisco, Calif.*]

*In this letter to his friends (and Fellowship Church members) Aubrey and Mar-
igold Burns,*[1] *Thurman describes the five lectures that comprised the inaugural
Mary L. Smith Memorial Lectures*[2] *at Samuel Huston College*[3] *in Austin, Texas,
from 11 to 16 April. Thurman delivered "The Religion of Jesus and the Disinherited"at the invitation of the college's president, Karl E. Downs.*[4] *These lectures
formed the basis of* Jesus and the Disinherited, *Thurman's first full-length book.
Thurman tells his friends that he was gratified at his overwhelming reception at
the lectures, calling it "a very fateful moment."*

*The lectures marked the culmination of two decades of thinking, speaking,
and writing on the topic of the religion of Jesus, which Thurman had first taught
at Spelman College in the late 1920s. As early as 1932 he was lecturing on the religion of Jesus (which he always carefully distinguished from formal Christianity),
which had received "much of its significance from the fact that its exponent was
a member of a despised circumscribed minority group."*[5] *A version of this lecture,
delivered in 1935 at Boston University, would be published that year as "Good
News for the Underprivileged."*[6] *Drawing on the earlier versions and expanding
them for possible publication, Thurman finally had the chance to present his
thinking on this subject in its definitive form.*

*One of the inducements and attractions of giving the lecture series for Thurman
was that its sponsor, Roy Smith, pledged to use his influence to get the lectures published. It was Thurman's understanding, as he writes here (and repeats in his autobiography), that Abingdon-Cokesbury Press*[7] *had the right of first refusal on the manuscript.*[8] *This does not appear to have been the case. Nonetheless, Abingdon-Cokesbury
Press was the first to see the manuscript, and though Thurman thought it "very likely"
that the press would not be interested "because of the southern bias in that organization," Abingdon-Cokesbury wanted to publish the lectures.*[9] *The editorial process, from
Thurman's perspective, would prove arduous but produced his best-known book.*

Mr. and Mrs. Aubrey Brown[10]
127 Cypress Drive
Fairfax, California

Dear Aubrey and Marigold:
     This is a belated note to say to you how deeply appreciative I am for your
share in making the Texas lectures possible. They were given with a deep sense

of freedom and inspiration. After I got there I decided that I would not read them from manuscript, but rather deliver them from the outline in my mind. It was a dangerous thing to do, but a very effective one. At the end of each lecture I had to take two or three bows and when the final lecture came there was the kind of ovation the like of which I have experienced only once before in my life. While the applause was going on a student arose to read a resolution from the student body requesting the administration to invite me to return next year to give the lectures. At the end of that the whole audience stood spontaneously and sang "God be with you until we meet again." It was a very fateful moment for me. I am sending today the completed manuscript to the college and from this point on the disposal of it is up to them. If for any reason Abbington Press feels that it cannot publish it, then I will send it to Eugene Exman at Harper's.

Did you see the quotation from "Cry The Beloved Country" in last week's Saturday Review of Literature?[11]

Many fascinating things are happening in the state of Texas. We must have a long session about what I saw and heard and felt while there. Incidentally, your friend at San Antonio is regarded by many people in the state as an outstanding liberal preacher. I hope he comes through finally in a favorable way as far as our request is concerned.

Once again, accept my thanks for your spirit and for your friendship.
Sincerely,
Howard Thurman
HT:is

                                                                   TLc.

NOTES

1. Aubrey Burns (1911–83), a writer and ordained Methodist minister, and his wife, Marigold Burns, are best known for their role in encouraging and facilitating the publication of Alan Paton's (1911–88) famous novel, *Cry, the Beloved Country* (New York: Scribner, 1948). In late 1946 Paton, a little-known South African penologist touring American reformatories and prisons, was invited, after a chance encounter with the Burnses at a party, to spend Christmas Day with them. He showed them the manuscript of his unpublished novel; they thought it a work of genius. Marigold typed the handwritten manuscript (she also typed the manuscript of *Jesus and the Disinherited*), and Aubrey and Marigold contacted numerous publishers, including Scribner, who agreed to publish the novel, which was dedicated to "Aubrey and Marigold Burns of Fairfax, Calif." For Paton's account of the Burnses' extraordinary work on his behalf, see *Cry, the Beloved Country*, vii–ix. Aubrey Burns's publications include "Segregation and the Church," *Southwest Review* (Spring 1949): 121–30; and a volume of poems, *Out of a Moving Mist* (Fairfax, Calif.: Tamal Land, 1977), with a foreword by Paton. Paton developed a connection to the church and became an international member. After attending a worship service with the Burnses, "the spirit of the church impressed Mr. Paton so deeply" that he requested an opportunity to address the church. His address on the racial situation in South Africa was printed as "The World at Our Doorstep," *Growing Edge* (Spring 1950): 7, 8–11.

2. The lectures had been endowed by the prominent Methodist minister and author Roy Lemon Smith (1887–1963), who from 1940 to 1948 was editor of the *Christian Advocate*, the official publication of the Methodist Episcopal Church. He was a prolific author, writing some ninety books. The lectures were dedicated to the memory of his mother and were intended to highlight "any phase of the Christian Faith and its Relevance to Society" (From Karl E. Downs, 5 January 1948). Smith intended the lectures to help highlight black ministers and aid in the publication of their works.

3. Samuel Huston College was founded in 1876 as Andrews Normal School by the West Texas Methodist Episcopal Conference. It was named in 1900 after Samuel Huston of Marengo, Iowa (not to be confused with the Texas politician Samuel Houston), who gave the fledgling institution nine thousand dollars. It began offering four-year degrees in 1926. It merged with the other historically black college in Austin, Tillotson College, in 1953 to become Huston-Tillotson College and has been known as Huston-Tillotson University since 2005.

4. Karl Everette Downs (1912–48) was born in Abeline, Texas; graduated from Samuel Huston College in 1933; and received graduate degrees from Gammon Theological Seminary in Atlanta (1936) and Boston University (1937). From about 1939 to 1943 he was pastor of Scott Methodist Church in Pasadena, California, where he established the Interracial Fellowship Church, a monthly meeting and forum. He became president of Samuel Huston College in 1943 and was widely praised for his accomplishments in increasing the size of the endowment and the student body before his death on 26 February 1948, less than two months before Thurman delivered the Mary L. Smith Lectures.

5. Jesse O. Thomas, "Urban League Weekly Bulletin," *Atlanta Constitution*, 28 February 1932.

6. "Tired of Being Underdog, Says Forum Speaker," *Baltimore Afro-American*, 19 December 1932; "Sincerity Will Not Work, Thurman Tells N.A.A.C.P.," *Baltimore Afro-American*, 4 April 1932; "Good News for the Underprivileged," in *PHWT*, 1:263–70. For a full discussion of the background to *Jesus and the Disinherited*, see Dixie and Eisenstadt, *Visions of a Better World*, 183–88.

7. Abingdon Press was established in 1914 by the Methodist Episcopal Book Committee as the book-publishing arm of the Methodist Publishing House. With the unification of the Methodist Episcopal Church in 1939, it joined with Cokesbury Press, the book-publishing division of the Southern Methodist Church. (It was in Abingdon, Maryland, in 1787 that Cokesbury College, the first Methodist institution of higher learning in the United States, opened.) Around 1953 the name reverted to Abingdon Press.

8. *WHAH*, 219. Abingdon-Cokesbury's right to publish was not a part of the original understanding (From Karl Downs, 5 January 1948). Nolan Harmon from Abingdon-Cokesbury wrote to Thurman on 23 April advising him that his press would be happy to review the manuscript for publication, but "if, of course, you have made other plans and are under obligations to other publishers, you will feel free to disregard this invitation" (From Nolan B. Harmon, 23 April 1948).

9. To Eugene Exman, 23 April 1948.

10. Thurman wrote the salutation incorrectly.

11. After Thurman read the Paton novel, he told the members of the Fellowship Church that "it is at once one of the most deeply moving and socially alerted books I have ever read. The story is laid in South Africa and it points up the terrible misery and the authentic terror of the ethical disintegration of white and black people in that land"; the prose

"sings, sighs, takes to wing, breathes fires and brimstone and prays—sometimes all in one stirring paragraph" (To Friends, 28 February 1948). Burns and the playwright Maxwell Anderson tried to recruit Thurman to depict Stephen Kumalo, the native South African Anglican priest who is the novel's main protagonist, in a stage adaptation, and Sue Bailey Thurman and the executive secretary of the Fellowship Church tried to encourage him to meet with Anderson; while Thurman was flattered, he felt that "there is not enough of me to go around" to consider it (To Aubrey and Marigold Burns, 6 May 1949; From Sue Bailey Thurman and Lynn Buchanan, 11 June 1949). However, Thurman's good friend and Fellowship Church benefactor Todd Duncan did create the role of Stephen Kumalo on Broadway in Kurt Weill's musical adaptation of the novel, *Lost in the Stars* (1949).

➥ To the Church for the Fellowship of All Peoples
3 May 1948
[*Iowa City, Iowa*]

Thurman spent the spring of 1948 at the University of Iowa, where he taught a course called "Men Who Walked with God";[1] some of his class lectures were broadcast on the university radio station.[2] While in Iowa, Thurman writes to his Fellowship Church community and proposes a new arrangement for Sunday services. In this letter he suggests that the service be divided into two parts, with the first forty-five minutes prepared in a way that would be "particularly useful for those individuals who want discipline and experience in quiet and meditation." The second part of the service would be largely devoted to a sermon.

Dear Friends:

It hardly seems possible that a month has passed since I was at home sharing in the fellowship of the church. First of all, accept my thanks for all of the little and big ways by which you gave welcome to me. It is no little thing to share the lives and confidence of other human beings. I assure you that the experience is mutual.

My term here is rapidly coming to an end. Final exams begin on the 27th of May and Commencement is June 5. This means that I shall be coming back home the week of the 6th of June and I am planning to be in the pulpit on Sunday, June 13. During the month of May, I shall be carrying a rather heavy weekend schedule in addition to my regular assignment in the university. May 2, I preach at Howard University; May 9, I preach for the Church of the Good Shepherd in Chicago; May 23, I give the Baccalaureate sermon at the State College for Negroes in Pine Bluff, Arkansas, and later that day dedicate a memorial library for rural ministers in Little Rock, a library in memory of Mrs. Thurman's father. May 30, I preach the Baccalaureate sermon for Fisk University in Nashville, Tennessee.

You will be interested to know, I am sure, that the Mary L. Smith lectures which I gave at Samuel Houston[3] College in Austin, Texas, during the second week in April, were very well received. They had to do with religion and the disinherited.[4] It is the plan that they shall be published either in the fall or next spring.

I am constantly encouraged by the good tidings that come to me from many of you concerning the life of the church and the varied dimensions of self-realization which are being experienced.

I share with you, I am sure, in extending sympathy to Mr. and Mrs. James due to the death of their mother, Mrs. Henderson. We shall miss her in our study groups and in the fellowship of the church generally. One of the joys always available to us is the realization that the church closes in to give comfort, reassurance, and support to each one of us in times of dire need and sorrow.

I have been thinking about a new experiment in connection with the morning service. What would be your reaction to this proposal: The morning service be divided into two parts of roughly 45 minutes each. The first period would be confined exclusively to worship, quiet music, meditation, listening, the deepening of one's private devotional life in fellowship together. This would require most careful preparation and would be particularly useful for those individuals who want discipline and experience in quiet and meditation. The second section of the service would come after a complete break and a five-minute intermission. This service would be dominated largely by the sermon or the religious address. It would include a minimum of music—just enough to provide a suitable atmosphere for the address. Those persons who have a chief interest in the development of ideas as they apply to the religious meaning of life would find their major stimulation in this period. We would begin about fifteen minutes earlier and both services would be over between fifteen minutes after 12:00 and 12:30. Will you think about this idea and let me know your minds when I return? I would like to try it. If it doesn't work, it doesn't work.

Blessings on each one of you.

Sincerely,

[*signed*] H. Thurman

Howard Thurman

                                                                        TLS. FC

Notes

1. Thurman's course was based on Sheldon Cheney's *Men Who Have Walked with God* (New York: Knopf, 1945). Cheney was a popular author who wrote on many subjects, including the history of art and sculpture. The book is a sweeping history of prominent mystics, concentrating on twelve major figures—among them Lao-Tse, the Buddha, Plotinus, Meister Eckhardt, and William Blake. The following year Thurman preached a twelve-part series of sermons based on the book. The other assigned texts for the course were John Baillie, *The Interpretation of Religion* (New York: Scribner, 1928); Charles Bennett, *The Dilemma of Religious Knowledge* (New Haven, Conn.: Yale University Press, 1931); E. A. Burtt,

Types of Religious Philosophy (New York: Harper, 1939); and E. S. Brightman, *A Philosophy of Religion* (New York: Prentice-Hall, 1940).

    2. "Dr. Thurman at Iowa University," *Chicago Defender,* 21 February 1948.

    3. Huston.

    4. Published as *Jesus and the Disinherited* in 1949.

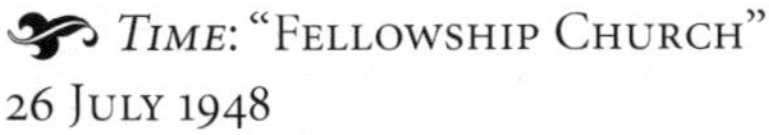 To Carl Murphy

24 July 1948

[*San Francisco, Calif.*]

Thurman sends a list of his favorite hymns to Carl Murphy, a prominent African American journalist.

Dear Mr. Murphy:

    The following is my list of favorite hymns:

  1. Dear Lord and Father of Mankind
  2. Still, Still With Thee
  3. O Master, Let Me Walk With Thee
  4. Breathe on Me Breath of God
  5. Spirit of God Descend Upon My Heart
  6. Be Still My Soul
  7. God of Our Life
  8. Faith of Our Fathers
  9. God Our Help In Ages Past
10. We are Climbing Jacob's Ladder

I hope this meets the request which you make of me.
Sincerely yours,
Howard Thurman

Mr. Carl Murphy
Afro-American Newspapers
628 N. Eutaw Street
Baltimore 1, Maryland

                                                 TLc.

Time: "Fellowship Church"

26 July 1948

From the time of Thurman's announcement of his intention to go to San Francisco to copastor the Fellowship Church, Time *magazine was interested in running an article about him and the new church. On 31 May 1944, the day after an interfaith testimonial dinner in Washington, D.C., honoring the Thurmans (with First Lady Eleanor Roosevelt in attendance), Thurman was interviewed by* Time *after a church service, with the intention that there would be a follow-up interview in San Francisco. An article about Thurman and the Fellowship Church in* Time *made perfect sense.* Time's *publisher, Henry R. Luce,[1] was the son of Presbyterian missionaries and, despite his generally conservative political opinions, was interested in new trends in liberal Protestantism and had relatively progressive racial views.[2] The article in* Time, *which was then at the peak of its popularity and had the largest circulation of any American newsmagazine, "would make a good story," thought Thurman, and would be a big boost in fund-raising.[3] At about the same time, both Alfred Fisk and Albert Cleage were interviewed for the article, though those at* Time *decided to postpone publishing it until Thurman arrived in San Francisco. As it happened, the article was delayed not for a few months but for four years. Although Thurman did "not at all like the photograph" that accompanied the article (depicting him smiling and looking quite cheerful), he allowed that the "reporting of the article was much better than* Time *usually does."[4]*

Religion: Fellowship Church

One day four years ago, Dr. Howard Thurman, dean of the chapel and professor of Christian theology at Washington, D.C.'s Howard University, got an unusually challenging letter. It was an invitation to help start an interracial, interdenominational church in San Francisco. There was no assurance that the colored people would take to the idea, or that white San Franciscans would approve. The pay would be negligible. Before long, Thurman had left Howard, where he had been twelve years, and was on his way to the Church for the Fellowship of All Peoples.

"The Strangest Thing . . ." In San Francisco last week some 250 men & women crowded into Fellowship Church's rented meeting hall. Half were white, more than a third were Negro, the rest Chinese, Japanese and Filipinos. Their religious backgrounds were also multicolored: Baptists, Quakers, Presbyterians, Roman Catholics, Jews, Episcopalians and many who claimed no church at all. The service last week was divided into two parts—half an hour of meditation, then 40 minutes of preaching and hymns.

Broad-chested Pastor Thurman spoke quietly in his rich baritone. "There is in each of us an innermost center," he began. "When we are concerned with our business and the details of living, this is difficult to discover . . . During these half hours together, let us enter into this experience and quiet . . ."

The silence seemed vibrant. From the street outside came the occasional voices of pedestrians. A cable car clanged at the corner. An air compressor muttered in the distance. A plane growled overhead. When the half hour was over, newcomers moved into empty seats for the second part of the service. Said one of them: "It was the strangest thing, the quiet when I came in . . . like coming into a cathedral."

No Dumping Ground. The church's first congregation numbered a scant 25 souls and was located in a section crammed with Negro war workers. Thurman persuaded them to move. "Until we became strong enough to have a character of our own, I thought we'd better get out of the atmosphere," he explains. The last thing he wanted was for the experiment to develop a settlement-house aura or become "a dumping ground for do-gooders who would get an uplift once a week by coming into the Negro community and helping a struggling interracial activity. I wanted people to come because of the contribution it makes to their lives."

During its first two years, Fellowship Church was sustained by an annual grant of $3,600 from the Board of National Missions of the Presbyterian Church (Northern). Now one-third of its $19,000 yearly budget is contributed by the congregation, the rest by friends and 185 "national associates" (who include such kindly lights as Mrs. Franklin D. Roosevelt, Mrs. Harper Sibley, president of the United Council of Church Women). In addition to his white Co-Pastor Robert Meyners, Thurman is assisted by a Nisei Methodist who preaches once a month.[5]

Last winter, Thurman feels, the experiment really came of age. With some misgivings he had gone to serve as visiting lecturer in philosophy and religion at the University of Iowa. When he returned he found that the congregation had stopped calling it "Fellowship Church" or "the church" and had begun to call it "our church." Says he: "Now comes the temptation to say, 'We have a very nice atmosphere here—let's freeze it.'"

No Buttons. Busy Dr. Thurman works night & day to keep it thawed out. He spends half his time in counseling, has conducted ten seven-week study groups during the past four years—mostly on mysticism as a dynamic source of action.

"Our hardest job," he says, "has been to keep our church from becoming a social whip. The radicals bear down, saying we are not in there fighting. Others want us to become an organization, a placement bureau, a mission that gets people jobs and gives away shoes." Thurman recently approved the decision of a member not to wear his Wallace button while welcoming people to church.[6] "We are a religious group," he insists. "It is important that we give strength to people working on interracial problems, but the interracial character of our own group is becoming the least significant part of it . . . We have remained a church."

Notes

1. Henry Robert Luce (1898–1967) cofounded *Time* in 1923, and as chief executive of Time, Inc., he oversaw such successful magazines as *Life, Fortune,* and *Sports Illustrated.*

2. Luce's father, Henry W. Luce, had heard Thurman speak in India in 1936 and wrote him concerning criticisms of his talk. See From Henry W. Luce, 12 February 1936, printed in *PHWT,* 1:325–27. In 1943 Luce had written his staff that "TIME is unshakably committed to a pro–Civil Rights policy and pro–square deal policy for Negroes" (quoted in Alan Brinkley, *The Publisher: Henry Luce and His American Century* [New York: Knopf, 2010], 412). For his liberal Protestantism, see ibid., 438.

3. To Alfred Fisk, 4 June 1944.

4. To Marion and Gilbert Banfield, 3 August 1948.

5. Hiroshi John Yamashita.

6. In 1948 Henry Wallace was the Progressive Party candidate for U.S. president. He opposed the increasingly anti-Soviet direction of American foreign policy, and his positions were widely seen as being closely aligned with the American Communist Party. Thurman wrote at the time: "There is some minor controversey [*sic*] about the reference to the Wallace button. The young man is one of the official greeters at the entrance to the church. It was his suggestion that he should not wear his Wallace button as he functioned in an official capacity at the church, because the church itself is not engaged in the political activity" (To Marion and Gilbert Banfield, 3 August 1948).

To Eleanor Roosevelt

27 July 1948
[*San Francisco, Calif.*]

Thurman writes to Eleanor Roosevelt, one of the national associate members of the Fellowship Church, to give her a progress report on the growth and needs of the institution. In this letter he does not ask her outright for a financial contribution. However, he does ask her to host an informal concert featuring the Fellowship Church Quintet at the Roosevelt mansion in Hyde Park, New York. It is not known whether such a concert took place. However, by 1949 the Fellowship Church had raised forty thousand dollars, of which thirty-five thousand dollars was used to purchase an ideal building on Larkin Street, where the church remains today. The church's national and international at-large members and the fund-raising group Friends of Fellowship Church raised almost all of the money donated.

My dear Mrs. Roosevelt:

I am enclosing a clipping from Time Magazine which in a sense is self-explanatory. I know that you have many urgent matters to which you must give your thought and attention, but I would like to know that you are finding room in your spirit for a continuing interest in our church. Much has happened since

Fellowship Church Quintet, 1949 (from left: Joseph Van Pelt, first tenor; Rokee Acevedo, second tenor; Corrine Barrow Williams, soprano and director; Raymond K. Fong, baritone; Emery Mellon, bass). Acevedo, of Mexican and Native American descent, and Fong, of Chinese ancestry, are dressed in native costumes. From the Bailey Thurman Family Papers; Manuscript, Archives, and Rare Book Library, Emory University.

the day in the White House when you were gracious enough to talk with me about the plan, prior to my leaving Howard University.

We are now under the great necessity for building our own home because our present rented quarters are being rapidly outgrown. The cost of a building lot alone will be in the neighborhood of $30,000. This letter is not an appeal to you for funds, but rather is it more in the nature of a report as to progress.

During the month of September our Quintet will be on a good-will tour in the East. They will be singing in Philadelphia about the 11th or 12th of September. I would like very much to have the group give an informal concert for you and your friends at Hyde Park if it could be arranged. The brochure explains the caliber of the group. They are in themselves an expression of the authentic genius of our church. If you are interested, and it is at all possible, may I hear from you?
Sincerely yours,
Howard Thurman

Mrs. Eleanor Roosevelt
Hyde Park
New York

TLc.

Untitled: Robert Meyners
August 1948

Robert Meyners joined the Fellowship Church as an assistant pastor in 1947, and his ordination service was held at the church in January 1948.[1] A new peace-time draft began in September 1948 (the Selective Service Act of 1940 had lapsed in 1947), and although Meyners was eligible for a ministerial deferment or could have registered as a conscientious objector, he chose neither of those paths. Rather, as a way of protesting the draft, he refused to register, choosing to accept whatever legal penalties were imposed. He believed that "the Christian way to combat evil is the way of redemptive suffering," and he wished to join the "many young men who choose the alternative of civil disobedience to the draft. They believe that this is the way of redemptive self-suffering, and they hope by this to convince others that conscription will lead to war." When he announced his decision, Meyners offered to resign from the church. His resignation was rejected by the church board because of their belief in "the freedom of the informed conscience in matters of behavior."[2] Meyners was not incarcerated, and he left the Fellowship Church in the summer of 1949. He soon went for an extended period to Europe, where he worked closely with Bayard Rustin and the European branch of the Fellowship of Reconciliation before returning to the United States and resuming his ministerial career.[3]

On August 30th, the national Peace-Time Conscription Act becomes effective with the registration of men in the twenty-five old bracket. Rev. Robert Meyners, the co-pastor of Fellowship Church falls within that classification. After much deliberation and reflection, he has decided that as a matter of conscience, he is not going to cooperate with the war system by complying to with this federal regulation. The result for him may be imprisonment. This alternative he has decided to take.

In view of what may be involved for the church in such a decision on his part, Bob offered to sever his relations with the fellowship prior to the registration. We did not encourage him in this position because of our fundamental belief in the freedom of the informed conscience in matters of behavior. While the position which he has taken is in no sense representative of the formal attitude of the board or the congregation, we are of one mind at the point of giving to Bob our confidence and moral support as he does what is to him the fulfillment of the demands of his Christian conscience.

It is our desire that the congregation will recognize that in this action, we are but fulfilling our commitment to close in around each other in all experiences of crisis which as individuals or as a group we may face. We must be prepared for whatever publicity may arise growing out of Bob's act. We must not permit ourselves to be thrown on the defensive but with intelligence and wisdom interpret to all and sundry that in our church we have a sustaining fellowship even at points of sharpest disagreement. It is a matter of terrible moment that within a few months after the formal close of a total war, our governor[4] began preparation for another war. The tragic responsibility for this must be shared by us all. Each of us is under great obligation to deal with the tremendous issues of war and peace in accordance with our profoundest spiritual insights and courage.

TD.

Notes

1. See To Charles C. Perrin, 10 January 1948, printed in the current volume.

2. Robert Meyers to Fellowship Church, 24 August 1948.

3. Bayard Rustin to Lynn Buchanan, 6 August 1949; Lynn Buchanan to Bayard Rustin, 24 August 1949.

4. Earl Warren (1891–1974).

➥ "The Grace of God"
21 August 1948
The Fellowship Church
San Francisco, Calif.

Thurman's lifelong theological project was characterized by practical responses to the philosophical and existential questions of dualism and implications for how the individual lived authentically and morally in the world. These questions of universality and particularity, spirit and matter, and freedom and finitude, according to Thurman, presented significant challenges for the early Christian doctrine of grace. The evolution of the concept of grace in Christian thought is part of this larger human struggle to capture what was first a quality of experience that added something extra to all human interactions, which he compares to a "grace-note" in musical performance. It is this "something extra," the "plus," or "something more," Thurman ruminates, that "becomes an expression finally, in religion, of a movement from God into the life of man that has as its purpose the development of and the maintenance of a creative and harmonious relationship between the individual and God." The grace of God, therefore, is universal, the part of everyone that makes us more than we seem to be, or more than we are, the part of ourselves for which we can take no credit and therefore the part that we hold in common with the rest of humanity, and with everything that is alive—the part of everything and everyone that is God's.[1]

About the Grace of God. It is a term that belongs in the history of all religious faiths and it belongs particularly to the history of the Christian religion because it represents in its theological implications one of the important interpretations given to the meaning and the significance of the life of Jesus Christ. Technically it is tied up with the whole doctrine of the atonement. The doctrine of the incarnation. It is a covenient bridge that explains one of the central mysteries of human life. And that mystery is, how does that which is spirit become matter? How does that which is mind become matter. This has harassed the thought of men so completely that they have—one man summarized it in a little ditty: "What is matter? Never mind. What is matter? No mind."[2] It is a central problem of human life—how does the infinite become finite? How does the universal become particular? How does the limitless become bounded? At what point does the universal cease being universal and become particular? It is a central problem of human thought and men have wrestled with it as a problem in Greek Philosophy, a problem of Plato [and] Aristotle—and all minds have been trying to answer it—a whole great system of religious and philosophic thought back some seven[teen] hundred years ago, known technically as Gnosticism, had to do with that problem. It confronted Christianity with its first great challenge. As a matter of fact, when Christianity met Gnosticism it was fundamentally threatened for the first time in its history and nothing has threatened it in any way that is comparable to the threat of Gnosticism until Christianity in our time has been brought face to face with the threat and the challenge of Communism.[3] And I shall not live long enough to see how this will end, of course, but it is a matter of fascinating speculation—but this is no place for it—as to how this issue will turn out. Now when Christianity faced Gnosticism, Gnosticism presented the world with an answer to this problem, you see of the finite and the infinite—the universal and the particular—the God and the man, you see. And they created a curious figure that was called the demiurge and he was halfway between the universal and the particular, and when he looked this way he was the universal, and when he looked that way he was particular.[4] And he became the bridge over which the universal and the particular got together. It met in him and all who understood him—it could meet in them. It was an interesting idea; and then Christianity picks this notion up, you see, because it had to face this same problem. And the creative thing that it did with it is expressed in the doctrine of the Grace of God. And let's examine it a little and see what it has to say to us today.

The word <u>grace</u> first meant something that was physical. It had to do with the quality of the physical, and that has remained in our definition. We say that this person moves gracefully, or is graceful as to her movements or as to some other physical manifestation of the personality. But always, you see, it is something more than what seems to be the fact. That's the clue to the meaning of grace. A human body, yes. But the human body has grace when it has this additional something that is delightful, that is beautiful, that is creative. The extra something. And then a little later the idea of grace became applicable to inner qualities, to qualities of mind and qualities of personality. And that is consistent in our use of the term in ordinary speech because we say of a person, "He is very gracious." And what do we mean when we say that a person is gracious? We mean that over and above the normal things that are characteristic of him, his behavior, etc., there is an extra something, a plus. And there's the clue again, you see. Always grace deals with this something-more-than what seems to be the apparent fact. Then in music, and if you will pardon this reference, because I do not know music; but there is a grace-note. It's a funny little note—it's somewhere around the lines. It has no particular status, but it gives a glow to the music. It's that extra something, you know—over and above what appears on the lines and the spaces and so forth and so on. You see a little grace-note, and you hear it—just a sound that makes a difference in the quality of the thing you're listening to. Extra.

Now, Christianity, as it has always done, brooded over this phrase and its use—this word and its use; and it found that here is something that has a universal significance and it is exactly the thing that it is trying—this is referring to Christianity—is trying to say about the meaning of the life in God. So in Christianity, grace means the extra quality that moves when our grace becomes active—that moves out from the mind and the personality of God, says the Christian dogma, focusing itself upon the human mind and the human and the human dilemma. Christianity takes this gross—gross in the sense of general—notion that it is a part and parcel of the experience of the whole universe; and says that when that quality becomes expressive of Divine intent, the individual is the recipient of the Grace of God. And it's an interesting thing.

Now it's tied up also with the conception of justice and you will see at once. Ordinarily in a religion like Christianity the concept of justice has to do with the re-establishing of an equilibrium that has been upset. The first American sociologist defined justice as the artificial equalization of unequals.[5] Don't bother—just forget that I said that but it's all right. If you will analyze it a little, you'll see what he is talking about but it's all right. Justice has to do with the maintenance of a balance, you see, of an equilibrium that is already true, that is status quo. Now when that is upset, justice means the restoration of the equilibrium. Now it has nothing to do with the original character of the thing that is in equilibrium, but its function is to restore the equilibrium. And that appears in all our courts. That is what we mean by justice—the restoration of equilibrium. Suppose you were being imposed upon by somebody and you stand it and stand it and stand it and then one day you run amuck, and if you inflict bodily injury on that person; and that person has you arrested, you are brought to court and the justice is to establish the equilibrium. Now the justice can't do much about keeping the man from annoying you within the frame of reference. He may keep up the pattern, but the justice penalizes you because you upset the equilibrium that was attained between you and the man. Now it doesn't say anything about the fact that the equilibrium was bad, that that relationship was bad, was negative, was anything else that we might say—you see the point. Now, justice, however, in the mind of Jesus, and subsequently in various ways it has moved into the genius of the Christian movement, does not have to do with the establishing of equilibrium. It insists, and this is the basis, and it insists in the words of Jesus that even the spirit of retaliation is wrong. That the equilibrium in itself will be an unjust thing, and therefore, he took issue with one aspect of the interpretation of justice in his own religion, which said that there should be "an eye for an eye, and a tooth for a tooth"—what they call the Lex Taliones[6]—there again the establishing of equilibrium. And Jesus looked at that and he said that what that issue means, it really means, is something else—that you have no right as you respond to another person's injury to you, to respond in kind. You should not want to break his head. But that which emanates from you should break his heart. And that's the difference. And that is the difference.

Now, grace, with that concept, becomes an expression finally, in religion, of a movement from God into the life of man that has as its purpose the development of and the maintenance of a creative and harmonious relationship between the individual and God. That's why our grace is always tied up with forgiveness for it says that a movement of God's is always towards man and then in a very, very interesting way says that is true because God is already in you and moving back towards himself. And that's how it bridges the gap between the finite and the infinite. It interprets human personality as being both infinite and finite. The movement of God toward the heart of man, towards the mind of man, stimulating it and inspiring it and judging it, a movement which is possible according to the Christian theory because God is already in the human spirit, in the human mind, moving back towards himself. It is the God in you that prays. It is the God in you that is moved to respond to God. Now, so much for the theological aspect of it, there are one or two practical things—more practical things—and I am through. Everybody is a recipient of the grace of God. Everybody. So it means that everybody has something that represents some kind of plus. There's more to you than I see or anybody else sees. And anytime anybody forgets it, there is a great possibility that you are reminded of it. And anything that you ever do, you see, is able to express the meaning of your intent because there is always something more—some brooding overtone, like a [*illegible*] that moves whenever you move—and you are never able quite to reduce to intent, to function, to deed, to act—always something more.

We are all recipients of the Grace of God. Suppose life dealt with you in accordance with what you deserved. Let's think about it for a minute, but don't think about it too hard because I don't want you to become morose. Suppose even that all the prayers that you have uttered were answered—gracious! Just suppose. Havelock Ellis[7] said when he was sixty years old that every day he thanked God that God did not answer the prayers of his youth. Suppose that you were immediately on the receiving end of much that you have passed out to others. Somewhere in the intricate matrix of your relationships with yourself and the world and all other human beings, there is another dimension always operating like a kind of transformer. Now that doesn't mean that eventually you will have to pay. It simply means that there is a mystery here that keeps you from ever having to strike an accurate, authentic and complete balance. That's all it says.

Now, that's why arrogance and pride stand at the top of the list of all the venal and vicious sins in any ethical religion, because the most important things about you, your talents, your gifts, your graces—you don't deserve any credit for it at all. Of course, you say, "I took what I had and I worked it over and I did this and so—." Yes, you did, but always there is something given, something extra for

which you do not deserve any credit, and therefore which must not ever become
for you the basis of your pride and your arrogance. It is for this reason that life
itself becomes the most radical expression of what is meant by the Grace of
God, Life, with all of the ways by which human beings, human nature, sustain
me—all of the overtones that surround my life because of individuals here and
there who send out into the stream of life qualities upon which I draw—this is
the Grace of God. If He dealt with me in accordance to my error and my sin, if
He dealt with you in accordance with your error and your sin, you would not
be sitting here this morning.

    "I care not where His islands lift their fronded palms in air;

    I only know I cannot drift beyond His love and care."[8]

TD.

NOTES

1. This 1948 sermon is substantially different from Thurman's sermon of the same
name delivered in Marsh Chapel at Boston University, reprinted as "The Grace of God," in
HT, *The Growing Edge* (New York: Harper, 1956), 70–76.

2. Thurman's version is a variant on its usual form: "What is matter? Never mind. What
is mind? No matter."

3. Gnosticism is a term for an amorphous group of religions that flourished in the early
centuries of Christianity, many of which were syncretistic mixtures of Christian, Jewish,
and polytheistic religious traditions. Gnostics generally believed in multiple levels of reality and that the apparent physical world was in some sense less important or "less real"
than the higher or secret levels of truth.

4. In many Gnostic cosmologies, the demiurge was the creator of the physical universe
and a lesser (and sometimes an evil) emanation from the highest spiritual reality.

5. In HT, *The Growing Edge*, 70, Thurman attributes the phrase to the American sociologist Lester Frank Ward (1841–1913). It is not clear if Ward used these exact words, but he
expressed himself in a similar vein, writing in 1898 that "individualism has created artificial inequalities" but "socialism seeks to create artificial equalities." See Lester Frank Ward,
Outlines of Sociology (New York: Macmillan, 1898), 292.

6. Latin for the "Law of Retaliation."

7. The British sex researcher Henry Havelock Ellis (1859–1939).

8. John Greenleaf Whittier (1807–92), "The Eternal Goodness."

≫ To NOLAN B. HARMON

24 AUGUST 1948

[San Francisco, Calif.]

On 28 May 1948 Nolan B. Harmon,[1] editorial director of Abingdon-Cokesbury
Press, wrote to Thurman telling him that the press had carefully read the man-
uscript of "The Religion of Jesus and the Disinherited" and stating that "you
have here the material for a very able and significant book."[2] Harmon expressed
an interest in publishing the book, pending revisions and changes to the man-

uscript. *His major suggestions for change were to expand the book by about 50 percent—he asked Thurman to increase its size from 83 pages to around 125, so that the book would be "standard in size," and to revise the final chapter on love, which Harmon felt was "not quite as strong, nor as convincing as are the others."[3] It is difficult to reconcile Thurman's account of the editorial process for* Jesus and the Disinherited *in his autobiography with the extant correspondence between Thurman and Abingdon-Cokesbury Press. In* With Head and Heart, *Thurman recalled that the process had been tense, drawn out, and bitterly contentious:*

> *[P]roblems surrounding the publishing of* Jesus and the Disinherited *were many and various. The editor had returned the manuscript, the pages covered with red ink—suggestions, criticisms, rephrasings. I was unaccustomed to this. Every comment, question, or criticism I took as a personal affront. My conference with the editor in New York was even more disconcerting. Ever critical, this man seemed nevertheless detached and indifferent. He was positive about nothing save the fact that the book could not be published without the suggested changes. At the end of our conference he returned the manuscript to me for revision and expressed his interest in its publication only after the changes were made. Eventually, we worked through our differences by compromise and capitulation.[4]*

Little of this bitterness is apparent in the surviving correspondence. Perhaps Thurman wisely chose not to commit his angriest and most harsh thoughts to paper. Possibly Thurman, always a sensitive man, was unprepared for the rigors of serious editing. As he wrote in his autobiography, "my experience with the editor at Cokesbury [sic] was my introduction to the world of commercial book publishing. The earlier work with the Ingersol [sic] Lecture ["The Negro Spiritual Speaks of Life and Death"] had been simple."[5] Another explanation perhaps lies in underlying tensions between Thurman and Harmon. Thurman had first thought that Abingdon-Cokesbury would be uninterested in publishing his manuscript because he believed that the press had a "southern bias."[6] Jesus and the Disinherited *is (save the autobiography) the most personal of Thurman's books, rooted in his experiences of growing up in the South. Harmon was at best a southern moderate whose racial paternalism and romanticized view of the old South would have been immediately apparent to Thurman, who could have easily taken offense at Harmon's "detached and indifferent" attitude and lack of positive comment during their editorial conference, viewing it as not merely personal criticism but as an example of the basic detachment and indifference of even many well-meaning southern whites to the true situation of southern blacks.*[7]

Whatever transpired between the two men, Thurman's original lecture manuscript is not extant, making it difficult to assess the scope of Harmon's editorial interventions and Thurman's subsequent changes. Thurman did resist Harmon's suggestion to expand the volume, though he did rewrite, per Harmon's insistence, the final chapter on love. On 7 October, Harmon wrote to Thurman accepting the manuscript for publication. Despite Harmon's concern over the brevity of the book, he suggested cutting it further, dropping Thurman's written prologue, which Harmon thought "somewhat lengthy and does not do what might be expected of it in introducing the reader at once to your main theme."[8] *Thurman accepted Harmon's suggestion, and the published version of* Jesus and the Disinherited *opens with a short two-page preface, with two paragraphs of acknowledgments, rather than a prologue, though it is possible that the bulk of the preface was placed in the first chapter.*[9] *The galley proofs were sent by Abingdon-Cokesbury Press to Thurman on 30 November, and he returned the galleys in mid-December.*[10] Jesus and the Disinherited *was published in the spring of 1949.*

Dear Dr. Harmon:

I am almost through with the work on the manuscript. The Chapter on LOVE has been entirely re-written and is a much more satisfactory piece of work than the original one. I find that the total manuscript is not much longer than it was originally. I suppose this has to stand because it says precisely what I want to say. Very carefully have I gone through the pages to cull out superfluities of one kind or another. The result seems cognizant and integrated.

I expect to mail the manuscript to you at the end of this week. I shall be leaving for the East on August 29th to be gone about twelve days. If my journey takes me to New York City, I shall call to see you. If it doesn't, you can correspond with me here with reference to contract and so forth.

It was a joy to meet you in the office, and I look forward to a renewal of our acquaintance.

Sincerely,

Howard Thurman

Dr. Nolan B. Harmon
Abingdon-Cokesbury Press
150 Fifth Avenue
New York 11, New York

TLc.

Notes

1. Nolan Bailey Harmon Jr. (1892–1993) was a native of Meridian, Mississippi. The son, grandson, and great-grandson of Methodist ministers, he was educated at Millsaps College, the Candler School of Theology, and Princeton University. He served as a chaplain in World War I and later was a circuit-riding minister in Maryland and Virginia. In 1940 he became book editor of the United Methodist Church, editorial director of Abingdon-Cokesbury Press, and editor of the journal *Religion in Life*. In 1956 he was elected as a bishop of the church, serving the conference in western North Carolina and after 1961 in north Alabama and retiring in 1964. He was the author of *The Famous Case of Myra Clark Gaines* (Baton Rouge: Louisiana State University Press, 1964) and chief editor of *The Encyclopedia of World Methodism* (Nashville: United Methodist Publishing House, 1974).

On 12 April 1963, Good Friday, Harmon was one of eight Alabama clergy members who issued a statement calling for the ongoing civil rights demonstrations in Birmingham to cease and for black leaders to seek redress through legal means and "observe the principles of law and order and common sense." In response, on 16 April, Martin Luther King, Jr. wrote his famous "Letter from Birmingham Jail." A careful student of Harmon's racial thinking has called it "inconsistent and bewildered," at once paternalistic and calling for basic rights for blacks, defending the status quo while criticizing segregation. Racial change, Harmon believed, would come about only through "the slow, slow, slow processes of time." See S. Jonathan Bass, *Blessed Are the Peacemakers: Martin Luther King Jr., Eight White Religious Leaders, and the "Letter from Birmingham Jail"* (Baton Rouge: Louisiana State University Press, 2001), 38–44, 233–36.

2. From Nolan B. Harmon, 28 May 1948.

3. From Nolan B. Harmon, 28 April 1948.

4. *WHAH*, 219–20.

5. Ibid.

6. To Eugene Exman, 23 April 1948.

7. Harmon had given sermons in the 1920s asking his congregation to set a good example for blacks because they were childlike and often imitated the "dominant" race. Whites must teach blacks; "how will they learn otherwise." He frequently gave sermons on the moral lessons to be found in the lives and careers of Stonewall Jackson and Robert E. Lee. See Bass, *Blessed Are the Peacemakers*, 40–41.

8. From Nolan B. Harmon, 7 October 1948.

9. Gordon B. Duncan, editorial assistant for the press, suggested this to Thurman (From Gordon B. Duncan, 30 November 1948).

10. Ibid.

🦕 From Nelson A. Rockefeller

18 October 1948

New York, N.Y.

Nelson A. Rockefeller[1] invites Thurman to participate as a "national leader" in the work of the National Conference of Christians and Jews.[2] On 21 November, Thurman responded to Rockefeller, telling him that he was unable to attend the luncheon but would be happy to serve on the committee.

Dear Dr. Thurman:

I have accepted the general chairmanship of the 1949 Brotherhood Week campaign of the National Conference of Christians and Jews and it would give me great pleasure if you would serve with me as a member of a special committee of national leaders. Your only responsibility would be to visit one city, speak to the prominent members of that community and present a plan worked out to express the principles of brotherhood in the everyday deeds and human relations of the individual and the community. Present world conditions highlight the importance of such a program at home and this, as you know, is the basis of the Brotherhood campaign. We hope to stimulate the educational, religious, community and media organizations to renew and expand their efforts toward this end, climaxed during Brotherhood Week, the week of Washington's Birthday, 1949.

I should like to have you join us at lunch on November eighth at the Rockefeller Center Luncheon Club, 30 Rockefeller Plaza, 65th floor, at 1 P.M. This will be the only organizational meeting which will be held. The national committee chairmen will be present at that meeting and you would hear more fully about the over-all plans. At the same time you could designate the city you would be willing to visit.

Your acceptance would be of tremendous help in furthering these vital objectives. I look forward to hearing from you and, in the meantime, with best wishes,
Sincerely,
[*signed*] Nelson A. Rockefeller
Nelson A. Rockefeller

Dr. Howard Thurman
2660 California Street
San Francisco, California

                                                                                    TLS.

Notes

1. Nelson Aldrich Rockefeller (1908–79), one of five sons of John D. Rockefeller Jr., had a notable career as a businessman, philanthropist, and politician. He served as assistant secretary of state for Latin American affairs (1944–45); undersecretary of health, education, and welfare (1953–54); governor of New York State (1959–73); and vice president of the United States (1974–77). At the time of this letter, Rockefeller was engaged in private business and philanthropic pursuits.

2. The National Conference of Jews and Christians was formed in 1927 and in 1938 was renamed the National Conference of Christians and Jews. Its roots are in the Goodwill Committee of the Federal Council of Churches, a liberal Protestant umbrella organization, and similar outreach efforts by the American Jewish Committee, which led to the founding

of the independent interfaith organization committed to promoting religious and racial tolerance. It sponsored its first Brotherhood Day in 1934. In 1998 the organization was renamed the National Conference for Community and Justice. The Rockefeller family had long been connected to liberal Protestant causes, among them Riverside Church in Manhattan.

❧ FROM PAT BEAIRD
1 NOVEMBER 1948
NASHVILLE, TENN.

In his letter of 7 October 1948 to Thurman accepting his manuscript, Nolan B. Harmon, editorial director of Abingdon-Cokesbury, wrote that it was the opinion of the press that "Jesus and the Disinherited" was a better title than "The Religion of Jesus and the Disinherited"—the salesmen thought it more commercial.[1] Although Thurman had long preferred the longer title, in part because it preserved the distinction between "the religion of Jesus" and Christianity,[2] he would agree to the new title but not before suggesting a completely different alternative, "The Hounds of Hell." Although the press rejected Thurman's suggestion out of hand, in many ways it was far closer to the spirit of the book than the final title and is perhaps the book's dominant image. The powerful image of the hound of hell, with its roots in both English poetry and African American folklore,[3] makes more than one appearance in Jesus and the Disinherited, *with Thurman reminding readers of "the persistent hounds of hell that dog the footsteps of the poor, the dispossessed, the disinherited."[4]*

Rev. Howard Thurman
The Church for the Fellowship of All Peoples
2142 Pierce Street
San Francisco 15, California

Dear Dr. Thurman:

Our staff was very glad to join Dr. Harmon in accepting your JESUS AND THE DISINHERITED. It was read by several members of our staff here and all are agreed that it is an excellent work, which probably can be distributed very widely.

Dr. Harmon has mentioned to you the matter of the prologue and title. Both are very important. Dr. Harmon tells me that you will supply a two-page preface which will overcome objections to the lengthy prologue. We are hoping that this preface will serve to arouse immediate interest so the reader will read straight through to the heart of your book. In its present form the prologue is an obstacle to be hurdled before one begins to appreciate the value of what you have to say. It would not hurt mail order sales particularly, but we know that it will hinder the sales in bookstores and at conference book tables where buyers sample books usually by reading the first few pages and studying the table of contents.

The title is even more important because most of your books will be sold by mail. The title must suggest the nature of your book, and the more accurately descriptive, the better.

Your suggestion THE HOUNDS OF HELL suggests a murder mystery of the Sherlock Holmes type rather than a serious study of an important social problem. Our staff is agreed that JESUS AND THE DISINHERITED is an excellent title and much to be preferred over any others that have been suggested. Indeed, we could not accept the book at all if it must be called THE HOUNDS OF HELL. The sale would not be sufficient to avoid a considerable loss.

I am enclosing our contract which provides for the payment to you of a royalty of ten per cent of the retail price of all books sold. If it is satisfactory in every way, please sign all three copies, returning them to me in the enclosed envelope. We will complete one copy with our signature and return to you for your files on receipt of copy for the two-page introduction approved by Dr. Harmon.

I am sorry I cannot give you at this time a definite schedule. We expect to put the book through as promptly as manufacturing and advance promotion requirements will permit. Very likely we will start selling the book to bookstores early in January with publication date sometime in April.

Sincerely yours,

[*signed*] Pat Beaird

Pat Beaird

Manager

PB: mv

enc.

TLS.

NOTES

1. From Nolan B. Harmon, 7 October 1949.

2. Thurman had proposed a lecture series on "The Message of the Religion of Jesus to the Disinherited" as early as 1938 (From Harold Pflug, 28 October 1938). Thurman did use his preferred title in an article that appeared at the same time as *Jesus and the Disinherited,* summarizing its first chapter. See Howard Thurman, "The Religion of Jesus and the Disinherited," in Thomas H. Johnson, *In Defense of Democracy* (New York: Putnam, 1949).

3. One of Thurman's favorite poems was the English religious poet Francis Thompson's "The Hound of Heaven" (1893), a description of a person being chased and hounded by God. The image of the hellhound has a prominent place in African American folk culture, perhaps most famously captured in "Hellhound on My Trail," written in 1937 by

the Delta bluesman Robert Johnson (1911–38): "I gotta keep movin / I gotta keep movin / Blues fallin down like hail / Blues fallin down like hail / Umm mmmm mmm mmmmmm / Blues fallin down like hail / Blues fallin down like hail / And the days keeps on worryin me / there's a hellhound on my trail / hellhound on my trail / hellhound on my trail."

    4. HT, *Jesus and the Disinherited*, 36.

꙳ "The Tragic Sense of Life"
28 November 1948
The Fellowship Church
San Francisco, Calif.

In this sermon Thurman speaks on human incompleteness, the unavoidable gaps between our aspirations and their realizations, human restlessness, and how all "life is trying to learn how to say 'God.'" The tragic sense of life was a key theme in Thurman's thought and practice. In a later manuscript he wrote, "The transition from innocence to knowledge is always perilous and fraught with hazard."[1] The extant transcription has a number of lacunae and other textual corruptions.

I sometimes think that the men of our generation or period in history have lost the sense of the tragic sense of life.[2] The tragic sense of life is the awareness that the sensitive individual has, his most staggering flights of imagination, of dreaming, of hoping, yearning, aspiring, taking place over a rather churning abyss. And if he falters or fails in the thing toward which he reaches, there is a penalty that life exacts from which there is no excuse; so that all of living really is against the background of the tragedy of life, all that we mean by evil in the world, all that men have experienced as evil takes place within the context of this tragic sense of life.

Stated another way: it is the difference between the thing that I seek to do, to achieve, to become, and that which actually I am able to do, to achieve, to become. Man's reach should exceed his grasp, or what are the heavens for.

There is a radical difference between the reach and what we are actually able to put our hands on as ours. All of life takes place in the midst of what seems to be a meaningless series of blind forces. Think about it a little while. There is a sense in which I am content, a sense always that I am able to achieve things, that I am able to do things that I can be bringing to bear upon the problems of my life, that which enables me to forget it. That is one side of [*missing words*]

On the other hand, I recognize that there is a sense in which I can't do anything much, that I do not have any power, that I seem to be buffeted about by meaningless blind circumstances. And you can see why man feels that way. We are born into the world without any choice. Nobody consulted me about this journey. Here I am in the midst of a family, with parents whom I didn't choose;

and they do the best they can under the circumstances, and that may not be much. All of our life they have been struggling to get something with which to find fulfillment. And in the midst of that sense of deep, and frustration, I come along. They give me the margin of what is left. I find that I am a human being that responds to stimuli, and I cannot react to the stimuli so this thing turns up in my environment. I react to it. All of these multitudinous experiences of my life are essentially raw materials that are part of the mystery of life. And with these raw materials, I can make something positive or negative—not in between. I built, in a sense, myself out of these raw materials. I am what I am at any particular moment because of the raw materials that have been beating in upon me even before my conception. And I have the responsibility of building a self, a me, out of these indiscriminate materials.

The interesting thing is that there is something about me, some part of me that started out full grown apparently. In the various myths there is always one having to do with someone being born full grown. The myth that puts its hands on what seems to be timeless truth about human beings, that there is a core of personality, something that was rich, mature, able, that has no beginning, no ending, that always was, that this core that seems to brood over all the raw material of life, that makes an enrichment of itself, that we call it self.

Deep within all of us there is one or the other of the two possible interpretations that I can give about the very nature and meaning of existence. One of them is this: that deep within me I am convinced that life is fixed, that life is finished; it is completed; it is hard; it is unyielding; it is rounded out. If I am convinced that life is finished, unyielding, unmalleable, then in my practical approaches to experience I become a victim of determinism. I know that everything is as it is, and I can't change it. I am fatalistic. I don't quite know what to do. I can not possibly die until my time comes. I will run any risk; I will do anything; for unless it is my moment, I can't die anyway. Winston Churchill felt that way all during the war, it is said. He would expose himself because he knew he couldn't die until his moment, and he had a deep feeling that his moment wouldn't be until the end of the war. His things were all in order, and all ordered complete.

Now, if you happen to be in a strong position, that is a wonderful feeling to have. If you are in an advantaged position, if you are a man who has all the things he thinks he needs, that is wonderful. But if you happen to be one who is not that way, then life becomes a hell, and there is no hope for such a person in his mind.

Now, the second position is that life is in its very structure fluid. It is that which is dynamic, that which is developing, which has growth. That is not the same thing as saying that progress is inevitable or that the longer we stay on the planet the better things would be; I am not talking about that. I am speaking of the conception that there is in life something that is on the make, unfolding. It represents the unfinished, not the underdeveloped, but the undeveloped. If that is man's position, then he can always attack the problems in his life with a certain sense of confidence because he knows that with his mind brooding over the apparently unyielding stuff of life he can hold his hope over the dead center; and, at last, by the sheer power of his imagination this stuff of life begins to take shape. That is why men keep on struggling, keep on working, keep on attacking; for they feel that the final word remains to be written. That is the background.

There are two or three things I want to say about the meaning of the tragic sense of life. One of the differences between life and things, between life and matter, is this: that life seems always to be going up. Life seems always to be integrating, moving from the simple to the complex, and more involved and more responsible; while matter seems always to be running down—so that is why a poet refers to a thing like a field as the gray hairs of the earth—a running down of the process. A curious thing the relationship is between this running down and the running up. It is the breaking down of matter that causes life to work toward integration.

One of the other characteristics of life is that life seems always to be involved in struggle. That seems to be the very nature of life—to work at things, to be involved in some measure of conflict, in the struggle for survival. There is tension in life; it never has all that it can use at any particular moment. It can always take on a little something more. There is at the very center in life something that doesn't stand still. It shakes like an aspen leaf. At the center of life there is agitation, so that when this stops, then life becomes all matter. Now, that is life when there is no mind in it. Apparently a just life in its very structure is agitation. It is struggle, reach, consume, and reaching for more. That which seems always to be restless—that is life in general.

Now, human life is the same way. There is struggle going on in our bodies now; the struggle between living and dying. As long as life is ahead, you are around. Sometimes it is equal; then we say life is in the balance. Then when the struggle ceases, the person is dead. You are aware of these cells that are living their private lives in your body. Suddenly when you lose this struggle, the word goes through all of you, and these cells suddenly don't have any nourishment and they die.

The psychic life of man is the same. The little child is always saying, "Why?" The answer satisfies only for a few days. But you know that if you are wise, you had better work in the interval. There is this restlessness in the mind, this reaching, this consuming and asking for more, so that when you are mature, one of the things your mind insists upon is that somehow things make sense. And you worry because the situation in which you are struggling doesn't fit into any scheme or pattern and you try to make the thing make sense.

In all of our personal relationships as human beings there is the same thing. I have a friend, and I enjoy my friend and my friend enjoys me; but there is something that I am always trying to do with him. It isn't quite ripe yet, and so I work at it sometimes, but not doing anything. This same restlessness is characteristic of the death of any relationship when we take it for granted.

The same thing is true in all of the things that we do; nothing that you have ever done was quite as accurate as the thing you thought you were doing. You always miss it. It is expressed in geometry. There is a law of the constant and variable. The law is that the variable approaches the constant as a limit. It never quite equals it. That is the principle that is operative in all human life. The really good cook is the one who understands this. There is a brittle moment as the first mouthful is taken. If nobody says anything, then you work the conversation around until finally someone will utter a remark that will tell you that it was all right. In your mind is the sneaking suspicion that the thing wasn't quite as you had in mind.

The final aspect of this moral struggle: I am never able to do the decent thing quite, because always, even in the deed that seems to me to be [the] most complete expression of my good will, of my kind heart, always lurking in the shadows of my ethical consciousness is something that isn't quite worthy of me, and I know that however good the deed is, it isn't quite a good deed because I am not sure that all of me believes in the integrity of goodness. That is why a man came to Jesus and said, "Good master, what shall I do?" "Don't call me good. There is none good but God."

Now, what is the meaning of all this restlessness? What is the essence of the moral struggle? What is the point of the tragic sense of life? The gulf between what I say and what I am able to achieve, the gulf that is never quite filled in. The religious significance seems to me to be simply this: that man finds that he can never be complete in himself, that life isn't and can never be complete in itself, that the meaning of all of the struggling of life is that life is trying to spell out an ultimate meaning. Life is trying to learn how to say "God."

That is why all religions of whatever kind or variety or degree, wherever located in any culture or age—all religions, in the last analysis, are trying to say the same thing. There is a poem that a friend of mind sent to me from a hospital in which she was located. It summarizes what I have been trying to say. It pictures the reaction of the world, the creation of man. God is weighing the problem of the creation of man, and he loves the little object he has made and he wants to give him everything. "I will give him a mind, memory, the ability to get tired." And then at the bottom of the basket containing his gifts to man, there is one thing left. "Shall I give him this or not?" And the thing left is spelled out REST. Then God decides that he will not give man rest, for if he gives him rest, then man will be content. "And I will lose him; so I will keep rest with me. He can never leave me because only with me will he find rest."

"Thou has made us for [thyself] and our souls are restless until they find their rest with thee."[3]

TD.

NOTES

1. HT, "When Knowledge Comes," in HT, *The Inward Journey* (New York: Harper, 1961), 16–17, 18.

2. The phrase is commonly associated in English with *The Tragic Sense of Life* (New York: Macmillan, 1921)—in the original "El Sentimento Trágico de la Vida"—by the Spanish author Miguel de Unamuno (1864–1936).

3. Augustine, *Confessions of St. Augustine*, bk. 1, chap. 4.

⌘ "Love Your Enemy"
January 1949
The Fellowship Church
San Francisco, Calif.

Thurman delivers a sermon on the techniques of learning how to love one's enemies through overcoming "the necessity" of hatred. The sermon appeared in the first issue of the Fellowship Church's new publication, The Growing Edge.

"Love your enemies that you may become children of your Father who is in heaven, who causeth the sun to shine on the just and the unjust, who causeth the rains to fall on the good and the bad."[1]

I want you to think very carefully with me about this this morning.

The first basic assumption that is present here is the fact that God expects men to be like Him. What an amazing concept! The creative mind and spirit of God <u>dares</u> to assume that it is within the range of possibility for human life that man shall become and shall behave and perform like God. Here is at once the most radical interpretation of the meaning of dignity and human worth.

It is important in the second place to point out the fact that, in God's relationship with human life, He does not share the gross guarantees of life on any basis of moral discrimination. A good man and a bad man, unless something has happened to their lungs, breathe the same air. If I have just killed a man and it rains on the block where I live, it rains in my yard just as it rains in the yard of my neighbor who has just saved a man's life. It seems to be fundamental to the creative guarantees of life that they operate without regard to moral character or moral considerations. Now the love of enemy begins at the same point at which all other loves begin; it begins with love of self. I love myself. I recognize how that sounds, but let us examine it. Do you love yourself? I recognize sometimes that I love myself, not wisely but too well. But always basic to the love of self with which we begin is what I would call a simple self-regarding impulse that makes me lay hold upon and remain in constant touch with myself with a kind of abiding enthusiasm.[2]

This love of self is rooted in my experience of myself, which is this: that to me I am of infinite worth. I may not be of very much value to X, or Y, or Z; but, to _me_, I am a creature of infinite worth. There is no external evaluation that you can place upon me, which evaluation in my judgment it is worth giving myself away for. I am of infinite worth to myself. Any basis of equality among human beings has, at long last, to rest upon this fundamental insight: that each man to himself is of infinite worth and value, and the only equality that is capable of standing up finally in human relationships is the equal—of infinite worth.

Out of this first concept comes a second to the effect that, because I am of infinite worth for an infinite series of reasons, I am worthy of respect. I have in myself a basic confidence that there is in me that which is holy and divine and beautiful. Therefore, when I begin with the love of myself, I am really saying this: that all of the things that I feel when I am uninhibited by my fears, by my own corruption, all of the feelings that I have for human beings become highly intensified and focused in the way I feel toward myself.

Now when I shift or broaden the base of my self-regard so as increasingly to include man, it means that I am <u>on my way</u> to fulfill the insistence that is implicit in our text: "Love Your Enemies, that you may become children of God who causes the sun to shine on the good man and the bad man."

Under the love of self come the love of friends. This is the second step in the process toward loving our enemies (though some of us don't go all the way). One of the difficulties about applying to friends the thing about which I have been talking is the general dinginess of familiarity.

We take friends for granted. That is, of course, the great tribute that we pay them; but in taking them for granted we do not provide enough oxygen in the air for them to keep breathing. When a person becomes a friend, it means that that person steps out of line with the great mass of human beings; that person takes one step forward so as to be singularly or intimately distinguished from the rest of the people of the world for whom I have an unfocused feeling of basic confidence, sympathy, interest and respect. When this person steps out from the mass, he or she becomes the focal point, the concentrating point for all of the good feelings I have for humanity, feelings which I discovered when I realized that I myself was a part of humanity. When you become my friend, I can bring together in some creative urge all of these elemental feelings that I have for the human race as well as for myself. I single you out and just pour them upon you. That is all right. That is friendship at its best, because I do not expect you perhaps at the same moment to single me out and pour them upon me. If I do, there is a leak in my hose somewhere. I don't quite give you all the things that my pretentions would indicate. I am holding some back so that I can reward you when you start pouring some in my direction.

Love of self; love of friend; now love of enemy: When a person becomes my enemy, be he a private or a public enemy, it means that he has stepped out from the mass just as a friend has. He is no longer in the context with the rest of the people for whom I have this gross feeling (gross in the sense of not being utterly refined, not gross in the sense of evil or bad) of oneness and understanding and fellowship that is my claim to being a member of the human race. When an individual steps out and is not the center or creative focus for all these good things, then he is the enemy, because I <u>then</u> underscore his sense of isolation and separateness from the mass of men; and in that underscoring I nullify any sense of moral obligation or moral responsibility or moral relationship to him.

Now, before I can love him I have to get him back into the context. So when I talk about loving my enemy, if he still remains my enemy, I have been just talking. Something must happen that will get this individual back into the context so that what is available in me, going out to others, will be available to him. If he is not in the context and is not singularly at the point of focus of all creative things as a friend is, then it means that there is no way by which I can get into communication with him until somehow he is restored to his place in the context.

Let us take this principle and see how it applies in the life of Jesus with reference to loving our enemies. There seems to me to be three kinds of enemies Jesus was dealing with all the time.

The first enemy was exemplified by Jesus when he said: "If you are offering your gift to God at the altar; and you remember that somebody who has been very much a part of your primary world is out of line, then leave your gift and go and find this person; juggle him back into position."[3] "Become reconciled with him," Jesus said, "and then go and resume your worship of God." This kind of enemy presupposes, you see, one with whom I had had specific, definitive, primary relationship and with whom that relationship is broken. Before I can do anything about it, I must somehow get the ground, the basis of this relationship that is ruptured, restored. (Obviously, if I have had no primary contact with the individual, there is no point in reconciliation, because there is nothing to reconcile.)

The second type of enemy is within a wider circle, but not quite the universal circle of oneness. Standing within that circle he has betrayed everything that you and the other people that are within that circle regard as being sound, righteous, decent, humane. In Jesus' experience, the tax collector was such a person. The tax collector in Jesus' world was a Jew who understood the psychology of the community, who knew exactly which stops to pull out and which stops to push in to get the last farthing for the Empire out of the Jewish community. He was a man who understood, and sold his understanding for a price. It may be that he was trying to forge some new basis for dignity for himself and his family. It may be that he felt so grossly insecure that, out of the depths of his insecurity, he fashioned what he thought was a new dimension of security by putting his talent at the disposal of the Empire. Whatever may be the reason, the fact is that he was within the family and sold the family out. So, he is the enemy. How then do you love him? You can't love him until you get him once again back into the context. That is why Jesus insisted that the tax collector is also a son of Abraham.[4] Thus you put at the disposal of the tax collector those forces which will make of the tax collector himself the severe judge of his own deed. That is why, when Jesus did this with Matthew, Matthew said, "If I have taken from anybody that which is not right, I will repay," and when I can see any tax collector within the context, then I know what it is to be bound by the tax collector necessity. I can't love him and get to him at all until somehow he is back in the context.

There is a third enemy. For Jesus it was Rome. It is the great impersonal enemy. How can you love such an enemy. I have seen, on the basis of the generalization which Jesus developed, how I can love Enemy No. 1 and Enemy No. 2. The same principle applies to No. 3. I must somehow develop in my relationship with Rome that which takes the Roman from under his Roman necessity. A centurion, a captain, came to Jesus and said, "My servant is sick. I have tried everything. Every available source has been tapped but he is still sick and dying."[5] Here was no garden variety of man but an official Roman, a centurion who felt himself to be the ambulating epitome of the essence of Rome. Now that man had something happening to him. Under the driving pressure of a great affection which was frustrated, he came out from under his Roman necessity and became just a man, a human being who loved another human being. Out of the desperation of his affection he sought help. This centurion thus became one with all of the mass of human beings who have experienced great affection and tremendous frustration in fulfillment of it. And when that happened, Jesus saw no longer just a Roman centurion, no longer even a Roman at all, but a human spirit emancipated by a selfless love.

Here, finally, is the only possible way to love one's enemy. Somehow I must work at the job of making my enemy come out from under the type of necessity that makes him my enemy. And I must come out from under the necessity that makes me his enemy. Then, together, we can see ourselves as children of God, who causes the sun to shine on the good men and on the bad man, who makes his rain to fall on the just and the unjust alike.

Sermon of the Month: "Love Your Enemy," *The Growing Edge—The Worship Supplement* (the bulletin of the Church for the Fellowship of All Peoples) 1, no. 1 (January 1949).

Notes

   1. Matt. 5:44–45.
   2. For a very different appraisal of love of self, see HT, "The Significance of Jesus III: Love," *PHWT,* 2:60–67.
   3. Paraphrase of Matt. 5:23–24.
   4. Luke 19:1–10.
   5. Matt. 8:5–13.

To Lorimer D. Milton
11 January 1949
[*San Francisco, Calif.*]

Thurman congratulates Lorimer Milton, his good friend, financial adviser, former teacher at Morehouse College, and longtime business adviser, on his appointment as chairman of the board of trustees of Howard University and expresses his dismay that a new biography of John Hope fails to mention his close relationship with Thurman.

Mr. L. D. Milton[1]
Citizens Trust Company
212 Auburn Avenue, N. E.
Atlanta, Georgia

Dear Laurel:

   I am sending this line to congratulate you upon your election to the chairman of the Board of Trustees of Howard University. This is a singular honor loaded with extremely arduous responsibilities. I want you to know what a constant inspiration you are to me because with simplicity and tremendous intelligence, you have worked at the issues of our common life with a creative enthusiasm.

   I have just seen Mr. Hope's biography.[2] Ed[3] sent it to me for Christmas. I am shocked and amazed that the biographer saw fit to give no place in his book to any facet of the very unique relationship which I had with Mr. Hope.[4] I suppose some influences were brought to bear upon him to see to it that that would not happen.[5] I think you know me well enough to know that I am not talking about a bid for honor in the book, but I mean that it is singularly unfortunate that no reference is made to our relationship which influenced so many things except that he met me in London and we spoke several days together.[6]

   My new book on "Jesus and the Disinherited" will be published by Abingdon-Cokesbury the first of May and it is the May selection of the Religious Pulpit Book Club.

   I hope to see you in June when I come east to give the baccalaureate sermon at Wellesley College.

By the way, we must raise $30,000. for our building into which we move January 29. I wish you would send a check for it. Make it out to The Church For the Fellowship of All Peoples. This will do your soul good.

Sincerely,

Howard Thurman

TLc.

NOTES

1. Lorimer D. Milton (1898–1986), one of the most successful African American entrepreneurs of his generation, was born in Prince William County, Virginia, and raised in Washington, D.C. He received his bachelor's and master's degrees from Brown University, and in 1920 John Hope (the first black graduate of Brown) recruited him to teach economics at Morehouse College, where he remained on the faculty for two decades, balancing his teaching with his business career. He was co-owner of the successful and fashionable Yates and Milton Drugstore, for black Atlantans, and from 1927 to 1971 he was co-owner and president of Citizen's Trust Bank, the largest black-owned bank in Atlanta. From 1941 to 1972 he was a member of the board of trustees of Howard University, serving as chairman after 1949.

2. Ridgely Torrence, *The Story of John Hope* (New York: Macmillan, 1948). Ridgely Torrence was a poet, playwright, editor, and leading white promoter of the Harlem Renaissance. He is best known for his *Three Plays for a Negro Theatre* (New York: Macmillan, 1917).

3. Edward S. Hope.

4. As an indication of their closeness and Hope's respect for Thurman, in 1926 Hope asked Thurman to write his biography. Thurman felt that he was not the right person for the task and declined (To John Hope, 13 July 1926). Hope offered Thurman a faculty position at Morehouse immediately after his graduation, but Thurman elected to go to Rochester Theological Seminary instead (*WHAH*, 43).

5. Possibly a reference to Thurman's bête noire Florence Reed, president of Spelman College from 1927 to 1953. Reed was a close associate of Hope's and was prominently thanked in the acknowledgments of Torrence's biography.

6. "In London he met Howard Thurman (a graduate of Morehouse and a professor there), who had been traveling in Scotland. The two men saw each other daily, went to the theatre, discussed racial problems" (Torrence, *Story of John Hope*, 329). This occurred during the summer of 1931, when Thurman was in Europe—the summer after the death of his first wife, Katie Kelley. It is the only reference to Thurman in the biography.

꩜ "THE GROWING EDGE"

FEBRUARY 1949

THE FELLOWSHIP CHURCH

SAN FRANCISCO, CALIF.

Thurman had been familiar with the phrase "the growing edge" since 1936, and in the 1940s it became one of his favorite catchphrases. Originally referring to the self-healing powers of all living things, it became for Thurman a sign of the purposiveness of life, always surmounting problems, always rising to new levels. "Life seems, at its heart," he argues here, "to be irritation, some form of agitation that is trying to reveal a hidden something not disclosed." This essentially Lamarckian view of evolution that Thurman held owed much to the influence of Olive Schreiner, whom he quotes at the end of this sermon.

Look well to the growing edge. All around us worlds are dying and new worlds are being born; all around us life is dying and life is being born. The fruit ripens on the tree, the roots are silently at work in the darkness of the earth against a time when there shall be new leaves, fresh blossoms, green fruit. Such is the growing edge! It is the extra breath from the exhausted lung, the one more thing to try when all else has failed, the upward reach of life when weariness closes in upon all endeavor. This is the basis of hope in moments of despair, the incentive to carry on when times are out of joint and men have lost their reason, the source of confidence when worlds crash and dreams whiten into ash. The birth of the child—life's most dramatic answer to death—this is the growing edge incarnate. Look well to the growing edge!

Many of you recall that the quotation just read was the Christmas card which our church distributed last year.

One person, reacting to our Christmas card, wrote a letter to a friend describing how, when he was an interne in a hospital, a woman who had been severely burned was brought to the hospital. When the interne and nurse moved in her direction to see about treating the injury, she screamed because of the pain and the anticipated pain. Finally, they were able to do something about it and treat the burned places. After about twenty-four hours, there appeared along the edges of the area that had been stripped by the intensity of the heat, a rim of pinkish redness that began to creep with definiteness and accuracy over the part of the body that had been burned; and, so fascinated was the injured woman by the apparently miraculous expression of rehabilitation on the part of the human body, that it became for her a source of inspiration and strength as she faced the days ahead.

Technically, the term, Growing Edge, is one that has to do with the way in which new flesh appears when old flesh has been destroyed.

The experience of the Growing Edge is universal. The Growing Edge is that sensitive margin which seems always to be pushing forward, to be reaching out beyond the present achievement or the present development. It has been experienced in many ways on this planet since life began. Several months ago, when a little boy was being dedicated, I noticed on his neck what looked like a dimple, and when I remarked about it, I was told that the doctor said it was the vestigial remains of a gill which would remain as a slight opening in the neck.[1] In time it would be removed by surgery. Here was an echo of the far-off day in the past when the waters that covered the earth began receding and dry land made its crucial and fateful appearance. When our forbears saw that the water was disappearing, and having through all their years been conditioned by water-breathing, they were faced with the necessity of either learning to get their air neat or dying. Some of them learned to push out and adapt themselves to the new conditions, while others burrowed themselves more deeply into the slimy ooze of primeval ocean beds, and either died or became something other than we are today. This push, this reaching out at that far-off moment is another dimension of the Growing Edge.

Centuries passed, millions of them. Then, when we became more nearly like the creatures that we are now, and began living in trees because that was much "healthier," we developed the use of our hands by leaping from limb to limb in quest of fruit and various other things. That process caused us to learn to measure distances and to know how much weight a particular limb could stand, etc. So something was beginning to happen to the processes of mind.

The forest began doing what the water had previously done. It was clear that if we were to survive, we would have to come down out of the trees and begin living the life of land dwellers and learn how to survive without the thick skin and horns and other protective means some other forms of life guaranteed themselves against destruction. Our minds continued pushing out, pushing, pushing, always pushing.

Then, after we settled ourselves in communities, towns, cities, countries, we began to experiment with those collective arrangements, political, economic, social, by which men have learned to live together with some measure of peace.

But deep within every setting of apparent tranquillity there were always, as a stirring within the womb of humanity, those dreamers, those people whose minds are always reaching out, whose minds are reproducing in creative fashion the mood of the Growing Edge by which life in its gross manifestations has guaranteed itself. Dreamers they are and they were restless creatures, always thinking of the possibility of alternatives, always saying that the present is wonderful but, "Somehow I keep thinking of what would happen if we did it this way instead of the way we are doing it." They are the men who became the stirrers of action, the enemies of the established order, a whole army of them; and we call them by various names, prophets, dreamers, seers, and sometimes we call them insane; but there they are, these dramatizers of the growing edge in the life of man.

One of the interesting things about the Growing Edge is that it seems always to be pushing for fulfillment, for realization of itself. It seems to be working on some hidden plan of revolution that it wants to see come to pass. It is unfinished, it is unrealized, it is unfashioned. But it is always trying to realize itself, trying to fashion itself, trying to arrive. Therefore, it seems that the growing edge is symbolic of life, a creative manifestation of life. Life seems, at its heart, to be irritation, some form of agitation that is trying to reveal a hidden something not disclosed.

The growing edge, then, seems to present one of the most amazingly interesting paradoxes about life, for it is working always for fulfillment, transcending the status quo, transcending that which is, in anticipation of that which is not. So it becomes symbolic of growth, and the destiny of the growing edge is finally "to get there." But as soon as everything is ready for it to be there, it shoots past the goal to the next thing. So the paradox is that the growing edge is always working to be finished, to stop being a growing edge, to settle down and be; and yet the very nature of the growing edge makes that state forever impossible. It is expressive of life. Nature is always finally against that which has arrived, that which is ripe, that which has completed itself. Life seems to withdraw its creative, dynamic process from that which has arrived, to be on the side of that which is on the make, which has not yet arrived, which is in process. If I want to live, life seems to suggest, I must always be working toward completing something that I never complete; for if I complete it, life is through with me. So when I round out this little dream that I have brooded over with all the creative processes of my mind until at last it begins to realize itself, in its full-orbed stature then I know that I had better begin looking beyond. If I tarry with that which has realized itself, then I will die. Tennyson puts on the lips of Ulysses—

> "I am a part of all that I have met;
> Yet all experience is an arch where thro'
> Gleams that untravell'd world whose margin fades
> Forever and forever when I move."[2]

And Robert Browning in *Paracelsus*—

> "I shall arrive! what time, what circuit first,
> I ask not; but unless God send his hail,
> Or blinding fireballs, sleet or stifling snow,
> In some time, his good time, I shall arrive.
> He guides me and the bird. In his good time!"[3]

For this reason, youth is of paramount importance, for youth seems to be the collective expression of the Growing Edge. (I recognize that youth is as much a state of mind as it is anything else. In the days when I worked on a college campus the thing that impressed me most was that the most conservative people on the campus were the students. If the faculty decided to change something, the students came down on us with the wrath of the established order.)

Quite logically, youth represents the Growing Edge because the life process, and for me, the mind of God, finds its maximum opening where the inhibitions are not too deeply laid. Therefore, if the Church for the Fellowship of All Peoples is to live, not only must it see always that its mood remain experimental but its deep responsibility is to see to it that its youth have a chance to believe that such an experience as we are having together this morning is a rational and normal experience. If we do that, then I think we may depend upon the living Presence of the living God to guide us, to give us confidence in the enterprise, to strengthen our hands, and, what is more important, to keep our minds always churning with ideas that have not been tried, with dreams that have not been fulfilled, with hopes that stagger us, but yet will not let us alone. There will be held over our heads a crown that we shall be trying to grow tall enough to wear.

We shall not be dismayed, then, even though our way is difficult, even though there are many things that guarantee for a season the limitations under which we operate. We shall be full of quiet courage and humility, confident that the dream of a friendly world in which men will not be hampered by race and national origin and creed is a rational dream. How do we know that it is a rational dream? Because in primary units of living together we can demonstrate it and feed our faith with the facts of our experience. That is our opportunity and our challenge.

I close with an allegory. A mother duck brought her ducklings down beside what had been a pond, but since her last brood of ducklings was born, this, that had been a pond was nothing now but baked mud; but the mother did not realize it. She stood on the banks, urging her ducklings to go down and swim around and disport themselves in the water and eat worms and chickweed, where there was no water and there were no worms and chickweed; while they, with their fresh, young instinct, smelled the chickweed and heard the water way up by the dam. And they said to their mother, "Mother, in your day and in the days of your other ducklings, this may have been good water, but if you and yours would swim again, it must be in other water."[4]

It is to this dream of the Growing Edge that we dedicate ourselves and give our thanksgiving to God, who is the strength of our lives.

Sermon of the Month: "The Growing Edge," *The Growing Edge—The Worship Supplement* (the bulletin of the Church for the Fellowship of All Peoples) 1, no. 2 (February 1949).

NOTES

1. A branchial or gill cleft—which in fish develop into gill structures—can appear on infants, usually on the neck, if incompletely eliminated during embryonic development.

2. Tennyson, Alfred Lord, "Ulysses" (1842), l.18–21, in Robert W. Hill, Jr., ed., *Tennyson's Poetry* (New York: W.W. Norton, 1999), 82–84.

3. Robert Browning, *Paracelsus* (London: Effingham Wilson, Royal Exchange, 1835), 28.

4. Paraphrase of Olive Schreiner, *Woman and Labor* (New York: Frederick A. Stokes, 1991), 49–50, in HT, *A Track to the Water's Edge: An Olive Schreiner Reader* (New York: Harper and Row, 1973), 100–101.

"The Commitment"
March 1949
The Fellowship Church
San Francisco, Calif.

The Commitment of the Fellowship Church, Thurman writes in this sermon, was not "the creation of any single mind" but was an act of creative collaboration, painstakingly crafted, and extensively discussed and debated. It exists in two earlier versions, replaced in 1948 by the third and most enduring iteration that opens the sermon. The three phrases Thurman explicates here remained unchanged through the three versions. Thurman was proud of what had been wrought in fashioning the Commitment and delivered many sermons on it. He gave a series of sermons on the first version of the Commitment in August 1944 and another series of sermons on the same topic in 1951, in addition to this 1949 sermon.[1] For Thurman, the Commitment was not a creed or a confession of faith but necessary architecture for the church, the building of a "floor upon which people of . . . radical diversities may stand together."

> I affirm my need for a growing understanding of all men as sons of God, and seek after a vital interpretation of God as revealed in Jesus of Nazareth whose fellowship with God was the foundation of his fellowship with men.
>
> I desire to have a part in the unfolding of the ideal of Christian fellowship through the union of men and women of varying national, cultural, racial, or credal heritage in Church communion.
>
> I desire the strength of corporate worship through membership in this Church for the Fellowship of All Peoples with the imperative of personal dedication to the working out of God's purposes here and in all places.

This commitment is not the creation of any single mind. About three years ago, the official status of our church was determined by the congregation. A committee of nine persons was appointed to spend as much time as necessary in thinking through the meaning of our undertaking and our proposal. This committee worked an average of five hours a week reporting every Sunday to the congregation. The congregation said what they liked or did not like, and then the committee worked for another week. That went on for some six weeks, until finally there emerged this commitment. It is not a creed; it is not, in some of its important aspects, a confession of faith; it does not represent a ceiling; but it does represent a floor upon which people of far-reaching and, in some ways, radical diversities may stand together in a common undertaking and a common dedication.

In this sermon I want to pick out three basic elements in our commitment that seem to me to summarize its essential genius.

The first is the phrase "a growing understanding of all men as sons of God." The assumption is that you don't ever quite understand anybody; you certainly don't ever quite understand yourself. But if one's traditions are creative, they are growing things—they are living things; they are organisms. This concept calls your attention, first of all, to the fact that understanding is a growing thing. It is not static. Complete understanding is a crown held over our heads that, for the rest of our lives, we shall be trying to grow tall enough to wear. "Understanding of all men as sons of God." Jesus thought of all men as sons of God, children of God, potentially. Deep within the recesses of his thinking there seemed always to appear the insistence that men achieve their sonship. "I say unto you," he says, "love your enemies. Do good to the people that do not do good to you, in order that you may become children of your Father, sons and daughters of your Father who is in heaven, who causes his sun to shine on the just and on the unjust, on the good man and on the bad alike."[2]

Now, our point of view here is that there is only one equality among men, and that equality is not equality of talents. It is not an equality of ability; it is not an equality of economic power or position or prestige. It is not an equality of gifts, however diversified those gifts be. It is not an equality of physique; it is not an equality of beauty of feature or life. It is not an equality of morality; nor is it an equality of conviction. But it is an equality of the infinite worth of every man.[3] Whatever he may say to you about what he thinks of himself, every man, however dilapidated he may be, every man, however stripped and cast down and desolate and broken in spirit and depressed he may be, every man is convinced that he himself is of infinite worth. You may have difficulty in getting him to admit it. You may have to dig around through all the wreckage of his life, all of the debris of his life, in order to come upon that spark. That is what the Salvation Army means when it insists that a man may be down but he is never out. That is what they are talking about—that there is in every man this sense of infinite worth, that he is a being, a creature whose worth can never be measured in any terms that are quantitative.

Now this fact creates a dilemma for man, of course, because the only way which we have for measuring things is in terms of quantity. We transpose values in terms that are tangible. But let us not be deceived by that fact. The quality of infinite significance and worth that I attach to myself is the fundamental basis of equality among men. It is that concept that is brought into focus here, for when religion says that a man is a son of God, it is expressing in religious terminology this basic psychological fact. If I am aware of myself in that dimension, then I must move out in my regard to and for my fellow man with the assumption that what I think of myself in terms of infinite worth, he thinks of himself; and therefore, in my relationship with him, I must always salute this infinite worth, this priceless ingredient that makes me know that I am a man, that makes him know that he is a man.

The second concept to which I call your attention is that of corporate worship, "the strength of corporate worship."[4] The center of our undertaking, the heart of our commitment, summarizes itself in terms of the worship of God. And I say very directly and very plainly, and with profound reverence, the details of which I cannot examine at the moment, that I do *not* mean the worship of Jesus Christ.[5] I mean the worship of God, the immediate awareness of the pushing out of the barriers of self, the moment when we flow together into one, when I am not male or female, yellow or green or black or white or brown, educated or illiterate, rich or poor, sick or well, righteous or unrighteous—but a naked human spirit that spills over into other human spirits as they spill over into me. Together, we become one under the transcending glory and power of the spirit of the living God. For there is a moment in this place that catches us up in breathless wonder, adoration, glory; the walls that shut us in with our little problems, with our little anxieties, with our heart hunger or our mind weariness—there is a moment here, Sunday morning after Sunday morning, when the barriers are pushed away. And even for those who are not believers, something happens, a sense of being related to a *power* that is more than I am, that is not the generation of *my* mind, that is not the projection of *my* desires, that is not merely the ground of *my* wishful thinking, but a vitalizing, purifying, exciting moment of Presence.

We believe that this may be the experience of every human spirit, whatever his particular credo, whatever may be the particular religious exclusiveness in which he has been bred and reared. We believe that God and the spirit of God can wipe out the walls that have separated us in worship; that men who, left to themselves, bow at another kind of altar, or at no altar at all, can be caught up in a moment of all-inclusive, all-pervading worship of God; that the ground of life, and the essence of life and of the brooding creative spirit that hovers over all the aspirations and the yearnings and the desires of men, can bring each man into His presence with a new and wonderful transcendence. We *believe* it in this church because *we experience it.*

The last thing to which I call your attention is "the imperative of personal dedication," the experience of worship pulling together one's resolves. Carl Sandburg wrote a poem about a man who was very discouraged and in despair; and he bought a gallery seat to hear Mischa Elman[6] play the violin. And when Mischa Elman finished playing, the man came down from the gallery where he had been listening to this Jewish musician "rake scraped horsehair over catgut." But, says Carl Sandburg, "when his feet hit the sidewalk, they hit the sidewalk in a new way."[7] Now, dimension is an aesthetic sense. The experience of unity in the presence of God, of the oneness of God, puts a scent in my nostrils that sends me, in all of the things that I do, trying to express it. In my work, in my relationships with people on the street, I look with new eyes on those with reference to whom, when I was imprisoned in my little narrow self, I had no experience of oneness. The fears that I had, that kept eating away at the basis of social security, are now removed, because I have let down my guards in an effort to move creatively into an understanding of other people and let them move creatively into an understanding of me. And in that moment of shuttling, they become a part of me forever.

To illustrate what I mean: a certain friend of this church worked overtime last Christmas trying to do a lot of things, helping us in connection with the holidays. So I said to him afterwards, "Let me pay you something for all of this time. It is not part of your agreement with us to do these extra things." And he said, "Oh, thank you very much. I need the money, and I need it desperately, but I can't take it." I said, "Why can't you?" He said, "When I meet people from Fellowship Church downtown, they treat me there just as they treat me here on Sunday morning. And anything I can do to help this along, it eases my own burden." If our commitment doesn't mean that, it means nothing.

Men, all kinds, sons of God; men, all kinds, achieving an experience of oneness in worship in the presence of God, and fulfilling the experience in their workaday world. Share in this fellowship, then, whether you feel unworthy or not. It will, through the fulfillment of its purpose, make of you a worthy sharer in it. This is our responsibility and our glory.

Sermon of the Month: "The Commitment," *The Growing Edge—The Worship Supplement* (the bulletin of the Church for the Fellowship of All Peoples) 1, no. 3 (March 1949).

NOTES

1. HT, *Footprints*, 39. The 1944 sermons on the Commitment are not extant. In 1951 Thurman preached six sermons on "The Meaning of Commitment." Four of these sermons survive: "Spiritual Awareness" (28 January); "A Vital Experience of God" (11 February); "The Bond That Unites" (1 April); and "The Strength of Corporate Worship" (8 April). They will be published in a later volume of *The Papers of Howard Washington Thurman* devoted to Thurman's sermon series from the Fellowship Church and Boston University years.

2. Matt. 5:44–45.

3. See To Henry A. Myers, 28 May 1945, printed in the current volume. Cf. Myers, *Are Men Equal?*, a book that Thurman much admired. "The idea of equality has its source in the private man's sense of his own infinite worth. All immortal souls are equally precious in the eyes of God." Myers, *Are Men Equal?*, 160.

4. On 8 April 1951 Thurman preached an entire sermon on "The Strength of Corporate Worship." It was reprinted in *The Growing Edge* (Summer 1951): 22–26. In it he makes clear that if he had a model for corporate worship, it was his participation in Quaker meetings. In the act of successful corporate worship, "the individual in the pew, the preacher in the pulpit, and the choir in the loft become one in a creative synthesis in which there is a common sharing, a pooling of desires and concerns, and a common awareness of inner need in the presence of God."

5. Thurman had been publicly making the distinction between the nonidentity of "the worship of Jesus Christ" and "the worship of God" since at least 1937. See HT, "The Sources of Power for Christian Action," 29 December 1937, printed in *PHWT*, 2:100.

6. Mischa Elman (1891–1967) was a prominent Russian American violinist of Jewish ancestry.

7. Carl Sandburg, "Bath," in Carl Sandburg, *Chicago Poems* (New York: Henry Holt, 1916), 55.

❧ "The Quest for Stability"

April 1949

From 7 to 14 March 1949 Thurman delivered four lectures in San Francisco at the eighteenth national convention of the YWCA of the U.S.A. (They were published as a single talk, with breaks between the four sections.) In the lectures Thurman argues that America of the Cold War era was still suffering from the spiritual and moral exhaustion and enervation of the total war. As a result, the commitment to democratic principles had lost some of its vitality and the sense of self was weakened. He contends that the only way to overcome such impulses is to reestablish a sense of self rooted in a common dignity and spirituality.

In an illuminating essay on character in his volume *Christ in the Ancient World*, T. R. Glover makes the telling point that men are made great by great responsibilities.[1] When they lack a sense of responsibility for the common life, they lose their morale. For what is morale, after all, but a belief, a faith in one's cause, in one's purpose—yes, even in one's activities.

The threat to our morale has its roots in three important aspects of modern life. In the first place, the spiritual and moral effects of total war have left us well-nigh exhausted. Everybody is tired. Even the freshmen in college are weary. By total war, I do not mean merely the radical demands that were made upon our physical and economic resources. But I do mean that primary and exhausting demands were made upon the total population.

War has always been regarded as the highly specialized activity of a particular group within the state, sometimes of the professional soldiers, those who have made military service their career. During the war we referred to the military group within the Japanese nation as those who were responsible for the war. The same reference was made concerning those who were close to Hitler and Mussolini. In this country, even during a total war, we were careful to make that old distinction in ascribing blame to the military men and not to a people, a distinction in contradiction to our own experience of war at the time.

The simple fact is that, during the war, we were all of us involved, men and women, old and young, rich and poor. It was total war. There was no spot on this planet which was not caught in the maelstrom. This meant that there was no group anywhere, and scarcely an individual that could brood creatively over the widespread tragedy with detachment sufficient to define the lines along which the world might move for its own salvation. Now we are so exhausted that there is scarcely enough energy left with which to believe in peace. Upon returning home from war, Mr. Anthrobus, in Thornton Wilder's *Skin of Our Teeth,* says that he has lost the one thing that had enabled him before to start again at the end of each destructive period in the race's history. He had lost his morale, for he no longer was convinced of his belief about man and his future on the planet.[2]

Yes, the experience of total war has undermined our stability with reference to the possibility of peace on the earth.

In the second place, we are wandering in the confusion arising from the challenge made by Axis totalitarianism to the easy-going democracy of the United Nations. It was possible during the first World War to meet the rather vague challenge of the Central Powers with the famous slogan "Make the World Safe for Democracy" as our rallying point. It was not mandatory to be more specific. But, in our struggle with the fascists of the Axis, we were faced with something new in our democracy. In fascism there was a clear, bold statement as to goals and means. The fascists stated clearly that they were working for a new order based upon the doctrine of the inequality of man. Before our very eyes, we saw this doctrine provide the individual with a basis for integrated action and a profound sense of participation in a collective destiny.

Faced with this challenge, the democracies found it absolutely necessary to be equally clear in the statement of their aims and ends. This had to be done, if for no other reason, in order to keep intellectual self-respect. Paradoxically enough, the more clearly the meaning of democracy was spelled out in contrast to that of fascism, the more actively was unrest created within the democracies themselves. One need only refer to the disagreement between Mr. Roosevelt and Mr. Churchill over the interpretation of the Atlantic Charter.[3] The unrest within the democracies had to be placated because a divided people could not wage total war successfully. The insistence that all differences made sharp by fascism should be suspended "for the duration" caused men to relax their belief in democracy, even as they gave their lives in its defense.

The fear of Axis fascism has been somewhat displaced by the fear of Russian communism. Mark you, I said, "the *fear* of Russian communism"; I did not say, "the recognition of the dangers of Russian communism." The fear of Russian communism is in direct proportion to our lack of faith in democracy. Hence the attack on our morale.

In the third place, our belief in institutional or organized religion is in danger of being destroyed. It is quite commonplace for one to remark these days that there is no validity in maintaining a belief in organized religion as a serious undertaking for the human spirit. A very good case can be made in defense of such a position. We must never forget, however, that organized religion in every society does call attention to certain "ideal points of reference" that shine as lighthouses in the surrounding darkness. It announces the age-old quest of the human spirit for values and meanings, and provides frames of reference that extend beyond the particular vicissitudes of fortune. There is something timeless about its announcement. When men forget that fact, they begin to settle for the immediate goal, the immediate end, and by so doing lose the "tragic sense of life"[4] without which there is no empirical ground for human dignity. The demand for relative values is urgent always, but those values must find their meaning ultimately in something that is beyond.

Something else has happened in this regard. A generation ago the Christian movement in this country was inspired by the great slogan "The Evangelization of the World in This Generation."[5] It swept through our country like a ball of fire. The result was that thousands of people scattered themselves all over the world, taking the Gospel with them. They discovered that there were other world religions that had been at work long before Christianity. They were sure that, out of one blood, God had created all men. This was the basis of human unity. In the course of their experiences around the world, it became increasingly clear that a common origin was not enough to guarantee the achievement of human unity; there must also be a common faith. There are many other factors in modern life pointing in this same direction.

The loss of our confidence in organized religion precisely at the moment when it is clear that we must find a common faith to guarantee the unity of the race, is, in effect, making a fundamental attack on our morale. What must we do to achieve stability in the midst of a climate that undermines morale?

*　*　*

The quest for stability is pursued against a background of threatening confusion and is impelled by a desire for personal morale. Its achievement results in a profound *sense of self.* It is important, therefore, to find out what a *sense of self* may mean as the object of our search.

In the first place, one's personal stability depends on his relationships with others. For, in order to answer the question, *Who am I?* the individual must go on to ask, To whom, to what, do I belong? This primary sense of belonging, of counting, of participation in situations, of sharing with the group, is the basis of all personal stability. And from [*illegible*] is derived the true *sense of self.*

We are all related either positively or negatively to some immediate social unit which provides the "other-than-self" reference which in turn undergirds the sense of self. Such a primary group confers *persona* upon the individual; it fashions and fortifies the character structure. It is so important that most of our choices, decisions and actions are taken in the light of their bearing upon our relationship with the group or groups that give to us dignity, self-respect, status, a sense of self.

Whenever I ask myself, "What do I wish—what do I want to do?" I am almost sure to raise the broader question, How will this affect my standing with others? For experience tells us that disapproval and criticisms are likely to emasculate or even to annihilate our sense of self and so to strip us of all personal significance. At such moments, if we can find a strong personality to lean on, we fasten upon him with such utter dependence that we become in important ways his reflection; and sometimes after a bitter humiliation, when we so greatly need help for our healing, for being made whole again, we are introduced to a personality who brings us what we need and stays with us, until slowly, and often with great pain, we are able to stand on our own feet once more. And so we regain personal stability.

Another question that we instinctively ask is, *What am I?* The answer rests in part with the quality of our achievements—our ability to express ourselves in effective action. Yet no one's deeds offer an adequate account of his entire personality. There is always a margin of self not quite involved in whatever he may be thinking, saying or doing at any particular moment. For each person is both a *participant* and a *spectator.* No self-expression can be perfectly complete.

When, therefore, I try to find an answer to the question, What am I? I should not only seek an external basis for my sense of self, but also look for the personal center within myself from which outward self-expression comes. And then I should bring them into a single focus. For, when I am divided between myself as participant and myself as observer, conflicts arise and increase in riotous irresolution. No wonder that Christianity places so great an emphasis upon wholeness, sincerity and genuineness; and that sin is seen as "missing the mark." Salvation comes to the individual through stability when the deed and the doer are integrated by the unifying power of God's Holy Spirit.

*　*　*

We may describe the sense of self and its development in still another way. A person feels his stability when he has "free flowing" access to that which is of paramount significance and worth to him. He finds the way to stability through a specific sense of his whole relationship to the world and to history. This may be called the *sense of context,* which gives perspective to individual life.

There is a faculty of mind, a principle of rationality running through the very structure of character, which insists that things must naturally make sense. We try to reduce the conglomerates of our experience, however vast they may be, to manageable units of comprehension. This explains the child's habit of asking, Why? why? why? Even when an answer is given, the satisfaction is only temporary and the insistent *why* soon reappears. The small personality is trying to stretch itself around the world, to take into its mind all that it is meeting, every day, in order that it may have what we have called a *sense of context*.

Self-respect is in reality this same sense of context, based primarily upon one's estimate of himself. Each person wishes to be convinced that he is a person of infinite worth. He may be a bad man, he may be an ugly man, he may be a poor man, he may be an ignorant man, he may be very wretched; yet even if he is stripped to the barest substance, his self-regard still persists to some degree. This is the basis of genuine democracy. There may not be equality among men in terms of ability, or power, or grace, or achievement, or spirituality, but the crucial point of reference for democracy is the fact that, to himself, each human being is a person of infinite worth.

The development of the human body illustrates the same sense of context in a physical dimension. Rodin's sculpture of the hand of God, with its gigantic palm holding a lump of clay out of which the shapes of human bodies are emerging, dramatizes the point.

A few months ago I dedicated a baby boy in baptism. Holding him in my arms, I noticed a dimple in his neck. The mother said that it was not really a dimple, but instead, according to the doctor, the vestigial remains of a gill. It was a token out of the prehistoric past, reminding us that, when the waters receded and our primeval forbears had to learn to breathe on land, it must have been extremely difficult for those who survived in the new context of existence.

Yet the human body has finally worked out a context in which all organs function as a whole. When an organ does not so behave, when it fails to perform its own task as it should, it falls out of context and we say that we are ill. And what the body has learned about context and its stability, the psyche also must learn.

We live in a time when psychopathic ailments are unprecedentedly common, indicating that the emotional elements in the personality are out of context in our characters. Unresolved frustrations, hates and fears will not accept the personal solution offered by our minds and wills, but remain outside of the integration of our rational and moral selves. This widespread loss of morale is due, no doubt, both to forces at work upon us from outside and to our inability to achieve and maintain an inward unity in the face of the many cross currents in our common life. A revived over-emphasis upon nationalism is, for example, the direct result of having given ourselves over to total war. The barriers being erected between peoples, the lines being drawn between Soviet Russia and the

West, the wall of rancor rising between Catholicism and Protestantism, all show to how great an extent we are failing to bring our world into its true context. And so our instability increases, while prophetic voices tell us that there is no hope of stability in our world until all the peoples and all the systems find their rightful places in a context which relaxes tension and makes for the wholeness of mankind.

It is important that each one of us, in his quest for lasting stability, should become sensitive to those things within himself and in his surroundings which may help him to achieve a feeling of context. The resources of religion and of healthy living serve as keys to the hidden contexts, opening secret doors to the room in which the human spirit enters into full integration with God. This is what St. Augustine meant when he exclaimed, "Thou hast made us for Thyself, and our souls are restless till they find their rest in Thee."[6]

*   *   *

It is obvious that no person can be serene, tranquil, composed or consistent unless he has found serenity, tranquility, composure and consistency in his experience of life beyond himself. Stability cannot be plucked out of the thin air nor conjured up by a sort of magic. It is a state of mind, a quality of being that has been drawn, and then personally distilled, out of one's own experience. It always contains an element of triumph when soundly won, being in this respect akin to goodness. For we do not correctly say that a child is good, since a child is only innocent. When the term is applied to a mature adult, it has a specific meaning in the realm of moral freedom. There is a "can't-help-it" quality about the "goodness" of a child, but a man is good to the extent that he has wrought beauty out of ugliness, has distilled purity out of stain, has winnowed peace out of chaos. Therein lies the triumph of goodness—always best-known by its scars.

The sense of presence shares something of this same character. It connotes a spiritual victory gained through a series of struggles for unity within and without. It is all-pervasive; it is whole; it is enveloping like the wind. It is, indeed, the Holy Spirit of God, wherein the quest for tranquility finds its ultimate fulfillment.

There lived in the Dark Ages a lively, isolated, brilliant person who undertook to clarify and to define the true meaning of tranquility as found in God. John Scotus[7] insisted that life is one, a living unity, and that life is characterized by creative process. And he taught that there is only one species of stability, the sort which is grounded in divine process. Scotus speaks of God as the source of life, that out of which life has come. He refers to God as the goal of life, toward which all living creatures move.

Conscious living is made up, therefore, of an infinite participation in this continuing process and expresses itself in a constant movement from ground to goal.

This process is a pulse beat of the eternal, quivering in spatial and temporal relationships. The unity of essence, the unity of being, the unity of process, fundamental to any merely private or collective sense of oneness of which we may be aware, is the divine stillness and motion generating the sense of presence which fills the man who prays and conducts his life with reverence.

We are now prepared to comprehend a principle which is fundamental to the entire quest. The experience of unity is more compelling than the dogmas and prejudices that tend to divide. And every such experience, on whatever level, is an intimation of that profound unity of all existence within the spatio-temporal continuum through which we discern an expression of the mind, the purpose and the will of God.

Those who wish to exercise decisive control over the lives of others are, for this reason, careful to keep them from experiencing unity. If walls of separation are to be maintained, this insight is sound. Men may not be permitted to experience full unity. For the experience of unity with other men and groups is the basis, the very essence of stability, of peace of mind, of security within. God is one—life is one. There are no divisions in the world except those that man has instituted. This is an important aspect of Jesus' teachings about singleness of mind and purity of heart. "Blessed are the pure in heart for they shall see God."[8] Herein lies the unity of self—here is felt the sense of Presence: nothing dividing, nothing separating us from our creator and redeemer.

Ethical religion always recognizes the place of suffering in human experience and its significance in the development of God awareness. The human spirit, in its supreme effort to incorporate into itself the pain and tragedy of all creation, achieves a wholeness that relaxes tension, that transcends turmoil and that makes for tranquility. Seeking to reduce pain to a manageable unit, man gains new strength through all the reaches of his being, and knows that he can endure anything that life may command.

"The Quest for Stability," *Woman's Press* 43, no. 4 (April 1949): 12–15.

Notes

1. "The thing that above all ruined ancient society was the increasing withdrawal of responsibility from the individual . . . ancient history teaches us that men are made great by great responsibilities." See T. R. Glover, *The Influence of Christ in the Ancient World* (New Haven, Conn.: Yale University Press, 1929), 78.

2. The following is from Thornton Wilder, *The Skin of Our Teeth* (1942), in Thornton Wilder, *Collected Plays and Writings on Theater* (New York: Library of America, 2007), 280:

Antrobus: Maggie, I've lost it. I've lost it.

Mrs. Antrobus: What have you lost?

Antrobus: The most important thing of all: The desire to begin again, to start building . . . when you're at war you think about a better life; when you're at peace you think about a more comfortable one. I've lost it.

Less than a month before these lectures, Thurman had given a sermon at the Fellowship Church devoted to "The Skin of Our Teeth." He said of this passage, "Life ceases to be tragic and merely becomes melodramatic. . . . You feel unclean, depressed, ashamed of the human race, and in that moment of intensity you wish you could resign, but you can't. That is what war does. War killed the ground of self-respect which is the raw material out of which the will to keep on is made" (HT, "Skin of Our Teeth," 27 February 1949).

3. The Atlantic Charter was a joint declaration issued by the United States and the United Kingdom on 14 August 1941 after a meeting between Churchill and Roosevelt off the coast of Newfoundland. There were many differences between the two leaders over the details of the Atlantic Charter, but Thurman is probably referring to the third clause, promising to ensure and protect "the rights of all peoples to choose the form of government under which they will live." Churchill's insistence that this did not apply to the peoples of the British Empire had previously provoked Thurman's passionate protest: "[I]f India cannot be given her freedom under the Atlantic Charter, then freedom of men everywhere can be throttled and side-stepped" (*PHWT*, 2:348).

4. Thurman is arguing that the essential dignity and worth of the individual are made possible or contingent upon the limitations posed by the tragic character of existence; therefore the question of freedom and equality, cornerstones of democratic life, in an ironic way are supported by the "tragic sense of life." See also "The Tragic Sense of Life," printed in the current volume.

5. This is a phrase associated with John R. Mott (1865–1955), longtime leader of the International YMCA and the World Student Christian Federation. See John R. Mott, *The Evangelization of the World in This Generation* (New York: Student Volunteer Movement for Foreign Missions, 1900).

6. Augustine, *Confessions of Saint Augustine*, bk. 1, chap. 1.

7. John Duns Scotus (c. 1266–1308) was a leading medieval theologian and philosopher who argued, in opposition to the view of his great predecessor Thomas Aquinas, that all being is univocal and not equivocal or analogical. That is, the attributes of God, such as goodness and wisdom, have the same lexical meaning when applied to humans, so that there is, in this sense, a unity to all being.

8. Matt. 5:8.

🪰 From Mary McLeod Bethune
29 April 1949

Bethune[1] acknowledges here the impending publication of Jesus and the Disinherited. *She shares Thurman's concern that Eleanor Roosevelt seems to be losing interest in the Fellowship Church idea.*

Dr. Howard Thurman
2041 Larkin Street
San Francisco, California

Dear Howard:

I have your note and I am very happy to know that your new book will soon be out. Remember I am cognizant of the fact that I have a large number of your books here unsold. They will be pushed out as soon as there is an opportunity to do so. I shall be very happy to receive an autographed copy of JESUS AND THE DISINHERITED.

It is strange that Mrs. Roosevelt has not seemingly shown the interest in the work that is so close to her heart and to which she gave a great deal of thought. I saw her at Hyde Park on the 12th of April. I shall, in my own way, make an approach to her about the work you are doing. I will say to her that both you and Sue are hoping that she is still keeping in mind the work out there. She has been busy.

When you go to Daytona, be sure and come in contact with the school. I may be there at that time.

I miss Sue. She should be near me right now. I need her every day.
Sincerely yours,
[*signed*] Mary McLeod Bethune
Mary Mcleod Bethune
Founder-President

TLS.

NOTE

1. Mary McLeod Bethune (1875–1955), a lifelong friend of Thurman, was born near Maysville, South Carolina, and attended Scotia Seminary and Dwight L. Moody's Institute for Home and Foreign Missions. After teaching in several schools in the South, in 1904 she founded the Daytona Educational and Industrial Training School for Negro Girls in Daytona Beach, Florida. In 1923 it merged with the Cookman Institute of Jacksonville, Florida to become a co-ed high school. In 1924 the school affiliated with the United Methodist Church and became a junior college called Bethune-Cookman College, in 1941 it began to offer four-year baccalaureate degrees, and in 2007 it became Bethune-Cookman University. Website of Bethune-Cookman University; http://www.cookman.edu/about_BCU/history/ (accessed 31 December 2014). Bethune was its president from its 1904 founding until 1942. She was president of the National Association of Colored Women from 1924 to 1928 and founded the National Council of Negro Women in 1935. She became a part-time staff member of the National Youth Administration in 1936 and director of its Division of Negro Affairs in 1938. A close friend of Eleanor Roosevelt, she was a leading figure in the "black cabinet," a group of black New Dealers who pushed for greater attention to the needs of blacks by the Roosevelt administration. Published widely in the black press, she was one of the most prominent African American leaders of her time.

⮞ FROM ALICE SAMS
4 MAY 1949
[*Daytona Beach*], FLA.

Thurman's mother acknowledges the receipt of a copy of Jesus and the Disinherited. *As she expresses concern for Madaline's health, her tremendous sense of faith in God and Thurman's abilities—which served as his foundation in his early years—shines through.*

My dear Son I thank god And you for the {book}It A great book I have only read A little my eyes Are not so good And I can t read to much It came the lass of lass week But It is A great book. I wonder where you got so much knowlege from God only Could give It to you I Am verry thankful to God for permiting me to be you mother I Am Asking him to spear me to see my sick Child I Am sick but but life is behind me And her life was before her to look At, It should Cause us to strive to look After Olive And Ann verry prayerful {&} Careful Im glad she is out where you Are I hafter pray to God for faith And strength to not go down under the strain but {he}is Able And willing to help us And surply us with for All of trial pray for me And her And you own selfe that you be strong Mr Sams is at the little school up to BCC[1] now love to Sue And the children most to you [Alice Sams]

AL.

Note

    1. Bethune-Cookman College.

✐ From Pauli Murray
5 May 1949
New York, N.Y.

Murray updates Thurman on her life since leaving California after obtaining her second law degree (LL.B.) from the University of California at Berkeley in 1945. She writes of her efforts to start a legal career in New York City and her deepening spirituality. Murray also acknowledges a debt of $150 to Thurman, a loan while she was in law school. The letter reveals Thurman's ongoing interest in financing educational opportunities for promising African Americans.

Reverend Howard Thurman
Fellowship Church, 2041 Larkin St.
San Francisco 9, California

Dear Howard Thurman:

I am answering your letter of April 29th immediately because I am so overjoyed to hear from you, and because it may get snowed under if I hold it.

Yes, I learned of Jessie Overholt's death[1] (which occurred while I was in the hospital undergoing a serious operation)[2] more than six months later, and it was more than a shock to me.[3] I immediately wrote to John Overholt[4] and part of that letter appears in the book of testimonials. Mr. Overholt also sent me copies of your memorial talk which I read with great appreciation.[5] The letter from which excerpts appear refers to Mrs. Overholt's visit to my mother in Durham, which will identify it for you.

First, let me clear my conscience. I have never forgotten that you forwarded to me the sum of $150.00 which was part of a scholarship fund Mrs. Overholt had given you for such needs as you felt must be met. I have considered that a debt of honor and have listed it among my debts, as required as part of my application for admission to the New York State Bar. I still carry it in my accounts payable.

You may recall that when I left California I was very ill and in need of surgical care. I was unable to give myself attention until April, 1947, and was not able to earn an income again until September, 1947. The result of these tribulations is that I started my career in private practice with a debt of more than $1300.00, {in} which your loan was included. I hope that it is not a pressing need with you at the moment. If not, I shall carry it along until I can clear my immediate expenses. Just know that I will repay it as soon as I can become anywhere near solvent.[6]

To face the private practice of law was a deep spiritual problem for me. My information and the accepted point of view seemed to be that in order to "get along" in the field of private practice one had to be "sharp" and to be dishonest. Few people believed that lawyers had integrity and could be guided by the two Commandments of the New Testament.[7] Curiously enough, until I was willing to face the logical outcome of my own ethical principles and was willing to enter the lists of practice determined not to compromise those standards which I set for myself, I could not resolve the conflict. Every step from that decision has been one of pure faith. Even my recent decision to get out on my own has little behind it more than a fragment of a "grain of mustard seed."[8]

I think it is going to work. At each point of utter discouragement something providential has come through which has given courage and the wherewithal to continue. The most dramatic of these has been an assignment which I have from the Women's Division of the Methodist Church. They have a subcommittee on Church and Social Relations, of which the executive director is Thelma Stevens,[9] whom you may have met. For the past several years they have been groping toward a racial policy in their various institutions more in keeping with their avowed social creed. This led to a review of their racial policies and a desire to know what they could or could not do toward integration without racial segregation under the laws of the various states.

The result is that I have embarked upon a study and compilation of the actual texts of the laws on race of the 48 states and the District of Columbia, a compilation which has never been done by any organization or individual to my knowledge. My deadline for completing the study is June 1, 1949, and if I can get it ready for the printer by then, I think by fall we will have a publication which will be exceedingly valuable in our quest for equality.[10] To actually be paid for doing the work that is nearest to my legal heart is God-guided to say the least!

My private practice is in its infancy, but growing. At first the choices in favor of integrity were hard. As time went on they became easier, and by now I hope they are axiomatic. I stress this fact because it has always been such a bugaboo among lawyers and pre-lawyers. They give the impression (and they apparently mean it) that they enter law primarily to "make money." I do not want to minimize the costliness of legal service or to pretend that my fees are cut-rate. They are not. Yet I am trying to steer a clear course between the ability of the client to pay for legal services and my own estimate of the worth of my services. As yet I have few guides because of my meager experience. And I do believe that in time my hazy preoccupation with spiritual values will be my greatest asset.

The writing suffers of course. The discipline of the law profession leaves little room for creative flights. I do hope that it can be renewed from time to time as I become more confident in my profession and have some leisure.

I think I can summarize this soliloquy by saying that I never read my Bible more intently than after I began practicing law. I am not sure this is what you wanted to know, and didn't expect this to come out—but here it is for what it is worth. In the meantime, please get in touch with me when you pass through again. I missed you when you spoke at Cambridge, and there are all too few people with whom one can speak "souls-up." It was Jessie's great gift—that one felt spiritually purified after sessions with her.

My warm greetings to Mrs. Thurman and the friends who remember me.
{Sincerely,}
[*signed*] Pauli
{P.S. This letter is extremely self-centered, but I'm sure you understand. Please place me on the mailing list for anything you think important and let me know what is happening out there. I still keep my active membership in the California [Bar?].}

TLS.

Notes

1. For Thurman's eulogy for Jessie Overholt, see To Fellowship Church, 7 July 1947.

2. Murray described her illness as "chronic subacute appendicitis aggravated by the strain of completing my graduate work and passing the bar." Pauli Murray, *Song in a Weary Throat: An American Pilgrimage* (New York: Harper and Row, 1987), 264. Sarah Azaransky wrote that Murray was hospitalized three times between 1937 and 1947 for what Murray described as "emotional breakdowns" brought about in part by her acute anxieties over her sexual and gender identity. Sarah Azaransky, *Pauli Murray and Democratic American Faith* (New York: Oxford, 2011), 23–25.

3. Murray wrote of Overholt that when she was a student at Howard Law School, she was lucky to have Overholt's financial support: "Mrs. Overholt had become interested in my desire to study law and sent periodic checks to supplement my earnings" (Murray, *Song in a Weary Throat*, 182). Overholt also gave financial assistance to the Workers' Defense League (where Murray had worked) and "contributed heavily to Odell Walker's defense" (ibid.). For the Odell Walker case, see *PHWT*, 2:315.

4. John Overholt (1893–1976), a businessman, was a graduate of Wooster College (1907) and Princeton University (1909).

5. Thurman's eulogy was printed in the self-published memorial pamphlet, *Jessie Wickwire Overholt: March 12 1892–May 6 1947* (Cleveland, 1947).

6. For the racial and gender barriers Murray encountered in starting her legal career, see Murray, *Song in a Weary Throat,* 270–77.

7. Mark 23:26.

8. Later that year Murray would further complicate her life by running as the Liberal Party candidate for a seat on the New York City Council (from Brooklyn); she would finish a respectable second.

9. Thelma Stevens (1902–90) was long involved in social action for the Methodist Church. She ran the Bethlehem Center—a community center for blacks—in Augusta, Georgia, from 1928 to 1939. From 1940 until her retirement in 1968, she headed the Women's Division of Christian Service for the Board of Missions of the United Methodist Church. Murray described Stevens as "a stalwart, dedicated Christian" who "defied my stereotype of a white Mississippian. Her commitment to the demise of racial segregation was as unswerving as my own" (Murray, *Song in a Weary Throat,* 286).

10. Murray was a bit overly optimistic about the publication date of her 746-page tome, *State Laws on Race and Color, and Appendices: Containing International Documents, Federal Laws and Regulations, Local Ordinances and Charts* (Cincinnati: Women's Division of Christian Service, Board of Missions and Church Service, Methodist Church, 1951). Over the succeeding decade, it would serve as a powerful tool for the NAACP and other organizations seeking redress to racial inequality through the courts.

❧ From J. Ed. Miller
10 May 1949
Connelly Springs, N.C.

After reading Jesus and the Disinherited, *J. Edward Miller, a Baptist pastor, questions whether Thurman believes that Jesus is God.*

Gal. 1:6–9.

Dr. Howard Thurman
Church for the Fellowship of All Peoples
San Francisco, Calif.

Dear Dr. Thurman:

This is my first experience in attempting to write to an author, but I have read your book, "Jesus and the Disinherited."

You gave me these impressions in your book:

1. You really do not believe that Jesus Christ is God, very God of very God.

2. You imply that Goliath died of fear (page 39). Read I Samuel 17:49.[1]

I appreciate your mention of the great faith of your mother, but can it be that you have drifted far from that faith yourself?

What is your purpose in trying to undermine the faith of God's people in his precious word?

I am expecting you to answer my letter and my questions.
Yours for Jesus' Sake
[*signed*] J. Ed. Miller

                                                                    ALS.

Note

1. "And David put his hand in his bag, and took thence a stone, and slung it, and smote the Philistine in his forehead, that the stone sunk into his forehead; and he fell upon his face to the earth." Thurman wrote in *Jesus and the Disinherited*, "When the great Goliath beheld David, and the full weight of the drama broke upon with force, it might well be literally true that under the tension growing out of a sense of outraged dignity he burst a blood vessel, resulting in apoplexy" (39).

∙⬗ To J. Ed. Miller
24 May 1949
[*San Francisco, Calif.*]

In his response to Miller, Thurman reminds him that the Bible warns Christians not to judge others.

The Rev. J. Ed. Miller
Rt. 2, Box 117
Connelly Springs
North Carolina

Dear Rev. Miller:
Please accept my thanks for your letter under date of May 10.

With reference to your comments on my book, relative to my interpretation of Jesus, I have nothing to add that is not stated in the first chapter: "Jesus An Interpretation."

I am grateful to you for an expression of your opinion, relative to my own faith, but please let me remind you that the words from the Book which means much to you are most appropriate which say "Judge not that ye be not judged."[1]
Sincerely yours
Howard Thurman

                                                                    TLc.

Note

1. Matt. 7:1; Luke 6:37.

Christian Century
12 September 1951

"Trumpet Ready in the West: San Francisco Church Successfully
Abolishes the Color Bar in Religious Life"

*This is the longest and most searching article published on the Fellowship
Church during the years of Thurman's tenure. For this reason the editors
thought it important to include it in the current volume of* The Papers of
Howard Washington Thurman, *which is primarily concerned with the Fellowship Church. The article, though published anonymously, was written by the
managing editor of the* Christian Century, *Harold E. Fey,[1] who had visited
the church over the summer.[2] Fey carefully discusses both the possibility of the
church and some of its potential problems, expressing the hope that the Fellowship Church might "raise the banner of a raceless Christianity and lay down
a challenge to the segregated, conscience-stricken ranks of American religious
life."*

> O get your trumpet, Gabriel,
> And come down to the sea.
> Now don't you sound your trumpet
> Till you get orders from me—
> I got a key to that kingdom,
> I got a key to that kingdom,
> And the world can't do me no harm.[3]

A richer, happier, more abundant spiritual life awaits the day when American
Christianity abolishes its almost universal practice of racial segregation. Those
who dispute this conclusion had better be prepared to deal with the Church
for the Fellowship of All Peoples in San Francisco. Because Fellowship Church
is surmounting the color bar in religious life, The Christian Century recently
made it the subject of careful study. As a result of this on-the-spot inquiry, we
are convinced that this church has, in the vivid imagery of the Negro spiritual,

Fellowship Church Choir. From the Bailey Thurman Family Papers; Manuscript, Archives, and Rare Book Library, Emory University.

called down the angel of judgment. Today Gabriel stands where the Pacific ocean, no longer a barrier but a bridge between peoples of different races, rolls through the Golden Gate. His trumpet is ready to sound.

Fellowship Church is demonstrating that it has "a key to that kingdom." It is proving that Christians of the three main races—Negro, Caucasian and Oriental —can, under the leadership of the Holy Spirit, develop the strong bonds of common life and inner discipline which are essential to a well rounded congregational life. It is revealing that a church so inspired and so organized can exert an influence out of all proportion to the size and wealth of its membership. It is showing that this influence flows directly from the power released in the lives of its members through Christian faith and not primarily through a frontal attack on a social injustice. One of its most remarkable achievements is that in its fellowship the consciousness of racial differences simply and quickly dissolves. Fellowship Church is far less disturbed over race than any similarly situated segregated church—white, Negro or Oriental—could possibly be. Consequently, it is better equipped to deal with persons as persons.

Fellowship Church UNESCO delegation, fall 1949 (from left, Sue Bailey Thurman, Emery Mellon, Corrine Barrow Williams, Lynn Buchanan, Ruth Acty, Arnold Nakajima, Sylvia Nichols, Raymond Fong, Carolyn Threlkeld, Joseph van Pelt). From the Bailey Thurman Family Papers; Manuscript, Archives, and Rare Book Library, Emory University.

Started Seven Years Ago

Fellowship Church is now carrying its living demonstration into the seventh year. It has survived the dangers which are inherent in the youth of any new enterprise and are particularly perilous to one that departs at many points from the conventional pattern. Segregation is an almost universal practice in American church life, yet this church thrives without segregation. That makes it of interest to Roman Catholicism, whose membership is only about one per cent colored, in spite of teachings of the church outlawing racism. It makes it of concern to Protestantism, which does no better. "The number of white and Negro persons who ever gather together for worship under the auspices of Protestant Christianity is almost microscopic," according to Frank Loescher, author of *The Protestant Church and the Negro*.[4] When even a single congregation proves that an almost universal practice is as unnecessary practically as it is disreputable spiritually, its achievement deserves study.

"Centering Down," Fellowship Church liturgical dance presentation. From
the Howard Thurman Collection, Howard Gotlieb Archival Research Center,
Boston University.

Few church members try to defend the practice of racial segregation on
grounds of Christian principle. It is justified on the basis of economic factors,
or for reasons of social expediency or personal preference. Such reasons do
not satisfy the awakening Protestant conscience on this matter. Its view was
expressed by the Amsterdam Assembly of the World Council of Churches. In
1948 this representative body declared that the church "has reflected and then
by its example sanctified the racial prejudice that is rampant in the world. . . .
It knows that it must call society away from prejudice based on race or color
and from the practices of discrimination and segregation, as denials of justice
and human dignity; but it cannot say a convincing word to society until it takes
steps to eliminate these from the Christian community because they contradict
all that it believes about God's love for his children."[5]

HERE COMES THE FUTURE

The American Christian conscience, as expressed through denominational
and interchurch assemblies, has condemned racial segregation as unworthy of
the Christian church. But such resolutions have had little effect, so far, on the

behavior of local congregations. In time a change is coming, and such actions forecast what form it will take. But Fellowship Church does more than that. Here one may meet the future in the present. Here the change has taken place. Here repentance is bearing fruit in life.

Fellowship Church was established in 1943 and was formally organized in 1944 to demonstrate that segregation is wrong in principle and must not be allowed to hinder the ministry of the gospel to all people. Today it has 345 resident members and 1,105 members at large. A little over half its members are white and around 40 per cent are Negroes. It has half a dozen Oriental members, but a larger proportion of those who attend its services are Orientals. It owns its own building and has a paid staff of three full-time and two part-time persons. It has overflow congregations practically every Sunday and is on its way to becoming one of the strong churches of San Francisco. A leading white minister of the city gave The Christian Century his opinion that Howard Thurman, minister of Fellowship Church, is probably the outstanding Protestant clergyman of San Francisco.

San Francisco is an excellent location for the Church for the Fellowship of All Peoples. It is one of the most cosmopolitan cities in the world. It was host to the international conference which produced the United Nations, and would have made an ideal permanent site for the world organization. It is America's principal doorway to the Orient. Men and women of Christian vision have long seen in this city with its unequaled harbor a mighty potential factor for good in the increasingly intimate relationships between the different peoples and races of the Pacific world.

Racial Mixture Changes

Among these Christian statesmen is Alfred Fisk, who teaches philosophy in San Francisco State College.[6] An ordained Presbyterian clergyman, Dr. Fisk is recognized for his work as a minister of reconciliation among the national and racial groups of his polyglot city. He and others opposed the racial hysteria which followed Pearl Harbor, but were unsuccessful in preventing the deportation of 100,000 Japanese-Americans from the west coast. Many of these had lived in San Francisco, and their removal left a vacuum in what is known as the Fillmore street area. Into the houses vacated by the Japanese-Americans moved large numbers of Negroes, drawn from Texas, Oklahoma and Arkansas by promises of wartime employment in bay area shipyards. From a prewar figure of 4,500, the Negro population of San Francisco multiplied 12 times in ten years. Today their number is estimated by the San Francisco Chronicle as 55,000, with another 70,000 living in communities across the bay.

This sudden change in the racial mixture caused many people to fear trouble. Among the many who moved to do something to head it off was Dr. Fisk. Backed by funds provided by his denomination (Presbyterian, U.S.A.), he and some associates started a "Neighborhood Church" among the newcomers and their neighbors. From the beginning its ministry was biracial. Professor Fisk and the Rev. Manly Johnson, a Negro student at the Berkeley Baptist Divinity School, carried on through part of 1943. Then Albert Cleage, a Congregational Christian clergyman, gave full time to the development of the church for six months.

A CRITICAL CHOICE

At this stage the church had a constituency but no formal membership. Its responsible board was a committee of the San Francisco presbytery and its working staff. The Presbyterian Board of National Missions provided, rent-free, the use of the former Japanese Presbyterian Church, an apartment for the resident minister and $3,600 for salaries. The rather uncertain nature of the project made it difficult to keep the interest of either members or ministers. In the fall of 1943 Professor Fisk wrote A. J. Muste, secretary of the Fellowship of Reconciliation in New York, asking for suggestions as to a successor to Mr. Cleage. This letter was referred to Howard Thurman, professor of theology and dean of the chapel at Howard University, Washington, D.C. Dr. Thurman attempted to find a man, but his efforts were unavailing. Then he volunteered his own services for the post. He arrived in San Francisco in July 1944.

Dr. Thurman's leadership has been so decisive a factor in the subsequent growth of Fellowship Church that his reasons for making this decision tell a good deal about the church as well as about himself. What could impel a man approaching 50 to leave a position of security and prestige, in which he had earned a life tenure, in the leading Negro university in the nation's capital? What could cause him to move himself, his wife and two daughters across the continent to assume the risks of an uncertain religious venture in an irreligious city at the edge of the Pacific? Dr. Thurman's answer, as given in a recent issue of the *Growing Edge,* a little mimeographed magazine published by the church, follows:[7]

> The cause of my acceptance goes much deeper and antedates Dr. Fisk's letter by many years. Ever since I began to give serious thought to the meaning of religion I have been deeply puzzled by its apparent inability to make a radical impact upon the tensions and the tragedies of human relations, particularly those obtaining between racial groups in America. Was this paralysis due to the nature of religious experience in particular? Or was it due to the breakdown in techniques and methods of implementation? Why cannot religion make a difference in the way groups deal with each other? More specifically, why was the church itself among the chief of sinners in the matter of racial separateness and prejudice?
>
> During the winter of 1936, while [I was][8] in India, the decision was reached that as soon as possible I would have to leave the relative particu-

larism of an academic atmosphere and move into a situation in an environment not under control where an honest attempt could be made to test the validity of the religious faith of men of good will, who drew their major inspiration from the genius of their own faith. It was obvious that a nucleus of interested and committed persons would have to be found and developed. My faith to make a bold venture without some such nucleus was too weak and indefinite. To do this would require becoming a part of a community somewhere and on the basis of belonging to seek to develop such a group. ... As soon as I heard about the group in San Francisco I felt that this was the opportunity if I dared to accept it. Mrs Thurman and I agreed that this was precisely the kind of opening for which we had hoped and prayed. The result was I secured a leave of absence from my work and sallied forth without any assurance beyond a dream in my heart and mind and a small group with which to work.

In April Mrs. Thurman had made a prospecting trip to San Francisco, had met members of the Neighborhood Church group and representatives of the Presbyterian Board, and had been favorably impressed. When the Thurman family arrived in July, the group consisted of about 30 men and women, Negro and white. Dr. Fisk continued to hold them together, but his copastor had departed long since. A temporary board without a chairman was the only nucleus of organization. Not only was there no formal membership, but there was no agreed basis of membership except attendance at Sunday worship and at "an occasional pot-luck supper." The relationship between the little group and the Presbyterian Church was uncertain as to both its meaning and its length. But there was a rent-free chapel for worship and an apartment above the meeting place where a minister might live. A summer camp for children was planned and the little group had faith in their mission.

Dr. Thurman rightly decided that the first job of the group was to decide what it was. It considered itself a church. But how could it be a church and nothing more? It was not easy to answer this question, "because," as Dr. Thurman said, "no provision is made in the genius of Protestantism for a church as such. It has to be some kind of church: Baptist, Methodist, Episcopal or something. It was my idea to project a church that would have a growing and creative basis of membership, rather than beginning from within the presupposition of a particular denomination. At first the idea seemed completely impossible."

Self-Inventory Taken

But with this man and this congregation complete impossibilities simply take a little longer to work out than do possibilities. Professor Fisk and Dr. Thurman wrote out a simple "basis of membership." When this was accepted by the provisional board, Dr. Thurman preached on it for several Sundays that summer while Dr. Fisk was away. By the fall of 1944 it had been discussed and thought through by those who were attending. So in September it became a "platform or floor but not a ceiling" for membership. The group became a church.

The platform has since been revised. In its present form it appears each Sunday on the cover of the mimeographed bulletin of the church as "The Commitment." Its three sentences follow:

> I affirm my need for a growing understanding of all men as sons of God, and I seek after a vital experience of God as revealed in Jesus of Nazareth and other great religious spirits whose fellowship with God was the foundation of their fellowship with man.

> I desire to share in the spiritual growth and ethical awareness of men and women of varied national, cultural, racial and creedal heritage united in a religious fellowship.

> I desire the strength of corporate worship through membership in the Church for the Fellowship of All Peoples, with the imperative [of] personal dedication to the working out of God's purposes here and in all places.

New members are received into the church every month after accepting this as their commitment. Each confers with Dr. Thurman and perhaps other members of the church staff. Each attends a long "orientation" session, where the meaning of the commitment is explained and discussed. Formal acceptance into membership comes at the morning service, when the congregation reads the commitment and each candidate comes forward as his name is called and signs the membership register in the presence of the congregation. A green ribbon or a sprig of ivy is pinned on the lapel of the new member for identification purposes. At the "coffee hour" which follows the church service, he is introduced to as many members as possible. "Members at large" are persons living anywhere who retain their connection with their own churches but accept the commitment and want to help the growth of Fellowship Church. There is also a loose group, numbering thousands, who have no formal relationship. They are called "Friends of Fellowship Church." Among the members at large are Alan Paton, author of *Cry, the Beloved Country,* which was partly written in San Francisco; Federal Judge and Mrs. Waites Waring[9] of South Carolina; Channing Tobias of the Phelps-Stokes Fund; Todd Duncan, the actor; and persons in India, Japan, South Africa, Iran, Formosa and the British Isles.

The next important decision concerned the location of the church. The neighboring Fillmore area was inhabited almost exclusively by nonwhites. Dr. Thurman and many members felt that their church was becoming segregated in spite of itself because of its location. But when it was proposed that the church move, some people felt this would mean that the church was running away from the

Negroes. Eventually the majority agreed to move. For a while the congregation met in the Japanese Methodist Church, then in the Theater Arts Colony. Then the church moved to its present location. From the first, attendance jumped and continued at a higher level, so the wisdom of the step was accepted. Soon the church began attracting people from throughout the bay area. Today some regular attendants come from Berkeley, an hour and 20 minutes away, or from Palo Alto, equally distant in another direction.

Declare Independence

The Presbyterian board continued to help the church, but the relationship became embarrassing to both sides. On the Presbyterian side, the mission board had difficulty in explaining its continued support for what was definitely not a Presbyterian church. The church and its principal minister found it hard to square their convictions with a denominational commitment, however tenuous. Finally the matter was put to a secret ballot of the 60 members the church then had. They were asked to vote on whether (1) they would become Presbyterians, or (2) join some other denomination, or (3) become independent with no provision for fellowship with any group, or (4) become independent "with provisions to be worked out for cooperation with other religious groups." The fourth proposition won by a large majority. The church has not yet carried out the provision for cooperation with a denomination, but Dr. Thurman thinks the time is likely to come when a union can be formed with some church group that is going their way.

When the church became independent, it had to make up the $3,600 the Presbyterian board had been allocating to its annual budget, and to do more than that if it was to survive and grow. But once more it was felt that the problem was primarily spiritual and only secondarily financial. A committee of nine—three Negroes, three Caucasians, two Japanese-Americans and one Chinese-American—held something like a dozen meetings. Each week they reported to a congregational meeting on their progress. Within five weeks the church had taken its present name, had elected a permanent board, and had proceeded under its own organizational plan, with by-laws and regulations.

Copastors Change

Originally the plan was to have copastors of different races. After a couple of years, however, Dr. Fisk resigned to devote full time to his teaching, which he had never given up, and to conduct his traveling seminars to Europe and the Far East during the summer.

Then Robert Meyners, a Congregational Christian minister, joined Dr. Thurman's staff as a one-year interne. He remained a second year. When his term was finished, the congregation decided to look again for a full-time copastor with indefinite tenure. Before he was found, Miss Adena Joy,[10] a Quaker with religious educational and college teaching experience, became assistant minister. She still retains this post. Lynn Buchanan,[11] formerly an advertising man, became administrative secretary of the church. A couple of years ago Mr. Buchanan organized and headed an interracial party of 12 members of the church for a journey to Paris to attend sessions of the United Nations Educational, Scientific and Cultural Organization.[12] This delegation was one of the few ever sent by a church to a meeting of this character. Its members learned as much from their experiences of racial discrimination on their way across America as they did from the sessions of UNESCO. They paid their own expenses.[13]

Where Will the Money Come From?

The financial problems of the early years of independency were serious and they have not yet been fully surmounted. At the beginning the major contributor to the Fellowship Church budget was Dr. Thurman. He is much sought after as a speaker to colleges and student assemblies, and at first devoted a considerable portion of his earnings to keeping the church going. This is no longer necessary, although he occasionally takes engagements with the proviso that the payment consist of a gift to the building fund of Fellowship Church, on which $12,500 is still owing. The regular budget is around $20,000 a year.

In 1949 the congregation purchased for $35,000 from the Evangelical and Reformed Church the building it now occupies at 2041 Larkin street. This neighborhood is inhabited chiefly by Italians and Chinese. In two years $22,500 has been paid on the building and $2,500 on its remodeling. Most of the money for the building has been raised outside the congregation. Arthur U. Crosby of Philadelphia and Gene K. Walker[14] of San Francisco—the latter the motion picture producer who is chairman of the board of Fellowship Church—have taken a leading part in this endeavor.

Citywide Constituency

When The Christian Century visited this church in the summer of 1951, it had 283 active and 62 inactive members in the bay area. About 25 per cent of its income comes by mail from outside the city. Of the sums which are contributed by the members in its huge parish, nearly half comes in the collection plates on Sunday morning. Around 200 persons pledge to give regularly through an envelope system. But many pledgers fall into arrears with their payments, so that the current expense budget suffers. This condition is not unknown in other churches, but it was causing concern at Fellowship Church.

At a meeting held in the church one evening, 30 members frankly faced the problem. Is Fellowship Church a charity which has to depend on outside contributions, or is it mature enough to carry its own program? Can a church be a real fellowship unless each member shares to the extent of his ability in its financing? Too many members of the church confine their participation to listening, more or less regularly, to sermons on Sunday morning. How can more members be interested in the general program which goes on seven days a week? The discussion lasted three hours, and the only person who noticed that members of all racial groups participated on an entirely equal basis was the visitor. The members long ago ceased to think in such terms.

Eventually a remarkable degree of consensus and group solidarity emerged. It was decided that the 30 would constitute themselves a committee to work for the welfare of the church on all fronts. Each member agreed to take names of persons whose pledges were in arrears, to call on them and renegotiate the pledges if necessary but try to get them "made current." They decided to recommend to the church for an experimental period the tithing of incomes, to ask for a special contribution from persons who do not pledge, and to have more frequent reports made to the congregation on its finances. Finally, they decided to have "another town meeting."

This referred to a general discussion by the congregation of questions affecting the church's "climate," program, organization and community relations. Last spring such a discussion was held by the whole church. Small groups gathered in members' homes for one or several evenings, developing a common mind on the future of the church. Then a prolonged session was held by a large portion of the membership in the church itself. Every kind of criticism as well as praise was debated, with complete democratic freedom. It proved a wholesome and liberating experience, and if not all questions were settled, there was at least the assurance that none was being suppressed or dodged.

Town Meeting Planned

Now a town meeting, to be held in August, was getting under way. One could immediately sense a quickening of interest. One member who had urged the adoption of a missionary program, helping other churches to follow where this one has pioneered, saw that this meeting would offer opportunity for advancing that idea. Another who had declared that the church is not sufficiently evangelistic—but who would have been horrified had his conviction that the church must double its membership been so designated—served notice that he wanted that topic discussed. Each stressed the point that the church can save itself only by a wholehearted commitment to save others.

Back of this is a serious concern which members discuss among themselves. Many people, they say, come to the church, grow enthusiastic and work hard for a few months, then drop out and are seen no more. Why does this happen as often as it does? In the last year the church seems to have struck a plateau, to be marking time. Why is it falling down, they ask, in fulfilling the promise which is implicit in the message of its great minister? "We are caught up in the power of a great idea," they say, "so why does not the church grow in a big way? Here is something so lacking in pretense, so genuine and right, that it should reach out without artificial promotion. It isn't doing that—yet. Why?"

An obvious answer is that the whole idea of a colorblind church is so new that it takes a while to catch on. This is particularly true because this church refuses to magnify its most distinctive characteristic into its one reason for existence. Its main quest is for spiritual illumination rather than to crusade against segregation or anything else. Yet this does not mean that this church turns its back on human need. In several cases members of the church have gallantly defied the peril of being evicted from their apartments because they have invited members of the church who were of other races to visit them. Every such encounter solidifies the fellowship of the church and deepens the desire for that quality of life which uncovers "that of God in every man."

Some people stumble over the kind of preaching they hear from the Fellowship Church pulpit, but many more find it one of the principal attractions of the church. Dr. Thurman is a Christian mystic. He acknowledges that Rufus Jones, the saintly philosopher of Haverford College, has had the greatest influence on him of any of his teachers. After graduating from Colgate-Rochester Divinity School, Howard Thurman studied with Dr. Jones for a year. Like the great Quaker, the pastor of Fellowship Church seeks the inner light of personal guidance and power. He does not strive nor cry, and a bruised reed he will not break. He refuses to press people unduly, to over-dramatize his message, to regiment folk in the strong harness of organization. He has often refused to tell representatives of other congregations how they can become like Fellowship Church. He says he is not seeking power of that kind. He has reverence for personality, but not much for the mass psychology of the typical American Christian group.

Dr. Thurman usually preaches to crowded congregations. He often follows one theme through many Sundays. He is most completely at home at the service of meditation which is held for a half-hour preceding the main church service. This period is marked by prayers and devotional readings and by the use of a meditation specially written by Dr. Thurman. Recently a series of these meditations was published by Harper under the title "Deep Is the Hunger."

The pastor of Fellowship Church spends a great deal of time in personal counseling. Sometimes he is so busy that people have difficulty in seeing him when they feel they need it most. In one case at least a man who tried to see him and failed is not in the church. In another, a woman telephoned for an appointment and was told that none was open for a fortnight. Not to be put off, she drove to the church in expectation that somebody on the minister's crowded calendar would not appear. Things worked out as she hoped. Today she is one of the most devoted members of the church. Because she found help when she needed it, she has been of great assistance to others.

Social Life Is a Concern

The aim of Fellowship Church is to give its members a complete and well rounded religious experience. As the church understands it, such an experience includes social life on a creative level. The church conducts social affairs ranging from "coffee hours" after the Sunday morning service to meetings in homes and beach picnics on Sunday afternoons. At the coffee hours the ministers and leaders of groups try particularly to spend their time visiting with new people, since they have discovered a tendency for old friends to spend too much time with each other. This has given rise to criticism concerning cliques, which the church is out to disprove.

This summer a Christian Century editor attended a Sunday afternoon Fellowship Church picnic on an ocean beach south of San Francisco. About 50 persons—young and old, Oriental, Negro and white—were there. Included in the number were several Japanese who had spent a year in the Carolinas studying textile production. They were about to embark for Japan and had elected to spend their last Sunday in America at Fellowship Church. There they had been invited to join the beach party. As they returned to Japan they had many stories to tell concerning the relations of the races in America. Some of these involved the church. Undoubtedly their account of what they saw at Fellowship Church would be set over against what they had seen in other places. When the attitude of Asiatics toward American racism is remembered, we can all be grateful that they found in San Francisco a church which believes that the Christian faith ought to make a difference in human relations.

Music and Arts Cultivated

Although the active congregation of Fellowship Church numbers less than 300 people, its program equals or exceeds that of most churches with a thousand members. Its educational work is continuous and creative. During the major part of the year, the church school meets in the church and in a house next door which has been bought and converted to educational needs. The excellent "new curriculum" of the Presbyterian Church, U.S.A., is used in many classes. In the summer months around 50 children attend a school of international understanding. This summer they studied Africa, using up-to-date methods and gaining an insight into many phases of African life.

Music and the arts play an important part in the life of Fellowship Church. Included in the excellent choir, to which members of the three main races belong, is a group of singers who are in considerable demand for appearances outside the church. This interracial group was formed on the journey of the

Fellowship Church delegation to the UNESCO meeting in Paris and has remained together ever since. Each week a choral dance class meets at the church, and its occasional concerts or exhibitions attract large audiences and respectful critical notices. An annual exhibition of paintings and other art objects is held in the church, and a continuous effort is made to keep the church attractive by using its members' artistic abilities.

Fellowship Church issues a little magazine, the *Growing Edge,* which has real merit as a literary and religious production. Some of its contributors are persons of international renown. Every weekly bulletin of the church is worth saving or passing on, for each contains a meditation by Dr. Thurman and other material of more than routine interest. The church has a library for the use of its members, and the titles of its books show that they were selected by persons of intelligence and a genuine appreciation of the best in the cultural heritage of the English-speaking world, and not of America only. When the total outreach of Fellowship Church is considered, the conclusion is inescapable that here is a Christian community which is not only concerned about the direction of American culture but is beginning to make an effective contribution to it.

What is the future of this church? Is that future bound up with Dr. Thurman, so that this Christian experiment in right human relations will end when he gives up its leadership? Opinions differ within the congregation. Many of the members continue to be so skeptical about the Christian integrity of other churches that they doubt Fellowship Church will have much influence on them. Most of the members of this church had dropped their former relations with any church long before they joined Fellowship. Many had never known what it meant to be a church member, and had never cared to know until they became members of this church. Some of those who are now the most active were openly agnostic. Throughout the membership there is a deep awareness of the difference between this church and other churches. Nearly every member feels that Fellowship Church is definitely more Christian—more what other churches ought to be and are not—and they do not hesitate to say so.

So far however they appear not to have decided what to do about this difference. They have not openly considered its significance. It is soft-pedaled, perhaps on grounds of charity, perhaps because criticism would seem narrow-minded. But this produces the tendency for Fellowship members to wrap their satisfaction with their church around themselves and to dismiss their responsibility for other Christians as of little importance. Fortunately this tendency is resisted, for most of the members have had plenty of opportunity to observe the cults which flourish in California and want to avoid anything resembling a cultish development. They may not be able to avoid it, however, unless they can develop stronger ties with other Christians than are now apparent.

A REVOLUTIONARY CHALLENGE

Fellowship Church might move in the opposite direction. It might raise the banner of a raceless Christianity and lay down a challenge to the segregated, conscience-stricken ranks of American religious life. Throughout America there are hundreds of urban situations like that in San Francisco, where the several races are cast into a new and closer relationship. With segregation breaking down in education, in employment, in housing, in labor unions, in politics, in the armed forces, the pressure on the church to follow where it has refused to lead is becoming very strong. The Christian faith continues to be a powerful leaven among people cast into these new relationships, even though large numbers of them have broken their relationship with the churches, as Fellowship Church has learned. They demand to know why the church should continue to be the only institution which refuses to change with its environment, especially when change conforms to its professions of faith.

What would happen if Fellowship Church were to initiate an aggressive campaign to evangelize these centers of disaffection for the church as it is? What if this congregation were to launch a mission for the conversion of American Protestantism to the gospel it professes to believe? What if it determined that the conviction which guides its life could no longer be endured unless it was shared? If its message became like Jeremiah's "burning fire in my bones,"[15] it might turn the religious life of this country upside down. If the past history of great religious changes is any criterion, something like that is going to be necessary if the grip of segregation is to be loosened on American churches.

On first acquaintance, Fellowship Church seems to be the polar opposite to anything revolutionary. Its members are probably above the average in culture. Few of them are the crusading type. They do not go in for drives, for noise, for breast-beating. They do more praying than broadcasting. They abhor pretense and heroics. They conduct the affairs of their church with dignity and fine sensitivity. And what is said of them applies of course to their minister.

Dr. Thurman reflects in everything he does the powerful influences of his Baptist and Quaker heritages, in which quietism continually struggles with a revolutionary urge to direct action. Both are reflected in his words:

> It is in this connection [segregation][16] that American Christianity has betrayed the religion of Jesus almost beyond redemption. . . . The result is that in the one place in which normal free contacts might be most naturally established and in which the relations of the individual to his God should take priority over conditions of class, race, power, status, wealth or the like—this place is one of the chief instruments for guaranteeing barriers. . . . The situation is so tragic that men of good will in all the spacious classifications

within our society find more cause for hope in the secular relations of life than in those of religion.

Perhaps the direction in which Fellowship Church will move will be a less spectacular but no less revolutionary middle way—that of winning acceptance and imitation through its success as a Christian congregation. It already has a point of contact with the great majority of American Protestantism. A considerable proportion of its members of all races are middle-class, quiet, very respectable people, as measured by ordinary American standards. It is this group which is staging what *Fortune* calls the "permanent revolution" of American life.[17] With barriers to employment at any level breaking down for minority races, they too are coming to share in the process of peaceful change which is characteristic of American living. Fellowship Church is pointing a way in which Christians of different races may express in terms of association for religious purposes their convictions concerning the nature of God and the relationships of men.

A Compelling Mission

This church is already a serious competitor for the interest and membership of newcomers to San Francisco, providing only that they are prepared to judge it on the basis of its preaching and its program and the Christian quality of its membership, without regard to other factors. In many respects it is an ordinary church with an extraordinary membership and a compelling mission. Its achievement in doing very well what other congregations do, and at the same time erasing the color line which they permit to stand, enables it to "speak to the condition" of an increasing number of churches in this country.

Much of destiny depends upon whether it is heard when it speaks. Fellowship Church is doing its best to build lines of communication. But that is too big a task for an independent congregation. It needs more help than it is getting from councils of churches, from denominational and interchurch associations. They have a stake in the success of the Church for the Fellowship of All Peoples— a stake that is much bigger than they can realize until they recognize the Spirit which broods over this church.

Editors of *Christian Century,* "Trumpet Ready in the West," *Christian Century,* 12 September 1951, 1040–45.
Copyright © 1951 by the *Christian Century.* Editors of *Christian Century,* "Trumpet Ready in the West," *Christian Century,* 12 September 1951, is reprinted by permission.

Notes

1. Harold E. Fey (1898–1990), a 1927 graduate of Yale Divinity School, was a Disciples of Christ minister who after a career in religious journalism joined the staff of the *Christian Century* in 1940. He served as editor in chief from 1956 to 1964, when he retired to take a

position at the Christian Theological Seminary in Indianapolis. Shortly before this article appeared, Fey wrote to Thurman telling him that he tried in the article "to indicate how much I am indebted to you" and that he hoped Thurman saw the article "as a warm and personal expression of gratitude to you and one-ness with you" (From Harold E. Fey, 5 September 1951).

2. Fey did not want his presence to be announced to the congregation, and Thurman and the board of trustees agreed. Thurman gave Fey complete freedom "to see anything [and] to look into anything, and [I] shall encourage you to talk to all and sundry." Thurman did want Fey to show him a draft of the article before publication, and Fey complied with the request, though Thurman did not see the final version before publication. See To Harold E. Fey, 19 May 1951; From Harold E. Fey, 5 September 1951.

3. Although many versions of the Negro spiritual "Blow Your Trumpet Gabriel" exist, this variant appears in HT, *Negro Spiritual Speaks of Life and Death*, 43.

4. Loescher, *Protestant Church and the Negro*, 76–78. Thurman quotes from the same passage in HT, *Footprints*, 12.

5. *The First Assembly of the World Council of Churches, August 22 to September 4, 1948* (New York: Harper, 1949), 81.

6. Fisk's connection to the Fellowship Church ended in the fall of 1946.

7. HT, "An International Church Is Born," *Growing Edge* (Spring 1950): 5–6.

8. Brackets are in original.

9. Julius Waites Waring (1880–1968), a Charleston, South Carolina, native, was a federal district court judge for the Eastern District of South Carolina from 1942 to 1952. He is best remembered for a series of notable decisions and opinions challenging racial discrimination, including his dissent in *Briggs v. Elliott*, 342 U.S. 330 (1952), the first case heard of the five that were eventually combined in *Brown v. Board of Education*, 347 U.S. 483 (1954). Most observers credited Judge Waring's transformation from a racial moderate to an outspoken civil rights advocate to his 1945 marriage to Elizabeth Avery Waring (1895–1968), a northern woman with strong progressive views. The couple were shunned by Charleston's white establishment, and after Judge Waring's retirement in 1952, they moved to New York City.

10. A native of Ashland, Oregon, Adena Joy graduated from Oregon State Agricultural College in 1933 and Chicago Theological Seminary in 1940, with a thesis on rural education. She later worked as a human relations and human life counselor and received a Ph.D. in criminology from the University of California at Berkeley in 1968.

11. Lynn Buchanan worked in advertising and public relations in the San Francisco area and had worked as executive secretary of a theater school in Beverly Hills.

12. Usually known by its acronym, UNESCO, the organization has been headquartered in Paris, France, since its inception in 1945.

13. For the UNESCO trip, see To Friend[s], January 1950 (annual Epiphany letter), in *PHWT*, Vol. 4.

14. Gene K. Walker (1903–97) was chief executive of Gene K. Walker Productions, an industrial and documentary film company based in San Francisco.

15. Jer. 20:9.

16. Brackets are in original.

17. Editors of *Fortune* magazine, *U.S.A.: The Permanent Revolution* (New York: Prentice-Hall, 1951).

Index

Page references in **bold** refer to illustrations or photographs; page references in *italics* refer to biographical information contained in the notes.